Working With Students With Disabilities

COUNSELING and
PROFESSIONAL IDENTITY

Working With Students With Disabilities

Preparing School Counselors

Editors

Vicki A. McGinley
West Chester University

Barbara C. Trolley
St. Bonaventure University

Los Angeles | London | New Delhi
Singapore | Washington DC

Los Angeles | London | New Delhi
Singapore | Washington DC

FOR INFORMATION

SAGE Publications, Inc.
2455 Teller Road
Thousand Oaks, California 91320
E-mail: order@sagepub.com

SAGE Publications Ltd.
1 Oliver's Yard
55 City Road
London, EC1Y 1SP
United Kingdom

SAGE Publications India Pvt. Ltd.
B 1/I 1 Mohan Cooperative Industrial Area
Mathura Road, New Delhi 110 044
India

SAGE Publications Asia-Pacific Pte. Ltd.
3 Church Street
#10–04 Samsung Hub
Singapore 049483

Publisher: Kassie Graves
Editorial Assistant: Carrie Montoya
Production Editor: Kelly DeRosa
Copy Editor: Patrice Sutton
Typesetter: Hurix Systems Pvt. Ltd.
Proofreader: Theresa Kay
Indexer: Scott Smiley
Cover Designer: Candice Harman
Marketing Manager: Johanna Swenson

Copyright © 2016 by SAGE Publications, Inc.

Printed in the United States of America

Library of Congress Cataloging-in-Publication Data

McGinley, Vicki A.

Working with students with disabilities : preparing school counselors / Vicki A. McGinley, West Chester University, Barbara C. Trolley, St. Bonaventure University.

pages cm

Includes bibliographical references and index.

ISBN 978-1-4833-5970-0 (pbk. : acid-free paper) 1. Students with disabilities—Counseling of—United States. 2. Children with disabilities—Education—United States. 3. Educational counseling—United States. 4. Student counselors—Training of—United States. I. Trolley, Barbara (Barbara C.) II. Title.

LC4031.M398 2015

371.9—dc23   2015015636

This book is printed on acid-free paper.

15 16 17 18 19 10 9 8 7 6 5 4 3 2 1

Brief Contents

Contents

Chapter 3: Laws and Ethics   51

Vicki A. McGinley

SECTION II: COLLABORATION

Chapter 4: Collaborative Teamwork and Advocacy   103

Diana Lawrence-Brown

SECTION III: APPLICATION

Chapter 7: ASCA Delivery Systems   175

Christopher Siuta and Alan Silliker

Chapter 9: Inclusion Considerations   233

Domenico Cavaiuolo

Introduction to the Series
Counseling and Professional Identity

While one can point to a number of historic events, such as the launch of Sputnik (1957), that have had a significant impact on public education in the United States, none have had and continue to have as profound effect as did Congress' enactment of the Education for All Handicapped Children Act (Public Law 94-142) of 1975. This landmark law, along with its subsequent modifications, provides evidence of our national commitment to a free appropriate public education for all students, regardless of their educational challenges.

Since its inception, the law has had a significant impact on the physical structure of our schools, the nature of our curriculum, our placement policies and procedures, our methods of teaching, and in a very real way—for many—our very job descriptions. This last point is certainly true of school counselors.

School counselors, whose mission is to support all children in their educational achievement, now find an increasing number of students with special needs on their caseloads. For many counselors, working with students with special needs was not part of their initial training, and as such they may quickly find themselves overwhelmed with the morass of jargon, the legal aspects, and more answers to the questions of best practices for supporting and facilitating their education. Meeting the needs of these children demands that counselors have a working knowledge of special education and the counselor's role with it. To this end, we are proud to be able to introduce *Working With Students With Disabilities: Preparing School Counselors* as part of our series: *Counseling and Professional Identity*.

Working With Students With Disabilities: Preparing School Counselors is a text written by true experts in the fields of Counseling and Special Education. What you are about to read is a text that addresses a significant void in the professional development of counselors. With the latest research supporting best practices and a clear understanding of the law and implications for all working within our schools, the chapters that follow provide the school counselors with a sound base of knowledge from which to facilitate the education of all students within their school.

This book, *Working With Students With Disabilities: Preparing School Counselors,* is more than an academic text that provides the latest research and theories. It is a text that will not only facilitate your developing knowledge and skills but also contribute to your development of professional identity.

However, one text, one learning experience, will not be sufficient for the development of a counselor's professional competency. The formation of both your *professional identity* and *practice* will be a lifelong process. It is a process that we hope to facilitate through the presentation of this text and the creation of our series: *Counseling and Professional Identity.*

Counseling and Professional Identity is a new—fresh—pedagogically sound series of texts targeting counselors in training. This series is *not* simply a compilation of isolated books matching that which is already on the market. Rather, each book, with its targeted knowledge and skills, will be presented as but a part of a larger whole. The focus and content of each text serves as a single lens through which a counselor can view his or her clients, engage in his or her practice, and articulate his or her own professional identity.

Counseling and Professional Identity is unique, not just in the fact that it "packaged" a series of traditional text, but that it provides as well an *integrated* curriculum targeting the formation of the readers' professional identity and efficient, ethical practice. Each book, within the series, is structured to facilitate the ongoing professional formation of the reader. The materials found within each text are organized in order to move the reader to higher levels of cognitive, affective, and psychomotor functioning, resulting in his or her assimilation of the materials presented into his or her professional identity and approach to professional practice.

We are proud to have served as coeditors of this series feeling sure that all of the text included, just like *Working With Students With Disabilities: Preparing School Counselors,* will serve as a significant resource to you and your development as a professional counselor.

Richard Parsons, PhD
Naijian Zhang, PhD

Editors' Preface

When we were first approached about coediting this book, we were both very excited to see more attention being addressed to the issues of students with disabilities from the worldview of school counselors. While those in special education and school counseling training programs receive excellent training in their respective fields of study, there is not often an exposure to course work in other disciplines due to the requirements of the individually chosen programs of study, and if there is, this coverage of material is most frequently conveyed in electives. Thus, not every school counselor will have access to specific special education information during their academic programs. Yet, with an increasing number of students with disabilities being included, school counselors are being asked to provide an increasing number of services to students with *Individualized Education Plans* (IEP). Whether these services are focused on such areas as counseling, parent/teacher consultation, or classroom psycho-educational lessons, it is imperative that they have a fundamental grasp of the language, laws, and issues in working with students in special education. As the American School Counselor Association (ASCA) and the Council for Accreditation of Counseling and Related Educational Programs (CACREP) have indicated, school counselors are responsible for working with *all* students, respecting their diverse backgrounds, and working toward improving their performance in academic, career, and personal-social domains.

Having an opportunity to develop this valuable resource for school counselors in training and in practice, which may also serve school professionals in related fields well, has been an honor and a privilege. In addition, being able to create this resource with our blended backgrounds in special education, legal advocacy, and school and rehabilitation counseling offers the reader a comprehensive, holistic perspective on working with these students.

The first section of this book, Foundation, establishes a baseline of special education, terminology, classifications, and principles. Specifically, Chapter 1 offers the reader an overview of the language and stereotypes associated with students with disabilities. This provides the novice counselor with a foundation in the field, and a review for those who already have some knowledge of special education. The *educational and professional standards* that guide the work of school counselors with respect to students with disabilities are addressed in Chapter 2, which is furthered by the *ethical and legal guidelines* presented in Chapter 3. The concepts of *free appropriate public education* (FAPE), *least restrictive environments* (LRE), and Individualized Education Plans (IEP) are also introduced in this third chapter.

Collaboration is the focus of the second section of the book. As the age old saying goes, "It takes a village to raise a child"; so too, it takes a community of educators, counselors, parents, and related professionals to adequately and effectively attend to the unique needs of children with disabilities. In Chapter 4, the reader is presented with a plethora of information with respect to the qualities of and skills required for effective partnerships, team-building suggestions, and co-teaching approaches. Chapter 5 provides more detailed information about the *multidisciplinary team* members, and the process; transition from *early intervention* programs; and discusses the concept of *response to intervention* (RTI). In addition, the "voices" of parents with children with disabilities are presented. This section is concluded with Chapter 6, which highlights the dynamics of home-school collaborations, diversity in parental perceptions, and ways school counselors can support this process.

The third section of the book pertains to *Applications.* Beginning with Chapter 7, the core principles and academic, career, and personal-social domains of ASCA's delivery systems are outlined, and tasks within direct, responsive, and indirect services provided by school counselors are described. Following, in Chapter 8, is a thorough discussion of assessment and evaluation processes and tools, and an overview of the MEASURE accountability system. RTI and IEPs are further discussed, and Functional Behavioral Assessments (FBA) is addressed. Chapter 9 presents a comprehensive overview of inclusion, including discussions of the preparation of all students for this educational process, parent and teacher expectations, communication essentials, attendance considerations, and interventions. The final chapter in this section, Chapter 10, addresses the various components of the transition process. Transition types, roles, tasks, and forms are discussed.

Cultural and Psychosocial Issues, the final section, begins with Chapter 11. Culturally responsive school programs and responding to the diverse learning styles of students are presented, and a review of school counselor roles and tasks in working with students with disabilities is shared. The final chapter of the book is Chapter 12, in which the psychosocial issues that students with disabilities and their parents and siblings face, such as stress, impact on the family, friendships, inclusion, and societal stigma, are described. This population being at higher risk for issues such as cyberbullying, substance abuse, physical and sexual abuse, obesity, depression, and suicide are defined. The chapter concludes with a summary of strategies and resources helpful for school counselors and all those working with students with disabilities.

We hope you find this book technically helpful and poignantly presented, providing both enhanced knowledge about and sensitivity to students with disabilities. There is so often a discussion of "normalcy" that arises when this population is addressed, and consciously or unconsciously, a sense of "different from" and "less than" emerges. We would like to leave the reader with the wisdom of Maya Angelou:

"If you are always trying to be normal, you will never know how amazing you can be."

*A dedication must go to those persons that understand you and
appreciate why you do what you do, so I first dedicate this to my immediate
family, my husband, Jim, and daughter Nora. However, a dedication also
goes out to those who have inspired you along the way, so I would have to say from a very
young age I have been compelled to look at things through a social justice lens, which
originates from my extended family, so I thank them also. I was lucky to have
great mentors and colleagues along the way, in particular, Dr. Diane Nelson Bryen from Temple
University has always taught and supported me, and my students at West Chester University
have kept me thinking and moving for many years, I thank them. Finally, there
are no better collaborators than Dr. Barbara Trolley, my coeditor.
It has been my extreme pleasure!*

Vicki A. McGinley

*I would like to dedicate this book first and foremost to my husband, Ron, and
my children, Ally, Nick, Zack, Hannah, and Sarah, who have been there to support me
while I pursued this professional endeavor. This book could not have been completed
without their patience and understanding. I would also like to acknowledge
Dr. Dwight Kauppi, my mentor, my colleague, and friend, who fueled my passion for working
with people with disabilities and taught me the importance of focusing
on the strengths of each individual, holistic assessment and intervention, and teamwork.
I would like to recognize all of the school counselors who dedicate their professional
lives to helping* all *children succeed. Lastly, for all students with disabilities,
believe in yourself and all that you can be!*

Barbara C. Trolley

Chapter 1

Introduction

BARBARA C. TROLLEY
St. Bonaventure University

HEATHER HASS
Mountain View Middle School, Goffston School District

TAMARA REYNOLDS
Cattaraugus-Allegany BOCES

"A true friend knows your weaknesses but shows you your strengths; feels your fears but fortifies your faith; sees your anxieties but frees your spirit; recognizes your disabilities but emphasizes your possibilities."

—William Arthur Ward, American Author, Pastor, and Teacher

In recent years, school counselors have seen more students in special education on their caseloads, especially with increased inclusion of these students in the classroom. While school counselors historically have had as their mission to serve *all* students, in many ways, this has been a new territory for these professionals, most of whom have not received any formalized training in special education. Discussion ensues as to what is the exact role of school counselors in working with students with special needs; that is, how much and what type of involvement will they have. In the meantime, these students are being seen by school counselors, as counseling is frequently a requirement in the educational plans of students in special education. While philosophical debates continue, and specific duties vary across school districts, it is *essential* that *all* school counselors have a basic, working knowledge of special education and that this area of service becomes part of their professional identity.

One of the most fundamental issues for school counselors to address in working with students with disabilities is establishing a clear comprehension of special education classifications and language. At times, it may seem like alphabet soup with the plethora of acronyms that swirl in special education verbal discussions and written reports. While it is very possible that some terms may get past any professional, at the very least, it is crucial that school counselors know how disabilities are classified, what each entails, common acronyms frequently utilized, and where to find additional information. In addition to the acquisition of technical terminology, it is essential that school counselors are familiar with the impact that language has had over time on children with disabilities and the stereotypes that exist. After reading this chapter, the reader will be able to accomplish the following:

1. Obtain an understanding of the classification of special education categories.

2. Learn commonly used acronyms in the special education field.

3. Explore common stereotypes of students with disabilities.

4. Examine negative language that persists today.

OVERVIEW

According to the Individuals with Disabilities Education Act (IDEA), the nation's special education law, a student with a disability must be educated in the least restrictive environment, to the maximum extent possible. (Note, as of 2004, this act is now identified as the Individuals with Disabilities Education Improvement Act, or IDEIA.) Within this federal law, classifications of disabilities exist that guide each state's definitions of disability and who is eligible for a *free appropriate public education* (FAPE). It is important to keep in mind that while there are specific criteria that pertain to each disability, how these disabilities are individually manifested may vary; that is, there is no absolute profile of a child with autism. These classifications are listed in Table 1.1.

In addition to the classifications, a plethora of acronyms exist which are commonly used in special education discourse. They are ever evolving and can be overwhelming to those who are just entering the special education system. While a sample list is presented in Table 1.2 below, please be aware that this list is not exhaustive or static.

Table 1.1   Thirteen Classifications of Disability According to IDEA; Part 300

(c) Definitions of disability terms. The terms used in this definition of a child with a disability are defined as follows:

(1)   (i)   Autism means a developmental disability significantly affecting verbal and nonverbal communication and social interaction, generally evident before age three, that adversely affects a child's educational performance. Other characteristics often associated with autism are engagement in repetitive activities and stereotyped movements, resistance to environmental change or change in daily routines, and unusual responses to sensory experiences.

   (ii)   Autism does not apply if a child's educational performance is adversely affected primarily because the child has an emotional disturbance, as defined in paragraph (c)(4) of this section.

   (iii)   A child who manifests the characteristics of autism after age three could be identified as having autism if the criteria in paragraph (c)(1)(i) of this section are satisfied.

(2)   Deaf-blindness means concomitant hearing and visual impairments, the combination of which causes such severe communication and other developmental and educational needs that they cannot be accommodated in special education programs solely for children with deafness or children with blindness.

(3)   Deafness means a hearing impairment that is so severe that the child is impaired in processing linguistic information through hearing, with or without amplification that adversely affects a child's educational performance.

(4)   (i)   Emotional disturbance means a condition exhibiting one or more of the following characteristics over a long period of time and to a marked degree that adversely affects a child's educational performance:

      (A)   An inability to learn that cannot be explained by intellectual, sensory, or health factors.

      (B)   An inability to build or maintain satisfactory interpersonal relationships with peers and teachers.

      (C)   Inappropriate types of behavior or feelings under normal circumstances.

      (D)   A general pervasive mood of unhappiness or depression.

      (E)   A tendency to develop physical symptoms or fears associated with personal or school problems.

   (ii)   Emotional disturbance includes schizophrenia. The term does not apply to children who are socially maladjusted, unless it is determined that they have an emotional disturbance under paragraph (c)(4)(i) of this section.

(5)   Hearing impairment means an impairment in hearing, whether permanent or fluctuating, that adversely affects a child's educational performance but that is not included under the definition of deafness in this section.

(6)   Mental retardation means significantly subaverage general intellectual functioning, existing concurrently with deficits in adaptive behavior and manifested during the developmental period, that adversely affects a child's educational performance.

(Continued)

Table 1.1   (Continued)

(7) Multiple disabilities means concomitant impairments (such as mental retardation-blindness or mental retardation-orthopedic impairment), the combination of which causes such severe educational needs that they cannot be accommodated in special education programs solely for one of the impairments. Multiple disabilities does not include deaf-blindness.

(8) Orthopedic impairment means a severe orthopedic impairment that adversely affects a child's educational performance. The term includes impairments caused by a congenital anomaly, impairments caused by disease (e.g., poliomyelitis, bone tuberculosis), and impairments from other causes (e.g., cerebral palsy, amputations, and fractures or burns that cause contractures).

(9) Other health impairment means having limited strength, vitality, or alertness, including a heightened alertness to environmental stimuli, that results in limited alertness with respect to the educational environment, that—

  (i) Is due to chronic or acute health problems such as asthma, attention deficit disorder or attention deficit hyperactivity disorder, diabetes, epilepsy, a heart condition, hemophilia, lead poisoning, leukemia, nephritis, rheumatic fever, sickle cell anemia, and Tourette syndrome; and

  (ii) Adversely affects a child's educational performance.

(10) Specific learning disability.

  (i) General. Specific learning disability means a disorder in one or more of the basic psychological processes involved in understanding or in using language, spoken or written, that may manifest itself in the imperfect ability to listen, think, speak, read, write, spell, or to do mathematical calculations, including conditions such as perceptual disabilities, brain injury, minimal brain dysfunction, dyslexia, and developmental aphasia.

  (ii) Disorders not included. Specific learning disability does not include learning problems that are primarily the result of visual, hearing, or motor disabilities, of mental retardation, of emotional disturbance, or of environmental, cultural, or economic disadvantage.

(11) Speech or language impairment means a communication disorder, such as stuttering, impaired articulation, a language impairment, or a voice impairment, that adversely affects a child's educational performance.

(12) Traumatic brain injury means an acquired injury to the brain caused by an external physical force, resulting in total or partial functional disability or psychosocial impairment, or both, that adversely affects a child's educational performance. Traumatic brain injury applies to open or closed head injuries resulting in impairments in one or more areas, such as cognition; language; memory; attention; reasoning; abstract thinking; judgment; problem-solving; sensory, perceptual, and motor abilities; psychosocial behavior; physical functions; information processing; and speech. Traumatic brain injury does not apply to brain injuries that are congenital or degenerative, or to brain injuries induced by birth trauma.

(13) Visual impairment including blindness means an impairment in vision that, even with correction, adversely affects a child's educational performance. The term includes both partial sight and blindness.

Source: Regulation 300.8c: Definitions of disability terms. *Building the Legacy: IDEA 2004.* U.S. Department of Education.

Table 1.2   Commonly Used Acronyms

AAC | Alternative Augmentative Communication
ABA | Applied Behavioral Analysis
ABC | Antecedent, Behavior, Consequence
ADA | Americans with Disabilities Act
ADD/ADHD | Attention Deficit/Attention-Deficit Hyperactivity Disorder
ADLs | Activities of Daily Living
ASD | Autism Spectrum Disorders
AT | Assistive Technology
AYP | Adequate Yearly Progress
BIP | Behavioral Intervention Plan
BOE | Board of Education
CAPD | Central Auditory Processing Disorder
CEC | Council for Exceptional Children
CP | Cerebral Palsy
CST | Child Study Team
DB | Deaf-Blind
DD | Developmental Delay
DIBELS | Dynamic Indicators of Basic Early Literacy
DSM | *Diagnostic and Statistical Manual of Mental Disorders* by the American Psychiatric
        Association
ECSE | Early Childhood Special Education
ED | Emotional Disturbance
EI | Early Intervention
ELL | English Language Learner
ESD | Extended School Day
ESEA | Elementary and Secondary Education Act
ESL | English as a Second Language
ESY or EYS | Extended School Year or Extended Year Services
FAPE | Free Appropriate Public Education
FAS | Fetal Alcohol Syndrome
FBA | Functional Behavioral Assessment
FERPA | Family Educational Rights and Privacy Act
HI | Hearing Impaired
HoH | Hard of Hearing
HQT | Highly Qualified Teacher
IAES | Interim Alternative Educational Setting
ID | Intellectual Disabilities*
IDEA | Individuals with Disabilities Education Act
IEP | Individualized Education Program
IFSP | Individualized Family Service Plan
LD | Learning Disability

(Continued)

Table 1.2 (Continued)

LEA | Local Education Agency
LEP | Limited English Proficiency
LRE | Least Restrictive Environment
MD | Muscular Dystrophy
MD or MH | Multiple Disabilities or Multiply Handicapped
MDR | Manifestation Determination Review
NASDSE | National Association of State Directors of Special Education
NCLB | No Child Left Behind Act (Elementary and Secondary Education Act)
OCD | Obsessive-Compulsive Disorder
OCR | Office of Civil Rights
ODD | Oppositional Defiant Disorder
OHI | Other Health Impairment
OI | Orthopedic Impairment
O & M | Orientation and Mobility
OSEP | Office of Special Education Programs
OT | Occupational Therapy
PBS | Positive Behavioral Supports
PD | Physical Disability
PDD | Pervasive Developmental Disorder
PLEP or PLP | Present Level of Educational Performance or Present Level of Performance
PT | Physical Therapy
RS | Related Services
RTI | Response to Intervention
SEA | State Education Agency
SEAC | Special Education Advisory Committee
Section 504 | Section 504 of the Rehabilitation Act
SED | Serious Emotional Disturbance
SI | Sensory Integration
SLD | Specific Learning Disability
SLI | Speech/Language Impairment
SLP | Speech/Language Pathologist
SST | Student Study Team
TBI | Traumatic Brain Injury
TDD | Telecommunication Devices for the Deaf
VI | Visual Impairment
Voc Ed | Vocational Education
VR | Vocational Rehabilitation

Source: Center for Parent Information and Resources (retrieved 3/12/15). Disability and Special Education Acronyms, Newark, NJ.

*Until October 2010, IDEA used the term *mental retardation*. In October 2010, Rosa's Law was signed into law by President Obama. Rosa's Law changed the term to be used in future to *intellectual disability*. The definition of the term itself did not change, only the use of "intellectual disability" instead of "mental retardation."

School counselors, as stated previously, must have the fundamental terminology in their vernacular, in order to effectively work with students with disabilities, students' parents, and colleagues. A related but distinct area to be aware of is how language regarding disability has evolved and impacted these students. The following are reflections from each of the authors of this chapter as to this notion of language and stereotypes which persist in regard to disability.

LANGUAGE AND STEREOTYPES

Haas Reflection

Using person-first language is a bugaboo of mine. Children are children and should be identified as such. IDEA itself uses the phrase "Child with a disability" in Section 300.8. So, rather than saying, the learning disabled student, it is better to use the phrase, "student with a learning disability." It sounds trite, but readers, consider the phrase "mentally retarded kid." What images does that conjure? Personally, as a special educator and advocate, I reflect on Willowbrook, a New York State run institution for people with disabilities, uncovered in 1972 as an inhumane and abusive residential facility, in which an overpopulated group endured unspeakable treatment. I am a firm believer that we must never forget how society used to treat our most fragile population, and we should remain proud of how far we have come, while never settling for where we are. Now reflect on the phrase "that mentally retarded kid" versus "the child with an intellectual disability." Some may say that it is just semantics or political correctness. By using child-first language, the mind will first consider the child and the disability second. Having an intellectual disability is just one aspect of a person and their character. Having worked with and taught students with intellectual disabilities, I can speak firsthand that my students are funny, bright, talented, inquisitive, stubborn, emotional, kind, friendly, and loving, to name just a few characteristics. When considering the educational programs students use, I am, again, a strong component for using student-first language. "The life skills kids" gives people an unspoken message that can pigeonhole students. It is better to say, "Students who access a life skills program," as there is much more to students than just a program in which they are enrolled. Another phrase commonly used is "confined to a wheelchair." By definition, confine means something that encloses or restrains. People are not confined *to*, they use a wheelchair for mobility. Language has power. We can all reflect on words that are unacceptable and offensive in our culture. Within special education and rights for people with disabilities, Rosa's Law, Public Law 111–256 changed the term *mental retardation* to *intellectual disability*. I am in hopeful anticipation of the change of the IDEA classification, Emotional Disturbance.

Trolley Reflections

In Chapter 11, the language and stereotypes associated with disability are further addressed. It is, however, important to introduce these concepts now in regard to students with disabilities, in order to set the stage for subsequent discussions. There is also an intimate tie with disability language and the previously discussed classification of students in special education. Diagnostic classifications are meant to shed light on the nature of the disorder, differentiate its existence from other disorders, and provide guidance to interventions. Unfortunately, such nomenclature is often used freely, and with negative connotations attached. Psychopath and Sociopath are just two examples of diagnostic disorders that have been applied to people's behavior, not as a clinical disorder but in terms of a derogatory statement being made. These images are daily reinforced in the media, whether it is a television show, a newspaper article, or a YouTube clip. This is demonstrated in the Guided Practice Exercise 1.1.

These misnomers also trickle down to youth. Most readers can remember one, if not numerous, time they heard the word *retard* on the school bus, playground, classroom, or neighborhood. Perhaps this is a word you yourself have used without a second thought. Furthermore, some educators, for example, may perceive learning disabilities to be a "catchall category" and that not everyone with that classification has a valid disability. Think back to a time when you heard a teacher state that a student was just "lazy" or "unorganized" or "unmotivated." If these assumptions abound, then appropriate accommodations may be lacking.

In addition to the negative psychosocial impact of these statements and perceptions, expectations of these students may be lowered and self-fulfilling prophecies

Guided Practice Exercise 1.1

MEDIA REPRESENTATIONS OF DIVERSITY

Over the next day or two, pay close attention to what you see on television shows, advertisements, and the news, as well as what appears in Internet stories, magazines, and the newspaper. Reflect back on the last movie you saw. What types of diversity were represented? Was a broad sample of people from diverse backgrounds included? Were these depictions accurate or stereotypical? If crimes had been committed, how were the alleged perpetrators described? If mental health issues were involved, how were these issues described (e.g., Were these issues the main focal point of the story? Was the act that occurred blamed on the mental health issue?)? If you were the writer of these stories and advertisements, what changes would you make?

(i.e., "I am disabled and have deficits, therefore, I will never be able to achieve my goals") developed, both of which can have far-reaching effect. Earle (2003) addressed the concerns that people with disabilities are less likely to go to college and get a job. Similarly, Corrigan and Watson (2002) poignantly discussed the challenges people with mental illness face, including limited opportunities for jobs, safe housing, health care, and interaction with diverse groups of people.

In addition, stereotypes of people with disabilities are associated with responses to them. Wolfensberger (1972), in his classic work on *normalization,* had addressed the connection of people's perceptions to treatment choices for persons with intellectual disabilities. For example, all are familiar with the inhumane conditions that people with mental illness suffered centuries ago. They were often seen as deranged and, subsequently, feared and locked away. Your first reaction might be, "But this was in the long distant past!" Now ask yourself, "Could similar things happen today?" This latter point is illustrated in Case Illustration 1.1.

In more recent times, there has been a movement away from the word *disabled* and cruel treatment of those with disabilities. I encourage all of the readers to take a moment and look up the word *disability* in a thesaurus. Just a few examples of what you will find are synonyms such as *disqualification*, *unfit*, and *defect*. It is no wonder that negative connotations of people with disabilities persist! Even though invisible disabilities are not excluded from stereotyping, they are often perceived as faking or lazy traits. Fortunately, there is now more emphasis on people's abilities,

CASE ILLUSTRATION 1.1

"IS THIS STUDENT *REALLY* WEIRD?"

Imagine you are a middle school student with a high-functioning autism diagnosis. You tend to focus on one topic, coin collecting. You have had this hobby for years and want to share this interest with your peers. Every day, you introduce this topic at the lunch table. In addition, you have a flat affect, and constantly interrupt others. You begin to notice that fewer people are sitting next to you at lunch, and you overheard some kids saying "weirdo" and "nerd" while they were pointing at you. The school counselor has noticed this behavior in the cafeteria and has called you into the office. You talk about what happened, as well as your desire to make friends. You begin to practice conversations with peers, doing role plays. The school counselor invites you to join a group.

as well as the use of person-first language. Person-first language appeared toward the end of the 20th century (Folkins, 1992; Snow, 2010; Staff, 1985). Bickford (2004) further discussed the intent of person-first language as a means of changing stereotypes and reducing bias against those with disabilities by focusing on the individual. Documents have even been written that address *disability etiquette* (United Cerebral Palsy Association, 2015; United Spinal Association, 2011). Instead of defining students by their disability (e.g., the crippled student), the focus is on who they are (the student with mobility impairment who has a great sense of humor). There is also a shift to asking how these students can achieve their maximum performance, often at the same level of their peers, albeit via an alternative format (e.g., with the assistance of a note taker, or having tests read). This does not mean that every educator will refrain from using older language and non-person-first terminology. Old habits die hard; it is a challenge after decades of speaking in a certain way to change. What is most important is not whether a slip of the tongue occurs but rather that sensitivity to students as people, not one characteristic (i.e., the disability), exists.

Language can perpetuate stereotypes, and stereotypes can prolong the use of negative jargon. Earle (2003), in addressing the Disability Rights Commission Campaign, raised the question, Is a person with a disability only half a person?, and discussed disability as a form of social oppression and stigma. Furthermore, Allison (2013) wrote an intriguing historical review titled "What Sorts of People Should There Be? From Descriptive to Normative Humanity." This author ends the article with a hope for more openness toward and greater recognition of the nontypical. Both of these publications point to the fact that while great progress has been made in terms of dispelling stereotypes and biases, many still remain. Many who are reading this text are familiar with the negative connotations students associate with classes held at Board of Cooperative Education Services (BOCES): "Only dummies go there." It is essential that early intervention occurs, not only with respect to the impairment but also in terms of developing a positive perception and treatment of students in special education. To further demonstrate these principles, consider Case Illustration 1.2.

School counselors can be key players in this mission, helping to educate, enhance the sensitivity of, and role model appropriate language and attitudes toward, and treatment of, students in special education. A first step may be the conduction of workshops at the start of each year for teachers, administrators, and staff. In addition to sharing specific knowledge, it is important that the audience be involved in experiential activities and that attitudes and biases are explored. Many scales exist that can assess attitudes toward disability (Ali, Strydom, Hassiotis, Williams, & King, 2008; Power & Green, 2010), as well as toward inclusion (Schwab, Gebhardt, Eder-Flick, & Klicpera, 2012). School counselors could also use less formal means of assessing attitudes such as the age old exercise of free

CASE ILLUSTRATION 1.2

"WHAT'S MY PROBLEM?"

Rashana is at the book fair. She is struggling to get between the aisles of books and is having a hard time holding all of her belongings, dropping some of them on the ground. Rashana appears anxious, frustrated, tired, and overwhelmed. She is not asking for help, but she appears to be talking to herself at times. Others are not offering her any help either. Rashana approaches the counter to purchase the books she selected, and her hand is trembling as she pulls out her money. Do you think Rashana has a disability, and, if so, what do you think it is and why? Many of you may have guessed an orthopedic impairment, others of you may have thought she has an emotional disorder. Some have thought she was under the influence of prescribed or other substances. Still others speculated that she may have tendencies similar to someone with schizophrenia. The ultimate point is that stereotypes abound, and our perceptions are colored by many things such as our past experiences, our own state at the time, values and beliefs, cultural backgrounds, and education. It is essential that these stereotypes are confronted. (By the way, the above is a description of myself, when I had the first of my five children in a stroller, and I was at the university bookstore trying to buy books for my doctoral program!)

association to words associated with disabilities. These activities could also be done with parents and students. (Note, standardized instruments would need to be chosen with respect to the norm age group of the instrument.) It is also important for school counselors to be aware of school policies and have a knowledge base and training with respect to specific topics, as Spears (2006) indicated in his discussion of the need for school professionals to have preparation before working with students with HIV/AIDS.

School counselors could additionally work with the student population. Indirectly, working within a team to assist students who are included would be of benefit. It has been found that inclusive education enhances social interaction among students and reduces negative stereotypes of students in special education (Ali, Mustapha, & Jelas, 2006). The more prepared and supported teachers are, the better the inclusion transition will be (Engelbrecht, Nel, & Pekka-Malinen, 2012; Mastin, 2010; Rodriguez, Saldana, & Moreno, 2012). Furthermore, if teachers are less stressed, they most likely will be role modeling more positive attitudes toward students in special education. Integrating disability education into the general curriculum is another task with which school counselors can assist. While they are not responsible for curriculum decisions or development, they can offer ideas and resources. Initially, teachers may resist as they feel overwhelmed with the current demands of the Common Core Standards and those associated with the No Child Left Behind Act. Can you imagine asking them to put something more on their plate? However, simplistic tasks such as the following could be manageable:

- Writing a book report on a person with a disability
- Discussing historical reactions to disability
- Showing a movie that addresses a disability and stereotypes
- Having a guest speaker with a disability
- Inviting a member of the team to address a disability topic
- Visiting a community center that serves people with disabilities such as a museum or an Independent Living Center
- Sponsoring an art contest about positive depictions of people with disabilities
- Having a child in special education share his or her disability (only with parental consent, and student assent)
- Searching the web, within appropriate limits set forth by the school district, for disability resources and depictions of people with disabilities

Ferguson (2001) postulated eight reasons why such infusion is important and describes 17 ways this can be done, some of which are described above. A creative activity was suggested by Seidler (2011). Students in middle school were first asked to explore stereotypes of disability and then challenge these views by the creation of comic strips. This study speaks to not only the content of disability education but also the chosen vehicle of its communication. Would students rather hear a lecture on disability or read a comic strip?

Knowledge is also important in facilitating better understanding of the disorder, minimizing fear, and decreasing stereotypes. Penn and Couture (2002), in their work which addressed people with psychiatric disabilities, supported the notion of knowledge decreasing stigmatization. These authors further discussed the problems with studies which suggest contact with people with disabilities can reduce stigmatization. Anyone who has held a door for someone with a disability and been yelled at can attest to the fact that simple contact in and of itself may be positive or negative in regard to stereotyping. Similarly, students who maximize the secondary gains of having a disability may leave educators and peers with negative perceptions. Imagine you are the gym teacher. One of your seventh-grade students, Tim, has been excused from taking physical education classes as he has an identified disability. You are walking down the hall one day, and you see Tim "goofing" off with his friends and sliding down the school stair banister. Besides being a liability issue for all students and a disciplinary issue (i.e., banister riding is against school policy), you are left wondering about the validity of his need to be excluded from all physical education activities. The question of whether Tim is taking advantage of his disability comes to mind. Or you are Samantha's teacher. She has a hearing impairment. One of her accommodations in her Individualized Education Program (IEP) is to have an interpreter. You are in constant communication with the interpreter to be sure that Samantha is clear about class notes, assignments, and homework. Yet Samantha continues to not turn in her homework, claiming she did not know what was expected. She continues to complain about a variety of class issues and indicates she can do very little by herself. In stepping back, you are struck by the possibility that she is obtaining secondary gains (receiving indirect benefits or social advantage from having a disability such as increased attention or release from chores) and is exhibiting learned helplessness (feeling powerless to change a situation and/or looking to others to complete her tasks, such as a student with a disability who is capable of walking up stairs and carrying his own books but insists on his need to use the elevator and have a peer helper).

As mentioned earlier, school counselors can role model positive behavior toward students in special education and use person-first language. Utilizing the philosophical underpinnings of the latter, school counselors, within individual and group counseling, can help students develop positive identities, seeing themselves beyond their disability. An excellent example of this process is found in the deaf culture. Often, people within this culture go to the end of the continuum and separate themselves from the disability concept (Jones, 2002). If they do not see themselves as being disabled, they are then not lacking in a human characteristic and can develop more positive self-esteem.

In the above discussion in regard to special education language and stereotypes, the multifaceted roles and tasks school counselors can assume, individually and within a team, to assist students with disabilities are addressed, and the importance of seeing and valuing these students as *children first,* not their disability, is stressed. Prior to the conclusion of this chapter, thoughts from a practicing school counselor working in an educational setting which serves students with disabilities are shared. In the following reflection, the positive impact of the willingness of school counselors to be diversified, flexible, and respectful in working with these students is illuminated.

Reynolds Reflection

School counseling and special education hold a special place in my heart. It can be rewarding and exasperating at the same time. Working with students who often see the world in a different way has pushed me to see beyond my own boundaries. Each student is unique; how his or her disability manifests is unique; the counseling program that is designed for him or her is created with these unique characteristics in mind. There is not a one-size-fits-all approach; it needs to be tailored to each student. How boring it would be if I used only one method for teaching frustration management or one way for increasing self-esteem! Because every student is different, I am able to be creative in my approaches.

My role in the realm of special education is incredibly multifaceted. A solid foundation in special education is paramount, including how to create an appropriate IEP as well as a 504 Plan, gather or know and apply the data needed for the least restrictive environment (LRE) decision process, understand discipline and how it relates to disabilities, apply guidelines for the academic intervention services (AIS) process and the response to intervention (RTI) process, and recognize the need for the collaborative team approach. Juggling all the different aspects can be overwhelming at times; this makes it apparent that there is a need for support for all participants. Consultation and collaboration provide the opportunity to share the workload.

The IEP/504 is the document to follow when counseling a student with special needs. My role is one of active participant in the IEP development. It should not fall on the shoulders of the school counselor to create the IEP; in fact, it needs to be a collaborative effort of a team consisting of the classroom teacher, special area teachers, school counselor, student support professionals (i.e., physical therapist, occupational therapist, speech therapist), and the parents. The team consists of professionals who know the children and are knowledgeable in their field. In order to create an accurate picture of the students, I need input from people who interact with the students on a regular basis. If there have been struggles on the bus, in the cafeteria, or in the nurse's office, it is vital to have a discussion with the staff in these areas. Data can be shared at the IEP meeting that is across all services, rather than just from the classroom.

According to the American School Counselor Association (ASCA), school counselors "help all students in the areas of academic achievement, personal/social development and career development" (ASCA, 2015, para. 4). In regard to students with special needs, we are governed by special education laws, which are in place to make sure the students receive what they need in order to level the playing field. It is vital for the school counselor to follow state and federal guidelines, board policies, and district policies and procedures. "Professional school counselors are committed to helping all students realize their potential and meet or exceed academic standards regardless of challenges resulting from disabilities and other special needs" (ASCA, 2013, p. 48). In order for students to realize their potential, a school counselor needs to advocate for placement in the least restrictive environment. Before placing students in a more restrictive setting, other options need to be attempted along with data collection. For example, a student who is struggling with the noise level in the cafeteria or in a hallway may find success when he or she utilizes sound canceling headphones. Rather than removing the student completely from the setting, providing strategies for the student to use so success can be more readily achieved is ultimately a better route. This is just one example of how the school environment can be disabling for a student, that is, a handicap that can easily be removed through a simple modification.

Data collection can be a tedious job, but without it, you have little to back up your words. It can be time consuming and even difficult to get team members on board with it. As a school counselor in a special education program, it is important to use a team approach when creating the goals and the data collection system; if classroom teachers do not buy into the collection system, there will be few data to report on. What can be frustrating is when it is readily apparent a student needs services, but data is lacking. With schools tightening the budget, they cannot be expected to provide services at a cost when there are no data to support the request. It is also difficult to attend a Committee on Special Education (CSE) meeting requesting services when there are few data to support the request for services. My job is to advocate for what my students need, and the best way I can do that is to bring data to the table. Through the years, I have used several different data information systems and with the increase in popularity of apps, a school counselor has a variety to choose from.

"A quality counseling program lies at the heart of an educational process committed to empowering students to realize their full academic potential" (Beale, 2003, p. 68). Through communications with the parents, special education department, teachers, student support professionals, and any outside professionals, I have to develop and implement effective counseling techniques with students receiving special education services. The counseling services must provide assistance to the students in order to meeting academic and social needs, but often this cannot be accomplished until behaviors that are interfering with the process are being managed. Assisting the teacher with behavior management planning is an important step to creating a system that will help the classroom run accordingly. Functional Behavioral Assessments (FBAs) and the development of Behavior Intervention Plans (BIPs), along with staff training, are duties that a school counselor needs to be familiar with. Observations across all services and at different times of day will provide the most accurate picture. The importance of this data collection has previously been emphasized. Creating data collection forms to track behaviors, including their antecedents and consequences, are part of the practice. In order to obtain accurate data, the forms need to work for the needs of the teacher. There are teachers who are more willing to maintain documentation than others; the data forms need to support the teacher and not be too cumbersome.

Students' needs are unique and personal to them. They bring their own experiences, strengths, and struggles into the counseling program. Consulting and collaborating with teachers, student support professionals, and parents help school counselors to understand the special needs of the student. It creates opportunities for team members to work on goals across all systems. This becomes an effective way for the delivery of services. Collaboration extends beyond the school building; working cooperatively with agencies lays the foundation for coordinating the use of community referral services. Again, advocating for the needs of the students both inside and outside of the school system is imperative. Utilizing cross systems meetings provides the opportunity to review data, share information, and brainstorm ideas and options to continue supporting the student as they progress in the school year. During these meetings, resources can be shared with the parents, and questions can be answered.

One important strategy that I teach across the board to my counseling students is *change begins with you.* You can choose to be happy. You can choose your attitude. You can choose your path in life. Your past does not have to dictate your future, unless you choose it to. Too often, I see students making excuses for their behaviors because of their disability; this is something learned, something they heard others state as a reason for the behaviors. It can be empowering for students to learn that they have a choice. It can be frustrating for school counselors when the students continue to blame the disability for the behaviors. It becomes a bit of a puzzle, at times, to figure out how to get the students to buy into a change in thought processes; it is much easier when the students decide it is their idea. Reality therapy, brief solution focused therapy, and cognitive behavioral therapy are all part of my "bag of tricks" for getting to the bottom of some issues. Sensory integration, in collaboration with the occupational therapist, has shown positive results in the counseling program. Teaching students how to regulate their own systems, based on their sensory issues, is the first part in teaching them they have a choice.

For example, Johnny is frustrated with his math worksheet. He is beginning to tense up his shoulders; he is gripping his pencil tighter; his neck is becoming sore and stiff. Johnny has been taught at the first signs of frustration to take a break and stretch. He asks for 2 minutes on the timer while he stretches the TheraBand with his arms and uses deep-breathing techniques. When the timer goes off, Johnny should be feeling less tense and uneasy.

This type of sensory break takes only a few minutes, but it provides relief from the stress the students are feeling. If Johnny is in a general education setting, he has other options to choose from: deep breathing in his seat, quiet stretching in his seat, and even asking for a 2-minute walk break in the hallway. The strategies are determined by the needs, as well as the responsibility level, of the students. After teaching strategies to students, I am able to attend general education classes with them. This provides the perfect opportunity to practice those strategies in the moment. This ability of school counselors to provide students support in a setting in which they have struggled provides more depth to the counseling program. In real time, I can walk these students through the struggle, so they are seeing success more quickly. The first time students are able to find that success becomes that moment they can reflect on. The students now have proof of their success and their ability to make positive choices.

School counseling in the special education arena can be very rewarding. There is something incredible about watching students with special needs achieve success over their struggles and give you that smile because they now know they can do it. Those successes may look small to people on the outside, but the baby steps add up quickly when the students make the connection between positive behavior choices and success.

SUMMARY

As indicated in the above discussions, "cookie cutter" approaches and labeling, which stereotypes and pigeonholes these students, are to be avoided at all costs. In contrast, individualized assessments and interventions, collaboration and consultation, and creativity and patience are essential ingredients in helping students with special needs achieve success, which is possible for and personal to them. Each child, even those with similar classifications, is a unique individual with varied needs that must be met in order to achieve his or her maximum potential.

In order to facilitate this positive development of students with special needs, it is important for school counselors to first examine their own attitudes, biases, life experiences, knowledge, and skills in regard to disability. Another classic book for all professionals to read is that by Beatrice Wright (1983): *Physical Disability: A Psychosocial Approach.* While it would be nice to assume that school counselors are positive role models all of the time, the truth is that they too are human and have their own "baggage." It is not uncommon for their perceptions of students with disabilities to be tainted by their own experiences and contact with this population, as well as by their lack of knowledge, resulting in assumptions and generalizations. For example, having held a door open for a student in a wheelchair which resulted in anger and resentment by the student may bias the school counselor in a future encounter and result in the development of negative perceptions of those using a wheelchair. Yet, like every person, this student reaction could easily be tied to his or her personality or prior events of the day and have nothing to do with the disability itself. Another example may involve the school counselor's lack of awareness of a disorder such as cerebral palsy, resulting, perhaps, in an assumption that these students are all also intellectually, not just physically, challenged (this illustrates the notion of *spread*). In reality, many students with cerebral palsy are well within the *normal* range of intellectual functioning. In both cases, it would behoove the school counselors to explore their reactions and obtain factual information.

In addition, school counselors need to be aware of guidelines set forth by their school districts and their professional organizations, such as the American School Counselor Association previously mentioned, as to their roles. While the multitude of varied tasks addressed in this and subsequent chapters can at first appear daunting and overwhelming, working from a framework that is based on employment and professional standards can provide clarity and structure. To this end, the standards of the accrediting body of school counselor preparation programs, the Council for Accreditation of Counseling and Related Educational Programs (CACREP), are woven throughout each chapter. To facilitate brevity and avoid repetition, the primary CACREP standards, which are infused throughout, are II.G.1;5 and those identified in the school counseling knowledge, skills, and practice domains. While this book is intended to assist school counselors in training, it is also an excellent resource for those practicing school counselors and professionals in related fields working with students with disabilities.

KEYSTONES

- All school counselors must have a basic, working knowledge of special education, so that this area of service becomes part of their professional identity.
- It is crucial that school counselors know how disabilities are classified, what each entails, common acronyms frequently utilized, and where to find additional information.
- It is essential that school counselors are familiar with the impact that language has had over time on children with disabilities and the stereotypes that still exist.
- Each student is unique; how his or her disability is manifested is unique, so the counseling program that is designed for the child is created with these unique characteristics in mind. There is no one-size-fits-all approach: it needs to be tailored to each student.
- Consultation and collaboration provide the opportunity to share the workload. The team consists of professionals who know the child and are knowledgeable

in their field. However, collaboration extends beyond the school building. It is important to cooperatively work with agencies and establish a foundation for the development of referral services within the community.

- In regard to students with special needs, we are governed by special education laws, which are in place to make sure the students receive what they need in order to level the playing field. It is vital for school counselors to follow state and federal guidelines, school board-district policies, and procedures.
- In order for students to realize their potential, school counselors need to advocate for placement in the least restrictive environment (LRE).

ADDITIONAL RESOURCES

Print

Geltner, J., & Leibforth, T. (2008). Advocacy in the IEP process: Strengths-based school counseling in action. *Professional School Counseling, 12*(2), 162–165.

Goffman, E. (1963). *Stigma: Notes on the management of spoiled ID*. New York, NY: Simon & Schuster.

Lam, W., Gunukula, S., McGuigan, Isiah, N., Symons, A., & Akl, E. (2010). Validated instruments used to measure attitudes of healthcare students and professionals towards patients with physical disability: A systematic review. *Journal of Neuroengineering and Rehabilitation, 7*(55). Retrieved from http://www.ncbi.nlm.nih.gov/pmc/articles/PMC2987969/

Milsom, A. (2002). Students with disabilities: School counselor involvement and preparation. *Professional School Counseling, 5*(5), 331–338.

Milsom, A., & Akos, P. (2011). Preparing school counselors to work with students with disabilities. *Counselor Education and Supervision, 43*(2), 86–95.

Milsom, A., Goodnough, G., & Akos, P. (2007). School counselor contributions to the Individualized Education Program (IEP) process. *Preventing School Failure, 52*(1), 19–24.

Wright, B. (1983). *Physical disability: A psychosocial approach.* New York, NY: Harper & Row.

Web Based

Activities

Classroom Activities to Teach Your Students About Disabilities: http://voices.yahoo.com/classroom-activities-teach-students-about-4674537.html

Highlighted Resource: In the Mix. What's Normal—Overcoming Obstacles and Stereotypes: http://www.pbs.org/inthemix/whatsnormal_index.html

Articles

Articles on Students with Disabilities: http://articles.baltimoresun.com/keyword/students-with-disabilities

Counseling in Middle/Secondary Schools: http://education-portal.com/academy/lesson/counseling-in-middle-secondary-schools.html#lesson

EngageNY (developed and maintained by the New York State Education Department-NYSED): https://www.engageny.org/

Improving Educational Outcomes for Students with Disabilities: file:///C:/Users/Owner/Downloads/Improving%20Educational%200utcomes%20(1).pdf

New York State Education Department (NYSED) Office of Special Education (OSE): http://www.p12.nysed.gov/specialed/

School Counselor Contributions to the Individualized Education Plan: http://www.redorbit.com/news/education/1137381/school_counselor_contributions_to_the_individualized_education_program_iep_process/

Scales

BioMedSearch: http://www.biomedsearch.com/nih/Validated-instruments-used-to-measure/21062438.html

Measurement of Attitudes Toward People With Disabilities: http://www-rohan.sdsu.edu/~mstover/tests/antonak.html

Stereotypes in Media

Common Portrayals of Persons with Disabilities: http://mediasmarts.ca/diversity-media/persons-disabilities/common-portrayals-persons-disabilities

REFERENCES

Ali, M., Mustapha, R., & Jelas, Z. (2006). An empirical study on teachers' perceptions towards inclusive education. *International Journal of Special Education, 21*(3), 36–44.

Ali, A., Strydom, A., Hassiotis, A., Williams, R., & King, M. (2008). A measure of perceived stigma in people with intellectual disability. *The British Journal of Psychiatry, 192,* 410–415.

Allison, K. (2013). What sorts of people should there be? From descriptive to normative humanity. *International Disability, Community and Rehabilitation Journal, 12*(2), n.p. Retrieved from http://www.ijdcr.ca/VOL12_02/articles/allison.shtml

American School Counselor Association (ASCA). (2013). *The professional school counselor and students with disabilities.* Retrieved from http://schoolcounselor.org/asca/media/asca/Position Statements/PS_Disabilities.pdf

American School Counselor Association (ASCA). (2015). *Careers/Roles.* Retrieved from http://schoolcounselor.org/school-counselors-members/careers-roles

Beale, A. (2003). The indispensable school counselor. *Principal Leadership.* Retrieved from http://www.principals.org/portals/0/content/46906.pdf

Bickford, J. (2004). Preferences of individuals with visual impairments for the use of person-first-language. *Rehabilitation and Education for Blindness and Visual Impairment, 36*(3), 120–126.

Corrigan, P., & Watson, A. (2002). Understanding the impact of stigma with mental illness. *World Psychiatry, 1*(1), 16–20.

Earle, S. (2003). Disability and stigma: An unequal life. *Speech and Language Therapy in Practice, 2*(33), 21–22.

Engelbrecht, P., Nel, M., & Pekka-Malinen, O. (2012). Understanding teachers' attitudes and self-efficacy in inclusive education: Implications for pre-service and in-service teacher education. *European Journal of Special Needs Education, 27*(1), 51–68.

Ferguson, P. (2001). *On infusing disability studies into the general curriculum. On point—Brief discussions in urban education.* Washington, DC: U.S. Dept. of Education, Office of Educational Research and Improvement, Educational Resources Information Center.

Folkins, J. (1992, December). Resource on person first language: The language used to describe individuals with disabilities. American Speech-Language Hearing Association (ASHA). Retrieved from http://www.asha.org/publications/journals/submissions/person_first.htm

Jones, M. (2002). Deafness as culture: A psychosocial perspective. *Disability Studies Quarterly, 22*(2), 51–60.

Mastin, D. (2010). *General and special education teachers' attitudes toward inclusion of Down syndrome students* (Doctoral dissertation, Walden University). Retrieved from ProQuest LLC database. (ERIC Document Reproduction Service No. ED514449).

Penn, D., & Couture, S. (2002). Strategies for reducing stigma towards persons with mental illness. *World Psychiatry, 1*(1), 20–21.

Power, M., & Green, A. (2010). The Attitudes to Disability Scale (ADS): Development and psychometric properties. *Journal of Intellectual Disability Research, 54*(9), 860–874.

Rodriguez, I., Saldana, D., & Moreno, F. (2012). Support, inclusion, and special education teachers' attitudes toward the education of students with autism spectrum disorders. *Autism Research and Treatment, 12.* doi:10.1155/2012/259468

Schwab, S., Gebhardt, M., Eder-Flick, E., & Klicpera, B. (2012). An examination of public opinion in Austria towards inclusion. Development of the "Attitudes Towards Inclusion Scale"—ATIS. *European Journal of Special Needs Education, 27*(3), 355–371.

Seidler, C. (2011). Fighting disability stereotypes with comic strips: "I cannot see you, but I know you are staring at me." *Art Education, 64*(6), 20–23.

Snow, K. (2010). *To ensure inclusion, freedom and respect for all, it's time to embrace person-first language.* Retrieved from http://sda.doe.louisiana.gov/ResourceFiles/Resources/PFL10.pdf

Spears, E. (2006). Students with HIV/AIDS and school considerations. *Teacher Education and Special Education, 29,* pp. 5–16.

Staff. (1985, March). NRA initiates campaign for language awareness. *NRA Newsletter*, pp. 1, 3–4.

United Cerebral Palsy Association. (2015). *Tools for reporters*: *Disability etiquette.* Retrieved from http://ucp.org/?s=Tools+for+reporters%3A+Disability+etiquette

United Spinal Association. (2011). *Disability etiquette.* Retrieved from http://www.unitedspinal.org/pdf/DisabilityEtiquette.pdf

Wolfensberger, W. (1972). *The principle of normalization in human services.* Toronto, Ontario, Canada: National Institute on Mental Retardation.

Chapter 2

Educational Initiatives and Professional Organization Standards

EDWARD A. MAINZER, EdD, LMHC
New York City Department of Education

"The peculiar disadvantage of change agents in education lies in applying methods which are largely educational to situations which are fundamentally political."

—Dale Mann, *Making Change Happen?* (Teachers College Press, 1978)

School counselors, like other educators, work in contexts shaped by both professional and political forces. This chapter explores how some major U.S. educational initiatives as well as standards promulgated by leading counseling professional organizations have helped shape the milieu in which school counselors serve students in general, and students with disabilities (SWD) in particular. It is critical that we understand these forces if we are to ensure the continued relevance of our work and effectively advocate for and deliver services to all of our children and youth.

In this chapter you will be introduced to some of today's major educational initiatives and professional organization standards. Note, this discussion is intended to give an overview of these areas. While it is essential to uphold these mandates and abide by the standards, diversity in the specific integration and application of these initiatives and standards, as well as in their value, may occur depending on such variables as the school's location, size, type, level, staffing, and funding. Specifically, after reading this chapter you will be able to achieve the following:

1. Identify the relevance of the Common Core State Standards for school counselors.

2. Compare and contrast positions taken by major counseling professional organizations and accreditation bodies related to school counseling.

3. Assess the significance of current educational initiatives and professional organization standards for school counselors serving students with disabilities.

EDUCATIONAL INITIATIVES

Educational initiatives have long been at the heart of the American experience. As was observed by Lawrence Cremin, American's greatest historian of education, "The movement of education to the core of the American experience, already discernible during the nineteenth century, accelerated during the twentieth" (1988, p. 12), and "political questions have been inescapable from the beginning" (p. 14). Thus, the national movement represented by the 21st century Common Core State Standards (CCSS) is part of a long political history, which in the words of Wiley and Rolstad "marks the most recent effort to create national standards" (2014, p. 38). A federal U.S. Office of Education was first established following the Civil War in 1867; however, despite adding some programs over the years, especially following World War I, major expansion of the federal role in education occurred only in the post–World War II period. The National Defense Education Act of 1958 and especially the Elementary and Secondary Education Act (ESEA) of 1965, which subsequently morphed into No Child Left Behind (NCLB) in 2002, have impacted almost every U.S. school child.

Two additional pieces of federal legislation are particularly critical to those serving students with disabilities (SWD). Following the adoption of Title IX in 1972 which prohibited discrimination based on gender, in 1973 Congress passed Section 504 of the Rehabilitation Act, prohibiting discrimination based on disability. And then in 1975, the Individuals with Disabilities Education Act (IDEA), also known then as public law (PL) 94–142, fundamentally changed the landscape, essentially creating special education as it exists nationally today. (Note, as of 2004, IDEA is now identified as the Individuals with Disabilities Education Improvement Act, or IDEIA.) As subsequently renewed (most recently in 2004), the law provides the legal mandate for special education programs throughout the United States, including the Individualized Education Program (IEP) process, and opens by stating,

Disability is a natural part of the human experience and in no way diminishes the right of individuals to participate in or contribute to society. Improving educational results for children with disabilities is an essential element of our national policy of ensuring equality of opportunity, full participation, independent living, and economic self-sufficiency for individuals with disabilities. (Individuals with Disabilities Improvement Education Act, 2004, pp. 2–3)

This was followed in 1990 by the wide-ranging Americans with Disabilities Act (ADA), which, unlike the IDEA, is not limited to education. Thus, it is enforced by the U.S. Departments of Labor, Transportation, and Justice as well as by the Federal Communications and Equal Employment Opportunity Commissions. See Chapter 3 of this volume for an extended discussion of Section 504, IDEA, and ADA.

In 1980, the U.S. Department of Education had become a cabinet-level agency, and a variety of reports and initiatives followed, perhaps most famously 1983's *A Nation at Risk,* issued by a commission appointed by the U.S. Secretary of Education, that warned of dire consequences in the absence of higher standards for U.S. students and helped fuel the changes that led to ESEA's transformation into NCLB. The CCSS are unlike these earlier efforts since despite enjoying considerable federal support, particularly with the federal Race to the Top (RTTT) grants of 2009, the CCSS were propagated by states' leaders, not the national government. An understanding of them is critical for school counselors.

COMMON CORE STATE STANDARDS (CCSS)

What Are the CCSS?

The Common Core State Standards (CCSS) were initiated by the National Governors Association (NGA) and Council of Chief State School Officers (CCSSO) between 2006 and 2010, growing out of the so-called standards and accountability movement in U.S. education. The CCSS took concrete form with the convening of teams to write K–12 standards in mathematics and literacy, which were issued in 2010. In their words, "The Standards are (1) research and evidence based, (2) aligned with college and work expectations, (3) rigorous, and (4) internationally benchmarked" (Common Core State Standards Initiative, 2010a, p. 3). CCSS are designed to address the concern to set consistent content standards for American education in a globalized world, ensuring that U.S. youth finish high school and college and are career ready to address the challenges faced by students who move between schools and districts in America's mobile society. The CCSS "define what all students are expected to know and be able to do, not how teachers should teach" (Common Core State Standards Initiative, 2010a, p. 6); nonetheless, "the Common Core represents a potential sea change in the highly fragmented, decentralized system of U.S. education" (Kornhaber, Griffith, & Tyler, 2014, p. 3).

An alphabet soup of organizations has since become involved with the CCSS, particularly in designing and marketing CCSS-aligned assessments, which have been among their most controversial components. These include the Partnership for Assessment of Readiness for College and Careers (PARCC). PARCC is in turn managed by Achieve, which was created by a group of governors and corporate leaders in 1996 "dedicated to supporting standards-based education reform efforts across the states" (Achieve, 2012, p. 1). PARCC received federal RTTT funding with which it is

> building a K–12 assessment system that: builds a pathway to college and career readiness for all students; creates high-quality assessments that measure the full range of the Common Core State Standards; supports educators in the classroom; makes better use of technology in assessments; and advances accountability at all levels. The first exams will be given in 2014–15. (Achieve, 2012, p. 2)

In a guide addressed specifically for school counselors, Achieve's leaders have written, "[f]or school leaders and counselors, implementing the CCSS is not about thinking out of the box. It is about transforming the box itself" (Achieve, 2013, p. 4).

An overlapping group of states (since some states have joined both groups) are affiliated with the Smarter Balanced Assessment Consortium (SBAC). They have also received RTTT funding but are specifically designing a technology-based assessment system:

> Smarter Balanced is developing a system of valid, reliable, and fair next-generation assessments aligned to the CCSS in English language arts/literacy (ELA/literacy) and mathematics for grades 3–8 and 11. The system—which includes both summative assessments for accountability purposes and optional interim assessments for instructional use—will use computer adaptive testing (CAT) technologies to the greatest extent possible to provide meaningful feedback and actionable data that teachers and other educators can use to help students succeed. (Smarter Balance, 2013, p. 1)

This has led to particular concerns that "without first addressing the current digital divide and opportunity gap amongst schools statewide, launching this nature of assessment will further increase the existing achievement gap between the wealthiest and poorest schools and districts" (Kawahata, 2013, p. 3). Smarter Balance has proactively articulated a system of supports for diverse learners, including English language learners (ELLs), students with disabilities (SWD), and ELLs with disabilities, through a system of universal tools available to all students; designated supports available to all students deemed to need them, and particularly SWD and ELLs with disabilities, in addition to accommodations specifically for SWD and ELLs with disabilities; and has developed extensive frequently asked questions (FAQs) specific to each population (Smarter Balance, 2014).

How CCSS Impacts on School Counselors

While acknowledging that "some view them as narrowing the curriculum and having been developed by corporate and political interests over the needs of students with a lack of evidence of success prior to usage" (Chen-Hayes, Ockerman, & Mason, 2014, p. 28), school counseling educators, such as Chen-Hayes, Ockerman, and Mason, have nonetheless called upon school counselors to find connections between the CCSS and the ASCA National Model and use them as opportunities to collaborate with classroom staff. Similarly, Achieve issued a statement on the role of the school counselor in implementing the CCSS, proclaiming that "knowing about the standards is important. Learning how schools must change to meet the CCSS is critical. School counselors need an understanding of how the standards will affect the three domains of professional school counselors—academic, career, and personal-social—in relation to the needs of their students" (2013, p. 7). Achieve continues by suggesting a range of ways for school counselors to engage the CCSS:

- Think across grade levels.
- Develop comprehensive school counseling plans.
- Provide focused professional support to teachers and academic supports to students.
- Work in alignment with American School Counselor Association (ASCA) national standards for professional school counseling.
- Create standards-based college- and career-focused lessons.
- Design clearer processes for course sequencing and credit articulation (p. 9).

Lawrence Jones, developer of The Career Key vocational assessment, has also written of the relationship between ASCA standards and CCSS as "a challenge and opportunity for school counselors" (2014, p. 3). In his analysis, they both share the goals of preparing students for college and careers and include identified student outcomes. However, unlike the CCSS, the ASCA standards overlap grades and provide more flexibility and discuss psychological development. Further, and touching upon issues in serving SWD, Jones expresses concern that "not all students are likely to have the ability or background to achieve the Common Core Standards at the same level, such as those students who are English Learners" (2014, p. 5). Nonetheless, Jones concludes that there are opportunities for both standards to complement each other in ensuring college and career success and that given their adoption by the vast majority of U.S. states and territories as well as the District of Columbia, it is critical that school counselors collaborate with other stakeholders around them. Thus, for example, school counselors can help students and parents understand them—particularly if CCSS aligned assessments are causing anxiety— and also incorporate alignments to CCSS when authoring plans for classroom-based school counseling lessons.

A self-described "action brief" issued by Achieve and other groups with funding from the MetLife Foundation calls on school counselors as school leaders to believe that "[t]he adoption of these standards means that **all, not just some students should be on the pathway to college and career readiness**" [emphasis in the original] (Achieve, 2013, p. 3). The American Counseling Association (ACA) has also issued a brief on the CCSS, calling on school counselors to familiarize themselves with them and how their school district implements them. The ACA also calls on counselors to not just "understand how their comprehensive, development counseling program integrates with Common Core, [as] that is how the components of their program support student outcomes and help students become college and career-ready," but as well—and particularly relevant to serving SWD— to "understand Common Core components and implementation so that they may facilitate the inclusion of all students as appropriate and advocate for those who might be excluded from activities needed for their success" (American Counseling Association, 2013, p. 1).

What Do the CCSS Say About SWD?

Early judgments regarding the impact of CCSS on SWD were varied, but there was no shortage of opinions. On the one hand, Haager and Vaughn wrote that "[t]he CCSS document and supporting appendices say very little about accommodating students with disabilities, only that some students may need extra supports to achieve competency" (2013, p. 1), and Kornhaber et al. wrote that "the Common Core's goals encompass equity. Yet, compared to No Child Left Behind, the role and meaning of equity within this reform are less sharply defined" (2014, p. 4). Similarly, analyzing the CCSS and SWD, the Center for Mental Health in Schools of the Department of Psychology at the University of California, Los Angeles, expressed concern that "the movement ignores the need to provide a unified and comprehensive system of student and learning supports to enable all students to benefit from the upgraded curriculum" (Center for Mental Health in Schools, 2012, p. 1).

By contrast, Thurlow (2012) has written more optimistically that "unlike many past educational efforts, the CCSS seem to have been developed with all students in mind" (p. 1). And looking specifically at writing skills and students with learning disabilities (LD)—the largest category of students within special education, Graham and Harris have written that although "[i]t will be years before we know if CCSS and its implementation make a difference in the improving education in the United States and more specifically the writing of students with and without LD," it is critical that "if evidence-based writing practices are to be a central component in the implementation of CCSS, we need to have a better understanding as well as more sophisticated models for how to prepare teachers to judiciously and intelligently implement such procedures and sustain their use" (2013, p. 36).

The opening to the CCSS ELA Standards includes that volume's only specific reference to SWD:

The Standards should also be read as allowing for the widest possible range of students to participate fully from the outset and as permitting appropriate accommodations to ensure maximum participation of students with special education needs. For example, for students with disabilities reading should allow for the use of Braille, screen-reader technology, or other assistive devices, while writing should include the use of a scribe, computer, or speech-to-text technology. In a similar vein, speaking and listening should be interpreted broadly to include sign language. (Common Core State Standards Initiative, 2010a, p. 6)

However, there is also a separate two-page CCSS document, "Application to Students With Disabilities," which states that

students with disabilities—students eligible under the Individuals with Disabilities Education Act (IDEA)—must be challenged to excel within the general curriculum and be prepared for success in their post-school lives, including college and/or careers. These common standards provide an historic opportunity to improve access to rigorous academic content standards for students with disabilities. (Common Core State Standards Initiative, 2010b, p. 1)

The statement then goes on to cite applicable federal guidelines and endorse supports based on the universal design for learning (UDL) strategies, instructional accommodations, and assistive technology devices. And while acknowledging that "some students with the most significant cognitive disabilities will require substantial supports and accommodations," the statement authors call for that to occur while nonetheless "retaining the rigor and high expectations of the Common Core State Standards" (Common Core State Standards Initiative, 2010b, p. 2). Similarly, the National Education Association (NEA), which was involved in their development, "believes the CCSS have the potential to provide access to a complete and challenging education for all children" (National Education Association, 2013, p. 3).

Their CCSS "Toolkit" includes a special section on SWD, and in addition to citing use of supports such as UDL, response to intervention (RTI), accommodations, and assistive technology, the NEA believes that the CCSS "provide a historic opportunity to improve access to rigorous academic content standards for students with disabilities" (2013, p. 49).

So How Does the School Counselor Ensure Success for SWD on the CCSS?

The role of the school counselor with regard to SWD and the CCSS speaks to a school counselor as part of the team of professionals in every school responsible for ensuring academic success for every student. It also speaks to the important role of the social justice roots of school counseling. Ultimately, it is about best practices to ensure that every student graduating from high school is college and career ready, including broadening the definition of *college* to include a more robust range of postsecondary opportunities since at least initially post–high school options other than a traditional 2- or 4-year college experience may be more appropriate for some individuals with different developmental abilities as well as differing interests. These principles are demonstrated in the Guided Practice Exercise 2.1.

Guided Practice Exercise 2.1

WHY DO THE CCSS MATTER FOR SCHOOL COUNSELORS?

Suppose you were part of the conversation that follows: What would you say next?

Counselor 1: "I'm so glad I'm not a teacher! I just couldn't be bothered to keep up with all these constant policy changes like these new common standards."

Counselor 2: "You mean the Common Core State Standards? They're important for counselors too."

Counselor 1: "Common core whatever; I made the choice not to be a classroom teacher, so I don't have to worry about them."

Counselor 2: "I have to disagree with you there; I think that as professionals working in educational institutions, school counselors need to be quite aware of these changes if they're going to be leaders in their schools."

Counselor 1: "Really, prove it! Give me examples of how those Common Core State Standards are relevant to what I do as a school counselor."

How do you respond?

COUNSELING PROFESSIONAL ORGANIZATIONS AND ACCREDITATION STANDARDS

The profession of school counseling, as Linda Foster writes, "is still a relatively new one and our identity as 'professionals' is still evolving" (2012, p. 42). Thus, it is not surprising that requirements for school counselor certification continue to evolve. "There is no single definition or scope of practice delineated in 50 diverse state licensing laws for professional counselors and requirements for school counselor certification" (Brady-Amoon, 2012, p. 191). Nonetheless, there are several major sources for recommendations regarding necessary skills for counselors. Unquestionably, the most influential recommendations for 21st century counselor skills come from the Council for Accreditation of Counseling and Related Educational Programs (CACREP), an organization which is itself an outgrowth of developments spearheaded by the American Counseling Association (ACA). Note, the specific organizations are individually discussed below. A summary of the Crosswalk of Selected Recommendations for School Counselor Competencies, based on CACREP, the American School Counselor Association (ASCA), and National Association for College Admission Counseling (NACAC), is presented in Table 2.1.

Table 2.1   Crosswalk of Selected Recommendations for School Counselor Competencies

CACREP	*ASCA*	*NACAC*
	Understanding of the organizational structure and governance of the educational system	
Legal and ethical considerations specific to school counseling	Addressing legal, ethical, and professional issues in PK–12 schools	Demonstration of appropriate ethical behavior and professional conduct
Human Growth and Development*	Developmental theory Identifying impediments to student learning; developing strategies to enhance learning	Possess a knowledge of the psychology of children, adolescence and young adults, human growth and development, and learning needs
Techniques of personal/social counseling in school settings	Counseling theory	Counseling and communication skills
Career Development*	Career counseling theory	Counsel students; full range of career options

(Continued)

Table 2.1   (Continued)

CACREP	ASCA	NACAC
Social and Cultural Diversity*	Social justice theory and multiculturalism	Recognize, appreciate, and serve cultural differences and the special needs of students and families
Characteristics, risk factors, and warning signs of students at risk for mental health and behavioral disorders	Mental health services including prevention and intervention	
Helping Relationships*	Individual counseling	Exemplary counseling and communication skills
Group Work*	Group counseling	Individual and group guidance sessions for students and parents
Curriculum design, lesson plan development, classroom management strategies, and differentiated instructional strategies	Classroom guidance	Workshops
Interventions to promote academic development; use of developmentally appropriate career counseling interventions and assessments; techniques of personal/social counseling in school settings	Promote academic achievement, personal/social growth, and career development	Addressing the personal, social, and emotional concerns and problems that may impede their educational development
Models of school-based collaboration and consultation	Collaboration and consultation with stakeholders	
School counselors as leaders, advocates, and system change agents	Using advocacy to close the achievement–opportunity gap	Advocacy and leadership in advancing the concerns of students
Use of accountability data to inform decision making; use of data to advocate for programs and students	Using data-driven school counseling practices	Develop, collect, analyze, and interpret data
Signs and symptoms of substance abuse in children and adolescents		
School emergency management plans, and crises, disasters, and other trauma-causing events		

Table 2.1   (Continued)

CACREP	ASCA	NACAC
Strategies to facilitate school and life transitions		Facilitate transitions and counsel students toward the realization of their full educational potential
Interventions to promote college readiness		Assist students in understanding the admission process
Assessment and Testing* Research and Program Evaluation*		

Source: Urofsky, R., Bobby, C.L., & Ritchie, M. (2013). CACREP: 30 years of quality assurance in counselor education. *Journal of Counseling & Development, 91*(1), 3–5; National Association for College Admission Counseling (2000) Statement on counselor competencies.

*This is a CACREP core curricular experience not restricted to school counseling.

AMERICAN COUNSELING ASSOCIATION (ACA)

The American Counseling Association (ACA) began in 1952 when the National Vocational Guidance Association, National Association of Guidance and Counselor Trainers, Student Personnel Association for Teacher Education, and American College Personnel Association (ACPA) convened a meeting that led to the birth of the American Personnel and Guidance Association (APGA). Although the word *counseling* was absent from APGA's name, "APGA's founding is usually referenced as the birth of the counseling profession" (Hodges, 2012, p. 192). APGA went through a series of name changes before assuming its current identity as the American Counseling Association (ACA), although in the process, it lost the ACPA, which disaffiliated in the 1990s, taking many members with it. As of 2015, ACA claimed 55,000 members.

Among the ACA's publications is *Code of Ethics* (American Counseling Association, 2014), which is regularly updated. In addition to a nondiscrimination clause that includes disability (Section C.5), it mandates appropriate accommodations for clients with disabilities when administering assessments (E.7.a) and includes counselors' obligation to recognize the impact of disability under Multicultural Issues/Diversity in Assessment (E.8). Additionally, the section on Distance Counseling, Technology, and Social Media requires counselors with websites to ensure access to persons with disabilities (H.5.d). Among the ACA's divisions is the American Rehabilitation Counseling Association (ARCA), which is dedicated to promoting life-span development of people with disabilities.

COUNCIL FOR ACCREDITATION OF COUNSELING AND RELATED EDUCATIONAL PROGRAMS (CACREP)

CACREP was founded in 1981 by the APGA working together with the Association for Counselor Education and Supervision (ACES) to accredit masters and doctoral programs in counseling. Although participation is voluntary, CACREP is a dominant force in counselor training programs. It accredits graduate-level programs in counseling fields including addiction counseling; career counseling; clinical mental health counseling; marriage, couple, and family counseling; school counseling; student affairs and college counseling; and counselor education and supervision. In October 2013, CACREP's position was further enhanced with the announcement that the Council on Rehabilitation Education (CORE), which was founded in 1971 by yet another set of professional organizations to accredit graduate study in rehabilitation counseling and eventually accredited undergraduate programs in the field as well, would become affiliated with CACREP.

By 2014, CACREP accredited 639 graduate programs in counseling, constituting almost two thirds of such programs in the United States (Kimbel, personal communication, February 27, 2014). They also reported that 27 states specifically cite CACREP in their rules or regulations (Ritchie & Bobby, 2011); this included, as of 2012, "22 states [which] have written graduation from a CACREP-accredited program into their guidelines as one pathway toward meeting the educational requirements for licensure" (Urofsky, Bobby, & Ritchie, 2013, p. 4). In addition to outlining the structure of credential requirements, CACREP has identified 31 specific competencies they believe necessary for school counselors, and which they divide into three domains: foundations, contextual dimensions, and practice (Council for Accreditation of Counseling and Related Educational Programs [CACREP], 2013, pp. 24–25). The current set of CACREP standards was issued in 2009; CACREP has since issued proposed revisions for public comment on new standards due to be finalized in 2016.

For CACREP accreditation, graduate programs must require that candidates complete a master's degree consisting of at least 48 credits, although as of the 2014 draft proposal, new CACREP requirements would increase that to a minimum of 60 credits effective July 1, 2020 (CACREP, 2013, p. 3). As part of the master's degree, CACREP requires that graduate students in approved counseling programs successfully complete an entry-level practicum of at least 100 hours over at least 10 weeks, including at least 40 hours of direct service with actual clients; and subsequently an internship of at least 600 hours, including at least 240 hours of direct service, which must include group leadership experiences; both the practicum and the internship include ongoing weekly professional supervision (CACREP, 2009, p. 16). The accreditation process itself involves the completion of a self-study of the given counselor preparation program within the particular institution of higher education; the institution completes the self-study of their program based on CACREP criteria, sending paperwork off to CACREP for its review, and ultimately having a site visit as well as opportunity for institutional response before a decision on whether or not to accredit a program is rendered.

The CACREP 2009 Standards contain very few explicit references to individuals with disabilities. The Professional Identity's section of the general standards calls for programs to ensure that the curricular experiences and demonstrated knowledge of understanding of human growth and development include "human behavior, including an understanding of developmental crises, disability, psychopathology, and situational and environmental factors that affect both normal and abnormal behavior" (Council for Accreditation of Counseling Related Educational Programs, 2009, p. 11). There are additional specific references to knowledge of "disability services" and the needs of "students with disabilities" in the standards for student affairs and college counseling, but the standards for school counseling reference students with disabilities only tangentially.

Under skills and practices, the school counselor should design and implement "prevention and intervention plans related to the effects of atypical growth and development," along with five other variables including "health and wellness" (CACREP, 2009, p. 41). Similarly, under the knowledge base for assessment, counselors are called on to understand "the influence of multiple factors (e.g., abuse, violence, eating disorders, attention deficit hyperactivity disorder, childhood depression)" (p. 42). By comparison, the second draft of CACREP 2016 Standards, which were open for public comment into 2014, proposed under human growth and development to add "theories of learning," "theories of normal and abnormal personality development," as well as "individual, biological, neurological, physiological, systemic, spiritual, and environmental factors that affect human development, functioning, and behavior" (CACREP, 2013, p. 8). Under assessment and testing counselors, it was also proposed that counselors know the "use of assessment results to diagnose developmental, behavioral, and mental disorders" (p. 10).

The second draft of the proposed CACREP 2016 Standards also made more explicit calls for counselors specializing in postsecondary counseling and particularly those earning degrees in clinical rehabilitation counseling to have specific skills around clients with "disabilities." As regards school counselors, the second draft of the proposed CACREP 2016 Standards suggested among other areas adding an understanding of the "characteristics, risk factors, and warning signs of students at risk for mental health and behavioral disorders" (p. 31) and the ability to engage in "classroom management strategies" (p. 32) as competencies.

NATIONAL BOARD FOR CERTIFIED COUNSELORS (NBCC)

The National Board for Certified Counselors (NBCC) was incorporated in 1982 and developed a national credential for counselors before the counselor licensure movement spread to all states across the nation. The advantage of NBCC is in being a single uniform national credential, unlike the patchwork of distinct state licensure requirements that now concurrently exist. NBCC credentials include National Certified Counselors (NCC), which is a prerequisite or co-requisite for their specialty credentials including Certified Clinical Mental Health Counselor (CCMHC), originally developed by the National Academy for Certified Clinical Mental Health Counselors in 1979 and taken over by NBCC in 1993; National Certified School Counselor (NCSC) developed in 1991 in cooperation with the American School Counselor Association (ASCA); and Master Addictions Counselor (MAC). Each of the credentials is based on a separate examination, and NBCC reports having certified over 80,000 counselors in the United States and internationally.

Hodges (2012) has noted that with the spread of counselor licensure nationwide in the early 21st century, the role of licensure organizations has shifted, and there has been "debate regarding NBCC's utility . . . in the post-licensure era," with defenders "arguing a license should be for general practice while national certification should identify specialty areas" (p. 192). As Hodges has also written, with the rise of licensed mental health counseling, there continues to be a struggle over the identity of unlicensed counselors, including school counselors, as well as with the more established clinical titles of social work and psychology.

THE EDUCATION TRUST AND NATIONAL OFFICE FOR SCHOOL COUNSELOR ADVOCACY (NOSCA)

In the 1990s, The Education Trust working with funding from the DeWitt Wallace-Reader's Digest Fund formed the National Center for Transforming School Counseling (NCTSC). They "argue[d] for the interdependence of the efforts of universities and district partners to reform the work of practicing school counselors and called for both schools and universities to address the disconnect between preparation and practice" (Seahorse, Jones, & Seppanen, 2001, p. 31). Following a national survey, they developed a grant process known as the Transforming School Counseling Initiative (TSCI), awarding funds to school counselor training programs dedicated to implementing programs "to reform public school counseling, especially in low-achieving schools, to ensure that counselors play a larger, more significant role in assuring the academic achievement of all children" (Seahorse et al., 2001, p. 3). The first participating universities in 1997, each paired with a cooperating school district, were in California, Indiana, Ohio, Georgia (two universities), and Florida. Writing the next year, NCTSC leaders proposed "a model of activism where counselors function as leaders, change agents, and as people willing to take risks" (House & Martin, 1998, p. 285), which they saw as an imperative for counselors based on the ASCA *Code of Ethics.*

As the 1990s turned into the 2000s, Patricia Martin was particularly significant to the impact of the NCTSC. Martin had a long history of advocacy as a school counselor, building principal, and school district leader when she was recruited by The Education Trust. In reflecting on what had been accomplished to date and calling for further action at the beginning of the new century, Martin (2002) wrote:

> The mission for schools in the 21st century focuses squarely on effective teaching and learning. Standards-based education reform, with a relentless call for accountability and increased academic achievement for all students, comes at a time of booming technological advances and rapidly changing diversity in the composition of U.S. schools. The convergence of these forces, coupled with a critical look at school counseling at the close of the 20th century, provided a perfect opportunity for re-thinking, re-framing, and transforming the role of school counseling in American schools. (p. 148)

And Martin and her colleagues at NCTSC believed that school counselors were "in a critical position to focus on issues, strategies, and interventions that will assist in closing the achievement gap between low-income and minority students and their more advantaged peers." Indeed, she argued, "issues of equity, access, and supporting conditions for success come to rest at the counselor's desk" (Martin, 2002, p. 149).

The NCTSC argued against those university programs that prepare school counselors primarily to serve as mental-health style individual therapists when they have caseloads that make it impossible to serve all students in such a manner and instead called for school counselor education programs to "teach students how to use data to support decision making, and develop strategies for removing institutional barriers to student success" (Hines & Lemons, 2011, p. 5). They identify five core competencies school counselors need to master in their "new vision": (a) leadership, (b) advocacy, (c) team and collaboration, (d) counseling and coordination, and (e) assessment and use of data.

Moving from The Education Trust, between 2002 and 2013 Martin continued her leadership at College Board, serving as an assistant vice president in its National Office of School Counselor Advocacy (NOSCA). Focused on promoting "the value of school counselors as leaders in school reform, student achievement and college readiness" (College Board, 2010b, p. 4), Martin went on to challenge school counselors to

> step away from being "maintainers of the status quo" and become "dream-makers and pathfinders" for all students navigating their way through K–12 schools today. They must have the courage to stand up for students who may be unable to stand up for themselves in systems that have produced disparate academic results and thus, few to no postsecondary options for many students in the past. (College Board, 2010a, p. 6)

Martin's work has influenced a generation of school counselor educators and their students (e.g., Chen-Hayes, Ockerman, & Mason, 2014; Dahir & Stone, 2012; Hatch, 2014; Ockerman, Mason, & Chen-Hayes, 2013).

NOSCA's Eight Components of College and Career Readiness Counseling are as follows:

1. College Aspirations ("build a college going culture")

2. Academic Planning for College and Career Readiness ("a rigorous academic program")

3. Enrichment and Extracurricular Engagement ("ensure equitable exposure")

4. College and Career Exploration and Selection Processes ("early and ongoing exposure")

5. College and Career Assessments ("for all students")

6. College Affordability Planning

7. College and Career Admission Processes ("so they can find the postsecondary options that are the best fit with their aspirations and interests")

8. Transition from High School Graduation to College Enrollment ("to help the students overcome barriers and ensure the successful transition from high school to college"; College Board, 2010a, p. 3).

The national advocacy office calls for the first six elements to begin at the elementary level and continue through middle school into high school where they should be joined by the final two components (College Board, 2010a). In regard to the learner with special needs, in writing about the culturally competent school counselor, NOSCA commented about a counselor being aware of how "my own group membership(s) (race/ethnicity, gender, disability, socio-economic status, nationality, and/or religion) can impact my group and other groups, especially groups that are traditionally underrepresented in college and career readiness" (College Board, 2011, p. 18), but the advocacy group does not specifically discuss students with disabilities, seeing adaptation to the students' needs as implicit in the broader advocacy role of the school counselor.

AMERICAN SCHOOL COUNSELOR ASSOCIATION (ASCA)

The American School Counselor Association (ASCA) was chartered in 1953 as the fifth division of what was then the American Personnel and Guidance Association and is now the American Counseling Association (ACA). Since then, ASCA has grown to become the dominant voice of the school counseling profession through an active program that includes professional publications, national conferences and awards, and lobbying and collaboration with other professional groups around the nation and even internationally. By 2015, ASCA represented over 30,000 members and had developed a strong identity and national presence independent of the ACA. Indeed, in January 2015 for the first time, ASCA's School Counselor of the Year ceremony was held in the White House, building on momentum established following First Lady Michelle Obama's address to ASCA's National Conference in July 2014 as part of her Reach Higher Initiative to promote postsecondary education.

Historically, counselors were required to join both the ACA and a division if they wished to belong to either, but reflective of the complexities in counselor identity, particularly among school and mental health counselors—who began to affiliate with the American Mental Health Counselor Association (AMHCA)—that requirement was dropped. Indeed, Hodges has written that

> while ASCA and AMHCA remain divisional affiliates of ACA, each collects separate membership dues, holds separate national conventions, retains their own lobbyists and publicizes themselves as primary organizations representing their respective counseling specialties. From an outside perspective, ASCA and AMHCA's relationship with ACA appears tenuous and one can only speculate whether they will remain divisional affiliates. (2012, p. 193)

Hodges has also noted that most U.S. counselors do not affiliate with any professional organization.

These tensions became particularly acute when the ACA started work in 2005 with the American Association of State Counseling Boards (AASCB) to develop a vision of the counseling profession in the year 2020. The so-called 20/20 Vision for the Future of Counseling (generally known as 20/20) intended to establish "the core set of principles that unify the various membership, certifying, accrediting, and honor society groups within the profession of counseling" (Kaplan, Tarvydas, & Gladding, 2011, p. 3). ACA divisions, including ASCA, were part of this process; however, the ASCA declined to sign off on 20/20's definition of counseling, questioning whether there is really one unified counseling profession (Studer, 2015, p. 23). Writing of the initial refusal in which the ASCA was at one point joined by Counselors for Social Justice (CSJ), the ACA leadership dismissed the refusal as representing only 6% of the ACA's "entities" (Kaplan et al., 2011, p. 10); however, ASCA continues to be the largest single division within the ACA. Writing in support of the ACA's position on 20/20, King and Stretch nonetheless concluded that "[t]he counseling profession is experiencing an identity crisis as the profession passes through Erikson's adolescent stage of development and asks, 'Who are we?'" (2013, p. 9).

Debate over the role of the school counselor continued in 2012 when the ASCA released a draft of the third edition of *The ASCA National Model* that listed "working with one student at a time in a therapeutic, clinical mode" (American School Counselor Association, 2012a, p. 21) as an inappropriate activity for school counselors. In an April 2012 letter on behalf of ACA, its then President Don W. Locke expressed disagreement, noting that "school counselors may be the first—and at times the only—mental health professionals students see and they must be able to provide individual counseling to students when appropriate. This counseling may be clinical in nature" (Locke to Burkhard, personal communication, April 18, 2012, p. 1). As finally published, the ASCA revised that portion of its third edition to indicate that only "providing therapy or long-term counseling in schools to address psychological disorders" was inappropriate (American School Counselor Association, 2012b, p. 45). Indeed, some research has suggested "that professional school counselors' least diffused and thus most unique role in the school setting is in the provision of direct counseling services to students" (Astramovich, Hoskins, Gutierrez, & Bartlett, 2013, p. 181), leading others to conclude that "both school counselor roles, that of educational leader and that of mental health professional, are necessary to address the overwhelming level of mental health needs of students" (DeKruyf, Auger, & Trice-Block, 2013, p. 274).

The ASCA National Model

The single most important development in professional school counseling in the last generation has been the creation and subsequent implementation of model-based counseling spearheaded by the ASCA. "Since the early 1990's, the majority of state school counselor associations have used elements of the comprehensive and/or developmental process as the underpinning for program design, delivery, and evaluation" (Dahir & Stone, 2007, p. 1). The ASCA published the first edition of *The ASCA National Model: A Framework for School Counseling Programs* in 2003, quickly followed by a second edition in 2005. The model recognizes the critical role of counselors in promoting students' growth in three areas: personal-social, academic, and career development. The model also speaks to the need for school counseling departments to consider program delivery and management systems, including data collection and accountability, as critical components of a comprehensive school counseling plan. "School counselors must be able to effectively show the results of their work with students in concrete and measurable ways, illustrating to others why having a school counseling program is critical to student success" (Curry & Lambie, 2007, p. 145). For example, show results by demonstrating the impact of targeted school counselor interventions on such metrics as state standardized test scores, discipline referrals, or student absences and tardiness for selected groups of students.

ASCA's third edition in 2012 contained revisions in both format and content. The CD-ROM, which had been included in the second edition, was replaced by a code to link with online forms and a digital version was published simultaneously. An important part of the third edition was recognition of the changed educational landscape since the model was first issued, exemplified by the proliferation of standards, including the CCSS. Student standards, which had been a key part of the previous edition, were omitted from the book, an acknowledgment of the increased pace of change and of ASCA's ongoing revision process, although they remained available on the ASCA website. Additions to the third edition included a series of 18 two-to-three-page special topic pieces written by a wide range of counseling researchers and practitioners on topics from collaboration and leadership to RTI and science, technology, engineering, and math (STEM) education.

In line with best practices in other areas of education, the model calls for school counselors to engage in needs analysis, recognizing that different communities served by different schools will have different needs and should receive different counseling services. The model also calls upon counseling departments to develop a written vision statement that builds on that of the school in which they serve and to engage students and families they serve in the process of developing this statement. Counselors are called upon to critically examine how they provide services by engaging in time analysis to ensure that, for example, they push into classrooms to provide group counseling that reaches all students, not just the most needy or most demanding students. Data are a particularly important component of a transformed school counselor for their power to establish why districts need counselors.

The model's advocates have suggested that it has significant implications for transforming school counseling and believe that the model speaks to recognizing the key role counseling staff and services can play in school reform. In the introduction to the first adaptation of the model for international schools, Judy Bowers, one of the coauthors of the first edition of the *ASCA Model*, noted that "[w]hen counselors react to the immediate school needs, frequently only a small group of students are served," while in a model-based program, "all students are served when the counselors teach classroom lessons based on National competencies in the academic, career, personal-social, and global perspective domains" (Brown, 2011, p. 5). Summarizing effectiveness studies conducted by researchers at the Center for School Counseling Outcome Research and Evaluation, Lapan concluded that "when highly trained, professional school counselors deliver ASCA National Model comprehensive school counseling program services, students receive measurable benefits. Furthermore, comprehensive program implementation may be most beneficial for youth living in poverty" (2012, p. 88). Another important aspect of the ASCA Model is the Recognized ASCA Model Program (RAMP). Schools and their counseling departments may apply to ASCA for RAMP recognition by submitting a rigorous self-study packet. To date, implementation of the ASCA Model has been particularly strong in several core states, notably Arizona, Georgia, Illinois, Indiana, North Carolina, Rhode Island, and Virginia.

ASCA and SWD

Many components of an ASCA Model–based school counseling program are responsive to the special needs of SWD. One example is the model's treatment of response to intervention (RTI), a technique which made its way into general education decades before the 2004 reauthorization of the IDEA approved it as an alternative method to identify learning disability (LD) and which others have hoped will address the overrepresentation of minorities and students with low socioeconomic status in special education (Bineham, Shelby, Pazey, & Yates, 2014). *The ASCA Model* states that "RTI represents a theoretical approach to identifying students who are struggling in reading, mathematics or in their behavior through action research" (American School Counselor Association, 2012b, p. 73). RTI is also one of the topics covered in an ASCA position statement, "The Professional School Counselor and Response to Intervention" (retitled "The Professional School Counselor and Multi-Tiered Systems of Support" in 2014), which states that "[p]rofessional school counselors work collaboratively with other educators to remove systemic barriers for all students and implement intervention programs that assist in student success" (American School Counselor Association, 2013, p. 40).

Another important ASCA resource is *ASCA Mindsets and Behaviors for Students Success* (2014). First issued in draft in time for ASCA's 2014 national conference, it replaced the *ASCA National Standards for Students* (2004), which had originally been issued in 1997 and served as a core document until the ASCA National Model was developed. Subtitled "K–12 College- and Career-Readiness Standards for Every Student," the *Mindsets and Behaviors* provide research-based competencies under the categories of learning strategies, self-management skills, and social skills, all aligned by grade level to the CCSS and designed to provide a framework for small-group and whole-class school counselor interventions. Particularly relevant to SWD, they are based on the premise "that content knowledge and academic skills are only part of the equation for student success" (American School Counselor Association, 2014, p. 1). They are also linked to searchable database(s), allowing counselors to both locate and contribute resources.

A separate ASCA position statement specifically addresses and is titled "The Professional School Counselor and Students with Disabilities." After noting the mandates of laws such as the IDEA and Section 504 of the Rehabilitation Act of 1973, ASCA states, "Professional school counselors recognize their strengths and limitations in working with students with disabilities. Professional school counselors also are aware of current research and seek to implement best practices in working with students presenting any disability category" (American School Counselor Association, 2013, p. 48). SWD is also a topic addressed in the ASCA *Code of Ethics*: from an introductory paragraph noting the right of each person to be treated with respect and have access to a comprehensive school counseling program without regard to a range of demographic characteristics including "abilities/disabilities," to affirming the particular rights to self-direction and self-development of those "who have historically not received adequate educational services" (American School Counselor Association, 2010, p. 1), to inclusion of advocacy for SWD under the section dedicated to and titled Multicultural and Social Justice Advocacy and Leadership. In Case Illustration 2.1, issues around

CASE ILLUSTRATION 2.1

SUSPENSION OF A STUDENT WITH A DISABILITY

Michael is an elementary school student in your school who has an IEP. He can be hyperactive, inattentive, and defiant and as such receives counseling from you one time per week according to his IEP as well as on an as needed basis. You identified him as having behavior problems out of control that at times could threaten the classroom both in terms of learning as well as safety. After a particular incident that sent Michael and another boy to the office, Michael was suspended from school for 3 days.

Michael's father called you and said that you were denying Michael his education through this suspension for 3 days. The principal said that suspending Michael for this incident was justifiable as he caused a fight where another child was hurt and that Michael had only been suspended one other time this academic year. Michael's father countered that if the teacher had been following Michael's behavior plan correctly, she would have sent Michael to you prior to things getting out of control.

First, what standards pertain to your involvement with Michael? (List.) Do you believe the school has the right to suspend Michael? If so, why? What supports your belief? Finally, how would you follow up with the parent, the teacher, the principal, Michael?

laws as addressed in Chapter 3, and school counselor strengths and limits within the educational process, as discussed in this chapter, are presented.

NATIONAL ASSOCIATION FOR COLLEGE ADMISSION COUNSELING (NACAC)

The National Association for College Admission Counseling (NACAC) was founded as the Association of College Admissions Officers in 1937 by a group of Midwestern colleges and universities. It incorporated in 1959, changed its name in 1968 (and again in 1995), and moved to Alexandria, Virginia, in 1987. It has since grown into an international organization with over 13,000 members now including a diverse range of college-access professionals, among them not only college admissions officers but also school counselors and independent counselors (Hoganson, 2012). During this evolution, the NACAC has also become involved in considering the skills and training needed by school counselors and has expressed concern that many "counselor education programs provide little or no attention to the precollege guidance and counseling aspect of the school guidance program" (National Association for College Admission Counseling, 2000, p. 1).

The NACAC therefore delineated specific competencies that they recommend as part of school counselor preparation programs including eight School Counselor and eight College Admission Counselor Competencies. One of the NACAC recommendations is that both school and college counselors should have the ability to develop, collect, analyze, and interpret data, including "tests of learning disabilities." They also call for counselors to "possess and demonstrate the counseling and consulting skills that will facilitate informed and responsive action in response to the cultural differences and special needs of students" (National Association for College Admission Counseling, 2000, pp. 5, 11). As regards SWD, the NACAC competencies state that both school and college counselors should be able to understand and interpret tests of learning disabilities as well as call for general advocacy regarding "the educational needs of students."

NACAC also issues and regularly updates a code of conduct known as the Statement of Principles of Good Practice (SPGP). A number of passages in the SPGP are particularly relevant to working with SWD, including the sixth of their six "Core Values," on "Social Responsibility," which states that "[w]e believe we have a duty to serve students responsibly, by safeguarding their rights and their access to and within postsecondary education" (National Association for College Admission Counseling, 2013, p. 2). Additionally, the second of their "member conventions" states that "members will evaluate students on the basis of their individual qualifications and strive for inclusion of all members of society in the admission process"

Guided Practice Exercise 2.2

DO THE DIFFERENT SCHOOL COUNSELING STANDARDS COME TOGETHER?

CACREP, ASCA, NACAC . . . there seem to be so many standards for school counselors to consider: Do these organizations even talk to one another?! Use Table 2.1 to compare and contrast how the proclamations of these different organizations do or do not relate to each other. Explain to what extent you see or do not see a unified vision of school counseling.

(p. 2). Finally, another section of the SPGP specifies that all postsecondary members agree to "providing accurate and specific descriptions of any special programs or support services available to students with handicapping conditions, physical and/or learning disabilities and/or other special needs" (p. 10). These concepts are illustrated in the Guided Practice Exercise 2.2.

KEYSTONES

- It is critical that school counselors keep abreast of changing trends, take ownership, and make their voices heard through membership and leadership in professional organizations, lobbying, and political activism in order to effectively advocate for diverse learners and ensure their inclusion.
- School counselors, like other educators, work in contexts shaped by both professional and political forces, and as such, it is critical that they understand these forces to ensure the continued relevance of our work and effectively advocate for and deliver services to students.
- Knowing about standards is important as school counselors need to develop and implement school counseling programs with respect to enhancing student competencies in three domains: academic, career, and personal-social.

ADDITIONAL RESOURCES

Print

American School Counselor Association. (2014). *ASCA mindsets and behaviors for student success: K–12 college- and career-readiness standards for every student.* Alexandria, VA: Author.

Chen-Hayes, S., Ockerman, M. S., & Mason, E. (2014). *101 solutions for school counselors and leaders in challenging times.* Thousand Oaks, CA: Corwin.

Dahir, C. A., & Stone, C. B. (2012). *The transformed school counselor* (2nd ed.). Belmont, CA: Brooks/Cole.

Hatch, T. (2014). *The uses of data in school counseling.* Thousand Oaks, CA: Corwin.

Struder, J. R. (2015). *The essential school counselor in a changing society.* Thousand Oaks, CA: Sage.

Web Based

American Counseling Association: http://www.counseling.org

American School Counselor Association: http://www.schoolcounselor.org

Center for School Counseling Outcome Research and Evaluation: http://www.umass.edu/schoolcounseling

Common Core State Standards: http://www.corestandards.org

Council for Accreditation of Counseling and Related Educational Programs: http://www.cacrep.org

REFERENCES

Achieve. (2012). Achieve & the American diploma project network. Washington, DC: Author. Retrieved from http://www.achieve.org/files/About%20AchieveADP-Apr2012.pdf

Achieve. (2013). Implementing the Common Core State Standards: The role of the school counselor. Washington, DC: Author. Retrieved from http://www.achieve.org/files/RevisedCounselor ActionBrief_Final_Feb.pdf

American Counseling Association (ACA). (2013). Common Core State Standards: Essential information for school counselors. Alexandria, VA: Author. Retrieved from http://www.counseling.org/docs/resources—school-counselors/common-core-state-standards.pdf?sfvrsn=2

American Counseling Association. (2014). *Code of ethics.* Alexandria, VA: Author. Retrieved from http://www.counseling.org/knowledge-center/ethics

American School Counselor Association. (2004). *ASCA National standards for students.* Alexandria, VA: Author.

American School Counselor Association. (2010). *Ethical standards for school counselors.* Alexandria, VA: Author.

American School Counselor Association. (2012a). *The ASCA National Model: Draft for Public Comment* (3rd ed.). Alexandria, VA: Author. Retrieved from http://www.academia.edu/4535157/ASCA_National_Model_THIRD_EDITION_Draft_for_Public_Comment

American School Counselor Association. (2012b). *The ASCA national model: A framework for school counseling programs* (3rd ed.). Alexandria, VA: Author.

American School Counselor Association. (2013). *ASCA position statements.* Alexandria, VA: Author.

American School Counselor Association. (2014). *ASCA mindsets and behaviors for student success: K–12 college- and career-readiness standards for every student.* Alexandria, VA: Author.

Astramovich, R. L., Hoskins, W. J., Gutierrez, A. P., & Bartlett, K. A. (2013). Identifying role diffusion in school counseling. *The Professional Counselor, 3*(3), 175–184.

Bineham, S. C., Shelby, L., Pazey, B. L., & Yates, J. R. (2014, March). Response to intervention: Perspectives of general and special education professionals. *Journal of School Leadership, 24*(2), 230–252.

Brady-Amoon, P. (2012). Further extending the humanistic vision for the future of counseling: A response to Hansen. *Journal of Humanistic Counseling, 59*(2), 184–196.

Brown, J. (2011). Introduction. In B. Fezler & C. Brown (Eds.), *The international model for school counseling programs* (p. 5). Pembroke Pines, FL: Association of American Schools in South America (AASSA). Retrieved from http://www.aassa.com/uploaded/Educational_ Research/US_Department_of_State/Counseling_Standards/International_Counseling_Model_ Handbook.pdf

Center for Mental Health in Schools. (2012, Summer). Common Core State Standards: What about student and learning supports? *Addressing Barriers to Learning, 17*(3). Los Angeles, CA: Author at UCLA Center. Retrieved from http://smhp.psych.ucla.edu/pdfdocs/newsletter/ summer12.pdf

Chen-Hayes, S., Ockerman, M. S., & Mason, E. C. M. (2014). *101 solutions for school counselors and leaders in challenging times*. Thousand Oaks, CA: Corwin.

College Board. (2010a). Eight components of college and career readiness counseling. Washington, DC: Author. Retrieved from http://media.collegeboard.com/digitalServices/pdf/ nosca/11b_4416_8_Components_WEB_111107.pdf

College Board. (2010b). Own the turf: NOSCA's national advocacy campaign [Slide 1]. Washington, DC: Author. Retrieved from http://advocacy.collegeboard.org/sites/default/files/Own-the-Turf PowerPoint.pdf

College Board. (2011). A transformative process: NOSCA's eight components of college and career readiness counseling for equity in student outcomes. Retrieved from http://professionals.college board.com/profdownload/rhodes-rob_noscas-8-components.pdf

Common Core State Standards Initiative. (2010a). Common Core State Standards for English language arts & literacy in history/social studies, science, and technical studies. Author. Retrieved from http://www.corestandards.org/ELA-Literacy

Common Core State Standards Initiative. (2010b). Application to students with disabilities. Author. Retrieved from http://www.corestandards.org/assets/application-to-students-witHdisabilities.pdf

Council for Accreditation of Counseling and Related Educational Programs (CACREP). (2009). CACREP 2009 Standards. Retrieved from http://www.cacrep.org/doc/2009%20Standards%20 with%20cover.pdf

Council for Accreditation of Counseling and Related Educational Programs (CACREP). (2013). Draft #2 of the 2016 CACREP Standards. Alexandria, VA: Author.

Cremin, L. A. (1988). *American education: The metropolitan experience 1876–1980*. New York, NY: Harper & Row.

Curry, J., & Lambie, G. W. (2007). Embracing school counselor accountability: The large group guidance portfolio. *Professional School Counseling, 11*(2), 145–148.

Dahir, C. A., & Stone, C. B. (2007). School counseling at the crossroads of change (ACAPCD-05). Alexandria, VA: American Counseling Association. Retrieved from http://counselingoutfitters. com/vistas/ACAPCD/ACAPCD-05.pdf

Dahir, C. A., & Stone, C. B. (2012). *The transformed school counselor* (2nd ed.). Belmont, CA: Brooks/Cole.

DeKruyf, L., Auger, R. K., & Trice-Block, S. (2013). The role of school counselors in meeting students' mental health needs: Examining issues of professional identity. *Professional School Counseling, 16*(5), 271–282.

Foster, L. H. (2012). Professional counselor credentialing and program accreditation in the United States: A historical review. *Journal for International Counselor Education, 4*(1), 42–56. Retrieved from http://digitalcommons.library.unlv.edu/jic

Graham, S., & Harris, K. R. (2013). Common Core State Standards, writing, and students with LD: Recommendations. *Learning Disabilities Research & Practice, 28*(1), 28–37.

Haager, D., & Vaughn, S. (2013). Common Core State Standards and students with learning disabilities: Introduction to the special issue. *Learning Disabilities Research & Practice, 28*(1), 1–4.

Hatch, T. (2014). *The use of data in school counseling: Hatching results for students, programs and the profession*. Thousand Oaks, CA: Corwin.

Hines, P., & Lemons, R. W. (2011). *Poised to lead: How school counselors can drive college and career readiness* [Report]. Washington, DC: The Education Trust. Retrieved from http://www.edtrust.org/dc/publication/poised-to-lead

Hodges, S. (2012, January). Through a glass darkly—Envisioning the future of the counseling profession: A commentary. *The Professional Counselor: Research and Practice, 1*(3), 191–200. Retrieved from http://tpcjournal.nbcc.org/wp-content/uploads/hodges

Hoganson, M. L. (2012). 75 years of history and service: National Association for College Admission Counseling. Arlington, VA: Author. Retrieved from http://www.nacacnet.org/about/history/Documents/nacachistory.pdf

House, R. M., & Martin, P. J. (1998, Winter). Advocating for better futures for all students: A new vision for school counselors. *Education, 119*(2), 284–291.

Individuals with Disabilities Improvement Education Act. Public Law 108–446. (2004).

Jones, L. K. (2014). Common Core State Standards: A challenge and opportunity for school counselors. The Career Key. Retrieved from http://www.careerkey.org/pdf/ASCA-National-Model-Common-Core-Standards-School-Counseling.pdf

Kaplan, D. M., Tarvydas, V. M., & Gladding, S. T. (2011). 20/20: A vision for the future of counseling: The new consensus definition of counseling. Retrieved from http://www.counseling.org/knowledge-center/20-20-a-vision-for-the-future-of counseling

Kawahata, C. (2013). Common Core assessment and the digital divide. Retrieved from http://webpages.csus.edu/~cindykawahata/251/Argumentative%20Paper.pd

King, J. H., & Stretch, L. S. (2013, Winter). A critical analysis of counseling's professional identity crisis. *Vistas*. Retrieved from http://elitepdf.com/vistas-online-welcome-to-counseling-outfitters.html

Kornhaber, M. L., Griffith, K., & Tyler, A. (2014). It's not education by zip code anymore—But what is it? Conceptions of equity under the Common Core. *Education Policy Analysis Archives, 22*(4). Retrieved from http://dx.doi.org/10.14507/epaa.v22n4.2014

Lapan, R. T. (2012). Comprehensive school counseling programs: In some schools for some students but not in all schools for all students. *Professional School Counseling, 16*(1), 84–88.

Martin, P. J. (2002, Summer). Transforming school counseling: A national perspective. *Theory into Practice, 41*(3), 148–153.

National Association for College Admission Counseling. (2000). Statement on counselor competencies. Retrieved from http://www.nacacnet.org/about/Governance/Policies/Documents/Counselor Competencies.pdf

National Association for College Admission Counseling. (2013). Statement of principles of good practice. Arlington, VA: Author. Retrieved from http://www.nacacnet.org/about/Governance/Policies/Documents/SPGP_9_2013.pdf

National Education Association. (2013). NEA Common Core State Standards toolkit. Washington, DC: Author. Retrieved from http://www.nea.org/assets/docs/14047CommonCore_Toolkit_14.pdf

Ockerman, M. S., Mason, E. C. M., & Chen-Hayes, S. F. (2013). School counseling supervision in challenging times: The CAFE supervisor model. *The Journal for Counselor Preparation and Supervision, 5*(2), 44–57. Retrieved from http://repository.wcsu.edu/jcps/v015/iss2/4

Ritchie, M., & Bobby, C. (2011). Working together hand in hand: The common goals of CACREP and state counselor licensure boards. Retrieved from http://www.cacrep.org/doc/State_Licensure_Board_presentation_8[1].2011.pdf

Seahorse, K. R., Jones, L. M., & Seppanen, P. (2001). *Transforming school counseling: A report on early evaluation findings*. Minneapolis: The College of Education and Human Development, University of Minnesota.

Smarter Balanced Assessment Consortium. (2013, December). Frequently asked questions: Higher education. Retrieved from http://www.smarterbalanced.org/wordpress/wp-content/uploads/2013/12/Smarter-Balanced-Higher-Education.pdf

Smarter Balanced Assessment Consortium. (2014, March). Guidelines: Frequently asked questions. Retrieved from http://www.smarterbalanced.org/wordpress/wp-content/uploads/2013/12/SmarterBalanced_Guidelines_FAQ.pdf

Studer, J. R. (2015). *The essential school counselor in a changing society*. Thousand Oaks, CA: Sage.

Thurlow, M. L. (2012). The promise and the peril for students with disabilities. *The Special Edge, 25*(3), 1, 6. Retrieved from http://www.calstat.org/publications/pdfs/Edge_summer_2012_newsletter.pdf

Urofsky, R. I., Bobby, C. L., & Ritchie, M. (2013). CACREP: 30 years of quality assurance in counselor education. *Journal of Counseling & Development, 91*(1), 3–5.

Wiley, T. G., & Rolstad, K. (2014). The Common Core State Standards and the Great Divide. *International Multilingual Research Journal, 8*(1), 38–55.

Chapter 3

Laws and Ethics

VICKI A. MCGINLEY

West Chester University

"We know that equality of individual ability has never existed and never will, but we do insist that equality of opportunity still must be sought."

—Franklin D. Roosevelt

School counselors are important members of multidisciplinary teams (MDTs) that provide services to an increasing number of students with disabilities in the K–12 classroom. This increase is due to both the number of identified students with disabilities, as well as the fact that most of these students are educated in their *least restrictive environment* (LRE); for many of these students, approximately 89.3%, that means the general education setting (U.S. Department of Education, 2004). It is due specifically to this increase, and the school counselors' role in schools, that they must be cognizant of legislation that governs students with disabilities (Erford, House, & Martin, 2003). Additionally, a school counselor may work with a particular student over a number of years and thus be the individual in the school who is best able to advocate for the student, overseeing services and plans, such as the Service Agreement Plan (SAP), also known as the Section 504 Plan, as designated under Section 504 of the 1973 Vocational Rehabilitation Act, or a student's Individualized Education Plan (IEP) as designated under the Individuals with Disabilities Education Improvement Act (IDEIA) of 2004 (Erford et al., 2003). These plans encompass the student's functional life skills, academics, the student's social and emotional growth, as well as career goals and postsecondary school outcomes. As the content and implementation of these plans are governed by regulation, it is critical that school counselors know the legislation relevant to serving students with disabilities and their families and know their role in implementing these laws.

After reading this chapter, you will be able to carry out the following:

1. Identify legislation and relevant case law to serving students with disabilities.

2. Identify legal and ethical issues encountered in schools.

3. Understand the ethical standards and principles needed to adhere to the legal aspects of their role.

4. Gain access to resources, which address relevant legislation.

FEDERAL LAWS AND LEGISLATION RELEVANT TO SERVING STUDENTS WITH DISABILITIES

There are two main statutes that impact school counselors' work with students with disabilities—the Education for All Handicapped Children Act of 1975 (reauthorized in 2004 as the Individuals with Disabilities Education Act [IDEA] and Section 504 of the Vocational Rehabilitation Act of 1973 (Section 504). Other important statutes that will be touched upon are the No Child Left Behind Act (NCLB), the Families Educational Rights and Privacy Act (FERPA), and the Americans with Disabilities Act (ADA). (Note, as of 2004, IDEA is now identified as the Individual with Disabilities Education Improvement Act, or IDEIA.)

Understanding the content and language and how to effectively and legally implement these laws will help to support students and assist schools to avoid liability. In addition, understanding the categories of disability, their definitions and characteristics is critical for the school counselors' role. A thorough understanding of the special education process includes screening, assessing and evaluating, goal setting and planning, and implementing the students' plan. School counselors will also need to know how to best advocate for students, in order to obtain resources, to interact with outside agencies, as well as to provide direct counseling. Counseling with students with disabilities may be coordinated with outside services (i.e., medical, related services, etc.), as well as with family members and the students themselves (Tarver-Behring & Spagna, 2004). Specific laws that school counselors need to know and their roles with respect to these laws will now be covered.

Section 504

Section 504 of the 1973 Rehabilitation Act provides that

[n]o otherwise qualified individual with a disability in the United States, as defined in §706(8) of this title, shall, solely by reason of her or his handicap,

be excluded from participation in, be denied the benefits of, or be subjected to discrimination under any program or activity receiving federal financial assistance or under any program or activity conducted by any executive agency or by the United States Postal Service . . . (29 U.S.C. § 794(a) (1973))

Section 504 is a Civil Rights Act that prohibits discrimination and requires that reasonable accommodations be provided to the students with disabilities so that they may access the general education curriculum. Thus, the Office for Civil Rights (OCR) is the governing body of this law. The definition of students served under Section 504 is very broad and includes any physical or mental impairment, which substantially limits a student's major life activity (29 U.S.C. § 794(a) (1973). Students who are not eligible under IDEA for special education may still be eligible for protection under Section 504. For example, students who are identified as having ADHD may be covered under Other Health Impairment (OHI) under IDEA, and receive an IEP due to their needing specially designed instruction (SDI) and related services. However, children identified as ADHD under Section 504 may be in need only of accommodations to access the general education curriculum. For special education services under IDEA, students must be eligible under one of the 13 disability categories outlined in Table 3.1 below, and they also need to be in need of SDI and related services. However, students served under Section 504 receive a SAP with modifications and/or accommodations to the general education curriculum so that they may access the general education curriculum. A sample Section 504 Plan may be found in Appendix A. Table 3.1 provides some common examples of students considered with disabilities (either temporary or long term) who may be protected under Section 504 and require such accommodations and/or modifications to the curriculum.

Table 3.1   Students Who May Require Accommodations Under Section 504

Type of Condition	*Possible Modification/Accommodation*
Students with allergies and/or asthma	Visits to nurse
Students with communicable diseases (e.g., AIDS)	Time away from class to rest
Students who are substance abusers	Medication administration
Students with attention-deficit hyperactivity disorder (ADHD)	Preferential seating
Students with chronic fatigue syndrome	Less questions to answer and problems to solve
Students with a terminal illness	Less homework
Students with physical impairments	Transition to classes early

Like IDEA, Section 504 has procedural safeguards that provide the family and the student with due process rights in the event that there may be disagreement with the schools in regard to eligibility, evaluation, and/or implementation of services. Parents also have the right to review relevant records and to receive notice regarding referral, evaluation, and placement of their child. Students served under Section 504 have the right to have access to all academic and co-curricular school activities, and to a free appropriate public education (FAPE) in the general education setting that includes accommodations and/or modifications. In the next section, the school counselors' role, with the constructs of Section 504 in mind, is discussed.

The role of school counselors under Section 504

One main role school counselors have under this statute is to conduct periodic evaluations for the purpose of establishing and continuing eligibility and for reassessing needs and continued eligibility (Owens, Thomas, & Strong, 2011). The Association for Assessment in Counseling and Education is an excellent resource that school counselors may utilize in regard to assessment competencies, which are required (http://aac.ncat.edu/documents/atsc_cmptncy.htm), as are the ethical standards in regard to testing outlined by both the American Counseling Association and the American School Counselor Association. In addition, counseling reference books, such as *Assessment in Counseling: A Guide to the Use of Psychological Assessment Procedures* (Hays, 2013), are very useful resources in which specific qualifications for test administration and interpretation are outlined. Typically, a school psychologist would be involved in conducting standardized testing, while school counselors would be doing such evaluations as classroom observations, structured interviews, and surveys. Specific examples of assessment measures used by school counselors are presented in Chapter 8. When the students are identified, another task is to work with the MDT to ensure that the accommodations that make up the students' Section 504 Plan are in place and implemented effectively. Accommodations and/or modifications may include

- how curriculum material is presented, such as providing audio tapes, large print, a designated reader, instructions read orally, and/or reducing the number of items on a page;
- ways in which the student is asked to respond, such as allowing for verbal responses, answers to be dictated, or recorded into a recording device or computer;
- changing the setting, such as providing preferential seating, special lighting or acoustics, a space with minimal distractions, or administering testing in small groups and/or in an alternative site;

- timing such as allowing for frequent breaks or extended time to complete tests or assignments; test scheduling, such as administering tests over several sessions, allowing subtests to be taken in a different order, administering a test at a specific time of day; and other, such as providing special test preparation, and focusing and tasks (Council of Administrators of Special Education, 2011).

Once the Section 504 Plan is in place, depending on the district of employment, school counselors may be responsible for monitoring and updating this plan and for serving as what is known as the Section 504 coordinator, the professional accountable for the development and oversight of implementation of the SAP. A SAP, developed by the Section 504 team, specifies the plan of services students need to have in order to have an equal opportunity to succeed.

Another role of school counselors in relation to Section 504 may be that of the school-based coordinator. In a study done by Madaus and Shaw (2008), data reflected that, in schools, Section 504 is not under special education but is under the auspices of general education administrators, *followed by school counselors*, school psychologists, social workers, and general educators, then, followed by special education teachers, in terms of coordinating Section 504 meetings and subsequently the Section 504 plans for students.

Thus, school counselors need to be familiar with the students, the evaluation process, and the data obtained from the evaluation, as well as accommodation options that students are entitled to (Owens et al., 2011). For example, if a student has broken his or her leg and needs extended time or use of an elevator to reach his or her classes, the school counselor could be a vital resource in collaborating with teachers and administrators in communicating these needs, obtaining approval for the elevator use, and in the exploration of how missed class time may be made up. In addition, if the student has been involved in team sports and is struggling with this temporary lack of involvement, the school counselor is a great asset in the provision of individual counseling to assist the student to adapt. Even though Section 504 is not a special education law, coordination with special education is critical, so no children *fall between the cracks.*

IDEA of 2004

For special education services under IDEA, a student must be eligible under one of the 13 disability categories outlined in Table 3.2.

From the inception of the first federal special education law, the Education For All Handicapped Children Act of 1975 (PL 94–142), services for students with disabilities and their parents have been mandated, and it has been recommended that

Table 3.2   Thirteen Categories of Disability Served Under IDEA
Autism
Deaf-Blindness
Deafness
Emotional Disturbance
Hearing Impairment
Intellectual Disability
Multiple Disabilities
Orthopedic Impairment
Other Health Impairment
Specific Learning Disability
Speech or Language Impairment
Traumatic Brain Injury
Visual Impairment including Blindness

Source: Regulation 300.8c: Definitions of disability terms. *Building the Legacy: IDEA 2004.* U.S. Department of Education.

school counselors be familiar with the special education process and procedural safeguards of the law (Helms & Katsiyannias, 1992). The Procedural Safeguard Notice (PSN) under IDEA is quite lengthy, as it covers in full all of the processes and procedures under the law for which families and students are entitled. School districts are required to provide parents (unless parents waive this right) a copy of the PSN at least one time per year, upon their filing of a complaint and/or upon request for the PSN. The PSN covers such things as access to records, how to handle complaints, discipline, dispute resolution, due process hearings, evaluation procedures, informed consent, and LRE. It also includes other areas that may apply to only some parents such as private school placements, surrogate parents, and transfer of parental rights after their child turns age 18. School counselors who know the procedural safeguards will support you in following this law, as well as in advocating for the students you serve. For example, school counselors would need to understand the difference between eligibility criteria under Section 504 and IDEA and how best to advocate for students who are deemed eligible under each act.

IDEA provides funds to states and subsequently their local education agencies (LEA) to provide services to those students who are classified under the statute of having one or more of the 13 defined disabilities listed in Table 3.2. The special education process includes pre-referral, evaluation, decision of eligibility, IEP development, implementation of the IEP, and re-evaluation.

Since its inception in 1975 as the Education for All Handicapped Children Act, there have been six defining principles that make up the law. They are the principles of zero reject, LRE, FAPE, parent and student participation, due process safeguards, and nondiscriminatory evaluation. These principles are described next in more detail (http://www.education.com/reference/article/six-major-principles-idea/).

Zero reject

Schools must educate all children with disabilities between the ages of 5 and 21; however, if a state educates children without disabilities between the ages of 3 to 5, it must also educate children with disabilities in that age range. This principle applies regardless of the nature or severity of the disability and essentially means *no* children with disabilities may be excluded from a public education. Each state education agency is responsible for locating, identifying, and evaluating all children with disabilities or those who are suspected of having disabilities. This requirement is also referred to as the Child Find system. In a recent reauthorization of the law in 1997, which occurred as a result of various court cases (i.e., *Doe v. Koger*, 1979; *Goss v. Lopez*, 1975, etc.), the principle of zero reject has been extended into the area of disciplining students with disabilities. In 1988, the U.S. Supreme Court heard *Honig v. Doe,* which further spoke to discipline of students with disabilities, and confirmed that suspensions of students with disabilities over 10 days is considered a change in placement. This case also called attention to the *stay put* provision of the law that asserts that students remain in their current education placement during the manifestation determination process (described in Chapter 9), which supports the decision as to whether or not the problem behavior was a manifestation of the student's disability; thus, they cannot be denied a free appropriate public education (FAPE) at any time.

Nondiscriminatory identification and evaluation

IDEA specifics that all schools must use nonbiased methods of evaluation to determine whether a child has a disability. Testing and evaluation procedures must not discriminate on the basis of race, culture, or native language. All tests must be administered in the child's native language, and identification and placement decisions cannot be made on the basis of a single test score. For certain disability types, further guidelines and procedures for diagnosis may be specified, such as the use of response to intervention (RTI; a tiered method of academic intervention used prior to diagnosing a child with a specific learning disability, described in more detail in Chapter 4) and a medical doctor's diagnosis required for diagnosis of a child with ADHD.

Free appropriate public education (FAPE)

All children with disabilities, regardless of the type or severity of their disability, must receive FAPE. This education must be provided at public expense, and an IEP must be developed and implemented to meet the unique needs of each student with a disability. The IEP specifies the student's individual needs, states present levels of performance in all areas of need, identifies measurable annual goals and short-term objectives to address such needs, and describes the specific special education and related services that will be provided to help the student attain those goals and benefit from education.

Least restrictive environment (LRE)

IDEA mandates that students with disabilities be educated with children without disabilities to the maximum extent appropriate. It further states that students with disabilities be removed to separate classes or schools only when the nature or severity of their disabilities is such that they cannot receive an appropriate education in a general education classroom with supplementary aids and services. IDEA creates a presumption in favor of inclusion in the general education classroom by requiring that a student's IEP contain a justification and explanation of the extent, if any, to which a child will not participate with peers without disabilities in the general academic curriculum, extracurricular activities, and other nonacademic activities (e.g., lunch, recess, transportation, and sports). However, since LRE is still the law, and under LRE a continuum of placements must be provided to ensure that all students with disabilities are educated in their LRE, school districts must provide a continuum of placement and service alternatives. Figure 3.1 provides the continuum of placements offered to students with disabilities.

Due process safeguards

Schools must provide due process safeguards to protect the rights of children with disabilities and their parents. For example, parental consent must be obtained for the initial and all subsequent evaluations of their child and for any placement decisions regarding special education. Schools must maintain the confidentiality of all records pertaining to children with disabilities and make those records available to the parents. When parents of children with disabilities disagree with the results of an evaluation performed by the school or an educational placement decision, they can obtain an independent evaluation at public expense. When the school and parents disagree on the identification, evaluation, placement, or recommended plan and related services, the parents may request a due process hearing, a formal hearing conducted by an impartial due process hearing officer who renders a binding decision. States are

Figure 3.1   Continuum of Placements

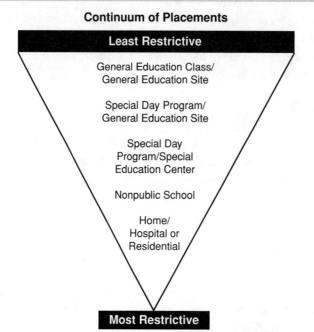

Continuum of Placements

Least Restrictive

General Education Class/
General Education Site

Special Day Program/
General Education Site

Special Day
Program/Special
Education Center

Nonpublic School

Home/
Hospital or
Residential

Most Restrictive

Source: Supporting Special Student Populations. (2006). *The Two-Way Immersion Toolkit.* Howard, E. R., Sugarman, J., Perdomo, M., & Adger, C. T. (Eds.).

also required to offer parents an opportunity to resolve the matter through mediation by a third party before holding a due process hearing. However, parents may elect to forgo the mediation and head directly to due process. Parents have the right to attorney's fees if they prevail in due process under IDEA. The law also includes provisions that allow the court to award reasonable attorney's fees to the prevailing school district against the attorney of a parent, or the parent who files a frivolous complaint. Although "due process hearings are a last resort to resolve conflicts or problems between school districts and parents" (Getty & Summey, 2004, p. 40), they occur with increasing frequency, and the majority of due process hearings are over placement or program issues (Newcomer & Zirkel, 1999).

Parent and student participation and shared decision making

As family members are a vital part of the MDT, the IDEA recognizes that schools must collaborate with parents and students with disabilities in the development and implementation of special education services. The parents' and, whenever appropriate, the students' input must be considered in the development of IEP goals and objectives, related-service needs, and placement decisions.

How school counselors may be involved in utilizing these six principles is demonstrated in Guided Practice Exercise 3.1.

Besides the six principles, the IDEA also guides states and LEAs in such things as components of the IEP, manifestation determination, and Functional Behaviorial Assessment. The IEP is mentioned in a number of the principles and thus is covered in more detail below.

Individualized Education Plan (IEP)

IDEA requires that the MDT create an IEP that provides an appropriate education for all students with disabilities whose educational performance is impacted and is in need of specially designed instruction and related services. (A sample IEP form may be found in Appendix B.) This instruction is to take place in the student's LRE. An IEP is a legal document that must be followed and must contain the following components:

- A statement of the child's present level of academic achievement and functional performance, including how the child's disabilities impact his or her involvement in general education
- A statement of measurable annual goals
- A description of how the child's progress toward meeting the annual goals will be measured and when progress reports will be provided
- A statement of the specially designed instruction (SDI) and related services and supplementary aids and services to be provided

---

Guided Practice Exercise 3.1

"HOW DO THE SIX MAIN PRINCIPLES GUIDING IDEA PERTAIN TO YOUR ROLE AS SCHOOL COUNSELOR?"

As the school counselor on your school's leadership team, you will be involved in making a presentation regarding the principles to your Parent Teacher Association. Your leadership team colleagues have asked you to focus on the six principles and your role as the school counselor in each.

You will have about 10 minutes for your part of the presentation. What will you say about these topics? How will you bring them to life in a manner that is responsive to parents?

- A statement of the program modification or supports for school personnel that will be provided to enable the student to advance appropriately toward meeting the annual goals
- An explanation of the *extent, if any, to which the child will not participate with nondisabled children* in the regular class and in extracurricular and nonacademic activities
- Individual accommodations that are necessary to measure the academic achievement and functional performance of the child on state and district assessments, or if the child participates in an alternative assessment, why that particular alternate assessment is selected
- If the child is 16 years old, a transition plan
- If the child is in need of it, a Behavior Intervention Plan (BIP)
- The projected date for the beginning of services and the anticipated frequency, location, and duration of those services and modifications (Friend, 2014)

Note: A sample IEP template may be found at http://www.sagepub.com/gargiulo4e/study/resources/plans/88919_siep.pdf.

With this understanding of the IEP, how school counselors can assist in this process is next described.

The Role of School Counselors in the IEP Process

The role of school counselors in the IEP process is increasing (Geltner & Leibforth, 2008). More children are being identified; thus, more are in need of those services that are typically provided by school counselors (i.e., referral, direct counseling, postsecondary school outcomes, etc.). Additionally, school counselors already possess unique knowledge, skills, and training that can be beneficial in guiding the MDT in the special education IEP process (Milsom, 2004). In the IEP process, school counselors can assist in developing relevant goals, specifying supports needed to obtain those goals, and making referrals to outside agencies for services. They also may provide direct service as indicated in the IEP such as individual or group counseling. Milsom (2004) found that 83% of school counselors engage in either individual or group counseling with students with disabilities at some point in the school year. In the next section, the No Child Left Behind Act (Milsom, 2004) is presented.

THE NO CHILD LEFT BEHIND ACT (NCLB)

NCLB is a reauthorization of a law passed in 1965, the Elementary and Secondary Education Act. The main thrust of this law is directed at making sure at-risk

youth are not left behind, and state and local education agencies are held account-able in carrying out that mandate through a standards-based reform movement. To accomplish this, many districts have instituted accountability standards through testing and adopting the Common Core Standards. Presently, 47 states have adopted Common Core State Standards (http://www.ascd.org/common-core-state-standards/common-core-state-standards-adoption-map.aspx). NCLB has made federal funding contingent on students' progress in regard to such standards, and it outlines corrective measures for schools that fail to maintain adequate yearly progress (AYP). Subgroups data (specifically, on those students at-risk due to, for example, their race or ethnicity, their migrant or income status, and those who are English language learners and have disabilities) are analyzed under this law (U.S. Department of Education, 2004). However, it should be noted at this time that due to many states and LEAs not meeting the goals of the law, there have been numerous state and LEA waivers granted, relieving schools of making the goal of all students proficient in reading and mathematics by the year 2014. In the next section, the role of school counselors in implementing NCLB is addressed.

The Role of School Counselors in Regard to NCLB

This emphasis on accountability has resulted in a significant change in the way schools do business and, thus, the way school counselors' responsibilities are defined (Dollarhide & Lemberger, 2014). In a study done by these authors, 210 school counselors responded to a survey that addressed perceptions regarding NCLB. Questions on the survey specifically explored school counselors' knowl-edge of NCLB, the effect of this legislation, and their role in relation to NCLB. Findings of this study included school counselors' reported knowledge of the legislation. Eighty-one percent of the school counselors identified student, parent, teacher, and/or community notification of test results as an activity and, positively, that data obtained from such testing resulted in educational changes for students. Most revealing was the school counselors' role in testing. The American School Counselor Association (ASCA) in 2005 stated that school counselors should coun-sel students about test anxiety and strategies, and they should interpret tests and analyze them in conjunction with multiple measures of student achievement. How-ever, in the aforementioned Dollarhide and Lemberger study, only 25.1% of the respondents described such involvement (2014). The majority listed their primary tasks as coordinating and administrating tests and serving as building test coordina-tor (29.2%) and possibly district coordinator (2.9%); proctoring tests and providing makeup testing (13.3%); and determining and monitoring for accommodations (3.3%). Academic remediation after testing was cited by 2.9% of the participants. Only 7.7% indicated that they did not participate in testing and/or analysis of data.

The concern raised by the participants of the study was that as more time is spent on these types of activities, less time is given to the emotional/social and academic needs of the students. School counselors identified the stressful effects of the legislation on teachers and students as resulting in *more* students having difficulties with teachers and teachers spending increased time on administrative types of paperwork and less on teaching. Thus, it is evident that school counselors may need to advocate for providing more direct services to teachers and students, such as the provision of direct counseling for test anxiety and test-taking strategies, and interpretation of test results in relation to the students' Section 504 Plan and/or IEP. In the next section, the Family Educational Rights and Privacy Act is addressed in relation to school counselors.

Family Educational Rights and Privacy Acts (FERPA)

School counselors must be aware of the rights afforded students and their parents regarding school records. Personal information about students in school records must be accurate, and access must be restricted to those with a justifiable purpose for use of that information. Confidentiality in schools and thus the protection of student privacy is given much needed attention, and has always been a component of the special education law. One of the main laws that govern the confidentiality of student information is the Family Educational Rights and Privacy Acts (FERPA; Fischer, Schimmel, & Stellman, 2003). This law is also known as the Buckley Amendment and addresses the legislation on who may and may not see student records, and how they are accessed and disclosed. The main components of this law are as follows:

- Parents, and students who have reached the age of majority or 18, have the right to review their school records.
- Schools must receive parental consent before evaluating or admitting students in school programs that would change their values or behavior.
- Schools must restrict unauthorized access to student information and protect the privacy of their records.
- Schools must protect children who are being used to gather data for federal surveys (Fischer et al., 2003).

FERPA is needed to deal with past abuses of student records that occurred, specifically providing access to outsiders and the denial of sharing records with the student and the family (Fischer et al., 2003).

According to Fischer et al. (2003), there are five main components of the act:

- Parents must be informed of their rights on an annual basis.
- Parents have the right to inspect and review records.

- Parents can challenge the accuracy of records.
- Students' records are confidential, and there is no disclosure of personal information without prior parental consent.
- Parents may file complaints with the U.S. Department of Education for lack of compliance with the act.

FERPA applies to all educational records, such as personal logs, treatment records (such as physician, psychiatrist, or psychologist notes), and directory information (such as dates of attendance, grades, and demographic information; Family Educational Rights and Privacy Act [FERPA], 1974; Underwood & Mead, 1995).

Schools must inform the parents before a disclosure of student information is made. Additionally, parents have the right to challenge the information contained in the records if they believe it to be inaccurate or misleading. The school must provide an opportunity for a hearing if they disagree or refuse to alter the record. There are exclusions in the law in terms of record handling. For example, amendments to FERPA clarify that a school may include, without prior consent, information in a student's records concerning disciplinary actions taken and disclosure of education records to certain state and local officials. An example would be if a child with a disability was removed from one school and moved to another for aggressive behavior; because the behavior was a manifestation of his disability, it did not result in expulsion.

The connections between FERPA and working with students with disabilities is evident in the IDEA in which clear guidelines for schools were set when collecting, storing, releasing, and destroying identifiable information for students with disabilities. Additionally, state education agencies (SEA) must have written procedures that notify parents of their right to inspect records and how such information is stored, disclosed, retained, and destroyed. In addition, annual notices must be given to parents on their rights to file a complaint or amend the child's records (Sealander, Schwiebert, Oren, & Weekley, 1999).

School districts must have a written release of information form in which it specifies the records to be released, reasons for release, and to whom the records would be released, and they must have an established procedure in the event parents resist giving consent. All other parties, other than who is designated to have access to records, must have parental consent. In the following section, the role of school counselor in relation to FERPA is presented.

The Role of School Counselors in Relation to FERPA

Confidentiality is a legal requirement and an ethical issue. How school counselors handle records of students may or may not establish trust. School counselors must be knowledgeable about the laws that govern the confidentially of school records, what are considered to be exceptions, and the nature of privileged communication. They must also be aware of their own professional organizations' ethical standards and practices regarding confidentiality (ASCA, 2005). School counselors may assist students and their parents in educating them as to the law, and in accessing student records which must be delivered within 45 days of the request. They may also refer them to knowledgeable professionals who can further address specific questions. Examples of these issues are illustrated in Case 3.1.

The final regulation, the Americans with Disabilities Act (ADA), is addressed in the next section.

AMERICANS WITH DISABILITIES ACT (ADA)

The ADA and Section 504 are both Civil Rights Acts and apply to all programs and activities offered by a school system, for example, school board meetings,

---

CASE ILLUSTRATION 3.1

"SHOULD SUSAN BE INCLUDED?"

Susan, age 7, spent her first 2 years in a segregated special education classroom for students labeled as intellectually disabled. The MDT had concerns about Susan's inappropriate behaviors that include elopement from the classroom; falling to the floor and screaming and crying when "she didn't" get her way; and aggressing toward classmates. Susan was verbal and tested in the moderate range of ID. At the most recent MDT meeting called by the special education teacher who has just completed a course at the local university, the question of including students in some general education class time was being discussed. Susan does not have a behavior intervention plan as part of her present IEP. In this meeting, a BIP was not discussed, but instead, it was decided that the school counselor, along with the psychologist, should conduct observations in Susan's classroom as well as the general educational setting in which Susan would be placed. The school counselor observes Susan on three different occasions for 45 minutes each and notices some environmental triggers really set Susan off—which, if addressed in the general education setting, could decrease the number of problem behaviors. The general education teacher is concerned and defensive, and in seeing this as Susan's problem, thinks that Susan should remain full-time in her special education class. What is the school counselor's role? What are his or her next steps?

extracurricular programs, teacher conferences, recreational activities, social and cultural activities, and summer school. Section 504 requires accommodations be provided to people with disabilities, when necessary, such as qualified interpreters, real-time captioning (CART), assistive listening devices, or other auxiliary aids, in order to ensure effective communication among all parties. These are services provided to all schools that receive federal funds. However, the ADA takes the law further in that Title II of the ADA requires comparable access by all state and local government programs, regardless of whether or not the programs get federal financial assistance. As such, it can be seen from the list of accommodations above (not an exhaustive list), any activity that the school is involved in must be accessible! The ADA discusses accessibility in relation to reasonable accommodation. A reasonable accommodation may include such things as making a facility accessible by adding a ramp, modifying a work schedule to take into consideration a person's stamina, and providing an interpreter.

Public schools must comply with the ADA in all of their services, programs, or activities, including those that are open to parents or to the public. For instance, public school systems must provide accessibility to parents and guardians with disabilities to these programs, activities, or services; and appropriate auxiliary aids (e.g., interpreters, note takers, transcription services, and written materials) as defined in the law below:

- services whenever necessary to ensure effective communication (56 Fed. Reg. 35696, July 26, 1991); and
- determination of what type of auxiliary aid and service is necessary, a public entity shall give primary consideration to the requests of the individual with disabilities (28 C.F.R. § 35.160). There is a lot of regulation in the ADA governing the provision of services to the deaf, as well as accessibility features for those persons with physical disabilities.

In the next section, the role of school counselors in implementing the ADA is addressed.

The Role of School Counselors Under ADA

As many school programs and services are supporting students with disabilities, the school counselors should see this provision as one of supports to the students they serve. All public trainings and communications must be accessible. School counselors need to know where to look to get support in implementing this law. Thus, they must be aware of needed resources and make the necessary referrals. Knowing the community and networking within that community will help.

All federal legislation has been presented above. However, prior to laws being passed there were many cases decided that helped to shape law. Cases are heard at the local, state, and circuit levels. See Appendix B for some of the more significant case rulings.

LEGAL AND ETHICAL ISSUES ENCOUNTERED BY SCHOOL COUNSELORS

School counselors will encounter legal and ethical dilemmas, all of which will be difficult, some more so than others. In a study done by Bodenhorn (2006), school counselors were asked to indicate their most common and challenging ethical dilemmas. Those areas participants identified most included student confidentiality, dual relationships with faculty, parental rights, and acting on student danger to themselves or others. In addition, Remley and Herlihy (2001) discussed reporting of child abuse as an issue that school counselors encounter far too often in their practice. These concerns are illustrated in Case 3.2.

Ethical dilemmas are extremely difficult with any child, but what happens when disability is a characteristic of the child? Although rules and regulations of reporting child abuse are clear, what happens when school counselors are working, for example, with a child who is nonverbal, such as a child on the autism spectrum may be, and/or one with multiple disabilities, where the decision of whether or not abuse may have occurred is not that easily identified? Other ethical and legal dilemmas emerge when working with children with disabilities. For example, with

---

CASE ILLUSTRATION 3.2

THE ISSUE OF MEDICATION

Susan, a 13-year-old girl with ADHD at her local middle school, splits time between her mother and father who were divorced last year. When with her father, she diligently takes her medication and "looks quite different in school." For example, she may concentrate, her grades are better, and she is more cooperative. However, when with her mother, who is spending a lot of time out of the home working and with a new boyfriend, Susan is given the message that it is "her body, and she can decide what she will and will not put into it." The teachers are complaining to the school counselor, indicating that Susan must take her medication. What are the next steps?

CASE ILLUSTRATION 3.3

BULLYING AND SEXUAL HARASSMENT

You are a school counselor who has been working with Stephanie, a 15-year-old child with learning disabilities, in direct counseling for a number of months since she came to you about possible bullying and sexual harassment outside of the school. It has been very difficult getting Stephanie to trust you, and now you are preparing for her IEP meeting in which you are not sure if the results of your counseling sessions should be shared or not as they may possibly lead to important goals being established on the IEP. What do you do?

---

respect to confidentiality as it relates to children with disabilities, FERPA and IDEA certainly give guidance and regulation; however, what about school counselor-student privilege, as all school counselors' records may be subpoenaed?

In a study done by Hermann (2002), of the 273 school counselors who were surveyed, over 90% indicated they felt they were well prepared to determine reported child abuse; 75% felt well prepared to determine whether a child would harm himself or herself; however, they felt least prepared to respond to being subpoenaed in a legal proceeding. It was not noted, however, as to whether or not any of these students were children with disabilities. With the consistently high and increased number of due process hearings for students with disabilities, school counselors must be prepared to deal with school records and legal proceedings and ethical conflicts that arise.

In addition, all school counselors are required to abide by the ethical standards of their personal organization, the American School Counselor Association (ASCA, 2005).

Table 3.3 provides an example of standards related to legal and ethical issues for school counselors.

According to Stone and Zirkel (2010), fulfilling the legal requirements and ethical standards may pose challenges for school counselors, as legal positions do not necessarily accompany ethical norms. What has been reported in the school counselor literature is that, in many situations, school counselors considered breaking confidentiality, based on the age and maturity level of the student (i.e., more likely to break confidentiality of the younger student and less so with increasing age; Isaacs & Stone, 1999). However, what has not been addressed is that when working with students with disabilities, the chronological age may not match the student's developmental/functional age; for example, a child with an intellectual disability may have a chronological age of 16 but function on a 5-year-old's age level cognitively.

Table 3.3 Ethical Standards

An example of a State's Competencies	1. Understand the role, function, and professional identity of the school counselor as a facilitator of the academic, career, and personal/social development of all students, and as a leader and advocate for systemic change within the school; 2. Are knowledgeable about current educational issues, local policy, administrative procedures, state and federal laws, and legislation relevant to school counseling. **IV.B Advocacy**—Studies involving the use of knowledge and competencies to advocate on the behalf of students and families of diverse and multicultural backgrounds, including understanding the advocacy process and the school counselor's role as an advocate for students and change within the school system to better meet the needs of students. Candidates: 1. Know the roles and processes of school counselors advocating on behalf of others; 2. Understand advocacy processes needed to address institutional barriers that impede access, equity, and success for students and families; 3. Demonstrate the ability to articulate, model, and advocate for an appropriate school counselor identity and program.
ASCA School Counselor Competencies	I-A-7. Legal, ethical, and professional issues in pre-K–12 schools I-A-8. Developmental theory, learning theories, social justice theory, I-B-3. Advocates for student success I-B-3d. Reviews advocacy models and develops a personal advocacy plan I-B-3e. Understands the process for development of policy and procedures at the building, district, state, and national levels Acts as a systems change agent to create an environment promoting and supporting student success I-B-5a. Defines and understands system change and its role in comprehensive school counseling programs I-B-5b. Develops a plan to deal with personal (emotional and cognitive) and institutional resistance impeding the change process I-B-5c. Understands the impact of school, district, and state educational policies, procedures, and practices supporting and/or impeding student success II-B-4. Applies the ethical standards and principles of the school counseling profession and adheres to the legal aspects of the role of the school counselor

(Continued)

Table 3.3 (Continued)	
	II-B-4c. Understands and practices in accordance with school district policy and local, state, and federal statutory requirements
	II-B-4d. Understands the unique legal and ethical nature of working with minor students in a school setting
	II-B-4e. Advocates responsibly for school board policy and local, state, and federal statutory requirements in students' best interests
	II-B-4i. Practices within the ethical and statutory limits of confidentiality
	II-B-4j. Continually seeks consultation and supervision to guide legal and ethical decision-making and to recognize and resolve ethical dilemmas
	II-B-4k. Understands and applies an ethical and legal obligation not only to students but to parents, administration, and teachers as well
CACREP	B. Skills and Practices
	1. Demonstrates the ability to apply and adhere to ethical and legal standards in school counseling.

Source: American School Counselor Association (2005). *The ASCA national model: A framework for schoolcounseling programs* (2nd ed.). Alexandria, VA: Author.

The answers will lie in ongoing professional development, developing cultural sensitivity, practicing within one's professional organization's standards, ongoing collaboration and communication with the MDT, and applying leadership and advocacy skills. Since school counselors must address the needs of all students they serve, they must assume responsibility for expanding and enhancing their own professional development (Scarborough & Deck, 1998). They must know and follow laws and policies and deal with ethical dilemmas, and as mentioned throughout this chapter, school counselors must serve as advocates for their students. According to Dahir and Stone (2009), the Transforming School Counseling Initiative (1997) placed emphasis on leadership and advocacy; school counselors are the professionals in schools to serve as *social justice advocates* to eliminate achievement gaps and ensure success. Since the inception of special education, the disproportionality of minorities placed in special education has been documented. An understanding of the challenges that race, ethnicity, and cultural barriers may place on a student is necessary knowledge for school counselors. How these variables impact evaluation and services is critical.

Within the ASCA (2005) model, school counselors are encouraged to pursue systemic change through leadership, advocacy, and collaboration. Advocating for students is an appropriate activity for school counselors, and it may be especially important to those students with disabilities to support empowerment of them and their families, and to advocate for their individual needs.

As a result of legislation, school counselors will be required to

- support the identification of students and the evaluation of students with disabilities,
- serve on MDTs,
- define and implement appropriate services for students with disabilities,
- counsel students with disabilities,
- provide the same services to students with disabilities that are provided to students without disabilities,
- consult with MDT members and outside agencies on the educational and affective needs of students with disabilities, and
- support staff development.

The work of school counselors is ever growing and exciting. All of their skills, knowledge, and dispositions are put to use on a daily basis in serving children and families. Being an important member of the MDT, many professionals, families, and, most importantly, students will turn to you for your support. Being knowledgeable of the legislation will ensure successful work with children and families with disabilities.

KEYSTONES

- Understanding the content and language of, and how to effectively and legally implement, laws will help to support students and to assist schools to avoid liability.
- A thorough understanding of the special education process includes screening, assessing and evaluating, goal setting and planning, and implementing the students' plan. The law governs us in all of these actions.
- School counselors will need to know how to best advocate for their students in order to be able to obtain resources, interact with outside agencies, and provide direct counseling.
- One main role school counselors have is to conduct periodic evaluations for the purpose of establishing and continuing eligibility of students for special education services and for reassessing their needs and continued eligibility.
- When the students are identified, school counselors work with the MDT to ensure that the legally sound plans are in place and implemented effectively.
- In the IEP process, school counselors can assist in developing relevant goals, specifying supports needed to obtain those goals, and making referrals to outside agencies for services. They also may provide direct counseling service as indicated in the IEP, such as individual or group counseling.

- Under NCLB, school counselors should counsel students about test anxiety and offer strategies, as well as interpret tests and analyze them in conjunction with multiple measures of student achievement. In some instances, they may also coordinate and proctor tests, serve as the building test coordinator, and, possibly, the district coordinator.
- School counselors must be aware of the rights afforded students and their parents regarding school records, such as the laws that govern the confidentiality of school records, what are considered to be exceptions, and the nature of privileged communication.
- School counselors must be aware of their own professional organizations' ethical standards and practices regarding confidentiality (ASCA, 2005).
- School counselors will encounter legal and ethical dilemmas, such as those pertaining to student confidentiality, dual relationships with faculty, parental rights, and acting on student danger to themselves or others.

ADDITIONAL RESOURCES

Print

Bartlett, L. D., Etscheidt, S., & Weistenstein, G. R. (2007). *Special education law and practice in public schools* (2nd ed.). Upper Saddle River, NJ: Pearson.

Norlin, J. W. (2007). *What do I do when: The answer book on special education law* (5th ed.). Horsham, PA: LRP.

Norlin, J. W., & Gorn, S. (2005). *What do I do when: The answer book on Section 504* (2nd ed.). Horsham, PA: LRP.

Yell, M. L. (2012). *The law and special education* (3rd ed.). Boston, MA: Pearson.

Web Based

ADA Document Center: http://adata.org/ada-document-portal

Federal Register Daily: https://www.federalregister.gov/

"The Office of the Federal Register informs citizens of their rights and obligations, documents the actions of Federal agencies, and provides a forum for public participation in the democratic process. Our publications provide access to a wide range of Federal benefits and opportunities for funding and contain comprehensive information about the various activities of the United States Government. In addition, we administer the Electoral College for Presidential elections and the Constitutional amendment process" (Mission section).

FindLaw: http://www.findlaw.com

Provides legal information and services for lawyers, businesses, and individuals.

IDEA Final Regulations: http://www.ed.gov/legislation/fedregister/finrule/index.html

Contains final regulations, priorities, and other rules and pdfs.

IDELR-Ed Admin online: http://www.lrp.com/ed/

"Obtain practical guidance, build professional capacity, and conduct legal/regulatory research about Autism, Behavior and Discipline, Early Childhood, IEPs, Inclusion, LRE, Specific Disabilities, Transition, and more!"

OSERS IDEA 97 Home Page: http://www.ed.gov/offices/OSERS/IDEA/

"An overview of the bill, a summary of the bill, and a brief set of frequently asked questions and answers are provided for people interested in having a broad understanding of some of the changes in IDEA'97."

Special Education Advocate: http://www.wrightslaw.com

"Parents, educators, advocates, and attorneys come to Wrightslaw for accurate, reliable information about special education law, education law, and advocacy for children with disabilities. You will find thousands of articles, cases, and resources about dozens of topics including IDEA 2004, Special Education, Law and Advocacy."

Types of Evaluations: http://www.concordspedpac.org/TypesEvals.html

"This website provides a sampling of evaluations that may be utilized by school systems."

U.S. Congress on the Net: http://thomas.loc.gov/

"Congress.gov is the official source for federal legislative information. It replaces the nearly 20-year-old THOMAS.gov site with a system that includes platform mobility, comprehensive information retrieval and user-friendly presentation. It currently includes all data sets available on THOMAS.gov except nominations, treaties and communications."

U.S. Department of Education: http://www.ed.gov/pubs/index.html

"ED's mission is to promote student achievement and preparation for global competitiveness by fostering educational excellence and ensuring equal access."

Wrights Law: http://www.wrightslaw.com/

Provides summaries of cases, resources, and references.

REFERENCES

American School Counselor Association (ASCA). (2005). *The ASCA national model: A framework for school counseling programs* (2nd ed.). Alexandria, VA: Author.

Bodenhorn, N. (2006). Exploratory study of common and challenging ethical dilemmas experienced by professional school counselors. *Professional School Counseling, 10*(2), 195–202.

Council of Administrators of Special Education. (2011). *Section 504 and ADA: Promoting students: A resource guide for educators.* Alexandria, VA: Author.

Dahir, C. A., & Stone, C. B. (2009). School counselor accountability: The path to social justice and systemic change. *Journal of Counseling & Development, 87*(1), 1556–6676.

Doe v. Koger, 480 F. Supp. 223 (N.D. Ind. 1979).

Dollarhide, C. T., & Lemberger, M. E. (2014). No Child Left Behind: Implications for school counselors. *Professional School Counseling, 9*(4), 295–304.

Elementary and Secondary Education Act, Pub. L. No. 9–10, 79 Stat, 27, 20 W.S.C. (1965).

Erford, B. T., House, R., & Martin, P. (2003). Transforming the school counseling profession. In B. T. Erford (Ed.), *Transforming the school counselor profession* (pp. 1–20). Upper Saddle River, NJ: Merrill Prentice Hall.

Family Educational Rights and Privacy Act (FERPA) of 1974 (20 U.S.C. § 1232g; 34 CFR Part 99).

Fischer, L., Schimmel, D., & Stellman, L. R. (2003). *Teachers and the law* (6th ed.). Boston, MA: Pearson.

Friend, M. (2014). *Special education: Contemporary perspectives for school professionals* (3rd ed.). Boston, MA: Pearson.

Geltner, J. A., & Leibforth, T. N. (2008). Advocacy in the IEP process: Strengths-based school counseling in action. *Professional School Counseling, 12*(2), 162–165.

Goss v. Lopez, 419 U.S. 566 (1975).

Hays, D. (2013). *Assessment in counseling: A guide to the use of psychological assessment procedures.* Alexandria, VA: American Counseling Association.

Helms, E., & Katsiyannis, A. (1992). Counselors in elementary schools: Making it work for students with disabilities. *The School Counselor, 39*(3), 232–237.

Hermann, M. A. (2002). A study of legal issues encountered by school counselors and perceptions of their preparedness to respond to legal challenges. *Professional School Counseling, 6*(1), 1096–2409.

Honig v. Doe, 484, U.S. 305 (1988). *Individuals with Disabilities Education Improvement Act,* H.R. 1350 (2004).

Isaacs, M. L., & Stone, C. (1999). School counselors and confidentiality: Factors affecting professional choices. *Professional School Counseling, 2*(4), 258–266.

Madaus, J. W., & Shaw, S. F. (2008, May). The role of school professionals in implementing section 504 for students with disabilities. *Educational Policy, 22,* pp. 363–378.

Milsom, A. S. (2004). Helping students with disabilities through multidisciplinary teams. In B. T. Erford (Ed.), *Professional school counseling: A handbook of theories, programs, & practices* (pp. 659–666). Austin, TX: Pro-Ed.

No Child Left Behind Act of 2001, Pub. L. No. 107–100 (2002).

Owens, D., Thomas, D., & Strong, L. (2011). School counselors assisting students with disabilities. *Education, 132*(2), 235–240.

Remley, T. P., Jr., & Herlihy, B. (2001). *Ethical, legal, and professional issues in counseling.* Upper Saddle River, NJ: Prentice Hall.

Scarborough, J. L., & Deck, M. D. (1998). The challenges of working for students with disabilities: A view from the front lines. *Professional School Counseling, 2*(1), 10.

Sealander, K. A., Schwiebert, V. L., Oren, T. A., & Weekley, J. L. (1999). Confidentiality and the law. *Professional school counseling, 3*(2), 122–128.

Stone, C. B., & Zirkel, P. A. (2010). School counselor advocacy: When law and ethics may collide. *Professional School Counseling, 13*(4), 244–247.

Tarver-Behring, S., & Spagna, M. E. (2004). Counseling with exceptional children. *Focus on Exceptional Children, 36*(8), 1–12.

Title II of the Americans with Disabilities Act (ADA), 56 Fed. Reg. 35696 (July 26, 1991).

Title II of the Americans with Disabilities Act (ADA), 28 C.F.R. § 35.160.

Underwood, J., & Mead, J. F. (1995). *Legal aspects of special education and pupil services.* Allyn & Bacon.

U.S. Department of Education. (2004). *Introduction: No Child Left Behind.* Retrieved from http://www.ed.gov/print/nclb/overview/intro/index.html

Appendix A

Sample Completed IEP (Created by Author's Legal Issue Class)

INDIVIDUALIZED EDUCATION PROGRAM (IEP)   SCHOOL AGE

Student's Name: _____ Michelle Smith _____

IEP Team Meeting Date (mm/dd/yy): _____ 12/17/2015 _____

IEP Implementation Date (Projected Date when Services and Programs Will Begin):   12/18/2015

Anticipated Duration of Services and Programs: 12/17/2016

Date of Birth: _____ 7/13/94 _____

Age: _____ 16 _____

Grade: _____ 10th _____

Anticipated Year of Graduation: _____ 2018 _____

Local Education Agency (LEA):   Delaware County 2

County of Residence: _____ Delaware County _____

Name and Address of Parent/Guardian/Surrogate: Phone (Home):   484-589-1234

    Mr. and Mrs. Kyle Smith   Phone (Work):   484-734-5678

    135 Joy Lane

    Chester, PA 19013

Other Information: _____

The LEA and parent have agreed to make the following changes to the IEP without convening an IEP meeting, as documented by these individuals:

Date of Revision(s)	Participants/Roles	IEP Section(s) Amended

IEP TEAM/SIGNATURES

The Individualized Education Program team makes the decisions about the student's program and placement. The student's parent(s), the student's special education teacher, and a representative from the Local Education Agency are required members of this team. Signature on this IEP documents attendance, not agreement.

Role	Printed Name	Signature
Parent/Guardian/Surrogate	Susan Smith	
Parent/Guardian/Surrogate	Kyle Smith	
Student*	Michelle Smith	
Regular Education Teacher**	Alisa Dianna – English Teacher	
Special Education Teacher	Alexander Hilliemeyer	
Local Ed Agency Rep	Mary Payne	
School Psychologist	M. Mei Lu PhD	

*   The IEP team must invite the student if transition services are being planned or if the parents choose to have the student participate.

**   If the student is, or may be, participating in the regular education environment

***   As determined by the LEA as needed for transition services and other community services

****   A teacher of the gifted is required when writing an *IEP* for a student with a disability who also is gifted.

One individual listed above must be able to interpret the instructional implications of any evaluation results.

Written input received from the following members:

Not applicable

Transfer of Rights at Age of Majority

For purposes of education, the age of majority is reached in Pennsylvania when the individual reaches 21 years of age. Likewise, for purposes of the Individuals with Disabilities Education Act, the age of majority is reached for students with disabilities when they reach 21 years of age.

PROCEDURAL SAFEGUARDS NOTICE

I have received a copy of the *Procedural Safeguards Notice* during this school year. The *Procedural Safe-guards Notice* provides information about my rights, including the process for disagreeing with the IEP. The school has informed me whom I may contact if I need more information.

Signature of Parent/Guardian/Surrogate: _____

I. SPECIAL CONSIDERATIONS THE IEP TEAM MUST CONSIDER BEFORE DEVELOPING THE IEP. ANY FACTORS CHECKED AS "YES" MUST BE ADDRESSED IN THE IEP.

Is the student blind or visually impaired?

☐ Yes   The IEP must include a description of the instruction in Braille and the use of Braille unless the IEP team determines, after an evaluation of the student's reading and writing skills, needs, and appropriate reading and writing media (including an evaluation of the student's future needs for instruction in Braille or the use of Braille), that instruction in Braille or the use of Braille is not appropriate for the student.

☒ No

Is the student deaf or hard of hearing?

☐ Yes   The IEP must include a communication plan to address the following: language and communication needs; opportunities for direct communications with peers and professional personnel in the student's language and communication mode; academic level; full range of needs, including opportunities for direct instruction in the student's language and communication mode; and assistive technology devices and services. Indicate in which section of the IEP these considerations are addressed. The Communication Plan must be completed and is available at www.pattan.net.

☒ No

Does the student have communication needs?

☐ Yes   Student needs must be addressed in the IEP (i.e., present levels, specially designed instruction [SDI], annual goals, etc.).

☒ No

Does the student need assistive technology devices and/or services?

☐ Yes   Student needs must be addressed in the IEP (i.e., present levels, specially designed instruction, annual goals, etc.).

☒ No

Does the student have limited English proficiency?

☐ Yes   The IEP team must address the student's language needs and how those needs relate to the IEP.

☒ No

Does the student exhibit behaviors that impede his/her learning or that of others?

[×] Yes   The IEP team must develop a Positive Behavior Support Plan that is based on a functional assessment of behavior and that utilizes positive behavior techniques. Results of the functional assessment of behavior may be listed in the Present Levels section of the IEP with a clear measurable plan to address the behavior in the Goals and Specially Designed Instruction sections of the IEP or in the Positive Behavior Support Plan if this is a separate document that is attached to the IEP. A Positive Behavior Support Plan and a Functional Behavioral Assessment form are available at www.pattan.net.

[ ] No

Other (specify):

Not applicable

II. PRESENT LEVELS OF ACADEMIC ACHIEVEMENT AND FUNCTIONAL PERFORMANCE

Include the following information related to the student:

- Present levels of academic achievement (e.g., most recent evaluation of the student, results of formative assessments, curriculum-based assessments, transition assessments, progress toward current goals)

Academic History:

On April 28, 2013, Michelle transferred to TCAHS, an emotional support school for the latter half of the 9th grade. She was referred for the out-of-district placement due to ongoing acts of aggression and, finally, two police arrests for fighting on school grounds. Before arriving at TCAHS, she was held at the Detention Center. The Notice of Recommended Education Placement (NOREP) dated 3/29/2011 stated that Michelle's current program at Chester High School did not have sufficient behavioral support to address her needs. At TCAHS, she is provided with accommodations, supports, and related services. There is a low teacher-to-student ratio, as well as a school-wide positive behavior support system. As part of her educational program at TCAHS, Michelle receives weekly individual therapy sessions (30–45 minutes/session) and bi-weekly group therapy (30 minutes/group). A vocational component, culinary arts, is embedded into Michelle's educational programming at TCAHS. She is currently in 10th grade.

Aptitude and Achievement Tests:

Michelle was initially evaluated in 2007 and began receiving full-time special education services in 5th grade. An evaluation was prompted by Michelle's difficulty in keeping up with classes, behavioral challenges, and poor ability to focus. In October 2009, she transferred to Wetherill School due to reported difficulties getting along with teachers at Smedley. Also at that time, Michelle was said to be emotionally affected by the decision to exclude her from the graduation ceremony after all expenses were paid in full.

Test of Word Reading Efficiency (TOWRE): 7/25/2010

Subtests	Standard Score	Percentile
Sight Word Efficiency	69	2
Phonemic Decoding Efficiency	75	5
Total Reading Efficiency	*66*	*1*

(Scaled Scores between 85 and 115 are within the Average range)

Grades

According to records, Michelle has earned 2.4375 credits to date. The following grades and comments were reported during her high school career:

TCAHS—10th grade (2011/2012)—1st marking period	
English	85
Reading	Pass
Math	94
Earth Science	95
Social Studies	95
Physical Education	85
Health	70
Vocational Shop (Food Prep)	85

A=90–100
B=80–89
C=70–79
D=60–69
F=50–59
Possible credits for year: 7.75

Comments: Completes class work, completes homework, cooperative/interacts positively, responsible/dependable, pride in achievement/appearance, making steady progress

TCAHS—9th grade (2010/2011)	
English	75
Reading	98
Math	95
Earth Science	90
Social Studies	87
Physical Education	85
Health	80
Vocational Shop (Food Prep)	60
Social Skills	Pass

A=90–100
B=80–89
C=70–79

D=60–69
F=50–59
Possible credits for year: 1.9375

Comments: Completes class work, completes homework, cooperative/interacts positively, responsible/dependable, making steady progress, frequently absent (English), careless/indifferent (Food Prep)

Reading

In Reading, Michelle was assessed on skills of oral fluency, rapid automatized naming (RAN), phonological awareness, sight word recognition, decoding, and reading comprehension.

Oral fluency is the ability to produce a series of words or ideas related to a specific criterion or visual cue rapidly by quickly retrieving information from long-term memory. Michelle completed two subtests in this category: Associational Fluency and Naming Facility. In Associational Fluency, she was verbally asked to provide words that were associated with a semantic criterion or initial phoneme sound, and she performed within the Average range (SS-97). On the second task, Naming Facility, Michelle also scored in the Average range (SS-95). Naming Facility is a task measuring rapid automatized naming (RAN), an important skill necessary for the quick and efficient retrieval of phonological information from long-term memory. RAN involved the ability to perceive visual stimuli (e.g., objects, colors, numbers, or letters) and to name it rapidly and accurately. It represents a very basic indicator of how fast the brain can integrate visual and verbal processes, which is an important part of reading.

Sound-symbol knowledge is the awareness, understanding, and store of information that an individual has of the association between sounds and print (also known as phonological awareness). This is the understanding that words are composed of individual phonemes, which are represented by letters of the alphabet. The Nonsense Word Decoding subtest measured Michelle's application of phonics by asking her to decode letter sequences that were not authentic words but made up of letter units that adhered to Standard English pronunciation; she performed in the Well Below Average range (SS-70). Michelle displayed ending sound confusion with /b/ for /p/ and difficulty with medial sounds.

The Letter and Word Recognition subtest measured both Michelle's ability to recognize vocabulary and her ability to decode unfamiliar words. She scored within the Significantly Below Average range (SS-66). She was not able to establish a basal point at her recommended grade level. On unfamiliar words, Michelle observably employed phonemic knowledge to assist with decoding; however, this is a weakness for her. Generally, she would break down parts in phonetic pieces and blend them as best as she could. She also appeared to rely on visual aspects to stimulus words (e.g., with → width, beard → bored).

Reading fluency tasks measured the speed, ease, and accuracy (i.e., automaticity) in which Michelle was able to read. On the Word Recognition Fluency subtest, she scored within the lower limits of the Well Below Average range (SS-66) due to poor word recognition and phonetic application skills.

Reading comprehension is the ability to extract meaning from printed text. On this subtest, Michelle was required to read a series of passages and to answer a number of literal and inferential questions regarding the passage's content. Her performance suggested much difficulty with questions that required reasoning and the integration of information, as opposed to responses that were explicitly provided in the text. In the most instances, she read silently to herself and referenced back to the text before providing an answer. The latter behavior indicated a lack of comprehension during her initial read; however, it is a good strategy to employ when comprehension is in question. Additionally, Michelle displayed difficulty searching and locating the appropriate place in the passage that contained the necessary information. As a result, she typically reread the entire passage before providing an answer. Michelle's reading comprehension score fell in the Significantly Below Average (SS-64).

At this time, Michelle demonstrated significant weakness in all major domains of reading. Precursory reading skills of oral fluency and rapid automatized naming were within the Average range. At this time, Michelle needs considerable remediation through an intense and explicit phonics-based reading program.

Group Reading Assessment and Diagnostic Evaluation (GRADE) 9/22/2011

Subtest	Stanine	Percentile
Listening Comprehension	1	—
Vocabulary	1	<1
Sentence Comprehension	1	—
Passage Comprehension	1	—
Comprehension Composite	1	<1
Total test	1	<1

Date	Lesson #	Score	
5/6/2011	5	122 wpm/0 errors	Pass
5/10/2011	10	137 wpm/2 errors	Pass
5/10/2011	15	146 wpm/ 1 errors	Pass
10/6/2011	20	152 wpm/1 errors	Pass
10/6/2011	25	125 wpm/1 errors	Pass
10/6/2011	30	130 wpm/2 errors	Pass
10/6/2011	35	130 wpm/ 2 errors	Pass

AIMSweb—8th grade probes
Computation
9/7/11 – 2/80
(Goal – 20/80)

Written Language
In the area of written language, Michelle was assessed in spelling and written expression. She scored comparably in both areas. On spelling tasks, Michelle displayed behaviors similar to those exhibited when reading. On several items, she wrote visually and/or aurally similar words despite the oral presentation of words in context-rich sentences. This consistent tendency to interchange homonyms and synonyms provides further evidence of lexical limitations. On the Spelling subtest, she obtained a score in the Well Above Average range (SS-74). On written expressive tasks, Michelle put forth much effort but had difficulty grasping lengthier and more complex items. As a result, further clarifications were sometimes needed after the standardized directions were provided. She scored in the Well Above Average range (SS-73) in this assessment of writing. Michelle needs improvement in the following areas: vocabulary, conventions, grammar usage, sentence structure, and theme development. Her written products often reflected her verbal expressive skills stylistically. For example, "I think yall doing a good job in spite of yall just need a little more work."
"Dear fan and Director which one of yall like the movie that bout to come out."

PSSA Writing Sample

A persuasive writing sample was collected on October 8, 2010, by Mr. Kappenstein. Michelle was asked to write an essay in response to a prompt, and a visual outline of the writing process was provided. The writing sample was scored by two raters according to the Pennsylvania System of School Assessment (PSSA) Scoring Guidelines, which rates each response according to five areas. Scores range from 1 to 4, with 4 indicating superb writing.

	Mr. Kappenstein Score	Comments	Mr. Maynard Score	Comments
Focus	1	Minimal focus	1	Very little focus
Content and Development	1	Superficial; no details	1	Unelaborated argument
Organization	1	Minimal organization	1	Lack of logical order and transitions
Style	1	Minimal variety in word choice and sentence structure	1	Minimal control of language and sentence structure
Convention	1	Minimal control in all areas	1	Minimal control, awkward sentences, many errors

Mathematics

In the area of mathematics, computational and mathematical reasoning skills were assessed. Michelle scored within the Well Above Average range in both domains (Math Concepts and Application, S-71; Math Computation, SS-70). Quantitative reasoning assessed her knowledge of math concepts and application to everyday situations such as time, money, reading graphs and charts, determining patterns, and creating and solving math problems. Some of the tasks required Michelle to listen to math problems while looking at coinciding pictures, to recognize the procedures to be followed, and then to perform the calculations. Michelle consistently had trouble with problems involving money, such as counting appropriate change. Although finger counting was observed, Michelle's performance on the Math Computation subtest did suggest a sufficient knowledge base with addition and subtraction math facts and algorithms. Problems were presented in a worksheet format, and Michelle was asked to complete as many problems as she could without time limitations. Michelle struggled with multiplication and division. She attempted to calculate the product of several multiplication problems; however, she was inconsistently successful. Michelle did not complete any division problems, including those for division facts (e.g., 8/2=). She stated that she does not understand the concept even though she had a general gist of multiplication. No problems involving fractions, decimals, percentages, or more complex items were attempted. At this time, Michelle should develop a conceptual knowledge base for these mathematical ideas before proceeding to complete worksheet-type problems involving those concepts. At this time, Michelle's history and pattern of development support the educational disability categories of Other Health Impaired and Emotional Disturbance. It appears that difficulties with ADHD and management of social-emotional-behavioral functioning have impeded her learning. Academic instruction for enhancing reading, writing, and math is highly recommended.

Curriculum-Based Measurement

9/17/11 – 2/25/114 CDPM
9/23/11 – 1/53 CDPM
(Goal – 12.5 Correct Digit Per Minute)

Concepts and Applications

9/15/11 – 0/42

9/30/11 – 1/42

10/7/11 – 3/42

10/15/11 – 4/42

10/21/11 – 0/42

Vocational Interests

Cluster	Cluster Quotient	Percentile	Rating
Mechanical	107	68	Average
Outdoor	97	42	Average
Mechanical-Outdoor	109	73	Average
Food Service-Handling Operations	123	94	High
Clerical-Social Service	81	10	Below Average

On the R-FVII:2, Michelle indicated a strong preference for vocations geared toward food service, housekeeping, and materials handling. She scored in the Above Average range for duties falling under food service. These occupations involve working in businesses and companies that are responsible for any meal prepared and serviced outside of the home. Her ratings also indicated a High level of interest for occupations in the housekeeping and materials handling sectors. Housekeeping involves the process of maintaining a building in neat and clean condition. These occupations involve receiving, moving, storing, packing, and shipping raw materials, components, and/or finished products. These scores are highly consistent with Michelle's desire to work in the food catering business since it incorporates tasks from each identified interest area.

Interest	T-Score	Percentile	Rating
Automotive	48	42	Average
Building Trades	57	75	Average
Clerical	41	18	Below Average
Animal Care	41	18	Below Average
Food Service	63	90	Above Average
Patient Care	27	1	Low
Horticulture	52	58	Average
Housekeeping	68	96	High
Personal Service	46	34	Average
Laundry Service	40	16	Below Average
Materials Handling	67	95	High

(T-scores between 43 and 57 are within the Average range)

- Present levels of functional performance (e.g., results from a functional behavioral assessment, results of ecological assessments, progress toward current goals)

According to Michelle's responses on the Conners CBRS, a Very Elevated score was found for the Oppositional Defiant Disorder diagnostic scale. She endorsed statements such as very frequently getting angered by other people and getting even when mad at someone and often arguing with adults and getting easily annoyed by others. An Elevated score was found for the ADHD, Predominately Hyperactive-Impulsive Type diagnostic scale, which indicated that Michelle may have high activity levels, restlessness, difficulty being quiet, and poor impulse control. Accordingly, Elevated scores were found for the following content scores: Aggressive Behaviors, Academic Difficulties, Hyperactivity/Impulsivity, and Violence Potential.

On the Conners CBRS, critical items requiring immediate attention included Michelle's report of hopelessness and knowledge of where to obtain a weapon. When queried, Michelle reported that there was no gun in her house. Her response to the question referred to a sharp weapon that she would use only if her life was threatened (i.e., "use for protection. Like if someone tries to kill"). Ms. Smith also noted Michelle's very frequent inclination to carry and occasional tendency to use a weapon. Ms. Smith expressed concerns regarding Michelle's thoughts of death and dying, ramifications of bullying victimization, feeling of helplessness, cruelty to animals, and disregard for others' rights. Clinical indicators include possible post-traumatic stress and phobic symptomology (e.g., bugs).

Functional Behavior Assessment
At TCAHS, Michelle's teachers completed a functional behavior assessment (FBA) to determine behaviors that may interfere with her ability to learn. If necessary, the data collected will help formulate a Positive Behavior Support Plan in which the identified behaviors will be addressed.

In Mr. Cruice's Food Preparation class, Michelle was reported to be a "perfect student in Food Prep." No behavior issue has been observed.

In Mr. Kappenstein's Social Studies class, Michelle will engage in verbal arguments with peers on an infrequent basis. At most, this targeted behavior occurs on a monthly basis. Argumentative behaviors last for approximately 10 to 15 minutes, and it takes varying amounts of time before Michelle is able to refocus after staff intervenes. The trigger of this behavior appears to be in response to the provocation of peers. According to Mr. Kappenstein, the identified behavior has the function of escaping from work or attention seeking. However, considering the context, the situation may be better interpreted as Michelle being disrupted from her work, feeling the need to defend herself, and seeking help from staff by engaging in escalated behaviors.

In Mr. Maynard's Science class, Michelle sometimes completes assignments quickly without demonstrating adequate effort toward other class activities. This occurs approximately once a week and is triggered by the assignment of independent seatwork. Teacher redirection has been successful in stopping the targeted behavior. Michelle's rush through work functions as a way to obtain a tangible reinforcement since she is allowed to work on the computer or other desirable activity once class work is complete.

In Mrs. Dianna's English class, Michelle has not demonstrated any behavior that interferes with learning at this point.

Classroom Observations:

Mrs. Alisa Dianna (English)

According to Mrs. Dianna, Michelle participates in class for 100% of the time. She follows class and school rules. She appears to have adjusted well to TCAHS despite a constant proclamation of her dislike for the school. Michelle is very motivated to do well at TCAHS for the possibility of transferring to another program. She is generally very focused despite any issues occurring in the class. She completes all assigned tasks. When frustrated, she is willing and able to ask for assistance. Her interactions with staff and peers are appropriate; however, when taunted, she will respond in a hostile manner. In English, Michelle works hard, completes assignments, and is kind to staff. Mrs. Dianna would like to see Michelle improve her reading and writing skills, including reading comprehension.

Mr. Alexander Hillemeyer (Math)

According to Mr. Hillemeyer, Michelle is very friendly and appropriately behaved. She completes work and follows directions. Her time on task is very high, and she demonstrates an excellent ability to focus. She is very motivated to do well in school and will ask for help when needed. Although she does not like the environment at TCAHS, Michelle does appear to like learning. She is very respectful of staff and is mature and appropriate with peers. Mr. Hillemeyer would like Michelle to improve her understanding of mathematical concepts and math fluency.

Mr. Eric Maynard (Science)

According to Mr. Maynard, Michelle is respectful, focused, and cooperative. Her affect, attitude, and social interactions have all been positive. Michelle follows rules and is invested in the school-wide behavior support system. She is on task and completes assignments about 95% of the time. So far, she has received good test scores on exams. Michelle is motivated to do well for the purpose of transferring to another educational placement. Mr. Maynard reports that she sometimes would rush through her work. Helpful educational techniques include positive reinforcement, praise, and one-on-one instruction.

Mr. Robert Kappenstein (Social Studies)

According to Mr. Kappenstein, Michelle is a highly motivated student. She is responsible and successful at getting work completed. She begins assignments immediately and can stay on task and focused until completion. Michelle is making excellent academic progress in Social Studies. She is not easily distracted. When distracted, Michelle is very good about making up any missed work. A strong desire to return to a within-district placement has been communicated, and it appears she is working hard and diligently toward that goal. She is able to follow rules and engage positively with staff and peers. Although Michelle initially had several "blowups" in school, she appears to have much better control over her emotions and behaviors this academic year. Mr. Kappenstein encourages Michelle to work on and maintain her level of self-control.

Mr. William Cruice (Vocational Shop-Food Prep)

According to Mr. Cruice, Michelle is polite, attentive, and hard working. She is focused and on-task about 99% of the time. She is motivated and demonstrates a great attitude in culinary class. The quality of her interactions with staff is very polite; however, Michelle does have some issues with peers who try to upset her or disrupt her day intentionally. Although Mr. Cruice never observed an incident of bad temper, he would like Michelle to receive anger management counseling to address past concerns of aggression.

Ms. Elizabeth Deegan (Mental Health Counselor)

According to Ms. Deegan, Michelle is respectful to adults, puts forth much effort in classes, has a strong desire to succeed in school and life, and has worked hard to change her behaviors. She does well in individual and group therapy sessions. She uses her individual sessions appropriately and works well with peers in group sessions. In class, she tries very hard to not get involved in any conflict, and for the most part, has been successful. Ms. Deegan believes Michelle may be able to function more easily in a smaller class setting. She does well with the majority of the students at TCAHS, but some students have persistently teased her. A prolonged period of taunting has caused Michelle to break down and misbehave in the past. Recommended goals for Michelle include anger management by activating resources that are available during difficult situations and improving her self-esteem. Michelle does not take any medication currently, and she enjoys gardening and working on creative projects.

Social-Emotional and Behavioral History:

In early childhood, Ms. Smith reported that Michelle was a happy, quiet, and well-behaved child. She was hesitant to leave her mother's side. Michelle continued to display good behaviors in Head Start and elementary school. However, beginning in middle school, a history of behavioral concerns emerged. Concerns included a quick temper, aggression, cutting class, running in the halls, issues with trust, and getting along with others. Difficulty maintaining relationships with certain teachers also started appearing. In high school, Michelle's aggression escalated and she began physically fighting with peers. In January and February 2013, she was arrested two separate occasions for a physical altercation during school. Since April 28, 2011, Michelle has been enrolled in an emotional support program at TCAHS.

According to both Ms. Smith and Michelle, she sometimes fights with her younger sister, Sally (aged 14 years). However, Michelle stated that she does not feel good when she and her sister are in conflict. Ms. Smith revealed that Michelle gets along well with family members as long as she is not annoyed by excessive questioning. She also stated that Michelle and her siblings might still be affected by the death of their maternal grandmother who passed away from illness in 2004. Michelle reportedly does not have a history of substance abuse.

Ms. Smith described Michelle's positive attributes as helpful (e.g., helps with chores, babysitting, and food preparation), affectionate, organized, protective, willingness to ask for assistance when needed, and her motivation to do well academically.

Attendance:
As of November 12, 2013, her current attendance for this school year

Days Present	41
Days Tardy	0
Excused Absences	4.5
Unexcused Absences	1.5
Out-of-School Suspension	1

For the previous school year (9th grade), Michelle's attendance from her date of enrollment at TCASH (April 28, 2011) through the last day

Days Present	38
Days Tardy	0
Excused Absences	1
Unexcused Absences	8

At Smith Upland High School, Michelle was absent 64.5 days before her withdrawal in January 2013.

- Present levels related to current postsecondary transition goals if the student's age is 14 or younger if determined appropriate by the IEP team (e.g., results of formative assessments, curriculum-based assessments, progress toward current goals)

> Michelle is currently in her 10th year of school. Currently, she is taking a food preparation course through TCAHS vocational program. She enjoys the class and has stated a career interest in culinary arts, possibly food catering. Mr. Cruice, her food prep teacher, stated that Michelle has demonstrated great potential in his class. Michelle has had the opportunity to partake in various catering events through her involvement in the food prep class. As part of this evaluation, Michelle completed a vocational assessment, which indicated employment interests in food service, housekeeping, and materials handling.
>
> **Transition Needs:**
> - Develop and maintain an appropriate plan for high school graduation
> - Develop and maintain ability to function independently and appropriately in a social environment
> - Develop and learn to spontaneously employ coping strategies
> - Develop positive social judgment
> - Develop life skills for independent living
> - Explore career interest in food service, housekeeping, and materials handling
> - Explore vocational training for desired occupation

- Parental concerns for enhancing the education of the student

> According to the Re-evaluation, Ms. Smith states she has concerns regarding Michelle's display of aggression, social aspects with her peers, and Michelle's nutritional diet. Parental concerns will be discussed further at the IEP meeting.

- How the student's disability affects involvement and progress in the general education curriculum

> Michelle qualifies for Special Education as a child with an Emotional Disturbance that [*sic*] the involvement and progress in the general education setting is not possible due to her high need for unique and specially designed instruction throughout the school day. Michelle exhibits inappropriate types of behavior or feelings under normal circumstances, and she has inappropriate verbal and physical behaviors. She qualifies for emotional support. Michelle qualifies for a secondary category of Special Education under the category of Other Health Impairment for ADHD and ODD.

- Strengths

> - Motivated to do well in school
> - Good attendance
> - Strong relationship with family
> - Ability to ignore negative behaviors of others
> - Willing to make up missed assignments
> - Respectful toward adults
> - Responsive to interventions

- Academic, developmental, and functional needs related to student's disability

  - To continue developing coping strategies for mood and behavior management
  - To improve academic achievement—in reading, writing, and mathematics
  - To enhance self-esteem and self-confidence
  - To begin setting and developing postsecondary goals and plans

III. TRANSITION SERVICES — This is required for students aged 14 or younger if determined appropriate by the IEP team. If the student does not attend the IEP meeting, the school must take other steps to ensure that the student's preferences and interests are considered. Transition services are a coordinated set of activities for a student with a disability that is designed to be within a results-oriented process; these services are focused on improving the academic and functional achievement of the student with a disability to facilitate the student's movement from school to postschool activities, including postsecondary education, vocational education, integrated employment (including supported employment), continuing and adult education, adult services, independent living, or community participation that is based on the individual student's needs, taking into account the student's strengths, preferences, and interests.

POST-SCHOOL GOALS—Based on age-appropriate assessment, define and project the appropriate measurable postsecondary goals that address education and training, employment, and, as needed, independent living. Under each area, list the services/activities and courses of study that support that goal. Include for each service/activity the location, frequency, projected beginning date, anticipated duration, and person/agency responsible.

For students in Career and Technology Centers, CIP Code:

Not applicable

Postsecondary Education and Training Goal: Michelle has the goal to attend postsecondary education in the interest of culinary arts upon graduation from high school.	Measurable Annual Goal **Yes**/No (Document in Section V)

Courses of Study: English, math, science, social studies, vocational shop-food prep, Emotional Support period

Service/Activity	Location	Frequency	Projected Beginning Date	Anticipated Duration	Person(s)/ Agency Responsible
One-on-one individual conference with school counselor to review graduation plan and program	TCAHS	One time per school year	12/18/2015	12/16/2016	School Counselor
Provide opportunity to attend Career Day	TCAHS	When offered by school	12/18/2015	12/16/2016	School Counselor
Support and instruction in behavior and social skills	TCAHS	One period per school day	12/18/2015	12/16/2016	Emotional Support Teacher

Support and instruction in computation and math reasoning skills	TCAHS	One period per school day	12/18/2015	12/16/2016	Learning Support Teacher
Support and instruction in expressive language (writing)	TCAHS	One period per school day	12/18/2015	12/16/2016	Learning Support Teacher
Support and instruction in reading fluency and comprehension	TCAHS	One period per school day	12/18/2015	12/16/2016	Learning Support Teacher

Employment Goal: Michelle has the goal to obtain competitive employment upon postsecondary education.	Measurable Annual Goal **Yes**/No (Document in Section V)

Courses of Study: English, math, science, social studies, vocational shop-food prep, Emotional Support period

IV. PARTICIPATION IN STATE AND LOCAL ASSESSMENTS

Instructions for IEP Teams:

Please check the appropriate assessments. If the student will be assessed using the PSSA or the PSSA-Modified, the IEP Team must choose which assessment will be administered for each content area (Reading, Mathematics, and Science). For example, a student may take the PSSA-Modified for Reading and the PSSA for Mathematics and Science. If the student will be assessed using the PASA, the IEP Team need not select content areas because ALL content areas will be assessed using the PASA.

- **PSSA** (Please choose the appropriate option and content areas for the student. A student may be eligible to be assessed using the PSSA-Modified assessment for one or more content areas and be assessed using the PSSA for other content areas.)

- **PSSA-Modified** (Please choose the appropriate option and content areas for the student. A student may be eligible to be assessed using the PSSA-Modified assessment for one or more content areas and be assessed using the PSSA for other content areas.)

Allowable accommodations may be found in the PSSA Accommodations Guidelines online: www.portal.state .pa.us/portal/server.pt/community/testing_accommodations__security/7448

Criteria regarding PSSA-Modified eligibility may be found in Guidelines for IEP Teams: Assigning Students with IEPs to State Tests (ASIST) online: www.education.state.pa.us/portal/server.pt/community/ special_education/7465/assessment/607491

Criteria regarding PASA eligibility may be found in Guidelines for IEP Teams: Assigning Students with IEPs to State Tests (ASIST) online: www.education.state.pa.us/portal/server.pt/community/special_education/7465/ assessment/607491

Not Assessed (Please select if student is not being assessed by a state assessment this year)

xxx	Assessment is not administered at this student's grade level

Reading (PSSA grades 3-8, 11; PSSA-M grades 4-8, 11)

	Student will participate in the PSSA without accommodations
	Student will participate in the PSSA with the following appropriate accommodations:

	Student will participate in the PSSA-Modified without accommodations
	Student will participate in the PSSA-Modified with the following appropriate accommodations:

Math (PSSA grades 3-8, 11; PSSA-M grades 4-8, 11)

	Student will participate in the PSSA without accommodations
	Student will participate in the PSSA with the following appropriate accommodations:
	Student will participate in the PSSA-Modified without accommodations
	Student will participate in the PSSA-Modified with the following appropriate accommodations:

Science (PSSA grades 4, 8, 11; PSSA-M grades 8, 11)

	Student will participate in the PSSA without accommodations
	Student will participate in the PSSA with the following appropriate accommodations:
	Student will participate in the PSSA-Modified without accommodations
	Student will participate in the PSSA-Modified with the following appropriate accommodations:

Writing (PSSA grades 5, 8, 11)

	Student will participate in the PSSA without accommodations
	Student will participate in the PSSA with the following appropriate accommodations:

PASA (PASA grades 3-8, 11 for Reading and Math; Grades 4, 8, 11 for Science)

	Student will participate in the PASA

Explain why the student cannot participate in the PSSA or the PSSA-M for Reading, Math, or Science:

Explain why the PASA is appropriate:

Choose how the student's performance on the PASA will be documented.

☐   Videotape (will be kept confidential as are all other school records)

☐   Written narrative (will be kept confidential as are all other school records)

Local Assessments

☐   Local assessment is not administered at this student's grade level; OR

☐   Student will participate in local assessments without accommodations; OR

xx	Student will participate in local assessments with the following accommodations; OR

> Extended time/Separate location

	The student will take an alternate local assessment.

> Explain why the student cannot participate in the regular assessment:

> Explain why the alternate assessment is appropriate:

V. GOALS AND OBJECTIVES – Include, as appropriate, academic and functional goals. Use as many copies of this page as needed to plan appropriately. Specially designed instruction may be listed with each goal/objective or listed in Section VI.

Short-term learning outcomes are required for students who are gifted. The short-term learning outcomes related to the student's gifted program may be listed under Goals or Short-Term Objectives.

MEASURABLE ANNUAL GOAL Include: Condition, Name, Behavior, and Criteria (Refer to Annotated IEP for description of these components)	Describe HOW the student's progress toward meeting this goal will be measured	Describe WHEN periodic reports on progress will be provided to parents	Report of Progress
Fluency Given 1 minute to read an unfamiliar passage at the 10th grade level, Michelle will increase her oral reading fluency from a baseline score of _____ correct words to a goal of _____ correct words for 3 consecutive probes assessed twice monthly. **Baseline:** to be determined within 10 days of implementation	Progress Monitoring, assessed twice a month	Quarterly with Report Cards	
Comprehension Given an unfamiliar 10th grade passage, Michelle will orally read the passage and answer comprehension questions increasing her baseline from _____ answers correct to _____ answers correct given twice monthly for 3 consecutive probes. **Baseline:** to be determined within 10 days of implementation	Progress Monitoring, assessed twice a month	Quarterly with Report Cards	

Written Language Given an unfamiliar writing prompt, 1 minute to think, and 3 minutes to write, Michelle will respond to the prompt increasing from a baseline of _____ total mechanical errors to a goal of _____ total mechanical errors for 3 consecutive probes assessed twice monthly. **Baseline:** to be determined within 10 days of implementation	Progress Monitoring, assessed twice a month	Quarterly with Report Cards	
Math Given a 10th grade level probe containing math computation problems (with point values increasing from 1 point for the easiest problems to 3 points for the most difficult, with the maximum points being 10) and 8 minutes to complete the problems, Michelle will write correct answers to computation problems increasing from a baseline score of 2 points to a goal of 20 points on 3 consecutive probes assessed twice monthly.	Progress Monitoring, assessed twice a month	Quarterly with Report Cards	
Behavior When provoked by a peer in the school setting, Michelle will increase her positive verbal and physical responses as mentioned in her BIP, from a baseline of _____ responses to a goal of _____ responses for 3 consecutive probes for 4 consecutive weeks. **Baseline:** to be determined within 10 days of implementation	Progress Monitoring, assessed twice a month	Quarterly with Report Cards	

SHORT-TERM OBJECTIVES – Required for students with disabilities who take alternate assessments aligned to alternate achievement standards (PASA).

Short-term objectives / Benchmarks

VI. SPECIAL EDUCATION / RELATED SERVICES / SUPPLEMENTARY AIDS AND SERVICES / PROGRAM MODIFICATIONS – Include, as appropriate, for nonacademic and extracurricular services and activities.

A. PROGRAM MODIFICATIONS AND SPECIALLY DESIGNED INSTRUCTION (SDI)
- SDI may be listed with each goal or as part of the table below.
- Include supplementary aids and services as appropriate.
- For a student who has a disability and is gifted, SDI also should include adaptations, accommodations, or modifications to the general education curriculum, as appropriate for a student with a disability.

Modifications and SDI	Location	Frequency	Projected Beginning Date	Anticipated Duration
Structured academic time – daily agenda written in the classroom, behavior expectations and consequences clearly displayed in the classroom	TCAHS, English, Math, Science, Social Studies, ES Class, Reading, Food Prep class	Daily, in all academic settings	12/18/2015	12/16/2016
Access to the Resource Room for remediation in material to check for Michelle's understanding	TCAHS, English, Math, Science, Social Studies, ES Class, Reading, Food Prep class	At least 60 minutes per school week	12/18/2015	12/16/2016
Provide academic materials at instructional level when guidance is available	TCAHS, English, Math, Science, Social Studies, ES Class, Reading, Food Prep class	When guidance is necessary for academic instruction	12/18/2015	12/16/2016
Provide academic materials at independent level for homework assignments	TCAHS, English, Math, Science, Social Studies, ES Class, Reading, Food Prep class	For each given homework assignment	12/18/2015	12/16/2016
Presentation of materials in manageable parts – assignments need to be broken down into monitored manageable steps	TCAHS, English, Math, Science, Social Studies, ES Class, Reading, Food Prep class	Per presentation and assignment	12/18/2015	12/16/2016
Materials should be presented visually and auditorily	TCAHS, English, Math, Science, Social Studies, ES Class, Reading, Food Prep class	During class when materials are being presented in front of the class	12/18/2015	12/16/2016
One-on-one instruction when needed	TCAHS, English, Math, Science, Social Studies, ES Class, Reading, Food Prep class	During class when one-on-one instruction is required/ requested by Michelle	12/18/2015	12/16/2016

Extended time for tasks and tests (up to 50%)	TCAHS, English, Math, Science, Social Studies, ES Class, Reading, Food Prep class	When extended time is needed for a given task or test	12/18/2015	12/16/2016
Calculator for math reasoning problems	Math	When given math reasoning work	12/18/2015	12/16/2016
Graphic organizers for reading and writing assignments	TCAHS, English, Math, Science, Social Studies, ES Class, Reading, Food Prep class	When given a reading or writing assignment	12/18/2015	12/16/2016
Completed modeled math problems	Math, Science	When expected to complete math problems both in and out of school	12/18/2015	12/16/2016
Support and instruction in behavior and social skills	Emotional Support Classroom	One class period per school day	12/18/2015	12/16/2016
Support and instruction in computation and math reasoning skills	DI Math Class	One class period per school day	12/18/2015	12/16/2016
Support and instruction in expressive language (writing)	DI English Class	One class period per school day	12/18/2015	12/16/2016
Support and instruction in reading fluency and comprehension	DI Reading Class	One class period per school day	12/18/2015	12/16/2016
Access to Emotional Support Classroom when feeling emotionally charged to discuss situation and apply learned coping strategies to cope with current situation	TCAHS, English, Math, Science, Social Studies, ES Class, Reading, Food Prep class	As needed by Michelle when feeling emotional	12/18/2015	12/16/2016

B. RELATED SERVICES – List the services that the student needs in order to benefit from his/her special education program.

Service	Location	Frequency	Projected Beginning Date	Anticipated Duration
Transportation to and from TCAHS	TCAHS	Daily, during the school year	12/18/2015	12/16/2016

C. SUPPORTS FOR SCHOOL PERSONNEL – List the staff to receive the supports and the supports needed to implement the student's IEP.

School Personnel to Receive Support	Support	Location	Frequency	Projected Beginning Date	Anticipated Duration
Teachers and staff working with Michelle	Michelle's teachers will receive a copy of her IEP at the beginning of her school year and upon any revisions	TCAHS	As noted in support	12/18/2015	12/16/2016
Teachers and staff working with Michelle	Ongoing consultation between special education case manager and general education teachers	TCAHS	Weekly consultation as a minimum – consultation can be more frequent if required or requested by the general education teacher	12/18/2015	12/16/2016
Teachers and staff working with Michelle	Consultation with Behavior Specialist and/or consultants for successful implementation of Michelle's FBA	TCAHS	At least one time per month	12/18/2015	12/16/2016

D. GIFTED SUPPORT SERVICES FOR A STUDENT IDENTIFIED AS GIFTED WHO ALSO IS IDENTIFIED AS A STUDENT WITH A DISABILITY – Support services are required to assist a gifted student to benefit from gifted education (e.g., psychological services, parent counseling and education, counseling services, transportation to and from gifted programs to classrooms in buildings operated by the school district).

Support Service	
Support Service	
Support Service	

E. EXTENDED SCHOOL YEAR (ESY) – The IEP team has considered and discussed ESY services, and determined eligibility:

Student IS eligible for ESY based on the following information or data reviewed by the IEP team:

OR

| xx | As of the date of this IEP, student is NOT eligible for ESY based on the following information or data reviewed by the IEP team: |

> A review of records will be completed to determine Michelle's eligibility for ESY by February 2016.

The Annual Goals and, when appropriate, Short-Term Objectives from this IEP that are to be addressed in the student's ESY Program:

If the IEP team has determined ESY is appropriate, complete the following:

ESY Service to Be Provided	Location	Frequency	Projected Beginning Date	Anticipated Duration

VII. EDUCATIONAL PLACEMENT

A. QUESTIONS FOR IEP TEAM – The following questions must be reviewed and discussed by the IEP team prior to providing the explanations regarding participation with students without disabilities.

It is the responsibility of each public agency to ensure that, to the maximum extent appropriate, students with disabilities, including those in public or private institutions or other care facilities, are educated with students who are not disabled. Special classes, separate schooling or other removal of students with disabilities from the general educational environment occurs only when the nature or severity of the disability is such that education in general education classes, EVEN WITH the use of supplementary aids and services, cannot be achieved satisfactorily.

- What supplementary aids and services were considered? What supplementary aids and services were rejected? Explain why the supplementary aids and services will or will not enable the student to make progress on the goals and objectives (if applicable) in this IEP in the general education class.
- What benefits are provided in the general education class with supplementary aids and services versus the benefits provided in the special education class?
- What potentially beneficial effects and/or harmful effects might be expected on the student with disabilities or the other students in the class, even with supplementary aids and services?
- To what extent, if any, will the student participate with nondisabled peers in extracurricular activities or other nonacademic activities?

Explanation of the extent, if any, to which the student will not participate with students without disabilities in the regular education class:

Michelle requires instruction to meet the outcomes identified in her measurable annual goals in reading, math, and behavior. This instruction will require a direct, explicit teacher of skills that are not within the scope of the general curriculum at her current grade level, and the time required for such instruction

> will supplant time during which she would otherwise participate in the general curriculum. The required replacement instruction will occur in a special education classroom, during which time Michelle will not be participating in regular education classroom instruction and activities.

Explanation of the extent, if any, to which the student will not participate with students without disabilities in the general education curriculum:

> Michelle requires direct instruction of skills and strategies in the areas of reading, math, and behavior that are not part of the general education curriculum at her grade level and cannot be meaningfully articulated within the curriculum, even with adaptations and support. She is included within the general education curriculum for all other subjects.

B. TYPE of SUPPORT

1. Amount of special education supports

☐ Itinerant: Special education supports and services provided by special education personnel for 20% or less of the school day

☒ Supplemental: Special education supports and services provided by special education personnel for more than 20% of the day but less than 80% of the school day

☐ Full Time: Special education supports and services provided by special education personnel for 80% or more of the school day

2. Type of special education supports

☐ Autistic Support

☐ Blind-Visually Impaired Support

☐ Deaf and Hard of Hearing Support

☒ Emotional Support

☐ Learning Support

☐ Life Skills Support

☐ Multiple Disabilities Support

☐ Physical Support

☐ Speech and Language Support

C. Location of student's program

Name of School District where the IEP will be implemented:	Smith Upland
Name of School Building where the IEP will be implemented:	The County Alternative High School

Is this school the student's neighborhood school (i.e., the school the student would attend if he/she did not have an IEP)?

☐ Yes

☒ No. If the answer is "no," select the reason why not.

   ☒ Special education supports and services required in the student's IEP cannot be provided in the neighborhood school.

   ☐ Other. Please explain:

_____

VIII. PENNDATA REPORTING: Educational Environment (Complete either Section A or B; Select only one Educational Environment)

To calculate the percentage of time inside the regular classroom, divide the number of hours the student spends inside the regular classroom by the total number of hours in the school day (including lunch, recess, study periods). The result is then multiplied by 100.

> **SECTION A: For Students Educated in Regular School Buildings with Nondisabled Peers – Indicate the percentage of time INSIDE the regular classroom for this student:**

Time spent outside the regular classroom receiving services unrelated to the student's disability (e.g., time receiving ESL services) should be considered time inside the regular classroom. Educational time spent in age-appropriate community-based settings that include individuals with and without disabilities, such as college campuses or vocational sites, should be counted as time spent inside the regular classroom.

Calculation for this Student:

Column 1	Column 2	Calculation	Indicate Percentage	Percentage Category
Total hours the student spends in the regular classroom per day	Total hours in a typical school day (including lunch, recess, & study periods)	(Hours inside regular classroom ÷ hours in school day) × 100 = % (Column 1 ÷ Column 2) × 100 = %	Section A: The percentage of time student spends inside the regular classroom:	Using the calculation result – select the appropriate percentage category
3.5	7.5	3.5/7.5 × 100 = 46%	$\boxed{46}$ % of the day	☐ INSIDE the Regular Classroom 80% or More of the Day ☒ INSIDE the Regular Classroom 79%-40% of the Day ☐ INSIDE the Regular Classroom Less Than 40% of the Day

SECTION B: This section required only for Students Educated OUTSIDE Regular School Buildings for more than 50% of the day – select and indicate the Name of School or Facility on the line corresponding with the appropriate selection: (If a student spends less than 50% of the day in one of these locations, the IEP team must do the calculation in Section A)

☐ Approved Private School (Non-Residential) _____

☐ Approved Private School (Residential) _____

☐ Other Private Facility (Non-Residential) _____

☐ Other Private Facility (Residential) _____

☐ Other Public Facility (Residential) _____

☐ Other Public Facility (Non-Residential) _____

☐ Hospital/Homebound _____

☐ Correctional Facility _____

☐ Out of State Facility _____

☐ Instruction Conducted in the Home _____

EXAMPLES for Section A: How to Calculate PennData – Educational Environment Percentages

	Column 1	Column 2	Calculation	Indicate Percentage
	Total hours the student spends in the regular classroom – per day	Total hours in a typical school day (including lunch, recess, & study periods)	(Hours inside regular classroom ÷ hours in school day) x 100 = % (Column 1 ÷ Column 2) x 100 = %	Section A: The percentage of time student spends inside the regular classroom:
Example 1	5.5	6.5	(5.5 ÷ 6.5) x 100 = 85%	85% of the day (Inside 80% or More of Day)
Example 2	3	5	(3 ÷ 5) x 100 = 60%	60% of the day (Inside 79%-40% of Day)
Example 3	1	5	(1 ÷ 5) x 100 = 20%	20% of the day (Inside Less Than 40% of Day)

Source: Adapted by author from "Student EP Assignment" from EDA 506 Course, Legal Issues in Special Education, (2013, July).

Appendix B

Decisions From U.S. Supreme Court

Brown v. Bd of Education, 347 U.S. 483 (1954). In this landmark decision, the Supreme Court found that segregated public schools are inherently unequal; decision is relevant to children in segregated special education placements.

Board of Ed. of Hendrick Hudson Central School Dist. V. Rowley, 458 U.S. 176 (1982). First decision in a special education case by the U. S. Supreme Court; defined "free appropriate public education."

Irving Independent Sch. Dist. v. Amber Tatro, 468 U.S. 883 (1984). The Supreme Court found that a medical treatment, such as clean intermittent catheterization (CIC), is a related service under the Education for All Handicapped Children Act and that the school is required to provide it.

Honig v. Doe, 484 U.S. 305 (1988). Strong decision in school discipline case on behalf of emotionally disturbed children who had academic and social problems. Court clarified procedural issues designed to protect children from school officials, parent role, and stay put rule and that schools shall not expel children for behaviors related to their disabilities.

Cedar Rapids v. Garret F., 526 U.S. 66 (1999). Supreme Court issued a favorable decision on behalf of child who needed related services to attend school.

Schaffer v. Weast, 546 U.S. (2005). Supreme Court held that the burden of proof in a due process hearing that challenges an IEP is placed upon the party seeking relief.

Winkelman v. Parma City School District (No. 05-983) (2007). Supreme Court rules that parents may represent their children's interests in special education cases and are not required to hire a lawyer before going to court. The Court held that parents have legal rights under the IDEA and can pursue IDEA claims on their own behalf, although they are not licensed attorneys.

Bd of Ed of City of New York v. Tom F (2007). The question before the Court was whether parents of a child who has never received special education from the public school district can obtain reimbursement for a unilateral private placement. The U.S. Supreme Court issued a split decision (4–4) in the case.

Forest Grove School District v. T.A. (2009). In a 6–3 decision, the Court held that IDEA allows reimbursement for private special education services, even when the child did not previously receive special education services from the public school.

U.S. Circuit Court of Appeals

Doug C. v. Hawaii (9th Cir. 2013). Important decision about parental participation at IEP meetings. "All special education staff who conduct IEP meetings should be familiar with this landmark ruling about IEP meetings and parental participation."

KM. Tustin Unified School District (9th Cir. 2013). Court of Appeals issued decision about the relationship between IDEA, Section 504 and ADA AA.

C.B. v. Garden Grove Unified Scho. Distt. (9th Cir. 2011). CA school failed to provide FAPE; guardian placed child in private program and requested reimbursement. The administrative law judge (ALJ) found that the child received "significant educational benefits" but ordered reimbursement for only half of tuition because private program did not meet all child's needs.

H.H. v. Moffett & Chesterfield School Bd. (4th Cir. 2009). Special ed teacher and an assistant restrained child in her wheelchair for hours during the school day while they ignored her, verbally abused her, and schemed to deprive her of educational services. In an unpublished decision, the court held that their conduct "violated H.H.'s clearly established right to freedom from undue restraint under the Fourteenth Amendment, and Appellants are therefore not entitled to qualified immunity as a matter of law."

Terrance D. and Wanda D. v. Sch. Dist. Philadelphia (E.D. Pa 2008). District failed to provide FAPE for many years, performed inadequate evaluations, misdiagnosed child as mentally retarded and emotionally disturbed, and misled the parent about her son's rights to autism services and ESY services.

J.D. v. Atlanta Independent School System (N.D. GA 2007). School district misdiagnosed a dyslexic boy as mentally retarded and placed him in a self-contained program for years where he did not learn to read. School district failed to complete 3-year reevaluation, as required by law. The court ordered the school system to provide J. D. with compensatory education at a private special education school for 4 years or until he graduates with a regular high school diploma.

Henrico County School Board v. R.T. (E.D. VA 2006). Tuition reimbursement case for young child with autism; comparison of TEACCH and ABA, comparison of FAPE and least restrictive environment, deference to decision of hearing officer, witness credibility, impact of low expectations, and "an insufficient focus on applying replicable research on proven methods of teaching and learning."

Winkelman v. Parma City Scho. Dist. (6th Cir. 2006). In a case on behalf of a child with autism, the court held that the school district's proposed placement was appropriate, that the parents' placement in a private school that educates children with autism was not the child's FAPE.

Legal cases retrieved from http://www.wrightslaw.com/.

Chapter 4

Collaborative Teamwork and Advocacy

Diana Lawrence-Brown

St. Bonaventure University

"Never doubt that a small group of thoughtful, committed citizens can change the world; indeed, it's the only thing that ever has."

—Margaret Mead, Anthropologist

School counselors need to be skilled communicators and collaborators for all students (CACREP, 2009) and, especially, for students with disabilities. No other students have so many professionals involved, both school and community based. *Effective services* for the student *depend* upon *effective teamwork* among service providers. Expectations for school counselors to work within a team approach have been increasing, and continue to do so. A counselor recognized for effective work with students with disabilities described the work this way: "collaborative, because almost nothing you do with special ed kids you are doing on your own. There are a lot of other professionals helping, so you have to keep the lines of communication open. So it's a collaborative process" (Frye, 2005, p. 447).

Some collaborative roles are legal requirements, for example, participation in IEP teams for students who receive counseling services as part of their special education plans. Others are being developed in an effort to provide more effective interventions for students with emotional, behavioral, and other disabilities. More and more often, these involve service providers who "push in" to the student's classroom.

Push-in services may be consultative (e.g., periodically observing a student and providing suggestions to teachers, parents, and others involved with the student), part-time (e.g., providing small-group counseling to students with disabilities and others that is integrated with classroom instruction, or teaching school counseling core curriculum lessons), or full-time (e.g., a counselor and special education teacher partnering as the main service providers for students with emotional and behavioral disabilities in a self-contained special education class). There is an increasing emphasis on push-in services in schools; in addition to their collaborative advantages, they have the practical benefit of providing students with access to counselors without missing instructional time.

Without effective teamwork, counselors and other service providers miss out on potent synergies available from collaboration and, even worse, risk working at cross-purposes to one another. School counselors experienced with collaboration describe being better able to meet challenging needs of students by brainstorming with and learning new strategies from other team members (Frye, 2005):

> It is very difficult working with students with disabilities, because you don't always see the positive results and sometimes they are hard to find; there will always be things [that] are issues that come up that you don't know how to help and the important thing to do is to keep trying until you find the right person to ask. (p. 447)

In addition, these counselors described collaboration as resulting in more people working toward the same goals.

In this chapter, issues around the need for school counselors to partner with fellow educators and service providers within the school and community and methods of accomplishing this mission are explored. Strategies are provided that are helpful for engaging and working with both professionals and parents. Throughout the chapter, important points are illustrated using quotes from experienced collaborators. These are drawn primarily from a study of school counselors recognized for their effectiveness with students with disabilities (Frye, 2005) and a study of a multidisciplinary collaborative team development project involving counselors, general and special education teachers, and administrators (Lawrence-Brown & Muschaweck, 2004). After working with the ideas in this chapter, the reader will be able to work out the following:

1. Understand key players' skills and processes necessary for effective partnerships for students with disabilities.

2. Identify potential barriers to the development of effective partnerships for students with disabilities.

3. Use resources provided to improve collaboration and communication skills and begin to apply this understanding of effective partnerships in work done on behalf of students with and without disabilities.

OVERVIEW OF PARTNERSHIPS

Purpose and Goals of Collaboration

As alluded to previously, the purpose of collaborative partnerships is improved quality of services, due to the synergistic nature of collaboration. According to Conoley and Conoley (2010), team members build a supportive relationship around accomplishing a specific purpose, where "each participant feels supported and more capable because of the interaction" (p. 79). Effective teams help maximize the success of students and families, and the personal and professional development of team members, by infusing greater energy, creativity, compassion, and resources (e.g., attention, information, assistance, material support) into the work. Here, experienced school counselors describe how collaboration around the needs of students with disabilities assisted in their work with other students, as well: "all the different special ed strategies, you can use in all aspects of your job. You can use them in a group that nobody has labeled special ed, but [where] they could all benefit" (Frye, 2005, p. 447).

While the specific endeavors of collaborative teams vary, a broad general goal is consensus decision making, leading to more effective problem solving. A solution is needed that all group members can at least live with (Morton et al., 1991). This is not a "majority rules" arrangement; any group member has veto power. Although it is not necessary for everyone to agree entirely, a prerequisite for any potential solution to be implemented is that everyone must be willing to support the solution for a specified length of time. Any decision that requires support from more than one person (directly or indirectly) to be implemented effectively should be approached collaboratively. Consider the following example of a collaborative team for a student with disabilities: Deborah is a new school counselor who would like to see individualized strategies used for Riki, a student who is experiencing social and behavioral difficulties in school. Riki is included in general education classes with push-in services from Deborah; Nita, his special education teacher; and Donal, a paraprofessional. Riki's parents have described similar problems outside of school, and Deborah is also recommending strategies to be carried over into the home and community. For Riki to receive the intended benefits of Deborah's suggestions, direct and indirect support will be needed from teachers and other professional service providers, administrators, parents, and paraprofessionals. Their support cannot be assumed; it needs to be won.

If one anticipated that collaborative decision making is more time consuming than either a majority rules arrangement or individual decision making, this is true.

But experienced team members learn (often the hard way) that decisions made without a consensus carry their own problems, often more serious than being time consuming. Group members who are not in agreement with the decision are unlikely to give it more than "lip service" and may even work actively against it. With collaborative decision making, not everyone has to be actively involved in implementing the decision, but before the process moves forward, everyone must agree not to undermine it. Otherwise, the group problem-solving process (next) continues.

QUALITIES OF EFFECTIVE COLLABORATORS

It has probably occurred to the reader by now that it is unlikely that all team members will be equally effective collaborators. That is true, but it does not mean that characteristics of effective collaborators are innate. While they may come more quickly and easily to some members than to others, we are all capable of becoming more effective collaborators. In this section, important qualities of effective collaborators are reviewed, drawing from Brown, Pryzwansky, and Schulte (2011); Morton et al. (1991); and Villa, Thousand, and Nevin (2008) except as otherwise noted.

Perspectives Toward and Interactions With Others

If most of us were asked to comment on likely qualities of effective collaborators, surely those associated with perspectives toward others would rank high on the list, including respect for team members and group ownership of problems and solutions. And in our increasingly diverse society, cross-cultural competence is critical to effective services and working relationships.

Respect for Team Members

Effective collaborators listen to and are respectful of all opinions and perspectives (Brown et al., 2011; Morton et al., 1991; Villa et al., 2008)—even those that they feel they could never agree with. Common procedures established by effective teams include use of a brainstorming phase when all ideas are recorded for future consideration by the team. In a subsequent evaluation phase, there is a conscious emphasis on evaluating ideas in relationship to a particular goal—and consciously on *not* evaluating people. If available synergies are to be capitalized upon, all ideas have a place in the process. Those not used directly may stimulate new ideas; those not used immediately may be helpful in the future. Team members whose ideas are not respected will sooner or later drop out of the process, if not physically, then psychologically. Creating an atmosphere where team members feel safe to think "outside the box" is critical for creative problem solving. Respectful interactions are needed both *in and outside of* meetings; much important work accomplished in team meetings can be quickly undone by thoughtless exchanges elsewhere.

Group Ownership of Problems and Solutions

Successful teams adopt an orientation of "we sink or swim together." As described by Ayers (1994), "The parties perceive themselves and each other as having a stake in the outcome, and, thus, each are willing to be responsible and accountable for its attainment" (p. 5).

It may seem obvious to suggest that responsibilities on the team should be divided fairly and in a way that takes advantage of each member's strengths and expertise, but it's not uncommon for some members to feel that most of the responsibility falls to them. For example, students with disabilities cannot attain expected outcomes through the effort of any one person on their own, yet special education teachers often feel that others expect them, as disability specialists, to "wave a magic wand" and "fix" the student. Here a special education teacher comments on the impact of teamwork on these feelings:

> Sometimes I feel like I'm solely responsible for making sure that my special ed. students are successful and that their needs are met and that their behavior is under control. . . . But, like now I feel like you know, as a team, we can all take a look at a child and say, "OK come on, let's do this. OK, he's gonna need X, and you know, here it is . . ." And, and that's good. (Lawrence-Brown & Muschaweck, 2004, p. 155)

In this case, the collaborative team process seems to have mitigated at least to some extent the sense of isolation sometimes associated with a special education teacher's position in a school.

Part of what makes teams that adopt a "sink or swim together" outlook more successful is that they tend to be more motivated and persistent. The feeling of not being alone builds perseverance, increasing the group's ability to persist through the failures that are inevitable in any difficult task that is long-term in nature (Brown et al., 2011).

Cross-Cultural Competence

As noted previously, cross-cultural competence is increasingly recognized as vital to effective working relationships and services in a diverse society. Cross-cultural competence is a process of valuing and understanding one's own and others' multiple and intersecting identities, worldviews, and behaviors, enabling mutually respectful, beneficial, and productive relationships (Brown et al., 2011; Lawrence-Brown & Sapon-Shevin, 2013). Professionals who effectively provide services cross-culturally are able and willing to adapt their methods to take into account the value systems and ways of being of those they are trying to serve. They take into consideration their students' and families' degrees of acculturation into the dominant European-American culture, along with their cultural origins (Kalyanpur & Harry, 2012).

Kalyanpur and Harry (2012) note that one indication that cultural differences may be at play is experiencing a "sense of strangeness" (p. 115), and suggest the following four steps of "cultural reciprocity" as a way that we can investigate and reflect upon both our own practices and the assumptions of our respective fields:

1. Analyze the cultural values underlying your perspectives and recommendations.

2. Determine if other stakeholders (especially the person to be served) share these assumptions; if not, analyze how their perspectives differ from yours.

3. Actively acknowledge and respect any differences; clarify the cultural bases of your personal and professional assumptions.

4. Engage in collaborative discussion to adapt your perspectives and recommendations to fit the value system of the person to be served.

These steps are especially important when our interactions prompt not only a sense of strangeness but also an initial reaction that the values and beliefs of another are "just wrong."

Be aware that, while cultural groups may noticeably differ from each other in their identities, beliefs, and practices, *individuals* within those groups vary markedly from each other. Consider your own cultural group and how wrong an outsider might be in assuming that your personal identities, beliefs, and practices would be the same as another member of that group. On a related note, individuals from *different* groups are more alike than different from each other. (Consider this response to the question, "What race are you?" Answer: "The human race.")

The message here is to be prepared to adjust your methods and recommendations to be more culturally responsive to your students, but be wary of generalizations suggesting that people from certain cultural groups uniformly think, believe, or behave in a particular way.

Just as we need to reflect upon and take into consideration perspectives of others, our perspectives toward ourselves are important as well; they are addressed in the next section.

PERSPECTIVES TOWARD SELF

Perspectives toward self are in some ways a less obvious consideration than perspectives toward others when analyzing effective collaboration, but they are also essential. As noted previously, self-analysis and understanding are important aspects of developing greater cross-cultural competence, as well as more effective collaboration skills (Brown et al., 2011). Blindness to one's own strengths, weaknesses, and cultural foundations can be just as damaging to a partnership as lack of respect for others' strengths, weaknesses, and culture.

Members of dominant cultural groups are particularly vulnerable to a lack of recognition of our own cultural foundations; as we are continually engulfed in them, they do not stand out to us.

Self-Awareness

Effective collaborators need to be simultaneously *aware of* their personal beliefs, strengths, weaknesses, and assumptions and self-confident *about* them (Brown et al., 2011). We need to be able to explain our areas of specialty, limitations, and ways that we can contribute to the task confronting the group; our own behavior should be a good model of our field for others. One of the most important qualities related to self-awareness is the ability to critically examine positions on issues (Brown et al., 2011) and explain our positions without defensiveness (Morton et al., 1991).

Openness

Also important to successful collaboration is being open to new ideas and able to compromise. Effective team members are willing to take risks and "go to bat" for students (Ferguson, Meyer, Jeanchild, Juniper, & Zingo, 1992).

SKILLS AND PROCESSES NECESSARY FOR EFFECTIVE PARTNERSHIPS

Skills and processes helpful for development of effective collaborative teams include the following, suggested by Morton et al. (1991):

1. Establishing the group's mission, ground rules, and a structured process for group problem solving

2. Rotating important roles among team members from meeting to meeting

3. Development of specific teaming skills

4. Self-evaluation of team functioning on a routine basis

Establish the Mission and Ground Rules for Group Interaction

Early on as the group is forming, members need to explicitly come to consensus about the purpose of their work together and the ground rules for group interaction. These prerequisites to group action are easily overlooked or viewed as too obvious to warrant the group's time. But team members often have not thought these issues through even from their own, individual perspectives; they are likely to assume that others share their partially formed understandings of how and why they should work together—until conflict arises. Extending our earlier example, a general educator may assume that the group's mission is to bring Riki up to grade level academically, while Deborah, the school counselor, may prioritize personal/social issues and Nita, his special education teacher, may emphasize supports and curriculum modifications needed for him to progress toward his IEP goals whether or not he's working at the same academic level as the rest of the class.

Collaborative teams cannot and should not avoid conflict entirely, as differing views are necessary to develop and realize the benefits of creative group synergies. Divergent perspectives are important for approaching difficult problems. In the example above, attention to all three perspectives is likely to produce the best outcomes for Riki. But conflicts stemming from a lack of shared vision or appropriate ground rules for interactions can produce very different outcomes. These problems may simmer along in the background, gradually fomenting, sometimes threatening the very existence of the team.

Common ground rules for interactions include an expectation that all group members should actively share their ideas and opinions, that others would hear them out respectfully (without interrupting, and while attending to body language), that all ideas are recorded without judgment during a brainstorming phase, and that ideas (rather than people) would be the focus of subsequent evaluation. Failure to establish ground rules for interactions may lead to unintended problems triggered by well-meaning team members, such as one person dominating the discussion or some members feeling that their ideas are not valued. When group members fail to share their ideas and opinions, others may come to view them with suspicion, for example, as being unable or unwilling to contribute to the work of the team, having hidden agendas (Villa et al., 2008), and so forth. Ultimately, failure to reach consensus on a shared purpose for the group is likely to lead to even more serious problems, as group members pull against each other, working in different directions.

Group Problem-Solving Process

Once your group has come to consensus on their mission and ground rules for interaction, it is ready to begin direct work on that mission. The following steps outline a group problem-solving process focused on consensus building through full member participation (cf. Brown et al., 2011; Conoley & Conoley, 2010; Friend & Bursuck, 2015; Morton et al., 1991).

1. Group readiness. Confirm members' readiness for problem solving; avoid important conversations when team members are already emotionally over-wrought and/or exhausted (Friend & Bursuck, 2015). Review the basic mission and ground rules of the group.

2. Fact-finding. Collect data concerning the specific problem currently being tackled by the group. Pay careful attention to (a) the goal, (b) the history of past efforts to solve the problem, and (c) constraints of the situation.

3. Appraise. Critically examine the data gathered, the premises underlying representations of the problem, and roles each group member is expected to play. Are there logical connections between identified problems, contributing factors, and problematic outcomes? Is the student to be served being blamed as the problem?

4. Outline problem and desired outcomes. Develop a problem summary and goal statement (expected outcomes). Keep in mind that there may be multiple problems emerging from interacting family, school, and community subsystems.

5. Idea generation. Brainstorm ideas without evaluating them—write everything down at this stage.

6. Short list. Develop criteria for choosing ideas to work with further. Outline competing hypotheses of the nature of the problem(s). Analyze the constraints on and consequences of the various possible solutions. Consider the degree to which proposed solutions are consistent with the group's mission and under the control of team members.

7. Come to consensus on course of action. Keep in mind that this is not a majority rule process; not only do various group members *have* veto power, but they should also *exercise* it if they are not willing to support the decision. Be culturally sensitive to different levels of comfort with various types of intervention, degrees of structure, individual or group emphases, and so on.

8. Refine course of action. Generate ideas to enhance or facilitate implementation of the most promising solution.

9. Prepare to implement plan. Develop a shared understanding and explanation of how the solution can be achieved. Consider problems that may arise from implementing the approach chosen and how they may be addressed.

10. Elaborate and implement plan. Include systematic and collaborative collection of monitoring and evaluation data. Allow for new information to come to light that may suggest modifications or new possibilities.

11. Evaluate plan. Consider results in terms of the problem summary and goal statement.

12. Revise as needed. Redesign the approach when data suggest that expected outcomes have not been achieved.

It is recommended that these steps be used in conjunction with structured role assignments, as discussed in the next section.

Roles of Team Members

A strategy that teams are routinely encouraged to use is assigning structured roles that rotate among group members from meeting to meeting (e.g., facilitator, timekeeper, recorder, observer), as described below (Friend & Bursuck, 2015; Morton et al., 1991):

Facilitator

Encourages each team member to participate, tries to keep the group working effectively together. Leads the use of problem-solving methods, conflict management strategies, et cetera. Ensures that the agenda is developed for the next meeting. All of the facilitating responsibilities can be assigned to one person for that day, or, in larger groups, everyone who does not have another role may be responsible to help.

Recorder

Takes and distributes public notes that include key points of the discussion and identify specific tasks, staff persons responsible to complete the tasks, and target dates for each.

Timekeeper

Keeps track of the agenda and how much time is left and helps keep the group on task.

Observer

Observes behaviors that encourage task achievement and good working relationships and leads discussion of this at predetermined intervals.

There are at least two benefits of assigning and rotating structured roles among team members. The first is ensuring that someone actually does keep track of the time, record notes, facilitate the team process, and so on. A second benefit is better understanding what it is like to be responsible for various aspects of team functioning, especially when members take on roles that may typically have been performed by someone else. Here, a team member illustrates this development:

> [Being] timekeeper has forced me to realize that I jabber way too much, because I was timekeeper, yet I'm the one that was continuing to draw this on and on and on. And so . . . I had a little self-reflection here, too. (Lawrence-Brown & Muschaweck, 2004, p. 152)

In many groups, fulfillment of these important roles is left to chance, waiting for someone spontaneously to both recognize the need and volunteer to fill the role. More often, however, no one fills the role unless there is a conscious, ongoing effort on the part of team members to ensure that someone is assigned to do it. In many team meetings, no one, for example, takes responsibility to redirect the team when the discussion gets offtrack, resulting in significant amounts of unproductive time. As another example, often the same person is repeatedly left to fill the same role, for example, developing the agenda, or recording public notes. In this case, the other team members may have little appreciation for or understanding of responsibilities in which they have played no part. These principles are demonstrated in Case Illustration 4.1.

Development of Specific Teaming Skills

Effective partners are made, not born; cultivating specific skills that facilitate collaborative teamwork creates more effective team members. Focused professional development is required, particularly in disciplines traditionally structured as individually provided services and interventions, rather than team based. These include both school counselors and the other school personnel with whom they need to collaborate.

Under a traditional professional development model, participants would hear about collaboration skills from a specialist and then be expected to develop and apply the skills independently at some point in the future. In contrast to this decontextualized approach, a sustained coaching process is recommended where team members learn specialized skills needed for successful collaboration in the context

CASE ILLUSTRATION 4.1

"WE NEED TO GET BETTER AT INCLUSION"

This case provides a more in-depth look at a collaborative team development effort undertaken by multidisciplinary teams at the elementary and secondary school levels (Lawrence-Brown & Muschaweck, 2004). Rather than taking time out to attend traditional, decontextualized professional development sessions, team members learned specialized skills needed for successful collaboration in the context of bringing about specific changes they deemed critical to the desired outcomes of their own inclusive schooling efforts (e.g., developing guidelines for curriculum adaptations, reporting progress, etc.).

In the beginning, communication among team members tended to be friendly, but not necessarily goal directed. For example, one team member commented, "Sometimes [we] would talk, about all kinds of stuff, but we don't always talk about what we need to do, to make sure that 'Child A' is successful, or what we've done that's been good or bad" (Lawrence-Brown & Muschaweck, 2004, p. 148). Participants also described a lack of shared vision of inclusive schooling. As this participant explains, "We all kind of came in [on] different pages and had no idea what was going to happen next year" (Lawrence-Brown & Muschaweck, 2004, p. 149).

A typical meeting involved brief training in a specific collaborative teamwork topic, followed by a work period during which the team addressed specific tasks that they had identified as being important for improved inclusive education within their schools (e.g., developing guidelines for curriculum adaptations, reporting progress, etc.). Collaboration skills also were modeled and encouraged during work sessions (e.g., full team participation, clarifying positions, etc.).

Common activities of the teams included analyzing past efforts, setting goals, and troubleshooting. For example, as this team member commented, "We have not accomplished goals in the past because we lacked direction. Now we have a direction to follow" (Lawrence-Brown & Muschaweck, 2004, p. 151). Another participant explained:

> [It's] proactive instead of reactive. . . . Everything was reactive when it first started. Because it was like . . . you know, "I could have changed *that*." . . . And then [the special education teacher] was like "All right . . . we've got to do something different for these guys here . . . so let's do *this*." . . . Whereas now we're actually doing it [proactive planning] in the beginning. (Lawrence-Brown & Muschaweck, 2004, p. 152)

Rather than merely waiting for problems to occur, then, teams began to look ahead to try to resolve potential problems in advance.

Participants identified the following outcomes of their work in collaborative team development: role clarification, acquisition of skills needed for effective collaborative teaming, development of shared vision, development of a schema for curriculum modifications and reporting progress, self-confidence in and enthusiasm for inclusive schooling efforts, a plan for expanding inclusive schooling efforts, and satisfaction with and commitment to a collaborative process.

Reflection Questions

1. How does this case connect with your experiences with teamwork (in or out of schools)? With professional development?

2. If you were the counselor on the team, how would you explain your perspectives, role, and potential contributions to the group to team members from other disciplines?

of their regular work together on projects of mutual importance to group members. For example, team members might participate in a brief "mini-lesson" about a specific aspect of collaborative teamwork and, then, receive immediate feedback and guidance from the coach about their use of collaboration skills as they work on practical problem-solving steps needed to bring about desired outcomes (cf. Lawrence-Brown & Muschaweck, 2004). The following sections describe several specific teamwork skills needed for building an increasingly creative and productive team.

Active listening

Active listening is a process of intentional and thoughtful attention to the person who is speaking; this means more than merely not talking (or texting) while he or she is speaking. Rather, the listeners' attention is communicated to the speaker using specific active listening strategies, including the following:

- Using open-ended questions to get more information about someone's opinion (e.g., "Will you tell me more about that?")
- Paraphrasing the opinion of the person who just spoke before stating your own
- Integrating what different people have said into a unified summary statement (Morton et al., 1991). An important skill in helping diverse groups of people come to consensus is the ability to draw the common threads of various perspectives together into a cohesive whole, emphasizing agreements while acknowledging areas still needing work.

Consensus building

This includes facilitating involvement by all team members, building upon the ideas of others, and supporting or criticizing ideas, not people: In many groups, a few relatively assertive team members dominate discussion and decision making. The contributions of quieter members are lost, and members who have not actively participated in decision making may be less committed to implementing those decisions. Effective collaborators recognize the value of divergent ideas and seeing the issue from someone else's viewpoint in obtaining the best solution, working to bring the perspectives and ideas of all stakeholders into the process, for example,

> I am hearing a little bit different ideas [from each of you]. . . . Why don't you each go around and say what you think—what's the goal of this? . . . And what's your vision at this point of how things would look? (Lawrence-Brown & Muschaweck, 2004, p. 149)

Here, a quieter team member comments on this strategy: "One benefit is the process [each member specifically asked to comment, 'round-robin' style]. I tend to be more of a—oh, maybe, onlooker you know sometimes. . . . So I thought that was beneficial" (Lawrence-Brown & Muschaweck, 2004, p. 154).

When the group reaches the stage of the process where ideas have been brainstormed and then must be evaluated, it is important to focus on evaluating the idea and not the person who mentioned it as a possibility. When necessary, raise important discrepancies gently; maintain focus on the student being served. Use "I" messages; for example, "I feel" versus "You are . . ." or "You do . . ."

Conflict resolution

Conflict is inevitable for any team, and learning to live with some discomfort is essential to the long-term survival of the group. Often, conflict results from simple misunderstandings among well-intentioned group members (Garcia, 2012). Teams are frequently advised to deal with conflict openly, honestly, and constructively (e.g., Morton et al., 1991; Villa et al., 2008). Discussing small conflicts as they arise can help prevent them from festering into more serious problems.

Groups are often conceived as functioning differently during different stages of their development (Friend & Bursuck, 2015); conflict may be more likely during some stages than others. As synthesized by Tuckman and Jensen (1977), groups may be expected to experience a period of "storming" relatively early in the process. This phase is characterized by intragroup conflict, emotional responses to task demands, and possibly catharsis. Teams whose work is long term in nature may expect to go through this phase more than once over the life of the group.

Conflict should not automatically be viewed as counterproductive, however. If there are no conflicting opinions, the team is almost certainly not taking full advantage of the varying perspectives of group members. Divergent ideas are necessary for the group to find a high-quality solution. Garcia (2012) discusses "a delicate balance to be achieved between adequate discomfort to produce insights and new learning and too much discomfort, which impedes the process" of being able to manage emotions well enough to allow for analysis, reflection, and development of more thoughtful responses to difficult situations (p. 168).

Conflict may occur both among and within collaborators (Kalyanpur & Harry, 2012). As an example of conflict within collaborators, Kalyanpur and Harry (2012) describe the dilemma of professionals wishing to develop a working relationship based on equality with family members whose culture encourages them to defer to authority. The authors further elaborate the possibility that those same professionals, while desiring an equitable relationship, may simultaneously hold a conflicting belief in expert knowledge, making it difficult to place as much value on the family's ideas as they place on their own.

Collaboration is an emergent process that takes time to develop, and conflict resolution skills in particular are among the more sophisticated to acquire. Skillful analysis of both oneself and others (discussed previously) is required. Friend and Bursuck (2015) suggest the following strategies:

- Maintain focus on the topic, avoiding interruptions and becoming sidetracked.
- Avoid offering unsolicited advice.
- Avoid speaking in absolute terms, for example, "the only way is . . ."; "there's no way to . . ."
- Avoid words and phrases that trigger emotional responses.

Noted previously (in connection with group readiness for problem solving), but worth repeating here, is to avoid important conversations when team members are already exhausted and/or emotionally overwrought.

Conoley and Conoley (2010) describe ways of encouraging collaborative behavior in others; imagine what a helpful skill this would be. They include

- identifying and focusing on the strengths of others,
- matching tasks to individual strengths,
- noticing the hidden advantages of negative situations, and
- perceiving and explaining the behavior of others in positive ways.

This includes both giving the benefit of the doubt and reframing neutral or negative behavior in positive ways. Such positive interpretations facilitate persistence on the part of group members in the face of difficult situations (Brown et al., 2011). Conoley and Conoley (2010) further describe those able to encourage collaborative behaviors in others as being intrinsically motivated by personal values and aspirations more than by monetary or status considerations.

In summary, although it may seem easier and more polite to avoid, ignore, or sidestep conflict, it is a necessary ingredient for finding the best solution. This does not mean that there is no place for courtesy. Communicating with team members in ways that are pleasant and engaging, and cultivating small gestures such as "noticing positive events, verbalizing complimentary observations to others, [and] being openly grateful for gestures of help" (Conoley & Conoley, 2010, p. 79) can make a real contribution to effective team functioning. As an example, consider the following scenario:

Deborah (the school counselor described in this chapter) has noticed that Riki's opportunities to develop relationships with peers are limited by the almost constant presence of Donal (the paraprofessional) at his elbow. Deborah hesitates to raise the issue, worrying that Donal may respond defensively. It may be helpful initially for Deborah to seek out other team members' perspectives on the situation. If they are in agreement, she might ask for their help in broaching the subject with Donal. (If they are not in agreement, this is an opportunity for Deborah to further explore both her own and others' perspectives, prior to further pursuing a change in approach.) The conversation may proceed in the following manner:

Deborah: "Donal, you are so conscientious in your work with Riki. You are always there for him, and it has really paid off in his academic skills. I really appreciate how you helped him use the study skills that we've been working on to prepare for his last test."

With help from other team members, she might go on to suggest that other students in the class might also benefit from some of Donal's support:

Deborah continues: "[Donal] Would you mind trying that same strategy out with some other students who didn't do as well as we'd hoped on that test?"

Donal: "Nita (Riki's teacher), is that all right with you? What if I'm working with someone else when Riki needs me? I'm supposed to be his 1:1 aide."

Nita: "I think the others would really benefit. You'll still be nearby, and we can all help keep an eye on Riki in case he needs more help."

Donal: "Well, if it's OK with his parents and the principal, I guess it's OK with me."

Deborah: "Good point. We can bring it up to them at our team meeting later this week. And this gives us the opportunity to pair Riki up more with peers; I think that will help with his social relationships."

By focusing on Donal's strengths, complimenting him in the presence of significant others, and showing her appreciation of his assistance in the past, Deborah helps build relationships and establish consensus (both in and outside of formal team meetings).

Self-evaluation of team functioning on a routine basis

Once the team has had the opportunity for professional development in specific teaming skills and processes such as group problem solving, active listening, consensus building, and conflict resolution, an ongoing system of formal self-evaluation should be scheduled to help the group monitor, practice, and maintain these skills. Areas in need of further development can in this way be identified, with follow-up instruction provided. Use of a structured self-evaluation tool is recommended, such as this one from the Institute on Community Integration (1990), which is illustrated in Figure 4.1.

Your team will find it a helpful exercise to use the previous sections of this chapter to flesh out the checklist items in Figure 4.1 with specific descriptors

Figure 4.1   Collaborative Teamwork Checklist

Answer each question "yes" (Y) or "not yet" (NY) for your team. "NY" indicates an area your team may wish to address to improve team functioning.

_____ Are all "key" players part of the team (e.g., family members, general educators, etc.)?
_____ Do all team members understand the purpose of the team?
_____ Does the team have a common goal or vision for inclusion of all students?
_____ Does the team identify student priorities together?
_____ Do team members have an interest in working together to accomplish their goal?
_____ Do team members understand the backgrounds and roles of fellow team members?
_____ Do team members share knowledge, skills, and resources with one another?
_____ Do team members respect and support one another professionally and personally?
_____ Are team members willing to work with one another to complete tasks?
_____ Do team members communicate in constructive ways, and is there respect for the contributions of each member?
_____ Do team members trust one another and feel safe in communicating?
_____ Do team members share responsibility for successes and setbacks?
_____ Do team members have regularly scheduled times to interact?
_____ Is an agenda developed before each meeting?
_____ Has the team decided upon a system of roles and procedures for team meetings?
_____ Does the team have an effective collaborative process for problem solving and consensus decision-making?
_____ Does the group have an effective method for resolving conflict?
_____ Are tasks assigned at the end of meetings?
_____ Is an effective record-keeping and dissemination system in place?
_____ Does the group take time on an ongoing basis to reflect on group functioning and evaluate group effectiveness?

Comments:

Source: Institute on Community Integration (1990). *Collaborative Teamwork: Working Together for the Inclusion of Students With Disabilities.* Minneapolis, MN. University of Minnesota, Institute on Community Integration.

to facilitate team discussion. During the self-evaluation process itself, the team should give examples to support each of their answers.

Utilize Guided Practice Exercise 4.1 to apply the principles in Figure 4.1.

The same "any member has veto power" guideline discussed previously should apply to decisions about self-evaluation of specific aspects of effective team functioning. These concepts are represented in Case Illustration 4.2.

CONSULTATIVE AND EDUCATIONAL APPROACHES TO PARTNERSHIPS

Among the activities recommended for school counselors by the American School Counselor Association (2008) is collaborating with teachers to present school

---

Guided Practice Exercise 4.1

BEST PRACTICES IN COLLABORATIVE PARTNERSHIPS

As the school year opens, record best practices that you observe being used in the area of collaborative partnerships. If possible, conduct this work with fellow team members or another small group of educators at the school. Use the Collaborative Teamwork Checklist (Figure 4.1) and the questions below to help structure your observations.

- In what ways are school counselors engaged in collaborative partnerships, and with whom?
- What qualities of effective collaborators do you see demonstrated, and how? Look for these qualities in interactions both in and out of formal meetings.
- What processes are used to facilitate productive group interaction and problem solving?
- What types of support for collaborative partnerships are provided? Look for professional development, scheduled collaboration time during the school day, administrative participation in collaborative decision making, administrative recognition of effective collaboration, and so on.

As the school year progresses, reflect on your list, highlighting the strengths that you have observed. Celebrate these with the group. Use any gaps identified to work with other group members and administrators to create a plan for supporting more effective partnerships in the future.

CASE ILLUSTRATION 4.2

ADVICE FROM AN EXPERIENCED TEAM PLAYER (KRISTIN N. SCHMICK)

This case is based on the experiences of a school counselor and a special education teacher. They were both assigned full-time to a special education classroom serving six students with intensive emotional and behavioral disabilities, and they were asked to comment on their experiences.

The special education teacher responded: "I can say that it was definitely a change for me. As teachers, we are usually the only person 'in charge' of a classroom and the decisions made within. When I started [here], I was unsure of how this program ran. I was coming into a program that taught a population of students with which I had little experience. [The counselor in my classroom] had already been working in this program and with most of these kids for an entire school year already.

"I wish I had more time to get to know the other professional that I was working with. I met [her] only a couple days before school was starting. In those couple of days, we spent time getting to know each other, which was great, but had I known some of the situations we would be dealing with regularly, our 'getting to know you' time would have been spent talking about our philosophies within the classroom."

Advice offered included the following:

- "Be honest with each other. Talk about situations after they happen. In the beginning, [we] struggled a bit because we were not on the same page with how to handle certain things; a 'power struggle' emerged. Eventually, we began to just openly say, 'I'm not sure why you handled that the way you did,' or 'Let me tell you my reasoning behind that choice.' This made things a lot easier because once I understood the reasoning, I was usually ok with her decision."
- "Let things go. It's not about your ego, or who is 'better.' It's about the students and what is going to work best to help them. When you let go of being 'right,' things flow a lot easier."
- "Don't blame. Not everything either of you decide will [always] work, and you can't blame the other person when their strategy didn't work. Never say, 'I told you so.'"
- "Have each other's back. Any decisions made should be a team effort when implementing."

(Continued)

(Continued)
Reflection Questions

1. As a new counselor, how would you respond if asked to take on the role of a full-time counselor in a special education class?

2. How might the skills, processes, strategies, research, and resources provided in this chapter be helpful?

3. What else would you want to know?

counseling core curriculum lessons. Such instruction could be provided by either the counselor alone, or by the teacher alone after consulting with the counselor, but a highly recommended practice in working with students with disabilities is co-teaching.

Co-Teaching Approaches

Co-teaching may take a number of forms; the following descriptions are adapted from Friend and Bursuck (2015) for use by a teacher and counselor. Partners should avoid reliance on a limited number of approaches, and on use of fixed groups, especially those that are deficit based.

One teach, one observe

In this approach, either the teacher or counselor may assume the primary instructional role. For example, the counselor may find it helpful to observe a student's social interactions within the group or the teacher's use of an instructional strategy. Similarly, the teacher may find it helpful to observe the counselor's use of behavioral, bullying, or crisis interventions; social skills training; study skills; and so on.

Station teaching

In this approach, the class is split into three groups; one group works with the counselor, one group works with the teacher, and the third group works without a teacher (e.g., at their seats or at a learning center).

Parallel teaching

The class is split in half, allowing all students to receive more individual attention. Similar instructional approaches may be taken with both groups, or groups may be organized according to factors such as interests and preferences.

Alternative teaching

One partner works with the majority of the students while the other works with a small group, for example, preteaching important skills or background knowledge, enrichment, and so on. Again, avoid routine use of deficit-based groupings, which tend to result in both stigma and lower levels of learning.

Teaming

Both partners work with the whole group simultaneously. This is considered by many experienced co-teachers to be the most exciting and rewarding model, but it does require greater compatibility than other approaches.

One teach, one assist

This approach should be used sparingly, with considerable attention to equality and rotation of roles. Otherwise, one of the partners may be routinely placed in a less active role more appropriate to an aide than to a professional.

As with other forms of partnership activities, co-teaching should be supported through specific professional development, guided practice, and a process for formal, ongoing self-evaluation. Opposition to co-teaching is often driven by limited understanding of the process and by lack of experience. When the supports noted above are not provided, partners may experience significant difficulties in implementing the model (Daane, Beirne-Smith, & Latham, 2000), including limited communication by participants uncomfortable with the co-teaching process.

In the next section, the importance of collaboration for school counselors engaged as advocates for students with disabilities is addressed.

ADVOCACY ON BEHALF OF STUDENTS WITH DISABILITIES

School counselors are recognized for their effectiveness in working with students with disabilities and employing advocacy to meet the personal/social needs of students on their caseload, which often centers around gaining access to the same counseling and school-wide activities and options made available to students without disabilities (Frye, 2005). Particular attention to collaboration skills and processes will be needed when advocating for inclusion in schools with a tradition of segregating students with disabilities. In these schools, other educators may assume that the needs of students with disabilities cannot be met in general education activities or that students without disabilities might suffer as a result.

A common advocacy need for students with disabilities, then, is having allies who understand the benefits to them and others of including them in general education classrooms. Contrary to common assumptions, students with disabilities do not usually learn more in self-contained special education classrooms; equal or superior results are obtained when appropriate supports are provided in general education classrooms (Affleck, Madge, Adams, & Lowenbraun, 1988; Banerji & Dailey, 1995; Bunch & Valeo, 1997; Cole & Meyer, 1991; Freeman & Alkin, 2000; Fryxell & Kennedy, 1995; Hunt & Goetz, 1997; Ingraham & Daugherty, 1995; Lipsky & Gartner, 1995; Logan & Keefe, 1997; Madden, Slavin, Karweit, Dolan, & Wasik, 1993; McGregor & Vogelsberg, 1998; Schulte, Osborne, & McKinney, 1990; Waldron & McLeskey, 1998; Wang & Birch, 1984; Willrodt & Claybrook, 1995). Of course, educators are also concerned about the progress of students *without* disabilities; here, the outcomes research is equally reassuring, with equal or superior academic, social, and behavioral outcomes for students without disabilities in inclusive general education classrooms compared to non-inclusive classrooms (Holloway, Salisbury, Rainforth, & Palombar, 1995; Peck, Donaldson, & Pezzoli, 1990; Salend & Duhaney, 1999; Sasso & Rude, 1988; Sharpe, York, & Knight, 1994).

In any advocacy effort, but especially when advocating on behalf of students from traditionally marginalized groups (including but not limited to those with disabilities), school counselors need to be aware of the micropolitics in play at the school and of their own level of power (or lack thereof). Effective collaboration is especially necessary to mitigate risks to untenured educators in situations where the needs of students from traditionally marginalized groups may suggest changes to the status quo that are likely to be unpopular among those with greater seniority, security, and/or power in the situation.

Collaboration on behalf of students with disabilities is important, but not always easy. In the next section, barriers to effective collaboration are addressed.

POTENTIAL BARRIERS TO EFFECTIVE PARTNERSHIPS FOR STUDENTS WITH DISABILITIES

Despite the many advantages of a collaborative approach, schools are notoriously slow to change, and ongoing collaborative teamwork is frequently neglected. Educators who are dissatisfied with inclusive schooling and other reform efforts within their schools often confess to the woefully insufficient, or even nonexistent, role of collaborative teamwork in their process. As noted by Ayers (1994), "While our times demand collaborative actions, in many cases our training, experiences, organizational structures, and traditions lead us to continue less successful patterns" (p. 5).

Specific barriers to effective partnerships include time and resources needed both for ongoing professional development and team meetings. Both of these barriers can be addressed with support from administrators. For example, scheduling changes are likely to be needed to support meetings of stakeholders on an ongoing basis (e.g., weekly common planning time for team members responsible for the same students). A regular meeting time that falls within the team's assigned workday is a critical support; without it, even the most skillful and enthusiastic teams are likely to break down over time. Be aware that scheduling and resource allocation are ongoing challenges for administrators; they need strong, unified messages from the team not only of the importance of these supports but also strong, unified messages of appreciation when they are provided.

The importance of administrative support in this process can scarcely be overestimated, including both "talking the talk" and "walking the walk." Important administrative activities associated with effective collaborative team functioning include at least periodic involvement in team meetings, and encouragement and reassurance both for staff who are enthusiastic about working on behalf of students with disabilities and those who are more hesitant.

Additional barriers to effective partnerships on behalf of students with disabilities may be associated with the ways that students are viewed at times by team members. For example, some school counselors feel that responsibility for students with disabilities should fall to special education teachers and that the provision of counseling services to students with disabilities constitutes a duplication of services (Frye, 2005). There is a double standard inherent in this assumption, in that the same assumption is not made about students without disabilities and their teachers (that is, it is rarely assumed that general education teachers would be able to meet the counseling needs of students without disabilities). These issues are demonstrated in Case Illustration 4.3.

Resources Helpful in Improving and Applying Partnership Skills

Now that the reader has a good sense of key ideas important to effective partnerships for students with disabilities, it is time to work with additional resources that will help to improve one's collaboration and communication skills and to apply this understanding of effective partnerships to work done on behalf of students with and without disabilities. These resources are organized into two main categories related to this chapter: (a) collaborative teamwork resources, to assist school counselors and their team members to develop their partnership skills, and (b) those that address cross-cultural competence (professional associations concerned with cross-cultural competence include the Association of Multicultural Counseling and Development and the National Association for Multicultural Education [NAME]. These resources are presented at the end of this chapter).

CASE ILLUSTRATION 4.3

"CAN THIS COLLABORATION BE SAVED?"

You are a school counselor known for your willingness to assist the principal in your building with school improvement efforts and are once more approached to help. As the situation is described by the principal, a new family has moved to the district. One of the family's children has significant disabilities and has been included in the old neighborhood school since kindergarten. The parents are insisting that the student continue to be included in your school; however, the only students with disabilities included in general education classes in your school have mild disabilities. The support that they receive has been limited to resource room services and, in some cases, counseling. Students with more significant needs have always been transferred to segregated special education classrooms elsewhere.

The principal is up front with you about both her opposition to including the student and her ignorance of strategies that might facilitate this process. As she explains it, "The parents have a lawyer, and we have no choice." Although she presents this as a project that you and she will work on jointly, your past experience suggests that most of the work will shift to you. Given her opposition, you can't help but wonder simultaneously if it would be better if she were involved as little as possible but also how this project could possibly be successful without her support.

Reflection Questions

1. How do you respond to the middle school principal's request for help?
2. How might the skills, processes, strategies, research (including outcomes of inclusion in the Advocacy on Behalf of Students with Disabilities section above), and other resources provided in this chapter be helpful?
3. What else would you want to know?

SUMMARY

In this chapter, issues around the need for school counselors to develop partnerships with fellow educators and service providers within the school and community and methods of accomplishing this mission have been explored. Key players, the purposes and goals of collaboration, and qualities of effective team members have been outlined. Strategies for engaging and working with collaborative teams of professionals, family, and other community stakeholders have been provided, including establishing the mission and ground rules for group interaction, a structured group problem-solving process, recommended roles for team members, and development of specific teaming skills.

Specific teaming skills addressed include active listening, consensus building, conflict resolution, and routine self-evaluation of team functioning. Consultative and educational approaches to partnerships have been outlined, along with related advocacy issues. Potential barriers to effective partnerships have been discussed, and resources and other suggestions for further development of your ability to develop effective partnerships on behalf of students with and without disabilities have been provided.

KEYSTONES

- School counselors are increasingly part of special education teams, and are valuable assets in assisting students to achieve optimal success.
- School counselors need to be skilled communicators and collaborators for *all* students, and especially for students with disabilities, as these latter students have an extensive number of school and community-based professionals involved.
- School counselors need to be familiar with effective strategies for engaging and working with collaborative teams of professionals, family members, and other community stakeholders. They need to be able to establish the mission of and ground rules for group interaction; foster a structured group problem-solving process; delineate recommended roles for team members; and develop specific team building skills.
- School counselors need to have specific team building skills including active listening, consensus building, and conflict resolution. They also need to conduct routine evaluation of the team functioning, as well as explore team building and co-teaching models within the classroom.

ADDITIONAL RESOURCES

Print

Blue-Banning, M., Summers, J., Frankland, H., Nelson, L., & Beegle, G. (2004). Dimensions of family and professional partnerships: Constructive guidelines for collaboration. *Exceptional Children, 70*(2), 167–184.

Foltos, L. (2013). *Peer coaching: Unlocking the power of collaboration.* Thousand Oaks, CA: Corwin.

Honigsfeld, A., & Dove, M. (2010). *Collaboration and co-teaching: Strategies for English learners.* Thousand Oaks, CA: Corwin.

Magiera, K., Lawrence-Brown, D., Bloomquist, K., Foster, C., Figueroa, A., Glatz, K., . . . Rodriguez, P. (2006). On the road to more collaborative teaching. *Teaching Exceptional Children Plus, 2*(5), 1–12. Retrieved from http://escholarship.bc.edu/education/tecplus/v0l2/iss5/art6

Robinson, K. (2007). Individual focus, systemic collaboration: The current attentional role of schools in the integrated delivery of mental health services. In D. Robertson, J. Anderson, & R. Meyer (Eds.), *Advances in school-based mental health interventions: Best practices and program models* (pp. 5–13). Kingston, NJ: Civic Research Institute.

Snell, M., & Janney, R. (2005). *Collaborative teaming* (2nd ed.). Baltimore, MD: Brookes.

Yawn, C., Hill, J., Obiakor, F., Gala, D., & Neu, J. (2013). Families and students with learning disabilities. *Advances in Special Education, 25,* 175–188.

Web Based

Collaborative teamwork resources

The Center for Effective Collaboration and Practice: http://cecp.air.org/

Devoted to fostering the development and the adjustment of children with or at risk of developing serious emotional disturbance through the production, exchange, and use of knowledge about effective practices.

New Conversations. Conflict Management Emergency Kit: http://www.newconversations.net/communication-skills-library-of-articles-and-teaching-materials/conflict-resolution-emergency-kit/

New Conversations. Seven Challenges Workbook with communication skills exercises: http://www.newconversations.net/

Co-Teaching Connection: http://coteach.com/

Provides resources for educators who want to know more about co-teaching, including a video, lesson plans, and common co-teaching problems and solutions. Online videos demonstrating the co-planning aspect of co-teaching are available from http://teachersnetwork.org/

Julian Treasure: Five ways to listen better: http://www.youtube.com/watch?v=cSohjlYQI2A)

Listening expert Julian Treasure shares five quick and interesting ways to retune your ears for conscious listening—to other people and the world around you.

Cross-cultural competence resources

The Equity Alliance: http://ea.niusileadscape.org/lc

Provides free, evidence-based, online resources and information about educational equity.

Center for International Rehabilitation Research Information and Exchange: http://cirrie.buffalo.edu/culture/

Cross-cultural competence resources include online cases and videos focusing on individuals with disabilities.

Teaching Tolerance: http://www.tolerance.org/

Provides a wide variety of free resources to educators interested in diversity, equal opportunity, and respect for differences in schools, including a magazine, film kits, and lesson plans.

For humorous, role reversal perspectives on stereotypes, take a look at these comedians' takes on stereotypes of European-Americans

Greg Proops: https://www.youtube.com/watch?v=aJYY1CFKzTg

John Oliver: https://www.youtube.com/watch?v=mwEGHlqbjw8

REFERENCES

Affleck, J., Madge, S., Adams, A., & Lowenbraun, S. (1988). Integrated classroom vs. resource model: Academic liability and effectiveness. *Exceptional Children, 54,* 339–348.

American School Counselor Association. (2008). *ASCA national model, executive summary.* Alexandria VA: American School Counselor Association. Retrieved from http://www.ascanationalmodel.org/

Ayers, G. E. (1994, Winter). They don't shoot collaborators anymore. *Teaching Exceptional Children, 26*(2), 5.

Banerji, M., & Dailey, R. (1995). A study of the effects of inclusion model on students with specific learning disabilities. *Journal of Learning Disabilities, 28,* 511–522.

Brown, D., Pryzwansky, W., & Schulte, A. (2011). The skills and characteristics of consultants and collaborators. *Psychological consultation and collaboration: Introduction to theory and practice.* Boston, MA: Pearson.

Bunch, G., & Valeo, A. (1997). *Inclusion: Recent research.* Toronto, Ontario, Canada: Inclusion Press.

CACREP. (2009). *Council for the accreditation of counseling and related educational programs 2009 Standards.* Retrieved from http://www.cacrep.org/wp-content/uploads/2013/12/2009-Standards.pdf

Cole, D., & Meyer, L. (1991). Social integration and severe disabilities: A longitudinal analysis of child outcomes. *The Journal of Special Education, 25*(3), 340–351.

Conoley, J., & Conoley, C. (2010). Why does collaboration work? Linking positive psychology and collaboration. *Journal of Educational & Psychological Consultation, 20*(1), 75–82.

Daane, C. J., Beirne-Smith, M., & Latham, D. (2000). Administrators' and teachers' perceptions of the collaborative efforts of inclusion in the elementary grades. *Education, 121*(2), 331–339. Retrieved from EBSCO Professional Development Collection.

Ferguson, D. L., Meyer, G., Jeanchild, J., Juniper, L., & Zingo, J. (1992). Figuring out what to do with the grown-ups: How teachers make inclusion "work" for students with disabilities. *Journal of the Association for Persons with Severe Handicaps, 17*(4), 218–226.

Freeman, S., & Alkin, M. (2000). Academic and social attainment of children with mental retardation in general education and special education settings. *Remedial and Special Education, 21*(1), 3–18.

Friend, M., & Bursuck, W. (2015). *Including students with special needs* (7th ed.). Boston, MA: Pearson.

Frye, H. N. (2005). How elementary school counselors can meet the needs of students with disabilities. *Professional School Counseling, 8*(5), 442–450.

Fryxell, D., & Kennedy, C. (1995). Placement along the continuum of services and its impact on students' social relationships. *Journal of the Association for Persons with Severe Handicaps, 20,* 259–269.

Garcia, S. B. (2012). The pre-service classroom as an intercultural space for experiencing a process of cultural reciprocity. In M. Kalyanpur & B. Harry, *Cultural reciprocity in special education* (pp. 155–174). Baltimore, MA: Brookes.

Holloway, T., Salisbury, C., Rainforth, B., & Palombar, M. (1995). Use of instructional time in classrooms serving students with and without severe disabilities. *Exceptional Children, 61*(3), 242–253.

Hunt, P., & Goetz, L. (1997). Research on inclusive educational programs, practices, and outcomes for students with severe disabilities. *Journal of Special Education, 31*(1), 3–29.

Ingraham, C. L., & Daugherty, K. M. (1995). The success of three gifted deaf-blind students in inclusive educational programs. *Journal of Visual Impairment & Blindness, 89*(3), 257.

Institute on Community Integration. (1990). *Collaborative teamwork: Working together for the inclusion of students with disabilities* [Brochure]. Minneapolis: Institute on Community Integration, University of Minnesota.

Kalyanpur, M., & Harry, B. (2012). *Cultural reciprocity in special education.* Baltimore, MA: Brookes.

Lawrence-Brown, D., & Muschaweck, M. (2004). Getting started with collaborative teamwork for inclusion. *Catholic Education, 8*(2), 146–161.

Lawrence-Brown, D., & Sapon-Shevin, M. (2013). *Condition critical: Key principles for equitable and inclusive schooling.* New York, NY: Teachers College Press.

Lipsky, D. K., & Gartner, A. (1995). The evaluation of inclusive education programs. *National Center on Restructuring and Inclusion Bulletin, 2*(2), 1–6.

Logan, K., & Keefe, E. (1997). A comparison of instructional context, teacher behavior, and engaged behavior for students with severe disabilities in general education and self-contained elementary classrooms. *Journal of the Association for Persons with Severe Handicaps, 22*(1), 16–27.

Madden, N., Slavin, R., Karweit, N., Dolan, L., & Wasik, B. (1993). Success for all: Longitudinal effects of a restructuring program for inner-city elementary schools. *American Educational Research Journal, 30,* 123–148.

McGregor, G., & Vogelsberg, R. (1998). *Inclusive schooling practices: Pedagogical and research foundations: A synthesis of the literature that informs best practices about inclusive schooling.* Baltimore, MA: Brookes.

Morton, M., Cotanch, B., Paetow, C., Rohn, C., Duncan, J., & Slavin, H. (1991). *Developing teaming skills.* Syracuse, NY: Division of Special Education and Rehabilitation, Syracuse University.

Peck, C., Donaldson, J., & Pezzoli, M. (1990). Some benefits non-handicapped adolescents perceive for themselves from their social relationships with peers who have severe handicaps. *Journal of the Association for Persons with Severe Handicaps, 15*(4), 241–249.

Salend, S., & Duhaney, L. M. G. (1999). The impact of inclusion on students with and without disabilities and their educators. *Remedial & Special Education, 20*(2), 114–126.

Sasso, G., & Rude, H. (1988). The social effects of integration on nonhandicapped children. *Education and Training in Mental Retardation, March,* pp. 18–23.

Schulte, A., Osborne, S., & McKinney, J. (1990). Academic outcomes for students with learning disabilities in consultation and resource programs. *Exceptional Children, 57,* 162–172.

Sharpe, M., York, J., & Knight, J. (1994). Effects of inclusion on the academic performance of classmates without disabilities: A preliminary study. *Remedial and Special Education, 15*(5), 281–287.

Tuckman, B., & Jensen, M. A. (1977). Stages of small-group development revisited. *Group and Organization Studies, 2*(4), 419–427.

Villa, R., Thousand, J., & Nevin, A. (2008). *A guide to co-teaching: Practical tips for facilitating student learning* (2nd ed.). Thousand Oaks, CA: Corwin.

Waldron, N., & McLeskey, J. (1998). The effects of an inclusive school program on students with mild and severe learning disabilities. *Exceptional Children, 64,* 395–405.

Wang, M., & Birch, J. (1984). Comparison of a full-time mainstreaming program and a resource room approach. *Exceptional Children, 5,* 33–40.

Willrodt, K., & Claybrook, S. (1995). *Effects of inclusion on academic outcomes* (Unpublished doctoral dissertation). Sam Houston State University, Texas. (Eric Document Reproduction Service No. ED 389102)

Chapter 5

Multidisciplinary Team Players and Process

K<small>AREN</small> D<small>ICKINSON</small>

West Chester University of Pennsylvania

"Alone we can do so little; together we can do so much."

—Helen Keller, American Author, Activist, and Lecturer

"Together we can do so much." This is such a simple phrase yet such a hope filled and powerful directive especially for those of us who work with, and are concerned about, the successful education and development of our children. While it could be argued that it truly *takes a village* to raise any child, the evidence is clear that engagement of those with special knowledge and skills, and the coordination of specialized services, is particularly effective when these efforts are in support of children with special needs. Nowhere is this more clearly demonstrated than in our schools and the coordinated, team-based programs provided to our children with special needs. This chapter explores both the "players" and the process of this collective, team-oriented approach to special education.

This chapter describes the nature of the unique roles and collaborative processes found within a *multidisciplinary team* (MDT) approach to supporting our students with special needs. More specifically, emphasis is given to detailing the role of school counselors and the unique knowledge and skills that they bring to the multidisciplinary team and the process of special education. School counselors, trained in both the theory and research highlighting the factors and processes that can inhibit or facilitate students' personal, social, and emotional development and academic performance, provide a unique and necessary skill set to the work of these MDTs.

By the end of this chapter, the reader will be able to carry out the following:

1. Identify what a multidisciplinary team (MDT) is and who may be on the team.
2. State at least three tasks the school counselor could do as a member of the MDT.
3. Identify the School Counselor Competencies issued by the Council for Accreditation of Counseling and Related Educational Programs (CACREP, 2016) and the American School Counselor Association (ASCA, 2012) as related to the counselor's roles and duties in the special education process.
4. Describe who is eligible to be considered to need special education and the steps to that process for your state.
5. Describe the high rates of the professionals working with students with disabilities as they relate to various educational levels.
6. Identify ways in which school counselors can help engage and support parents in the special education process.

[handwritten: MDT Team — cognitive physical socioemotional > data]

PLAYERS: MULTIDISCIPLINARY TEAM

While it may be obvious when children are struggling in their academic journey, knowing that there is a problem is only a small part of the process of remediation. School counselors are aware of the importance of gathering as much information as possible to discern the cause and effects of student behavior in order to help change what is needed. This process of understanding is not based on intuition or speculation. It is a data-based investigation, which is directed by the MDT. This process results in the gathering of information from every domain of the students' lives (e.g., cognitive, physical, socioemotional). This information will help identify needs and provide the foundation for successful interventions (U.S. Department of Education, 2006a).

In some states, the MDT may be referred to with a different title. For example, in Michigan, the name of the team is the Multi-disciplinary Evaluation Team (MET). Like the MDT, MET reviews important information such as school records, academic test results, medical history, and information the parent may share about the student (Plymouth-Canton Community Schools, Michigan, 2011). And in New York, the team is appointed by the Board of Education and is referred to as the Committee on Special Education (CSE; New York State Education Department, 2002).

In the next section, the specific details of the makeup and the workings of the multi-disciplinary team (cited as MDT for the remainder of the chapter) will be discussed.

MDT: The Mission

As gleaned from the Individuals with Disabilities Education Act (IDEA), the mission of the MDT is to gather information to assess the areas of strengths and need in the students in order to create an educational program in which the students will be successful (U.S. Department of Education, 2006a). The team decides on the types of data to collect based on the type of suspected disability. For example, take the case of a student who was having difficulty with math and reading yet has had good social skills and appropriate behavior with her peers and in the classroom. The team would want to complete assessments for cognitive and academic ability to examine the learning difficulties. However, they would not necessarily need to do a behavioral assessment or a perceptual or visual-motor test because those are not apparent needs. Or consider the student who is magnificently academically achieving in school but is yelling at the teacher, turning desks over, and running out of class when he is frustrated. This scenario would call for behavioral and socioemotional assessments, and quite possibly a psychiatric referral. Figure 5.1 is provided to show you examples of referral concerns and different types of assessments.

The purpose of these assessments is to obtain relevant functional, developmental, and academic data for the team to analyze the needs of the whole child. These

---

Figure 5.1   Examples of Referral Concerns and Assessments

Specific Concerns Include:

____articulation	____reading comprehension	____attention
____language	____listening comprehension	____spelling
____phonemic awareness	____math concepts	____writing
____enrichment	____written expression	____memory
____reading	____reading fluency	____other: ____

Specific Procedures:

____standardized cognitive assessments	____curricular based assessments
____standardized academic assessments	____classroom observation
____standardized perceptual assessments	____speech/language probe(s), screening(s) standardized assessment(s) and/or review of records
____standardized behavioral assessments	as deemed by speech-language pathologist
____standardized socioemotional assessments	____psychiatric assessments
____standardized memory assessments	____other: _____

assessments will lead to data-driven decisions, which secure accountability in this process. Information on the function or the cause of the child's behavior is gathered through collecting data specific to the individuals, their relationships, and their environments (Martin, 2012). By completing observational and standardized tests, the team will have information on the developmental and academic skills of the children in question. This information will allow the team to be better informed when developing teaching and intervention strategies for the students. All of these data are compiled into a report called a *Multidisciplinary Evaluation* (MDE), or an *Evaluation Report* (ER), which is then presented at a meeting to discuss the results and decide on further action. It is important to remember that we are here not only to support teachers with appropriate strategies and interventions, but we are also here to help students and their families in understanding the unique strengths and areas of need of individuals and the process.

MDT: Membership

As noted above, the types of data sought will vary as related to the identified needs of each child considered at risk. Similarly, the membership of the MDT will vary in relation to the specific needs of the students and the types of data sought. Typically, the team includes the classroom teacher, the school psychologist, or someone who can conduct assessments for diagnostic purposes; all are professionals who are qualified to assess children in the areas of need. Although there will be variations across the states in regard to members, the one constant within the MDT is that the parent will always be a team member (U.S. Department of Education, 2006b). Guided Practice Exercise 5.1 invites you to gather data on your MDT.

Guided Practice Exercise 5.1

MDT AT YOUR SCHOOL

Directions: Interview a school counselor or school psychologist at your site in order to answer the following questions. Share your findings with your classmates.

1. Who typically participates in the MDT, and what do their roles entail?

2. Are some members always constant?

3. Under what conditions might the membership change?

4. How do the differences in membership affect the types of data gathered?

Specific members of the MDT bring unique expertise to the assessment process. School counselors, when included on the team, bring a different perspective and understanding of the whole child including his or her functioning in the academic, social, and personal arenas. Case Illustration 5.1 provides one example of the school counselor's unique contribution to the work of the MDT.

CASE ILLUSTRATION 5.1

JANIE

Original Referral:

Janie is a 6-year-old, first-grade student. Her classroom teacher has identified the following as challenges for Janie.

a. She has difficulty in decoding words.
b. She has limited sight vocabulary.
c. Janie appears frustrated during reading class.
d. Although she has had supplemental help from the reading specialist, she appears to be getting even more frustrated.

Her frustration appears to be manifested in her refusal to do homework and her increasing aggressiveness toward her peers.

Counselor:

Ms. Phillips, the elementary school counselor, is quite familiar with Janie having initially seen her at the request of her parents. Ms. Phillips has observed Janie in the classroom, as well as on the playground. She has noticed a difference in Janie's social interaction in the two settings. Within the classroom, Janie appears to daydream instead of engaging in her directed activity and often appears as if she is attempting to escape or hide from teacher and/or peer recognition. This is contrasted to her behavior on the playground. Unlike her "under-the-radar" style exhibited in the classroom, Janie is quite assertive, often aggressive, in her attempts at directing the social interaction in the playground.

Over the course of the past 6 weeks, Ms. Phillips has been able to meet individually with Janie and has come to the following conclusions:

a. Janie is very sad and defensive about what she reports as "being dumb."
b. Janie is resistant to engaging with the reading specialist, feeling that this identifies her as "different" from her friends.

(Continued)

(Continued)

c. Janie reports that she gets upset and cries whenever her parents ask her to start homework. Further, it appears the crying is effective in that the parents succumb to her tears and allow her to avoid the challenges presented in the homework.

d. Janie complains that her peers avoid her and often make fun of her . . . calling her "mean."

Valuable Insights for the MDT:

With her special perspective on Janie, Ms. Phillips highlights the following as data to be considered by the MDT:

a. Janie has internalized her weak skills in reading as being dumb and incapable. This has put her on the defensive for receiving support from the reading teacher and, hence, does not want to engage in the extra instruction.

b. Janie's parents unwittingly have negatively reinforced Janie's notion of inadequacy by allowing her to avoid her homework by excusing her from it when she cries.

c. Janie's frustration has manifested into controlling and inpatient behaviors when she interacts with her peers, thus, causing them to turn away from her.

MDT: Roles

Many of the members of the MDT will take part in gathering information for the *Evaluation Report* (ER). Information about the students' present performance will be given by the classroom teachers or any specialists or support teachers who have worked with the students. The school psychologist, speech-language pathologist, or someone qualified to conduct individual diagnostic examinations of children will do the standardized assessments (U.S. Department of Education, 2006b). As seen next in the MDT: Data Collection section, school counselors do have a role in collecting data. Although school counselors are skilled in selecting appropriate assessment strategies that can be used to evaluate a student's academic development (CACREP, 2009), there are states that mandate that school psychologists do the standardized assessments.

In addition to assisting with the data collection, school counselors, with their knowledge and skill in group dynamics, are well positioned to serve in a leadership role facilitating the work of the MDT (ASCA, 2012; CACREP, 2009). School counselors can facilitate the meeting by inviting all participants to share information and helping the team understand what is being discussed. Education has its own language and terms that may not be known to all people at the meeting.

School counselors can promote understanding by taking the time to explain what terms and acronyms mean, particularly to parents who may not be familiar with educational jargon. Along with terms that may be unfamiliar, the interpretation of the data being shared may need clarification, and the acceptance of what is revealed may take time. These discussions can be emotional and are more productive when led by an individual with a calm, caring voice, such as a school counselor's. Case Illustration 5.2 will demonstrate the value of the school counselor in

CASE ILLUSTRATION 5.2

TIMMY

The MDT has just convened in order to decide which assessments will be conducted for an evaluation for Timmy, a second-grade student suspected to have a learning disability. Timmy has been having difficulty with focusing in the classroom, completing his work, and writing legibly. His demeanor has remained pleasant and positive; however, his grades have suffered in every subject. The team are discussing their ideas with Timmy's parents, Mr. and Mrs. Dewar.

School Psychologist: I'm so glad you were able to come in today and hear how Timmy has been doing. We have implemented many new strategies, and although Timmy tries very hard and has such a wonderful disposition, he is continuing to struggle. We are recommending a multidisciplinary evaluation for him.

Mr. Dewar: Well, we do want him to get help, but that sounds too intensive.

Counselor: I guess it can sound intensive! We're so glad you are both involved and want what's best for Timmy. We are looking at the same goal, to help Timmy. The multidisciplinary evaluation will allow all of us from various specialties to collect information regarding Timmy's strengths and needs. It's referred to as a multidisciplinary evaluation because members of the team from different disciplines, or areas of training, can gather data from a variety of perspectives to understand Timmy's needs (reflecting content and summarizing information).

Mrs. Dewar: Oh, so you *all* will work with him?

Counselor: Yes, it sounds like you think that seems like a lot of people . . . (reflecting feeling).

(Continued)

(Continued)

> Let me give you some examples. The school psychologist will assess Timmy's cognitive ability and the level he is achieving, or presently working on, right now. The reading specialist will share data on his reading progress. The teacher can give ideas as to what learning strategies have or have not worked. I can gather behavioral data by observing during the times Timmy is working and writing, and you can give input on what strategies work at home and when Timmy is most successful (summarizing information).

Teacher: And, I think there ought to be an OT screening, as well.

Counselor: I see that may sound confusing (reflecting feeling).

> An OT screening sounds appropriate. The OT, occupational therapist, will come and observe Timmy when he writes and offer some suggestions for Timmy's handwriting. We are looking for strategies, so he doesn't fatigue as quickly when writing (summarizing information).

Mrs. Dewar: Well, I've been wondering what to do to improve his handwriting!

In summary, the counselor has been able to reflect the feelings of the parents and, quite possibly, de-escalated their anxieties over having their son evaluated. Further, the counselor has been able to better inform the parents of the process their son is about to go through by explaining with greater detail, and in terms more familiar to folks who are not education majors!

facilitating the data being shared in the meeting. He is very aware of the anxiety parents may have when attending this meeting and how that anxiety could interfere with their understanding of the information presented and decisions made. In this case illustration, the counselor uses his skills of reflection and summarization.

As seen from the case above, school counselors are often involved in meetings which can be emotional. It may be prudent to think of the following four stages for presenting difficult information to parents as suggested by Auger (2006). When presenting information to parents that may be difficult to hear, understand, or accept, Auger suggested thinking of the delivery in four stages: (a) preparation, (b) delivering the news, (c) engaging the parents in a therapeutic dialogue about the news, and (d) follow-up.

Preparation for the meeting involves the invitation to the meeting, which needs to be in the parents' language, and making sure parents know what the meeting is for without going into too much detail before you are face-to-face. Imagine being invited to school to talk about your child. That alone could evoke feelings similar to being called down to the principal's office! You can inform the parents that you'd like to speak to them about some important concerns and will go into detail at the meeting. Although this could raise parental anxiety, reassure the parents that you are looking forward to meeting with them to hear how they believe their child is progressing. It would also be helpful to consider scheduling the meeting at a convenient time and the physical environment where the meeting will be held. It should be comfortable and private and allow for parents to be seated so that they are fully included, such as at a large, round table.

Starting and ending with a positive comment can lower defenses and, thus, is a productive way to start the meeting. In delivering the news, it is helpful to find out what the parents already know about the concerns and build on that information. "What do you know about your daughter's progress this year?" is a way to open the discussion in a nonthreatening way. Auger (2006) also suggested checking in periodically to make sure parents comprehend what is being said and to see if there are any questions.

I concluded that parents should be encouraged to express their feelings, individually, as the school counselor remains calm and continues to focus on reflecting those feelings. This is about the parents and helping them come to terms with information that they may not want to hear. It is helpful if the school counselor is available to continue to talk after the meeting is over if the parents are still upset or have questions. An invitation from the school counselor to the parents to call with any questions after leaving the meeting will leave the door open for communication and trust in the fact that someone cares about them and their child. A follow-up call by the school counselor would also help keep communication open and build a positive, working relationship.

MDT: Data Collection

As suggested above, the primary role of the MDT is the gathering of information that will guide decision making and educational programming. Data must be collected to show that the student is not achieving grade-level standards, that the student has had appropriate instruction and that the student has had research-based intervention (U.S. Department of Education, 2006b); that is, the *response to intervention* (RTI) strategies need to be documented.

The MDT gathers information through standardized tests (e.g., intelligence test, achievement test) and nonstandardized measures such as observations and interviews. The school psychologist typically assesses the child's cognitive ability and academic achievement. School counselors, on the other hand, can gather information through interviewing and observations. Interview data can be collected from parents, teachers, and staff who interact with the student. In addition to these data, observational data are also essential and mandated by IDEA (U.S. Department of Education, 2006a). In order to document the child's academic performance and behavior in the area or areas of difficulty, the child must be observed in his or her learning environment. The MDT must either "(A) use information obtained from an observation in routine classroom instruction and monitoring of the child's performance that was done before the child was referred for an evaluation, or (B) have at least one member of the [MDT] conduct an observation of the child's academic performance in the regular classroom after the child has been referred for an evaluation and parental consent is obtained" (U.S. Department of Education, 2006b, p. 3). School counselors are quite adept at observing behavior and environmental elements, which may have an effect on behavior (such as teacher-student interactions and internal and external distractions) and which thus positions them to collect these data (ASCA, 2012). When appropriate and given the referral, school counselors can collect data for a Functional Behavioral Assessment (FBA). These data would include identifying the problem behavior, the antecedents and consequences related to the behavior, and hypotheses as to why the behavior is occurring.

Along with these assessments, the law requires that we include the child's responses to previous interventions as additional data to be analyzed (U.S. Department of Education, 2006b). For example, the child in Case Illustration 5.1 (Janie) had needs in reading. The intervention employed was to receive support from the reading specialist. The effectiveness and response to this intervention would be used in the evaluation report. At times, the school counselor may be working directly with students through individual or small group counseling. They may conduct psycho-educational developmental classroom lessons, using strategies that may include behavioral interventions, such as learning coping skills, or self-management, and the use of positive reinforcement. School counselors can report on the students' response to these interventions. In addition, school counselors may report on the effectiveness of any other accommodations or strategies that were attempted, such as preferred seating, shortened assignments, and teacher check-ins.

Depending on the child's needs, other specialists may conduct assessments for areas such as speech and language or motor skills. In addition, other data gathering techniques such as surveys and behavior rating scales may be administered. Each state may vary in the guidelines as to who may administer and report out on these assessments. Therefore, it is important to be aware of the individual needs of the child at risk and how your state and school define the roles of the MDT.

The last section provided you with an understanding of the purpose and membership of the MDT and the roles and duties the MDT will typically perform. In the next section, the process for identifying needs and interventions for children at risk is explored.

PROCESS: SPECIAL EDUCATION

We have identified the players, and now will examine the special education process in which they are engaged. The IDEA has detailed the process to be employed in identifying and intervening with those children who are facing challenges within the regular classroom and its curriculum. This process engages school personnel in a variety of strategies that will help them identify children who, because of physical, psycho-emotional, social, or cognitive challenges, experience difficulty in achieving standards as expected by their age chronology or grade placement.

As will be detailed next, the process starts with a broad spectrum of analyses of all students' performances in hopes of achieving early identification of those students at risk who are exhibiting difficulty. While we in education have, and continue to employ, curricular modification and provision of supplemental support in hopes of assisting students who struggle, we find that some of these interventions are less than adequate and that additional analytical data are needed in order to craft a meaningful and effective intervention.

The process, as described in the subsequent section, moves us from a general population assessment and screening to the eventual formulation of an individually tailored remedial plan. It is a process for which school counselors can serve a central and valued role.

Child Find

As professionals who work to ensure the growth and development of all students, we want to find any student who may need specialized services and provide those services as early as possible. By federal law, the state must identify, locate, and evaluate all children with disabilities in the state who need special education and related services (Küpper, 2011). This is referred to as Child Find. Data are collected in a variety of ways. Screening for children at risk can occur with the analysis of normative school data including attendance, grades, test scores, and discipline records. While these data may have always existed, school personnel are now mandated by law to review and use this information for identifying children at risk.

In addition to screening by way of school-wide data, often Child Find occurs as a result of a concern specifically made known by a parent or one who is working directly with a student. School counselors are often called upon to meet with children who are angry, sad, or struggling. These could be red flags for children who may need further support. For these children who could be identified as at risk, a team of school personnel will identify interventions to be employed to meet the needs of the child. The effectiveness of these interventions will be monitored (see Response to Intervention [RTI] section).

Screening

In addition to analysis of typical school-based data, IDEA requires that starting in kindergarten, all students are to be assessed several times a year to obtain data to make sure grade-level benchmarks are being met (U.S. Department of Education, 2006a). This universal screening is an additional method to identify or predict students who may be at risk for poor learning outcomes. These assessments are typically brief and conducted with all students at a given grade level. For those children who may be identified as at risk, a team of school personnel will identify interventions to be employed to meet the needs of the child. The effectiveness of these interventions will be monitored, to be discussed further in the Response to Intervention section. This may be followed by additional testing or short-term progress monitoring to further identify students' risk status (Center on Response to Intervention at American Institutes for Research, 2007). School counselors may be part of the universal screening team. They can be particularly helpful when assessing new students or students with anxiety, as school counselors often have a rapport with many of these students, which may decrease stress associated with assessment.

Response to Intervention (RTI)

As noted previously, for those children who do not score at or above benchmark, there is to be a change of instruction or an intervention is to occur. With RTI, schools identify students at risk for poor learning outcomes, monitor student progress, provide evidence-based interventions, adjust the intensity and nature of those interventions depending on students' responsiveness, and identify students with learning disabilities or other disabilities (National Center on Response to Intervention [NCRTI], 2010). These interventions are often provided in tiers, with Tier 1 providing standard-aligned instruction for all students, Tier 2 providing interventions for some students, and Tier 3 providing instruction for just a few students who were not successful with interventions from the first two tiers.

Both the 2004 reauthorization of IDEA and the 2001 No Child Left Behind Act (NCLB) call for scientifically based instructional practices to be provided for a student who is struggling before a referral can be made for a special education evaluation (Cummings, Atkins, Allison, & Cole, 2008). Consider the following example. A second-grade student, Alia, did not reach benchmark scores during the first reading assessment at the start of school. She was moved to a Tier 2 reading group and given reading instruction using a different teaching method. Alia had progress monitoring for 2 months in the area of reading, and the results showed her scores remained below benchmark. Thus, Alia had an intervention in her area of need, and her progress was monitored. Due to her lack of progress and poor response to intervention, the MDT will take a closer look at her needs, as seen in the next section.

Multidisciplinary Team (MDT)

The process, up to this point, has resulted in the identification of students at risk and has even directed school personnel to the development and implementation of "scientifically based" interventions. For some students, however, their response to this intervention (RTI) is less than desirable and, as such, additional steps need to be taken to facilitate their learning and adjustment.

Children who still do not make benchmark, or adequate progress after they have received intervention with repeated assessments of achievement at reasonable intervals, will be recommended for an evaluation to determine the need for special education (U.S. Department of Education, 2006b). Special education consists of federal and state mandates to support children with disabilities with the programs and services needed to provide equal opportunity and access to be fully included in school (U.S. Department of Education, 2014).

As noted in the previous section, the MDT will meet to review current data on students and request parental permission to conduct evaluations (U.S. Department of Education, 2006b). The team will then decide what assessments will be needed to evaluate the students' strengths and needs. The process for special education has mandated timelines from referral to evaluation to programming to review (National Dissemination Center for Children with Disabilities, 2014). One example of a flow chart depicting the special education process can be found at the AZ.gov site (http://www .azed.gov/special-education/files/2012/02/special-education-process-flow-chart.pdf).

Multidisciplinary Evaluation (MDE)

The MDT has collected a vast amount of information over the past few months in an effort to diagnose the strengths and needs of the student in question. At this point, all the information is compiled into a written report typically referred to as an *Evaluation Report* (ER), or *Multidisciplinary Evaluation* (MDE). If the child is suspected of having a disability, the MDE must include

- a statement of whether the child qualifies as a child with a disability,
- the child's educational needs,
- the basis for making the determination, and
- a list of the MDT members. Each team member must certify in writing that the report reflects his or her conclusion. If the report does not, then the team member must submit a separate statement presenting his or her conclusion (U.S. Department of Education, 2006a).

In the case when children are suspected to have a specific learning disability, the MDE must also include relevant behavior noted while the MDT observed the child, whether that behavior affects the child's academic functioning, and any educationally relevant medical findings. Figure 5.2 provides an illustration of the

Figure 5.2   Sample Components of an *Evaluation Report* (ER)

SAMPLE COMPONENTS OF AN EVALUATION REPORT (ER)

Student Name: Janie   Date of Birth: 5/21/   Grade: 1

Date of Report: 1/10/   Date Report Provided to Parents: 1/15/

Local Education Agency (LEA): Seaside School District

School the Child Is Attending: Seagull Elementary

Current Educational Program: General Education

Name and Address of Parent/Guardian/Surrogate: John & Karen Smythe

Contact Information: Home Phone: 555-555-1234 Cell Phone: 555-555-4321

Complete Sections 1 through 6 for all students.

If determining eligibility for Specific Learning Disability (SLD), the SLD component near the end of this document must be completed and used to complete Sections 5 and 6.

1. **REASON(S) FOR REFERRAL: Janie has not progressed at an adequate rate and remains below state and local benchmarks in reading at the first grade level.**
2. **SOURCES OF EVALUATION DATA** (includes: observations, teacher recommendation, data provided by parents, and all assessments)
3. **IF AN ASSESSMENT IS NOT CONDUCTED UNDER STANDARD CONDITIONS, DESCRIBE THE EXTENT TO WHICH IT VARIED FROM STANDARD CONDITIONS** (including if the assessment was given in the student's native language or other mode of communication):
4. **DETERMINING FACTORS** – A student must not be found to be eligible for special education and related services if the determining factor for the student's disability is any of those listed below. Respond Yes or No to, and provide evidence for, each determining factor below.

   Yes   No   Lack of appropriate instruction in reading, including the essential
              components of reading instruction. Provide evidence:
         X   **Janie has received intervention through supplemental reading support
              and a change in reading instruction.**

   Yes   No   Lack of appropriate instruction in math. Provide evidence:
         X   **Janie is above state and local benchmarks in math.**

   Yes   No   Limited English proficiency. Provide evidence:
         X   **English is Janie's primary and only language.**

5. **SUMMARY OF FINDINGS/INTERPRETATION OF EVALUATION RESULTS** – Considering all available evaluation data, record the team's analyses of the student's functioning levels.

A. PRESENT LEVELS OF ACADEMIC ACHIEVEMENT – Describe the student's present levels, strengths, and the resulting academic needs, when appropriate. Include communicative status, motor abilities, and transition needs as appropriate. For students with limited English proficiency (LEP), include current level(s) of English language proficiency in reading, writing, speaking, and understanding/listening: **Janie needs direct instruction in reading in the areas of decoding and sight vocabulary.**

B. PRESENT LEVELS OF FUNCTIONAL PERFORMANCE – Describe the student's present levels, strengths, and the resulting functional and developmental needs, when appropriate:

C. [X] The student has a disability AND is in need of specially designed instruction and therefore IS ELIGIBLE for special education.

    1. Disability Category
       Primary disability Category: **Specific Learning Disability**
       Secondary disability category(ies), if any:

    2. Recommendations for consideration by the IEP team to enable the student to participate as appropriate in the general education curriculum (including special considerations the IEP team must consider before developing the IEP, measurable annual goals, specially designed instruction, and supplementary aids and services:

Evaluation Team Participation *(note: all participants will list name, title, and in case of a student with specific learning disabilities, whether they agree or disagree)*	**Agreement/Disagreement** *(note: in situations where evaluating students for specific learning disabilities, participants must note agreement or disagreement)*		
Name	Role/Title	Agree	Disagree
Ms. T. Porambo	School Counselor	X	
Mrs. J. Baselice	School Psychologist	X	
Etc. . . .			
Mr. & Mrs. Smythe	Parent	X	

DETERMINATION OF SPECIFIC LEARNING DISABILITY

NOTE: Additional information and documentation will be provided in those situations where the student is identified as having a specific learning disability. Data to be collected would include

1. *Evidence that the student does not achieve adequately for the student's age or does not meet State-approved grade-level standards in one or more of the following areas when provided with learning experiences and scientifically based instruction appropriate for the student's age or State-approved grade level standards and level of English language proficiency: oral expression, listening comprehension, written expression, basic reading skill, reading fluency skills, reading comprehension, mathematics calculation, and mathematics problem solving.*

2. *Description of the process(es) used to determine eligibility.*

(Continued)

Figure 5.2   (Continued)

3. *Data demonstrating that prior to referral or as part of the referral process for a specific learning disability, the student's regular education instruction was delivered by qualified personnel, including the English as a Second Language (ESL) program, if applicable:*
4. *Data based documentation of repeated assessments of achievement at reasonable intervals, reflecting progress during instruction, which was provided to the parents:*
5. *An observation in the student's learning environment (including the regular classroom setting) to document the student's academic performance and behavior in the areas of difficulty. Note the relationship of that behavior to the student's academic functioning:*
6. *Other data, if needed, as determined by the evaluation team.*

Source: Adapted by author from "Evaluation Report" [Form], (2008, July). Retrieved from http://pattan.net-website .s3.amazonaws.com/files/materials/forms/ER-070108.pdf

components or sections that would typically be included within an ER or MDE. The specific elements, as well as the configuration of those elements, would be defined by district and state policies.

The *Multidisciplinary Evaluation* (MDE) report must also include a recommendation stating whether the child is eligible to receive special education services. For example, it is the conclusion of the MDE that Janie from Case Illustration 5.1 has a learning disability and can start receiving special education services because she needs specially designed instruction.

Having collected the data and written them into a report, the *Multidisciplinary Evaluation* report will be presented to the parents at a meeting referred to as the Multidisciplinary Evaluation Meeting.

Multidisciplinary Evaluation (MDE) Meeting

Prior to meeting, the parents will have been provided the results of the MDE. Imagine how parents would feel when they receive the report concluding if their child has a disability or not. For some, this could be a time to rejoice in that there is finally an answer to what has been making school so difficult, and there will be help and support! For others, the conclusions could be disappointing or sad, or even provoke anger. Some parents may become angry with the idea that the school team is concluding their child has a disability. They may blame the school curriculum for being too difficult, or they may accuse the teacher of not providing appropriate instruction. Or some parents may deny that there is a disability and say that the results of the report are inaccurate. Whatever the emotions, it is important to remember that when speaking with the parents, this is *their* child we are diagnosing and discussing.

School counselors can be very helpful and proactive by sensitizing the team to possible parental reactions before the meeting occurs while avoiding bias. Parents need to feel that their voice is being heard, that their fears are being recognized, and that their questions are being answered. It would be helpful to have an initial discussion before the entire team meets. Having the school counselor and school psychologist available before the MDE meeting to go over the findings allows for a smaller and more intimate conversation, one in which parents may feel freer to ask questions, and cry if needed.

As the MDT meets to review the results of the evaluation report, school counselors can once again serve as leaders by making sure the parents' feelings are noticed and affirmed, and all team members have a good understanding of what is being discussed. Envision now, you are sitting at a meeting with an entire team of education professionals who have assessed your child and will now be talking about conclusions and recommendations. Even when the news is encouraging, this can be an overwhelming situation for parents. School counselors are there to reflect feeling, identify confusion, and help clarify information, not just for the parents but also for the entire team.

At this point, the team, which includes the parents, decides if the child is a "child with a disability," as defined by the IDEA (U.S. Department of Education, 2006a). While we need to work with the legal terminology, "child with a disability," we need to be cognizant that the parents are thinking of their child, not a label. A child is an extension of his or her parents, and some parents see their child as a reflection of themselves. Thus, some parents may feel guilty or at fault for their child's disability, and they may see their own struggles replaying in their child, creating angst. Some parents will agree with the findings and welcome the support. Yet others will find fault with the results and fail to see any relevance to their child. Under these types of conditions, there are times when parents may not agree with the evaluation and/or the decision of a disability. If parents do not agree with the decision, they may ask for a hearing to challenge the eligibility decision. If the parents disagree with the evaluation, they have the right to take their child for an Independent Educational Evaluation (IEE) and can ask that the school system pay for this evaluation (Küpper, 2011).

Services in Response to the Multidisciplinary Evaluation (MDE)

The results of the evaluation report will dictate the next action of the MDT. For those children who are found not to have a disability and thus ineligible to receive special education, the process is not yet over. The team must still consider what these students need to successfully learn. At times, it will be appropriate for students to continue to receive the same general education curriculum and the interventions and monitoring that were in place prior to the evaluation. This could occur when students have matured physically, cognitively, or emotionally or have become more efficient in new strategies and are no longer struggling.

While not eligible for special education, students might receive accommodations through a 504 Plan (U.S. Department of Education, 2010; see Chapter 3), or for those students who are found to have a disability, special education and related services may be provided, as will be identified in their Individualized Education Plan (IEP; see Chapter 3).

For a look at how a 504 Plan might work, consider Timmy in Case Illustration 5.2. The MDE concluded that Timmy does not have a disability for which he needs special education. Instead, the decision was that Timmy has Attention-Deficit Hyperactivity Disorder (ADHD), and while that can be disabling for some students, Timmy did not need a specially designed program. He did, however, need some accommodations in order to be successful in school. To help with his difficulty with focusing, the teacher is to state his name before she gives a direction or starts instruction, and he is to sit at a desk in the front row of the classroom. In order to help Timmy complete his work, the teacher has Timmy check-in with her after completing the first sentence or problem, then, every subsequent 10 minutes when a timer goes off. Finally, the use of a pencil grip and shorter written assignments were put into the plan as accommodations for Timmy's poor fine motor skills. It is helpful to explain the reasoning for these accommodations to Timmy so that he does not see them as punishment but as helpful supports. These accommodations enabled Timmy to work more independently and successfully. The teacher, parents, and the student experienced less frustration, and everyone was happier.

Consider another case of a student for whom a 504 Plan was written. Jenny, a bright, dedicated ninth-grade student, had excelled in every class and was every teacher's dream student until this year. When her grades plummeted and she began staying home from school complaining of severe stomach aches, the MDT at her school recommended an evaluation. From the data gathered for the *Multidisciplinary Evaluation* report, it was discovered that Jenny had a great fear of public speaking, which she needed to do in Speech Class and for presentations in many other classes. The decision of the team was that Jenny was not eligible for special education services; however, she did need accommodations to help her get through her school day. The accommodations included a pass to the counselor's office when she felt anxious, modified speaking assignments, such as video taping her presentation, and scheduled visits to the counselor's office to learn and practice stress reduction and coping skills.

In developing the IEP, school counselors bring a perspective of the whole child to this plan, and they can complement the skills of other school personnel by implementing specific interventions in the academic, career, and personal-social areas, as needed (Milson, Goodnough, & Akos, 2007). While much attention is often given to the academic area, attention must also be given to the child's emotional responses. This affective area is not always considered as a crucial component when looking at academic needs; however, this domain can affect all other domains, and school counselors have strategies to help this area develop (ASCA, 2012). Examples of these approaches include conducting individual and group counseling and contributing to the IEP process by extending support into the nonacademic and affective areas (Milson et al., 2007).

In developing and implementing the IEP, it is important to involve the parents. We want the parents to be able to attend the meeting and feel informed about the plan that will be implemented. The idea of parental engagement is more than a good idea; it is mandated under federal law (IDEA; U.S. Department of Education, 2006b). Beyond the mandate of the law, our concern for the student and the parents calls us to ensure engagement and understanding. The school counselors' skills of communication and collaboration can be effective in ensuring the parents know about the meeting, what will take place at the meeting, and making sure the parents can understand the language in the meeting. This care and concern is demonstrated in Case Illustration 5.3.

CASE ILLUSTRATION 5.3

SUPPORTING THE PARENTS

The IEP team is meeting to develop a plan for Keisha, who has been identified as having a specific learning disability in reading. The following is an example of the possible interactions in the IEP meeting between Mr. and Mrs. Johnson, Keisha's parents; the school counselor, Mrs. Lane; and the IEP team.

Mrs. Johnson: I understand that Keisha will be getting extra help, but how will we know how she's doing?

Special Education Teacher: We'll have progress monitoring data on her, and you'll receive a quarterly report.

Mrs. Lane: I can see that may sound confusing. Every week, Keisha will have an assessment that measures how many skills she has learned in reading. Every 3 months, you'll receive a summary of how she has progressed.

Mr. Johnson: Well, that's good, but how will we know if we need to change something in this plan?

(Continued)

(Continued)

Mrs. Lane: That's a great question! We will meet at least once a year to go over the goals we set and see what we need to change. However, if any of us feel we need to add or change anything within that year, we can meet to discuss it.

Mrs. Johnson: That sounds reasonable. What about these SDIs you keep talking about?

Classroom Teacher: Oh, you remember, those are strategies that will help Keisha in the learning environment. We've put a lot of those in place already.

Mr. Johnson: Well, if they're already in place, why isn't the problem fixed? Why should she have to do something different? She's going to get teased for doing something different, and I don't know if I like this plan.

Mrs. Lane: This is a lot of new information and is a different way of looking at Keisha's education from what you might have expected. We would all like Keisha to experience less frustration and feel more successful in school. You bring up some very important questions and concerns about Keisha's academic needs and learning in a new way. Let's review what Keisha needs and how different instruction can help with that. Let's also take a look at how we can help Keisha understand her learning style and how to cope with any reactions from her peers.

ADDITIONAL OPPORTUNITIES FOR COUNSELOR SUPPORT

While there may be subtle variations to the process described above, it is fair to say that it is a general template depicting the special education process and the role of the school counselors. There are additional opportunities when school counselors can provide support to the child and the family. These will be addressed below.

School Counselor Support: Transitioning From Early Intervention

There are several valuable contributions school counselors can make for children entering into the public school system for the first time. These are children with disabilities that are entering a formal education. This can be both an exciting and anxiety provoking experience for children and parents. School counselors can provide support by having a transition meeting with the parents of the children who have received support in early intervention. Speaking with the parents regarding their goals and their journey thus far provides invaluable insight into expectations and can make collaboration much easier. This is the first meeting of what could be many meetings over several years and an excellent opportunity to build a working relationship. Perhaps the child is not ready for kindergarten and requires another year of early intervention. Or maybe the school can provide needed support, and the child will enter school in the fall. Case Illustration 5.4 provides an example of the value of this transition meeting.

CASE ILLUSTRATION 5.4

FREDDIE COMES TO SCHOOL

Freddie is a 6-year-old Caucasian male who is diagnosed with high functioning autism. He has received early intervention special education services for the past 3 years in a preschool with typically developing children. Freddie has had behavior intervention strategies taught and monitored by a special education teacher in his preschool classroom. He has also received speech and language services to learn pragmatic language skills (social language) and occupational therapy services for sensory issues. When your team meets with Freddie's parents in the spring before Freddie is scheduled to come to your school, they tell you how worried they are about Freddie coming to school.

Freddie's parents explain that Freddie has had a wonderful experience at his preschool and he responds well to his teachers and therapists. However, that was not always the case. It has taken time for Freddie to feel comfortable with his school and everyone he works with, and he does not handle transitions well. They are also very comfortable with the teachers and specialists and are worried if all the new staff and faculty will be as friendly and accommodating as the people they are working with now. In addition, they mention that Freddie's older sister, Alana, is dreading the fact that Freddie is coming to her school. She is going into fifth grade in your school, and she is nervous about Freddie coming to the school. She has described Freddie's behavior as loud and odd, and she does not want to be embarrassed.

You thank the parents for sharing their concerns and ask them to also share their goals for Freddie. They reply that they really want him to fit in, be happy, and make a friend. As you gather information on current goals, you ask about Freddie's interests and strengths. Oh, say his parents, he is quite the artist! And, he loves to be read to and listen to music, as long as it isn't loud. As the meeting continues, you discover the following needs for Freddie:

- Structured routine
- Immediate feedback for good and bad choices

(Continued)

(Continued)

- Someone to explain social interactions and prompt appropriate responses
- Help maintaining focus on instruction and tasks
- Time and an area for doing heavy work or exercises for sensory needs
- A space in his classroom for quiet time

As you are writing down Freddie's needs you think of your kindergarten teacher, Ms. Coldwell. She has been teaching for over 25 years and has plenty of strategies for classroom management; however, this will be the first student with autism in her class. In fact, Freddie will be the first student with autism to be fully included in the educational program in the school. You start thinking about what you can do ahead of time to help Freddie and his family transition into your school.

In addition to a transition meeting, planning and preparing for a new student with a disability is another important task. The child may have physical needs such as a walker, academic needs such as for slow processing time, or behavioral needs such as for an inability to attend. By knowing what these needs are and preparing for them ahead of time, there is a greater chance for success as school starts. Preparing may include getting the environment ready; training for the teacher, other school personnel, and extra staff such as aides, cafeteria helpers, and bus drivers; or allowing for individual or small group counseling time. Guided Practice Exercise 5.2 invites you to reflect on how to prepare for Freddie in Case Illustration 5.4.

Guided Practice Exercise 5.2

PREPARING FOR FREDDIE (SEE CASE ILLUSTRATION 5.4)

Look at Case Illustration 5.4, Freddie Comes to School. As the school counselor, what preparations and accommodations can you make to smooth Freddie's transition into kindergarten? Consider

physical environment

social connections for Freddie

family connections and needs for parents and siblings

the meetings that would be appropriate

if any training is required, and if so, for whom?

actions you might take in the delivery system of your counseling program

School Counselor Support: K–12

School counselors have a great understanding of what it takes to develop and implement transition planning services for students with disabilities (CACREP, 2009). Through direct service activities, advocating for support services, coordinating the efforts of others, or directly providing services to students with disabilities through classroom guidance, small group counseling sessions, and individual counseling sessions, school counselors possess the skills and knowledge to make a difference by providing prevention and intervention activities during times of transition (Milsom, 2007). Meetings and trainings can help faculty and staff become familiar with certain characteristics associated with some disabilities, as well as gaining knowledge in goals, strategies, and accommodations. School counselors can make sure the physical environment is ready for equipment and any extra space which is needed. In addition to preparing the environment, allowing for personal interaction between students and between parents will set the stage for increasing comfort and a feeling of belonging. Examples of the types of transition tasks that can be implemented are illustrated in Table 5.1.

Throughout the K–12 school experience, school counselors can teach and reinforce the skills needed to be successful after high school. Self-advocacy, decision making, and career guidance are part of a comprehensive counseling program and are essential for all students.

SUMMARY

School personnel have an obligation to ensure every child can learn. When a child is struggling in school, there is a mandated process to follow so that the child receives

Table 5.1   Strategies to Help Prepare for Transitions*

Meetings	Environment	Social	Training
Hold IEP meeting with old and new team	Invite student for a tour of the school prior to starting	Facilitate an orientation for new students	Train Faculty/Staff on disability and accommodations
Hold meeting with new teacher	Create a space for breaks or alone time	Plan small group for new students	Train teacher on goals and strategies
Hold meeting with new aide	Designate a room for sensory activities	Arrange connections with other parents	Train aide on goals and strategies
Schedule appointments with the school counselor	Make sure classrooms have clearance for wheelchairs		Provide training on how to implement behavior plans

*Created by author

the services to which he or she is entitled. Part of this process includes a team of school professionals with varying expertise in how children learn and behave. As a member of this MDT, school counselors can support not only the process but also the child and other members involved in the process.

School counselors can help gather data; however, they can also do much more! By using active listening skills and taking on leadership roles by facilitating and mediating meetings, school counselors can help to clarify information, affirm, and process feelings; include all members; and empower parents to be involved team members. In every step of the process and in all transitions, school counselors can help prepare students and parents for what will occur and initiate any changes that will help to bring about success.

KEYSTONES

- The MDT is a team of professionals who gather data regarding a child's functioning in many areas, in order to understand his or her strengths and weaknesses.
- Parents play a vital role on this team and need to be included in every step of the special education process.
- The data assessed by the MDT will provide recommendations in order to plan an appropriate educational program through which the child can be successful.
- School counselors have unique skills that can help facilitate the special education process and enable parents to feel heard and affirmed.

ADDITIONAL RESOURCES

Print

Bartlett, L., Etscheidt, S., & Weisenstein, G. (2007). *School education law and practice in public schools* (2nd ed.). Upper Saddle River, NJ: Pearson Higher Education.

Fisher, G., & Cummings, R. *The survival guide for kids with LD*(*Learning differences)* (Revised and updated). Minneapolis, MN: Free Spirit.

Friend, M. (2010). *Special education: Contemporary perspectives for school professionals* (3rd ed.). Upper Saddle River, NJ: Pearson Higher Education.

Turnbull, A., Turnbull, H., Erwin, E., Soodak, L., & Shogren, K. (2015). *Families, professionals, and exceptionality: Positive outcomes through partnerships and trust*. Upper Saddle River, NJ: Pearson Higher Education.

Web Based

U.S. Department of Education's *504 Plans: Free appropriate public education for students with disabilities: Requirements under Section 504 of The Rehabilitation Act of 1973*: http://www2 .ed.gov/about/offices/list/ocr/docs/edlite-FAPE504.html

This site provides information on eligibility for a 504 plan and possible services which are available to those with a 504 plan.

Education World: http://www.educationworld.com/a_special/parent_involvement.shtml

An array of ideas and strategies for connecting parents to school are found on this site.

Great Schools: http://www.greatschools.org/special-education/legal-rights/666-special-education-evaluation-an-overview.gs

This site provides an overview of the purpose, procedures, and laws for evaluating a child for special education services.

IDEA: http://idea.ed.gov/

The Individuals with Disabilities Education Act is explored and explained on this site.

National Center for Learning Disabilities: http://www.ncld.org

This site offers news, events, information, and resources for learning disabilities.

National Dissemination Center for Children with Disabilities (NICHCY): http://www.nichcy.org

Site provides publications and training curriculum for children with disabilities.

REFERENCES

American School Counselor Association (ASCA). (2012). *The ASCA National Model: A framework for school counseling programs* (3rd ed.). Alexandria, VA: Author.

Auger, R. (2006). Delivering difficult news to parents: Guidelines for school counselors. *Professional School Counseling, 10*(2), 139–145.

Center on Response to Intervention at American Institutes for Research. (2007). *Essential components of RTI—A closer look at response to intervention.* Retrieved from http://www.rti4success .org/essential-components-rti/universal-screening

Council for Accreditation of Counseling and Related Educational Programs (CACREP). (2009). *2009 Standards.* Retrieved from http://www.cacrep.org/wp-content/uploads/2013/12/2009-Standards.pdf

Cummings, K., Atkins, T., Allison, R., & Cole, C., (2008). Response to intervention: Investigating the new role of special educators. *Teaching Exceptional Children, 40*(4), 24–31.

Küpper, L. (2011). *Communicating with your child's school through letter writing.* (Parent's Guide 9). Washington, DC: National Dissemination Center for Children with Disabilities (NICHCY). Retrieved from http://www.nichcy.org/schoolage/steps/

Martin, D. (2012). What is a functional assessment? Retrieved from Alberta Council of Disability Service (ACDS) website: www.acds.ca

Milsom, A. (2007). Interventions to assist students with disabilities through school transitions. *Professional School Counseling, 10*(3), 273–278.

Milsom, A., Goodnough, G., & Akos, P. (2007). School counselor contributions to the Individualized Education Program (IEP) process. *Preventing School Failure, 52*(1), 19–24.

National Center on Response to Intervention (NCRTI). (2010). *Essential components of RTI—A closer look at response to intervention.* Retrieved from http://www.rti4success.org/sites/default/files/rtiessentialcomponents_042710.pdf

National Dissemination Center for Children with Disabilities. (2014). Retrieved from www .nichcy.org

New York State Education Department. (2002). *Special education in New York State for children ages 3–21: A parent's guide.* Retrieved from http://www.p12.nysed.gov/specialed/publications/policy/parentguide.htm#cpse/cse

Plymouth-Canton Community Schools, Michigan. (2011). Home page: Special education—Tanger Center. Retrieved from http://specialeducation.pccs.k12.mi.us/

U.S. Department of Education. (2006a). *Building the legacy: IDEA 2004.* Retrieved from http://idea.ed.gov/

U.S. Department of Education. (2006b). IDEA Regulations, identification of specific learning disabilities. Retrieved from http://www.ideapartnership.org/index.php?option=com_content&view=article&id=844&oseppage=1

U.S. Department of Education. (2010). *Free appropriate public education for students with disabilities: Requirements under Section 504 of the Rehabilitation Act of 1973.* Retrieved from http://www2.ed.gov/about/offices/list/ocr/docs/edlite-FAPE504.html

U.S. Department of Education. (2014). About ED: Office of Special Education and Rehabilitative Services. Retrieved from http://www2.ed.gov/about/offices/list/osers/index.html

Chapter 6

Family Perspectives and Home-School Collaboration

KAREN DICKINSON
West Chester University

VICKI A. McGINLEY
West Chester University

> *"The central struggle of parenthood is to let our hopes for our children outweigh our fears."*
>
> —Ellen Goodman

All parents have hopes and dreams for their children, and expectations may be high when children are first born. For those parents who are told their child has a disability, life changes in an instant. There are many feelings parents may experience as their journey takes on a new path, and struggles that were not anticipated may make that journey more difficult than expected. Having a child with a disability in the family can impact the whole family dynamic as well. This chapter will investigate how the child and the disability are perceived within their family, and how that affects the family and the home-school relationship.

Attention is given to the grief process of the family in Chapter 12. This chapter will examine family issues in more depth such as taking a personal look at how parents view the school and educational journey in relation to their child with special needs. You will notice that families with a child with a disability are impacted in different ways. We will examine how parental perspectives may help or hinder this journey. The attitudes of school personnel who work with children with disabilities can also have quite an impact on the success of these children. We will look specifically at how school counselors can be supportive to the family and be an integral part of this journey.

Specifically, after reading this chapter you will be able to determine the following:

- Identify differences in how parents feel about and perceive their child's disability.
- Name at least two ways that collaboration between parents and the school counselor can promote the child's success.
- State at least three ways the school counselor can help support the parents and siblings of a child with a disability.

In the next section, factors within the family constellation and dynamics which can impact them are discussed.

FAMILY DYNAMICS

When children are in our purview at school, it behooves us to remember that their families are a large part of who they are, how they act, and who they are becoming. With family counseling typically beyond the scope of the school counselor role and access to family information and engagement often limited, the more school counselors can ascertain how the family is responding to the child with a disability and what their expectations and needs are, the better able the school counselors are to assist the child with special needs in the educational arena. A starting point is obtaining a glimpse into the world of families with a child with special needs and the sensitivity to some of their universal strain.

Counseling students with disabilities and their families in a systems-oriented way can improve relationships among family members and between the family and other systems in which the family interacts (Thomas & Ray, 2006). The school counselor may see the school system contributing to a family's situation and be able to intervene and support by adding more information to the discussion or help to change the context of the problem by identifying and affirming feelings or reframing the situation. Using systems-oriented counseling consists of assessing the family for its perspectives of the disability and family interactions, as well as providing strategies or techniques for change. By using systems-based models, such as the Belin-Blank Center model, the structural-strategic model, and the imaginative-postmodern model, school counselors can better understand the dynamics of the family and be able to make appropriate referrals for family counseling, if appropriate (Thomas & Ray, 2006).

When parents first learn their child has a disability, they may feel alone while grappling with an alternative view of their child's development and future. Discovering your child has a disability may close the doors to some expectations, or it may alter a path on the journey. A myriad of feelings may be felt when parents learn of a disability. There may be denial, fear, and confusion.

Parents may be ready to accept their child with special needs, or they may have great difficulty in doing so (Leyser & Kirk, 2011). Dreams for the future may be altered or shattered. When parents are hesitant to admit that their child may learn or act differently, it can cause pressure in the family and stress on the child and can hinder the identification of the disability and the ability to implement interventions. Case Illustration 6.1 is an example of what may happen when parents do not accept their child's disability.

CASE ILLUSTRATION 6.1

I DON'T WANT TO HEAR IT!

This example shows how difficult it can be for parents to accept the diagnosis of a disability. The MDE recommendation is that Marcus has a specific learning disability in reading and the MDT has gathered to decide if Marcus is eligible for special education. Marcus's parents, Drs. Rita and Mark Robbins, are both in attendance. The following is a conversation at the MDE meeting.

Dr. Rita Robbins (Marcus's mother): I don't care what the report says, I know that Marcus does not have a disability and does not need special education. He just needs more time to learn. And that classroom has way too many distractions, so of course he can't concentrate.

Dr. Mark Robbins (Marcus's father): Right. I remember students in special education going to a room and never seeing them all day. Marcus is a social boy, and he is well behaved. There's no way he has a learning disability, he's smart!

Counselor: This sounds like it's hard for you to believe, and it may be disappointing for you. It is true that Marcus does have very good ability to

(Continued)

(Continued)

> learn; however, as hard as he is trying, he is not making good progress. I imagine it must be frustrating for him, and you.

Dr. Mark Robbins: Absolutely, he is capable! I was in the gifted program when I was in school, and I see a lot of me in Marcus. There must be something wrong with the way you all are teaching him.

Dr. Rita Robbins: He's right! Marcus's grandfather is a recognized scholar, and Marcus says he wants to be just like him!

School Psychologist: We would like Marcus and you to continue to have goals for his long-term success in school. For now, we need to look at developing a plan that allows Marcus to learn and remember what he learns without so much difficulty.

Dr. Mark Robbins: We want that, too. Couldn't you do that without calling him disabled?

This conversation shows how sensitive school personnel need to be to parents when discussing their child and his or her disability. Parents may feel like all their plans for their child have come to a screeching halt and, at times, may be embarrassed by the fact that their child has a disability.

In addition, each member of a family impacts the whole family. Thus, when one member has special needs or requires extra attention, the entire family is affected. Homeostasis of the family is altered, compounding the day-to-day stressors with which most families are confronted. While all parents are concerned with childrearing and education, parents of children with disabilities have additional duties and concerns related to the disabilities (Taub, 2006), for example, work and school schedules, household chores, activities, and appointments. As such, siblings and extended family members may be involved in child care and take on the role of the main caregiver at points. This role transition could trigger issues with family members in regard to boundaries, similar to that of being a stepparent. When a child with a disability is a member of the family, numerous additional stressors may be added. For example, parents may be stressed time-wise, psychologically, and financially as they encounter conflicts between work expectations and the need to spend a good deal of time at specialist appointments, which can also interfere with work (Murphy, Christian, Caplin, & Young, 2006). This stress can be exacerbated if coworkers and supervisors are not permitted to leave for child care responsibilities, as per the request of the parent of a child with a disability, and instead face insensitivity and ultimatums.

In addition, the child's disability may impact the family life in broader ways such as issues related to having children with serious behavioral and/or medical concerns.

Parental time and energy may need to be devoted to the child with the disability, leaving little time for family fun, siblings' needs, or parental relaxation. Getting a break, such as arranging for respite care breaks from 24-hour duties, can be difficult (Murphy et al., 2006) as respite care services may be limited in the area where the family resides and/or finding qualified persons to provide respite care may be difficult due to the child's needs as a result of his or her disability. As a result of the day-to-day demands, these parents may experience more burnout, and they often will have less energy to devote to educational and transition concerns by the time their child with special needs reaches adolescence. Guided Practice Exercise 6.1 invites you to personally explore how families are impacted by a child with special needs.

In the next section, some voices of families are heard in order to enhance the awareness of school counselors as to some of the experiences and roadblocks these families may face.

Guided Practice Exercise 6.1

HOW ARE FAMILIES IMPACTED BY A CHILD WITH SPECIAL NEEDS?

Interview a parent(s) who has a child with special needs. Explore how the parent felt when learning the child had a disability as well as current feelings and thoughts about living with the child with a disability. The following questions may help to lead the discussion:

1. What are some of the thoughts and feelings you had when you learned your child had a disability? How about currently?

2. How do you feel your family has been impacted by your child's disability?

3. What are some of your expectations for your child?

4. How do you think your other children have been impacted by your child's disability?

Bring your information back to class for a group discussion on the various feelings parents have and the many ways families are impacted by a child with a disability.

Voices of Families

There is much more to a child than a child's disability. Oftentimes, the discussions between parents and the school team are focused on the diagnosis. While it is important to understand the diagnosis, parents want others in the school to know and discuss more about their child than just a diagnosis; they want to share their hopes for and understand the capabilities of their children (Leyser & Kirk, 2011). Several examples of personal communications the first coauthor had with several parents of children with special needs, which illustrate these points, are now shared.

One parent explained: "We don't like to hear all negatives or problems or 'can't.' We want to hear what worked, what you'll try next and that you recognize our child's strengths" (B. Siegel, personal communication, January 14, 2014). Another parent made a resounding appeal, "Yes, emphasize the strengths and the progress!" (T. Everitt, personal communication, January 20, 2014). This theme sounds like it would be easy to accomplish; however, with time constraints and coverage issues for meetings, school teams do not always take the time to begin and end discussions with strengths and celebrations. In addition, the day-to-day strain of a child's challenging behavior in school may deplete the ability of school staff to focus on positives; thus, *baby steps* of progress may be overlooked.

In other situations, not only do parents accept their child, but they want also to help other parents understand the special gifts their child can bring to the world. One parent shared, "From a parent perspective, I would love to reassure other parents of younger children . . . I would encourage them to have their children with special needs to do the same things as their siblings do, whether it's household chores, sports, or extracurricular activities. These activities may need to be modified, but it can be done. It may take longer for our children to learn to do some things, but many of them will get it" (B. Siegel, personal communication, January 14, 2014).

Another area that parents address frequently is their need to protect their child. Many parents may become overprotective of their child with disabilities. Sheltering them may avoid short-term pain (e.g., from rejection, from bullies, from failure), but alternately, the avoidance of these situations may end up slowing their development and their ability to deal with life's challenges.

Issues discussed in the prior communications between parents and professionals were similar to themes identified in a study done by McGinley and Wandry (2013). This research involved an innovative program whereby graduate students in a family systems course were placed with host families with a child with a disability. The following questions were posed to host mentor parents during focus groups:

- In what ways do students and families benefit from the mentoring partnership?
- How can a graduate course on working with families be enhanced to meet the dynamic needs of the family-teacher partnership?
- What suggestions do you have for students to effectively work with parents?

As stated previously, many of the themes identified in this study supported the prior parental comments. Examples of these themes follow:

- Increased exposure to and awareness of challenges for children and parents outside of the classroom
- Development of an appreciation for the value of life skills within curriculum
- Establishment of a holistic understanding of the life of a child with disabilities and their family
- Recognition of the interaction between home life and what occurs at school

In addition, there was much discussion in this study around the topics of bullying and medication, as these are at the root of many issues that parents and their children with disabilities faced frequently. Parents shared that because of their child's disability, their child was targeted by bullies, yet teachers could not always substantiate the bullying behaviors of their students, and parents did not always want the information disclosed. Along similar lines, changes in medication often contributed to changes in their child's behavior and temperament. In Table 6.1 are illustrated some of the conversations shared by the parents in this study; these discussions illustrate and provide further support for the need of the communication and collaboration between parents and schools.

In summary, listening to parental voices gives us an understanding of how important it is to work with parents' expectations, hopes, and dreams and to understand their challenges.

As school counselors, it is essential that (a) we listen to parental expectations, (b) work with the MDT to move those parental and student expectations into reality, and (c) help parents realize different hopes and dreams if the original ones are not obtainable due to the limits of the child or school resources. Before moving on to the focus on the school piece of the partnership, it is important to acknowledge the needs of siblings of students with disabilities in the next section.

Sibling Impact

Parents are not the only members of the family impacted by a student with disabilities. In a study done by Macks and Reeve (2007), which compared and explored the adjustment of siblings of children with autism and siblings of nondisabled

Table 6.1   Families' Voices

"I think a big part is to help them realize that even more so than with neurologically typical kids, you're teaching kids things they are going to use in real life, *and really to think about the kids' life outside of school and it's not about how did they score on the reading test or do they know when the revolutionary war was fought. It's about can you—if you're giving written directions, can you follow them, if you're given a map, can you follow it . . . it's life and I think that was one of the greatest things about having the grad student with us over the summer was unless the students have people with special needs in their own lives, they probably don't really get how pervasive this is and to be able to see the kids in different environments and see* what works and what doesn't *work and the sort of problems that they face—I think that gives the grad students a more* holistic view *of the kids."*

—Parent of a child with intellectual disabilities

"I think it's perfectly appropriate to ask me, 'how did you feel when your son was diagnosed?' I think what they need to be prepared for is it's a very emotional topic. I had one apologizing for making me cry and it's like, no you didn't make me cry, the memories made me cry—so they need to be prepared for that . . . none of the questions were intrusive . . . they all seemed to make perfect sense within the context of the class . . ."

—Parent of a child with intellectual disabilities

"Use the parents as resources because we are walking encyclopedias not only of our kids' disabilities, but of their abilities *and what programs work and what programs don't work so we're such an* invaluable resource *and we are always very willing to share."*

—Parent of a student with dyslexia, ADHD, and anxiety

"It's ok to ask if the student is on medication . . . my daughter's teacher emailed me 'she's like really, really sleepy in the morning' and I wrote her back well one of the side effects of her medication is tiredness, can you please let me know if there are certain periods where she's tired so I can tell her doctor."

—Parent with a student with emotional disturbance

children and explored parental reports, results indicated that the presence of a child with autism appears to enhance the psychosocial and emotional development of nondisabled siblings when environmental risk factors are limited. However, the presence of a child with autism increases an unfavorable impact on a nondisabled sibling as environmental risk factors increase.

Day-to-day environmental factors may be impacted for siblings of children with disabilities; thus, they may have to make adjustments to their activities and schedules. Parents may need to spend extra time in relation to their child with a disability by going to meetings, support services or therapies, or helping the child with daily tasks and schoolwork. Imagine having a sibling with a disability and always hearing about his or her behavior, or progress, or having to always go to his or her appointments. School plays and sports events of the children who are typically developing may be missed. How might the siblings feel?

In a study done by Begum and Blacher (2011), sibling relationship of adolescents with and without intellectual disabilities was examined via parental report. Results revealed that for typically developing adolescents, mothers reported more warmth in the sibling relationship for opposite sex dyads but status or power differences when the sibling was younger. However, for adolescents with intellectual disabilities, mothers reported more warmth in sibling relationship for same sex dyads, while birth order did not affect status or power in the sibling relationship.

Siblings will need to learn how to cope with living with a sibling with a disability, yet their needs and feelings also need to be addressed. As one parent shared, "Being in middle school with a sibling with a disability is not fun. Being a parent of those two children is not fun either. My daughter wanted to be like everyone else, and having a 'special' brother made her feel very different. Being different or feeling different is the horrible plague of middle school. As a result, she did not always treat her brother well while she was in middle school, and he started avoiding her instead of giving her the endless hugs which happened in elementary school. This was a painful time for all" (B. Siegel, personal communication, January 14, 2014).

It is also important for parents to recognize and acknowledge the positive reactions of the sibling toward the brother or sister with a disability. For example, one parent explained, "I remember when my daughter was in late elementary school and my son was in first or second grade. My son still gave his sister a huge hug and told her he loved her every time he saw her. My daughter's friends would witness this and tell her how lucky she was that her little brother treated her that way since their little brothers never did that" (B. Siegel, personal communication, January 14, 2014).

Therefore, an additional focus of school counselors is to be aware of and address the needs of the siblings of students with disabilities. Running small groups for such children is an ideal way that school counselors may be supportive. Small groups can empower siblings by developing a greater understanding of and empathy for the sibling with a disability, while affirming the nondisabled sibling's feelings. The Sibshops Curriculum (Meyer & Vadasy, 2008) provides opportunities for siblings of children with disability to connect and obtain peer support and education within a recreational format. School counselors are provided with a curriculum guide, which is easy to implement and is a great solution for addressing the siblings' needs. The following case illustration, 6.2, is an example of how a small counseling group could benefit students who have a sibling with a disability.

CASE ILLUSTRATION 6.2

MY BROTHER IS SO FRUSTRATING!

This case shares examples of the perspectives from siblings of children with a disability and how the school counselor can help reflect feelings and encourage healthy coping skills in a group setting.

Ms. Santoro (School Counselor): Thank you all for coming back to group this week. Last week you all shared what disabilities your brothers and sisters are challenged by and how it affects your families.

Leo: Yea! Jerry's therapies and appointments make all of us change our schedules, and it always has to be what he needs first. I always have to find a ride to my baseball practice.

Ms. Santoro: That sounds like it can be very frustrating, Leo. Does anyone else feel like that?

Amelia: Well, I can take the schedule revolving around Eddie, but does he have to be so embarrassing? He is so frustrating! He says things that make people mad all the time. Can't he just be quiet?!

Ben: Yea! Just because Eddie has Asperger's syndrome doesn't mean he has to be nasty, does it?

Leo: Geez, my friends don't even like to come to my house because they don't know what my brother will do next. We never go out as a family. In fact, my parents don't ever have a chance to go out at all.

Ms. Santoro: It does sound like many of you not only have to deal with a demanding family schedule, but you are also dealing with situations in which you are frustrated by your sibling's behavior. It may be a good idea to use today's group to discuss how to cope with your sibling's behavior and how to deal with your friend's reactions.

Leo: That would be great!

The school counselor facilitates the discussion to elicit examples of solutions that have worked for the group members in the past. The realization that members are not alone in their frustration helps to affirm feelings, and the ideas for coping become very supportive. In addition, the school counselor hands out community resource ideas for the students to bring home to their families, which includes support groups for parents and agencies that have child care for children with disabilities.

In this discussion, an overview of family dynamics and perspectives of having a child with a disability was reviewed. These responses can impact the nature of the home-school collaboration, which is addressed in the next section.

HOME-SCHOOL COLLABORATION

Overview

The Education for All Handicapped Children Act in 1975 and additional amendments in 1987 (PL 99-457) are legislative efforts that by their very nature involved family-school partnerships. As a result of these mandated educational services, parents and school professionals have been placed into relationships that require communication between the home and school in order to achieve the best interests of the child (Turnbull, Turnbull, & Wehmeyer, 2009).

Effective parent-professional collaboration has been shown to improve outcomes for students with disabilities (Whitbread, Bruder, Fleming, & Park, 2007). When school counselors establish effective communication with family members, their mutual knowledge and expertise can be shared as a vehicle to advance the child's success. When examining the collaboration of parents of children with disabilities and school personnel, trust is a key factor and may be a key ingredient in establishing positive student achievement (Martin, 2004; Smith, Hoy, & Sweetland, 2001). Lack of trust may result in hesitation from parents to accept suggestions from professionals and potentially less than adequate services for the child (Lake & Billingsley, 2000). In contrast, positive relationships can result in more parental input, which is particularly important in multidisciplinary (MDT) meetings (Turnbull et al., 2009).

Building positive parent-professional relationships is important for the student's success in school and for the student's future outside of the school system. For example, transition planning is a critical step in ensuring future success outside of the classroom and in everyday life once the student graduates. Transition planning works to improve the quality of life of not only the student but also of their family. Therefore, it is necessary to consider the family when implementing services (Ankeny, Wilkins, & Spain, 2009). Research in transition planning has shown that family participation and student self-determination are linked with increased graduation rates, employment, and achievement of positive postschool outcomes (Mason, McGahee-Kovac, Johnson, & Stillerman, 2002; Wehmeyer & Palmer, 2003). By developing important parent-professional relationships as early as possible, both groups will be better equipped to provide the needed support to the student throughout his or her academic journey and set the foundation for a smoother transitional planning process.

As previously discussed, improving communication and the partnership between the school counselor and parents are associated with educational advantages for the student (Whitbread et al., 2007). Therefore, it is important to have specific strategies in order to effectively engage parents in the decision-making process, to follow through, and to establish conflict resolution approaches that will assist all parties to work together for the greatest benefit of the student (Martin, 2004).

The importance of this collaboration has been empirically addressed. In one study, the results of a survey of deans of colleges of education found that while almost 90% felt parent-school collaboration was important, only 30% felt their graduates were well prepared to work with parents (Flanigan, 2005). A subsequent study of 116 schools, colleges, and departments of education revealed concerns that most graduates were not prepared to successfully initiate and engage in parent and community partnerships (Epstein & Sanders, 2006). The sampled group of deans also felt that graduates were too judgmental toward families and, to an extent, blamed parents' lack of care for their child's difficulties (Flanigan, 2005).

The significance of parent-school collaborations to the success of the student has been further supported by various professional and accrediting organizations. The national professional organization for school counselors, the American School Counselors Association (ASCA), has included several standards to reflect the importance of collaborating with parents to promote and support student success. For example, the school counselors' role is to not only be able to engage parents to collaborate with them on their children's development but also to know strategies and methods for working with parents in order to empower the parents to act on behalf of their children.

In addition, school counselors are expected to demonstrate competence in the development and conduction of parent trainings and workshops designed to enhance student success (American School Counselor Association [ASCA], 2012). Similarly, the accrediting body for academic institutions that train counselors, the Council for Accreditation of Counseling and Related Educational Programs (CACREP), calls for the engagement of parents in order to enhance teamwork with school professionals in an attempt to promote the success of students. Similar to the ASCA mission of parental empowerment, school counselors in training are expected to learn interventions that will assist all parties, parents and the community alike, to advocate for students with disabilities (Council for Accreditation of Counseling and Related Educational Programs [CACREP], 2009). For example, school counselors could contact community resources that specialize in communication programs to train school staff and parents on devices that help children with auditory processing disorders. School counselors could also support parents by providing workshops to give strategies for behavior management and connecting parents who have children with disabilities, so they can network and not feel alone.

In this section, the essential nature of parent-school collaboration has been highlighted. This collaborative effort is needed in order to enhance the potential for maximum educational success of the student with a disability. The specifics that are involved in this collaborative endeavor are further delineated in the next section.

Working With Families

In the prior section, an overview of the home-school collaboration was shared. In this section, specifications as to how school counselors can assist families of students with disabilities are addressed.

As previously stated, parents may be on different places on the spectrum regarding the acknowledgment and comprehension of their child's disability. School counselors can begin to help parents by helping parents to understand and accept their child's disability. This most likely entails consultation with medical resources, discussion of possible school services, referrals to outside services, and/or linkage with parental supports. In addition, it is essential that parents have a clear understanding of the MDT. The school counselor, in collaboration with the school's special education director and the school psychologist, can help with this endeavor.

Different levels of parental involvement in regard to determination of special education eligibility and the planning process have also been reported. There can be many reasons for this differential involvement such as lack of understanding; feeling overwhelmed, helpless, or not heard; and/or struggling with one's own issues. The more that parents can be involved in this process, the better. This level of participation can make a huge difference in parents either feeling like something is "being done" to the child and family, or feeling like they have an advocate (Hess, Molina, & Kozleski, 2006). Making sure that parents are aware and knowledgeable regarding the special education process will help to lead to a more successful program.

As previously mentioned, communication is vital to understanding the special education process. This is particularly important when using educational terms. One mother of a child with disabilities explained it this way: "Be aware of inadvertent misunderstanding, especially with 'special education jargon.' Sometimes parents don't understand the definitions of the terminology used, and whenever possible, jargon should be 'translated' into layman's terms to ensure the understanding amongst the entire team" (B. Siegel, personal communication, January 14, 2014). This will invite conversation and questions without worrying about feeling inadequate due to not knowing the vocabulary and terms. This same parent also offered this advice concerning communication: "If there are ever questions or apparent disagreements, ask the team to describe the behavior." Instead of "Tommy doesn't understand," it is more helpful to say, "Tommy starts tapping his pencil and humming."

Another way to maintain parental input involves the scheduling of such MDT meetings. Parents have to be informed of these meetings, and arrangements must be made for pertinent school staff to attend. A father of a child with disabilities expressed his satisfaction with the fact that the school counselor or case manager "makes sure everyone always knows about and can attend the meeting, or gets input from those who cannot attend" (B. Everitt, personal communication, January 20, 2014). It is important to gain input from everyone who works with the student, so progress in every area can be monitored, and new goals can be established. Making every effort to secure a meeting time when the most team members are available will make a more productive meeting. This parent reminds us that "parents may want to make meetings, but find it hard to always take off of work." Another parent provided further insight, "Be willing to be flexible when parents are stressed about losing their job due to the amount of time they take off because of their child with special needs. I know of at least three people who have lost their jobs because of [the] time demand of their children and missing work" (B. Siegel, personal communication, January 14, 2014). Schools need to be cognizant of the demands such as employment that may impact the capacity to parent effectively (Broomhead, 2013). Flexibility in meeting the needs of parents regarding meeting times and devoting time to communication and understanding will be beneficial to the student and entire team. Remember that by starting a meeting with signs of growth and progress, and with an anecdote in which care for the student is shown, will help to set the tone for a more positive interaction and lower defenses. Doing this will show the parent that you know and care for their child and are not just getting through some paperwork. School counselors, as can be seen in the prior discussion, have many roles in working with families. These professionals can also be of service to their colleagues in the school in working with students with disabilities. This role is addressed in the next section.

Working With School Educators/Staff

Not all teachers are comfortable having children with disabilities in their class. There are already many demands on teachers due to new curriculum and testing, which could increase stress. Inclusive education often causes extra work, and it could create behavioral issues in the classroom for the teacher. In addition, not every teacher has been prepared to work with individuals with special needs. This training has been tied to teacher responses to children with disabilities. In one study, attitudes of teachers working with children with disabilities were found to be more favorable when teachers had training and were more knowledgeable about special education (Gokdere, 2012). School counselors can assist in this area by the provision of continuing education workshops that deal with sensitivity to and awareness of disability.

Counseling students with disabilities and their families in a systems-oriented way can improve relationships among family members and between the family and other systems in which the family interacts (Thomas & Ray, 2006). The school counselor may see the school system contributing to a family's situation and be able to intervene and support by adding more information to the discussion or help to change the context of the problem by identifying and affirming feelings or reframing the situation. Using systems-oriented counseling consists of assessing the family members for their perspectives of the disability and family interactions, as well as providing strategies, or techniques, for change. By using systems-based models, such as the Belin-Blank Center model, the structural-strategic model, and the imaginative-postmodern model, school counselors can better understand the dynamics of the family and be able to make appropriate referrals for family counseling, if appropriate (Thomas & Ray, 2006). Both of these models, which were developed and adapted for use with gifted students, due to their flexibility have been applied to the population of students with disabilities, viewing family systems issues from a developmental perspective.

Additionally, school counselors can draw from their training and conduct needs assessments to identify potential areas for needed change in order to create a more positive classroom environment for students with disabilities as well as to convey important information to the teacher about potential modifications and knowledge about the disability. In collaboration with other school personnel, such as administrators, school psychologists, and social workers, they can also help to establish school policies that communicate respect, high expectations, and interest in equitable outcomes for *all* students (Milsom, 2006).

Above all, children with disabilities want to fit in, and their parents want a school environment where their child is accepted and welcomed and has an opportunity to learn with children who do not have special needs (Hess et al., 2006). One student with disabilities remarked, "I just want to fit in, and have friends and have people like me . . . I don't like to be around bullies" (B. Siegel, personal communication, January 14, 2014). School counselors can be helpful in providing activities to encourage understanding of differences and prevent intolerance behavior, such as name calling and relational aggression. By teaching about diversity, cooperation, and conflict resolution in classroom psycho-educational lessons, children will have a deeper appreciation of differences in people. In returning to the communications that occurred with parents, one suggested that the counselor provide "training for the whole school" when a student has a disability for which the staff is not familiar. She added on to that idea by pointing out, "This is really important for 'hidden disabilities' where a student can look 'normal' but still be struggling; such as children with a mild hearing loss, auditory processing disorder, traumatic brain injury or on the autism spectrum" (B. Siegel, personal communication, January 14, 2014).

In the course of one author's tenure as a school counselor, many parents remarked that when the school counselor worked with their child to do a classroom presentation regarding the child's disability, it made a world of difference in the understanding and accepting of their child.

SUMMARY

Having a child with disabilities affects the entire family in many ways. As a school counselor, it is vital to remember you can support not only the student but also the parents, siblings, educators, and staff. Your comprehensive counseling program can include training for parents to help with behavioral, academic(s), and career planning for their child. It can also include individual and/or group counseling for the student with a disability and for siblings. Additionally, school counselors can assist with the establishment of connections with community support services and referral networks.

Using your active listening skills, you can hear the concerns and the desires of the parents and help them understand the program that is designed for their child to be successful. Taking the time to involve parents in every step of their child's educational journey will build a strong relationship between the school and home. Remember that the language and the process of special education can be confusing and, at times, frustrating or upsetting. Listen to parents' thoughts and affirm their feelings, being careful to not reinforce inappropriate or unrealistic expectations. Make sure parents understand what is being said and what is being planned. You can set the stage for a welcoming, positive experience for children with disabilities and their families. Help the school climate to be one of acceptance and understanding, and the journey will be an exciting one!

KEYSTONES

- Families with children with disabilities are impacted in many and various ways.
- School counselors can be supportive of families by affirming feelings and being cognizant of work schedules when planning meetings.
- School counselors can support siblings of children with disabilities by providing group counseling opportunities for the siblings.
- Raising awareness of disabilities and how families are impacted is a task that the school counselor can help with by providing training to school staff and faculty.
- Creating a climate of acceptance and tolerance for all diverse learners can be achieved through professional development opportunities for the staff and faculty, and through the developmental guidance curriculum for the students.

ADDITIONAL RESOURCES

Print

Graves, J., & Graves, C. (2014). *Parents have the power to make special education work: An insider guide.* Philadelphia, PA: Jessica Kingsley. ISBN: 978-1-84905-970-1
  A guide for parents for understanding the special education process and programs in schools.

Lavoie, R., Reiner, M., Reiner, R., & Levine, M. (2006). *It's so much work to be your friend: Helping the child with learning disabilities find social success.* New York, NY: Touchstone. ISBN 9780743254656.
  Information and strategies for understanding and improving social skills for children with special needs.

Whiteman, N., & Roan-Yager, L. (2007). *Building a joyful life with your child who has special needs.* Philadelphia, PA: Jessica Kingsley: ISBN-13: 9781843108412; ISBN-10: 1843108410.
  Passages written by parents of children with special needs help bring understanding and acceptance to raising children with disabilities.

Web Based

American School Counselor Association: http://www.schoolcounselor.org

This site provides the student standards recommended for school counselors to follow, as well as research and practical-based resources to use in school and with families.

Family Voices: http://www.familyvoices.org

Family Voices focuses on a family perspective to improve health care programs and policies and ensure that health care systems include, listen to, and honor the voices of families.

Federation for Children with Special Needs: http://fcsn.org/

A website to inform, educate, and empower families with children with special needs.

National Association of School Psychologists: http://www.nasponline.org

The website for school psychologists has links to many resources for working with parents.

Our-Kids: http://www.our-kids.org/

Our-Kids is a "Family" of parents, caregivers, and others who are working with children with physical and/or mental disabilities and delays.

Parenting Children with Special Needs: http://specialchildren.about.com/

Links and resources for supporting children with special needs.

Parenting Special Needs: http://parentingspecialneeds.org/

Helps parents navigate the uncharted waters of raising a special needs child by providing practical tips, sharing life's lessons, and sharing how to tackle challenges.

REFERENCES

American School Counselor Association (ASCA). (2012). *The ASCA National Model: A framework for school counseling programs* (3rd ed.). Alexandria, VA: Author.

Ankeny, E. M., Wilkins, J., & Spain, J. (2009). Mothers' experiences of transition planning for their children with disabilities. *Teaching Exceptional Children, 41*(6), 26–36.

Begum, G., & Blacher, J. (2011). The siblings relationship of adolescents with and without intellectual disabilities. *Research in Developmental Disabilities, 32*(5), 1580–1588.

Broomhead, K. (2013). Blame, guilt and the needs for "labels": Insights from parents of children with special educational needs and educational practitioners. *British Journal of Special Education, 40*(1), 14–21.

Council for Accreditation of Counseling and Related Educational Programs (CACREP). (2009). Welcome to CACREP. Retrieved from http://www.cacrep.org/template/index.cfm

Epstein, J. L., & Sanders, M. G. (2006). Prospects for change: Preparing educators for school, family, and community partnerships. *Peabody Journal of Education, 81*(2), 81–120.

Flanigan, C. B. (2005). *Partnering with parents and communities: Are preservice teachers adequately prepared?* Cambridge, MA: Harvard Family Research Project.

Gokdere, M. (2012). A comparative study of the attitude, concern, and interaction levels of elementary school teachers and teacher candidates toward inclusive education. *Educational Sciences: Theory and Practice, 12*(4), 2800–2806.

Hess, R., Molina, A., & Kozleski, E. (2006). Until somebody hears me: Parent voice and advocacy in special education decision making. *British Journal of Special Education, 33*(3), 148–157.

Lake, J. F., & Billingsley, B. S. (2000). An analysis of factors that contribute to parent-school conflict in special education. *Remedial and Special Education, 21*(4), 240–252.

Leyser, Y., & Kirk, R. (2011). Parents' perspectives on inclusion and schooling of students with Angelman syndrome: Suggestions for educators. *International Journal of Special Education, 26*(2), 79–91.

Macks, R. J., & Reeve, R. E. (2007). The adjustment of non-disabled siblings of children with autism. *Journal of Autism and Developmental Disorders, 37*, 1060–1067.

Martin, N. R. M. (2004). *Strengthening relationships: When our children have special needs.* Arlington, TX: Future Horizons.

Mason, C. Y., McGahee-Kovac, M., Johnson, L., & Stillerman, S. (2002). Implementing student-led IEP's: Student participation and student and teacher reaction. *Career Development for Exceptional Individuals, 25*(2), 171–192.

McGinley, V. A., & Wandry, D. (2013, July). *Families views on the teacher personnel preparation curriculum.* Paper presented at the IASE Conference, July 6–11, Vancouver, Canada.

Meyer, D. J., & Vadasy, P. F. (2008). *The Sibshop Curriculum—Sibshops: Workshops for siblings of children with special needs.* Baltimore: Paul H. Brookes.

Milsom, A. (2006). Creating positive school experiences for students with disabilities. *Professional School Counseling, 10*(1), 66–71.

Murphy, N. A., Christian, D. B., Caplin, D. A., & Young, P. C. (2006). The health of caregivers for children with disabilities: Caregiver perspectives. *Child Care Health and Development, 33*, 180–187.

Smith, P., Hoy, W., & Sweetland, S. (2001). Organizational health of high schools and dimensions of faculty trust. *Journal of School Leadership, 11*(2), 135–151.

Taub, D. (2006). Understanding the concerns of parents of students with disabilities: Challenges and roles for school counselors. *Professional School Counseling, 10*(1), 52–57.

Thomas, V., & Ray, K. (2006). Counseling exceptional individuals and their families: A systems perspective. *Professional School Counseling, 10*(1), 58–65.

Turnbull, A., Turnbull, R., & Wehmeyer, M. L. (2009). *Exceptional lives: Special exceptional lives: Special education in today's schools* (6th ed.). Upper Saddle River, NJ: Merrill.

Wehmeyer, M. L., & Palmer, S. B. (2003). Adult outcomes for students with cognitive disabilities three years after high school: The impact of self-determination. *Education and Training in Developmental Disabilities, 38*(2), 131–144.

Whitbread, K. M., Bruder, M. B., Fleming, G., & Park, H. J. (2007). Collaboration in special education: Parent-professional training. *Teaching Exceptional Children, 39*(4), 6–14.

Chapter 7

ASCA Delivery Systems

CHRISTOPHER SIUTA

St. Bonaventure University

ALAN SILLIKER

St. Bonaventure University

"Know me for my abilities, not my disability."

—Robert M. Hensel, Disability Activist and Poet

The American School Counseling Association (ASCA) is the professional group representing school counselors. ASCA (2012) has articulated a national model for the practice of school counseling. That model was published to standardize school counseling programs and to promote service to all students. ASCA's position statement on school counselors and students with disabilities follows:

> *"Professional school counselors encourage and support the academic, career and personal/social development for all students through comprehensive school counseling programs. Professional school counselors are committed to helping all students realize their potential and meet or exceed academic standards regardless of challenges resulting from disabilities and other special needs" (ASCA, 2013, "Position" section, para. 1).*

This ASCA position makes reference to the Individuals with Disabilities Education Improvement Act (IDEIA of 2004) and the finding that individuals with disabilities have often received less than adequate support and services in educational settings (ASCA, 2013). IDEA (of 2004, PL 108-446) identifies 13 disability categories, as described in detail in Chapter 1, this volume: autism; deaf-blindness; developmental delay; emotional disturbance; hearing impairments (including deafness); intellectual disability (formerly mental retardation); multiple disabilities; orthopedic impairments; other health impairments; specific learning disabilities; speech or language impairments; traumatic brain injury; visual impairments (including blindness). These individuals who, by reason thereof, need special education and related services are emphasized in this chapter in relation to the types of services they may be provided by school counselors.

ASCA's position is that school counselors serve all students, including those with disabilities. That stance is reinforced with a statement of professional school counselors' roles (ASCA, 2013). Those roles include such activities as Individualized Education Plan (IEP)-based counseling, collaboration with family members, multidisciplinary team (MDT) membership, advocacy, and collaboration with student support professionals. Furthermore, specific roles for school counselors are delineated in more detail within the ASCA National Model (2012).

The ASCA Model comprises four themes and four components. The four themes are leadership, advocacy, collaboration, and systemic change while the four components of the model are foundation, management, delivery, and accountability. The focus of this chapter is the delivery system component of the ASCA National Model. An examination of research-based school counselor interventions for students with disabilities is of particular need since school counselors report being inadequately prepared to provide service to students with disabilities (Milsom, 2002; Praisner, 2003). Moreover, needs of these students are often neglected by school counselors (Hatch, Shelton, & Monk, 2009).

The delivery system comprises both direct student services and indirect student services. Direct student services include three activities: instructing a school counseling core curriculum, facilitating individual student planning, and responding to immediate student needs. Indirect services consist of consultation and collaboration. All of these services should be connected to student needs. Student needs and competencies required to achieve those needs are categorized into three developmental domains in *ASCA National Standards for Students*: academic, career, and personal-social (ASCA, 2004).

All students encounter a variety of developmental challenges during their years in school. However, students with disabilities may experience extraordinary barriers in their academic, career, and personal-social development. These barriers exist in such diverse aspects of life as employment, learning, social relationships, self-concept, human sexuality, housing, transportation, and mobility. Marshak,

Dandeneau, Prezant, and L'Amoreaux (2009) suggested that such obstacles demand the same school counseling support but at "amplified" levels.

The structure of this chapter includes a section for each of the four delivery systems partitioned into interventions for all students and amplified or augmented interventions for students with disabilities. As such, after reading this chapter, the following objectives, which are tied to the four areas of delivery system service, will be met by readers:

1. Knowledge of the school counseling core curriculum

2. Knowledge of individual student planning

3. Identification of responsive services

4. Knowledge of consultation and collaboration

DIRECT STUDENT SERVICES

School Counseling Core Curriculum

The School Counseling Core Curriculum delivery system (ASCA, 2012) is defined as an instructional program conveyed to all students to promote optimal academic development in academic, career, and personal-social domains. It is designed to be appropriate to students' developmental level and needs. Typical strategies include classroom instruction and smaller group activities.

Implementing a school counseling core curriculum may push some counselors out of their comfort zone since functioning in a classroom as a teacher necessitates a very different skill set than does individual and small group work. Cobia and Henderson (2007) have compiled 17 helpful ideas for presenting lessons. Practical suggestions that compose this list include the following: begin the lesson with something interesting, tell students the basic goal of the lesson, move around the room, make an effort to draw all students into the learning, and use several learning formats. As an additional resource, Tollerud and Nejedlo (2004) have a chapter on the process of designing a counseling curriculum.

An integral step in the design of a school counseling curriculum is a needs assessment. Preventive and developmental school guidance is best implemented when specific needs of students and the community are addressed. Needs assessment can be conducted informally via interviews with constituents and stakeholders including students, teachers, parents, administrators, and community members. More formal assessments do exist, including Berube and Berube's (1997) Survey of Student Concerns (cited in Berube & Berube, 1997).

Rowley, Stroh, and Sink (2005) conducted a study to examine the curricular materials used most by school counselors. Their analysis demonstrated that personal-social domain lessons were prevalent, while academic curriculum items were least reported. Particular assets of this article include a list of published school counseling curricula and recommendations for the implementation of a guidance curriculum. Those recommendations focused on such issues as financial considerations in purchasing materials, collaboration with colleges and universities, infusing curriculum within teachers' classroom lessons, and selecting curricula that may enhance the academic mission of the school.

Books, videos, and classroom materials are among curricular materials used by school counselors. Common student issues addressed by school counselor curricula are study skills, bullying, social skills, self-esteem, divorce, and drug/alcohol use (Rowley et al., 2005). This same study identified a broad array of curricula in use by school counselors but found only four programs that had been utilized by multiple respondents. Those four programs were (a) The Missouri Comprehensive Guidance and Counseling Program, (b) Here's Looking at You, (c) Second Step, and (d) Talking About Touching.

Academic Domain School Counseling Core Curriculum

Instruction by school counselors in the academic domain

Classroom guidance to promote academic success has typically focused upon teaching organizational and study skills. Several studies have demonstrated that classroom guidance lessons can have a positive impact on students' academic performance. However, curricula with a focus upon socioemotional education also have demonstrated a positive relationship with academic success (Zins, Weissberg, Wang, & Walberg, 2004). Student Success Skills, a program that includes personal-social classroom lessons, has emerged as a particular means to lessen academic gaps among students (Brigman, Webb, & Campbell, 2007). Student Success Skills curriculum lesson plans cover varied socioemotional and academic topics such as memory processes, test anxiety, interpersonal skills, goal setting, and teamwork (Brigman & Webb, 2004).

Group activities by school counselors in the academic domain

Small groups of students who are failing academically benefit from study skills and tutoring in specific subject areas. Group processing to enhance academic skills and performance enables students to identify their strengths and weaknesses, monitor progress toward goals, practice anger management techniques, and share success stories (Brigman, Campbell, & Webb, 2010).

Amplified curricular interventions in the academic domain

Students with disabilities should have full access to academic intervention services that are available to other students. IEPs enable school counselors to personalize academic strategies for individuals with disabilities.

Career Domain School Counseling Core Curriculum

Instruction by school counselors in the career domain

Many resources exist for career-oriented curriculum materials that can be easily accessed and implemented by school counselors (Center for School Counseling Outcome Research & Evaluation, 2014). Brown and Krane (2000) conducted a meta-analysis of career development interventions and discovered five components of those studies that were significantly related to intervention effectiveness. These components included the following:

1. Allow students to clarify career and life goals in writing.

2. Provide students with individualized interpretations and feedback.

3. Give up-to-date information on the requirements and likely consequences of considered career paths.

4. Include models that demonstrate effective planning and coping strategies.

5. Help students develop support networks that will facilitate their abilities to pursue their aspirations.

Much of college and career readiness involves social and emotional competence including communication skills and interpersonal relationships. Dymnicki, Sambolt, and Kidron (2013) described the concept of *social and emotional learning* (SEL) and demonstrated how a socioemotional-oriented curriculum can promote college and career readiness. In particular, college and career readiness includes socioemotional strengths, such as stress management skills, grit, paying attention, and the ability to regulate one's emotions. As for curriculum materials that are specifically career-oriented, Jarvis and Keely (2003) conducted a literature review on career development issues, including in their article a summary of promising guidance-related curricula or programs. Even though very few were mentioned, the authors singled out *The Real Game Series* as a valuable set of programs for student career building.

Group activities by school counselors in the career domain

Most career curriculum activities can be implemented in both classroom and small group settings. As with instructional activities, many resources exist for career-oriented curriculum materials that can be easily accessed and implemented by school counselors (Florida Department of Education, 2014; Missouri Career Education, 2014; Vocational Information Center, 2012). Activities are often organized within the nine elements of career education: career awareness, self-awareness, appreciations, attitudes/life roles, decision-making skills, economic awareness, skill awareness and beginning competence, employability skills, and educational awareness (Brown, 2012). Specific career domain activities include course selection and scheduling, transition planning, career interest assessment, job shadowing, resume and interviewing skills, preparation for Scholastic Assessment Test/American College Test (SAT)/(ACT) testing, and college visits.

Amplified curricular interventions in the career domain

Career development needs of students with disabilities are often neglected by school counselors (Hatch et al., 2009). As with other students, counselors should share information about high school graduation requirements and postgraduate options within education and employment. School counselors ignore many students with disabilities when they have more severe disabilities and are not included (Milsom, 2007). Students with disabilities should have access to career development activities that are available to all other students. School counselors working with students with disabilities on career development should be sensitive to special needs that are faced by these students, which may include confidence-building, self-advocacy, and architectural barriers.

School counselors working with students with disabilities are advised by Milsom (2007) to attend IEP meetings, teach self-advocacy skills, discuss disability services and legislation, and provide input for transition plans. Two particular targets for career transitions are those preparations for postsecondary education and transition planning for postsecondary employment. School counselor curricular topics for those students with disabilities anticipating higher education focus on college awareness, educational options, the college admissions process, disability support services in higher education, and legislation regarding students' rights (Naugle, Campbell, & Gray, 2010). Educating students-with-disabilities' families can be another important curricular approach for school counselors. One such approach involved the distribution of information packets to parents that described specific disability support services at selected colleges (Roberts, Bouknight, & Karen, 2010). Transition plans for college should also include curricular topics such as emotional adjustment strategies, anxiety reduction, and test-taking skills (Dipeolu, Storlie, & Johnson, 2014).

Transitions to postsecondary employment for students with disabilities should comprise topics centered on beginning competence skills and approaches to successfully obtaining a job. McEachern and Kenny (2007) recommend themes such as finding the right job, the application process, interview skills, and financial management. The Marriott Foundation's (2008) Bridges Program is a school-to-work approach with an excellent track record for youth with disabilities. The Bridges curriculum includes interviewing skills, appropriate dress, resume development, matching students' skills with jobs, and independent travel.

The Vocational Information Center (2012) offers many resources for school counselors and students with disabilities. Those resources are cataloged as career exploration, accommodations for students with disabilities, career counseling interventions, career resources for people with disabilities or barriers, transitions for special needs students, employment resources for disabled people, and guides and activities for students with disabilities.

Personal-Social Domain School Counseling Core Curriculum

Instruction by school counselors in the personal-social domain

School counseling curricula have been demonstrated to foster positive social and emotional development in students (Brigman & Campbell, 2003; Jarvis & Keeley, 2003; Sears, 2005). Moreover, social and emotional learning fosters academic success (Zinsser, Weissberg, & Dusenbury, 2013). Durlak and Weissburg (2007) reviewed 73 after-school programs that had been designed to promote personal-social skills. Problem-solving, conflict resolution, self-control, and self-efficacy were among the positive benefits of these programs. In general, socioemotional learning has been demonstrated to promote and enhance students' academic performance and positive social behavior (Collaborative for Academic, Social, and Emotional Learning [CASEL], 2012; Durlak, Weissberg, Dymnicki, Taylor, & Schellinger, 2011; Payton et al., 2008).

School counselor instructional strategies to promote socioemotional learning include the primary personal-social student competencies identified by ASCA Model standards:

1. Acquire self-knowledge and interpersonal skills.

2. Apply self-knowledge using decision-making and problem-solving skills.

3. Acquire personal safety and survival skills to cope with such challenges as peer pressure, conflict, inappropriate physical contact, and a full spectrum of life events (ASCA, 2012).

These same student socioemotional issues are consistent with Council for Accreditation of Counseling and Related Educational Programs (CACREP) standards for the preparation of school counselors (CACREP, 2009).

Specific socioemotional instructional materials are listed and reviewed by the Collaborative for Academic, Social, and Emotional Learning (CASEL, 2012). Those materials focus upon classroom guidance discussions of drugs and alcohol, peer pressure, loss and grief, and interpersonal skills. CASEL promotes five socio-emotional competencies of self-awareness, self-management, social awareness, social skills, and responsible decision making (CASEL, 2014). Additional resources for social skills training and socioemotional learning highlight the use of such strategies as modeling, role playing, and performance feedback (McGinnis, 2011).

Group curricular activities by school counselors in the personal-social domain

School counselors use small groups to promote knowledge and skills about personal-social issues such as divorce, bullying, development of friendships, and social skills development. Group and classroom curricular approaches to personal-social development are promoted by both CACREP and ASCA competencies.

Amplified curricular interventions in the personal-social domain

The personal-social needs of students with disabilities are often neglected (Hatch et al., 2009). However, teaching friendship skills and promoting a positive learner attitude has been shown to be an effective strategy for school counselors (Hatch et al., 2009).

Individual Student Planning

ASCA National Standards in the academic domain guide school counselors to promote students' success in school (ASCA, 2004). Individual student planning services is one of five areas included in those school counseling programs and activities that are intended to assist students with their personal goals and future plans. Such planning targets may include achievement of competencies in academic, career, and personal-social domains; developmental transitions such as movement along different educational levels (e.g., elementary school to middle school; high school to work or higher education); and personal goal setting (e.g., learning plans, high school graduation, or acceptance to college).

Two standard strategies for individual planning are appraisals and advisement. Appraisals involve any measurement or assessment by school counselors of students' strengths and weaknesses. Examples of appraisal results are academic grades, interests, learning style, and self-esteem. School counselor directed advisement entails a merging of appraisal data with educational and career information so as to guide students' future placement and goal setting. Both appraisal and advisement occur in the context of academic performance, career preparation, and personal-social development. The issue of appraisal is more thoroughly discussed in the subsequent chapter, Chapter 8. In regard to advisement, school counselors, for example, often meet with students for academic scheduling. These sessions tend to be brief and may occur as infrequently as once per year. Some individual planning sessions such as postsecondary advisement occur in the context of small groups, and most school counselors involve students' parents in the planning process. Students with disabilities often encounter more complicated life transitions than their nondisabled peers and therefore may require amplified individual planning services and interventions. Various types of individual planning, as they pertain to the academic, career, and personal-social domains, are addressed further in the next section.

Academic Domain Individual Student Planning

Appraisal interventions in the academic domain

School counselors typically meet individually with students to discuss academic performance issues and course scheduling. These meetings may occur quarterly, annually, and as individual needs dictate. Subject area grades together with achievement test scores are often a starting point for individual planning. Additional measurements of students' academic abilities that may be considered include classroom teacher reports, student learning style, academic self-concept, academic self-efficacy, and career interests. Assessment of a student's learning style is recommended as an aid to both teachers and individual students as they each attempt to identify academic strengths and weaknesses. Another important focus for assessment is students' level of motivation. Individual results on interest inventories can be a rich source of data to leverage students' academic motivation.

Amplified appraisal interventions in the academic domain

Students with disabilities may benefit from various test accommodations including individualized administration and flexible time arrangements. Individual achievement tests rather than group tests may be another helpful accommodation for students with disabilities. School counselors may administer tests individually to disabled students or may rather refer such specialized assessment to school psychologists or other professionals. Similarly, students with disabilities may require more time, effort, and support to complete homework. Additionally, Marshak et al. (2009) reported that students with disabilities may experience disengagement from the educational environment because of difficult relationships with peers and adults at school. Therefore, school counselors are advised to assess socioemotional needs of students with disabilities with respect to their academic performance.

Advisement interventions in the academic domain

As mentioned above, school counselors meet regularly with students to both schedule courses and to monitor academic performance. Future career goals and personal-social issues in and out of school are often incorporated into these individual planning sessions. In particular, ASCA National Standards recommend that school counselors assist students to relate school to life experiences outside of school (ASCA, 2004). A failure to understand the relevance of schoolwork can be a contributor to disengagement from education in general.

Amplified advisement interventions in the academic domain

School counselors are advised to provide resources to parents of students with disabilities so that they can support their children (Milsom & Hartley, 2005). Academic advisement and scheduling of classes is a particular way to start this collaboration with parents. Discussions of study skills, time management, and organizational skills are other advisement topics that can be shared with all students. School counselors can also begin advisement discussions about adaptive technology options and other assistive resources in the classroom for students with disabilities. Advisement should also be a setting to review appraisal results regarding interests, academic performance progress, and learning styles as well as students' strengths and weaknesses academically. The next section covers individual career planning.

Career Domain Individual Student Planning

Appraisal interventions in the career domain

School counselors are involved with career assessments of their students. Both ASCA National Model and CACREP standards (ASCA, 2012; CACREP, 2009) promote career assessment of interests, abilities, and aptitudes. College and career readiness are particular appraisal areas that have been gaining attention via Common Core Standards. School counselors in most schools are involved with test selection, administration, and interpretation.

Amplified appraisal interventions in the career domain

Sensitivity to test accommodations for students with disabilities is an obvious extraordinary feature of career assessment. These students may require untimed administration, assistance with item readings and responses, as well as selection of adapted and individual appraisal instruments. A particular need for students with disabilities is a realistic assessment of their abilities. Students, their families, school faculty/staff, and community members may attend overly to disabilities and obstacles to the exclusion of strengths and abilities.

Advisement interventions in the career domain

School counselors as career advisors promote occupational awareness, employment readiness, career goals, and the skills necessary to achieve those goals. ASCA (2004) National Standards in the career domain reinforce these categories of career advisement by school counselors. Additionally, the CACREP standards (2009) speak to preparation for school counseling that includes knowledge of transition programs, school-to-work, postsecondary planning, and college admissions counseling (SC.C.4 [standards], CACREP, 2009, "Knowledge and Skill Requirement" section).

Amplified advisement interventions in the career domain

School counselors as advisors for students with disabilities are in need of career exploration resources for these students. All students benefit from career information, yet special advisement needs of students with disabilities demand enhanced occupational information. For example, Washington State sponsors their Do-It Disability Mentoring Day each year for students with disabilities to meet with employees and mentors, many of whom have disabilities themselves. Such companies as Boeing and Microsoft are involved in this activity (University of Washington, 2013). Research from these activities has shown that students with disabilities benefit from work-based learning experiences as much as, if not more than, their peers without disabilities.

The Monadnock Center for Successful Transitions in New Hampshire also promotes career exploration for students with disabilities, using job shadowing (Street, Bigaj, & Mahon, 2010). The Monadnock Center provides guides for career advisors who wish to replicate the center's activities with students with disabilities. The next section covers the personal-social domain.

Personal-Social Domain Individual Student Planning

Appraisal interventions in the personal-social domain

Individual planning sessions with all students tend to focus primarily upon academic performance and, secondarily, upon career goals. Personal-social issues may emerge as a side effect of these sessions. For example, a student might share stories about problems at home and/or with peers. Such issues as domestic violence, neglect, and bullying affect academic performance and career development. Personal-social difficulties that materialize usually result in transition to responsive services such as counseling or indirect services such as referrals or consultation with other professionals or family.

An increase in the awareness that personal-social issues affect academic performance (CASEL, 2014) has resulted in a proactive appraisal approach at some schools to personal-social issues. For example, assessment of personal-social assets using the 40 assets model has been used to identify students' needs (Galassi & Akos, 2004; Stevens & Wilkerson, 2010). School counselors can easily assess the number of assets for individual students and then make plans to add assets. Another approach to assessment of personal-social needs is the use of behavior ratings and disciplinary reports. These measures of personal-social issues can be used to identify students' needs and prompt individual planning and goal setting.

Amplified appraisal interventions in the personal-social domain

As with all students, students with disabilities should be meeting regularly with their school counselor to make future plans. Personal-social needs of students with disabilities both reflect the general public and may include special considerations. For example, students on the autism spectrum can be expected to require augmented assistance with social skills development. Utilization of a group to address social skills of students is illustrated in Case Illustration 7.1.

CASE ILLUSTRATION 7.1

BRIAN

Brian is a 10-year-old male in an inclusive classroom. This student has an IEP and is classified as "Learning Disabled." He has been referred to the school counselor for an assist with some academic and behavioral concerns toward the teacher and other students. The student is brought in initially for individual counseling. Brian reports that he cannot keep up with the pace of the teaching that happens daily in the classroom. Furthermore, he says that he is distracted all of the time and that the other kids are always making fun of him. The teacher does not see what is happening because he sits in the back of the classroom. He reported this to the teacher, but she said, "You just need to figure it out." The counselor asked how long this has been going on, and he said, "All year!" The student is also saying his parents are getting a divorce, and that is making everything even worse. He is not handling any of these stressors effectively but is open to any assistance that the school counselor can provide. Counseling interventions for Brian include the following:

1. Discuss problems with teacher directly, without the student present.

2. Bring student in to discuss issues with the teacher after counselor meeting with teacher.

3. Move student desk to the front of the classroom.

4. Teacher will provide individual tutoring for student after school.

5. School counselor will continue to see this student individually once per week.

6. Student is referred to a social skills group with the school counselor. The group will run for 8 weeks.

7. Family will be brought in to discuss how family issues are impacting performance at school.

8. The school counselor provides referral for outside individual and family counseling with the parents.

9. School counselor and teacher will monitor attention issues and see if interventions assist him. If not, a referral to an outside professional will be warranted to assess for attention deficit disorder (ADD) or attention-deficit hyperactivity disorder (ADHD).

Additionally, assessment of personal-social needs may include more extensive measures such as the conduction of a Functional Behavior Assessment (Trolley, Haas, & Patti, 2009).

Advisement interventions in the personal-social domain

Transitions for students occur at various points during school years including entry to elementary school and later moves to middle school, high school, and postsecondary settings. All students can be expected to need adjustment to different academic challenges, peer interactions, and physical settings. Elementary school may be a first exposure to being away from home, interacting with teachers, and competing with peers. Middle school is a setting where homework demands are raised, students experience multiple teachers, and peer pressures increase including an increase in the possibility of bullying. High school ups the ante still further with an escalation in opposite gender interactions, more pressure for success in school, and a growth in extracurricular activity options. Finally, transition to postsecondary education and/or work demands that students manage a whole new array of personal-social challenges. For example, workers must adjust to employer-employee interactions. Additionally, postgraduates may deal with an unsupervised social life for the first time in their lives.

Amplified advisement interventions in the personal-social domain

Transitions for students with disabilities can be even more intense than for the general population. In addition to new settings, peers, and teachers or supervisors, students with disabilities may experience heightened barriers to learning and social life. School counselors can be instrumental in preparing students for their new lives. Special challenges for students with disabilities include architectural barriers, the impact of diagnoses and labeling, and new peer relationships. Some students with disabilities may experience discrimination and social rejection (Marshak et al., 2009).

Particular advisement needs for students with disabilities' transition to middle school include challenges in developing new friendships, how to disclose aspects of their disability to new acquaintances, stress management, dealing with feelings of jealousy toward nondisabled friends, and reliance on support from family (Fleischman et al., 2011).

Students with disabilities can be helped to flourish when school counselors become more sensitive to the influence of the characteristics of students' disability types on their level of academic and socioemotional development. This section aims to achieve this objective in an informative and experiential manner for all those interested in helping facilitate a less bumpy transition from year to year for students with disabilities, charting the uneven course that oftentimes occurs when active IEPs are implemented for students.

It helps to distinguish a student's struggles based on the various disabilities, according to the IDEA law, such as autism, mental retardation (now called intellectual disability), and so on. Staff will then strive to equip school counselors with practical strategies to reach out and impart knowledge to such students individually, in groups, or within the classroom setting. Furthermore, by understanding the classifications as they are described, oftentimes the school counselor is supporting and assisting the students' primary classroom teachers in an effort to streamline services. School counselors as advisors to students with disabilities can assist adolescents in identifying their strengths, especially during the transition to high school (Hamlet, Gergar, & Schaefer, 2011). This is also a good time to help these students develop self-advocacy skills. The next section addresses responsive services, another critical variable in the ASCA delivery system framework.

Responsive Services

Responsive services are those activities that are designed to address the immediate needs of students (ASCA, 2012). Such student needs can be categorized within the three domains of academic performance, career development, and personal-social issues (*ASCA National Standards for Students*, ASCA, 2004). Responsive services activities within each domain include individual counseling strategies, group counseling, crisis counseling, conflict resolution, and student support activities. Several of these responsive services are illustrated in the Guided Practice Exercise 7.1.

Students With disabilities

School counselors are finding increasing numbers of students with IEPs on their counseling caseloads (Owens, Thomas, & Strong, 2011). Particular concerns of

---

Guided Practice Exercise 7.1

SAL

Sal is a 15-year-old freshman in high school. This student had been to the school counselor based on a lack of motivation and unwillingness to take responsibility for his academic tasks. He skips school quite a bit and was caught smoking marijuana on school grounds. Upon discussion, the student reports that he does not like himself and wants to "kill himself." He has not been able to keep up with the other students and cannot concentrate at all. He says that these problems started in middle school and are worse now. The parents are well educated and wealthy. The father is a physician. Sal has an older brother who just entered college on a full academic scholarship to a reputable university. This student reports a great deal of pressure from family members. The school counselor meets individually with Sal, during his lunch period. Upon discussion, Sal reports that he is not happy with how school is going and hates himself. A lethality assessment is completed, and the student has risk factors for suicidal behavior, one being he had thought about taking all of his father's sleeping pills. The teacher is informed that the student will not be back to class that day. Sal's parents are called immediately and are invited to the school to discuss the issues face-to-face. Upon discussion, the student is given a referral to a local mental health agency for a full counseling assessment to take place. The parents are also notified that their child will be referred to the Instructional Support Team to discuss possible accommodations for the student moving forward during the school year. A release of information is signed so that there can be collaboration between the school and mental health agency. The parents and school counselor will communicate weekly to discuss progress. The school counselor will see this student twice per week individually and look to involve Sal in a group counseling process to assist with self-esteem, peer issues, and social skills.

students with disabilities include stressors that typically developing students do not commonly experience. For example, such concerns include negative body image, stigma, and the impact of the disability on their quality of life. As complex issues such as these enter the daily lives of school counselors, a variety of mental health interventions, usually short term, may be required. Sink (2011) described many of these approaches relative to specific client issues including some disabilities categories.

Responsive school counseling interventions can be enhanced when counselors are aware of the needs of their students. Livneh, Wilson, and Pullo (2004) listed eight major categories in enumerating common needs of people with disabilities:

1. Physical needs (e.g., mobility, activities of daily living, pain control)

2. Psychological needs (e.g., alleviation of anxiety and depression, anger control, frustration tolerance)

3. Social needs (e.g., appropriate interpersonal communication, assertive behavior, managing stigma)

4. Vocational needs (e.g., employment training, job interviewing, job maintenance)

5. Financial needs (e.g., disability benefits, gainful employment)

6. Environmental barriers (e.g., accessibility, transportation, shopping)

7. Attitudinal barriers (e.g., inappropriate language, social prejudice, disability-related stigma)

8. Recreational needs (e.g., leisure-time activities)

School counseling professionals have long been known to take a multifaceted approach when working with students in school districts. Most are known as the "go- to" school personnel within a school building when day-to-day problems arise. One aspect that school counselors can employ is assessing school climate in relation to students with disabilities and initiating interventions or advocating for change when appropriate (Milsom, 2006). Based on the aforementioned classifications of those students with disabilities, there are stigmas and attitudinal barriers to be mindful of when protecting them from discrimination and prejudice. School counselors can employ strategies and support school personnel when it is determined that there are areas for intervention and respond based on those needs.

School counselors have been educated in their academic programs to work effectively with students who have disabilities. There has been a positive shift within graduate programs to do so based on the need for counselors to become more comfortable in working with them and creating a more positive school culture surrounding them. Research by Praisner (2003) suggested that one reason school personnel might possess negative attitudes toward students with disabilities is that they did not receive adequate training regarding those individuals and therefore feel unprepared to provide services to students with disabilities effectively. School counselors surveyed by Milsom (2002) reported completing minimal formal training related to students with disabilities prior to being employed as school counselors and indicated they felt only somewhat prepared to provide services to students with disabilities.

Goals and plans

When school counselors meet with students, goals and treatment planning should be at the forefront because goals are directly related to the counselor's choice of strategy and intervention. As it pertains to responsive services, the school counselor begins with treatment planning to provide a roadmap for the particular interventions to be formulated. In essence, school counselors are taught that in order to be responsive, a clear, concise, realistic student treatment plan must be put in place. Many school districts are requiring "lesson/treatment" plans to be submitted to school administrators to describe and delineate the responsive services being provided to students. The goals within these plans may be classified as immediate, intermediate, or long term. A combination of those goals will be reflected immediately within the treatment plan. Exceptions may occur when working with students in crisis where those goals may be reflected as short term in nature. Once those goals are developed by the counselor and student, the treatment plan is developed.

The treatment plan has often been missed as an integral strategy in treatment planning for students. Although it is not the same as a mental health case conceptualization model, it is important nonetheless for success of all students. Professional school counselors will encounter psychopathology on several scales, and this corresponding document will provide perspective on the issues that the students face. Treatment plans should include four types of information including these:

1. The goals that have been established

2. The kinds of interventions that will help students realize their goals

3. The length of time it would reasonably take to achieve success

4. The format that will be used to deliver interventions (mode of treatment)

Also, the student characteristics may also affect the outcome of a strategy and thus affect goal attainment, so those characteristics become a part of the planning process that leads to the treatment plan. Many believe these student characteristics are the most powerful sources of influence affecting the outcome of treatment.

Cormier and Nurius (2003) provided guiding principles in the preparation of student plans that reflect appropriate student characteristics:

- The plan is culturally and clinically literate and reflects the values and worldviews of the student's cultural identity.
- The plan addresses the needs and impact of the student's social system including any oppressive conditions within the student's system.
- Consideration is given to the role of important subsystems and resources in the student's life, such as the family structure and external support systems.
- The plan addresses the student's view of health, resilience, and ways of problem solving, as well as the student's level of acculturation and language dominance.
- Preference in planning treatment is included, as well as making sure the length of the counselor's proposed treatment matches the needs and time perspective held by the student.

Due to this plan being a guide to assess progress, there are further descriptions of important characteristics for counselors to consider when formulating treatment plans (Cormier & Nurius, 2003):

- A description of all relevant and potentially useful treatment approaches
- A rationale for each procedure that will be used
- A description of the counselor's role in each intervention
- A description of the student's role in each intervention
- Possible discomforts or risks that may occur as a result of the intervention
- Expected benefits that will occur as a result of the intervention
- The estimated time for each given intervention

School counselors can break these plans down into four intervention categories for students. The first is that of *affective interventions*. These strategies elicit and respond primarily to feelings and emotions, possibly involving body awareness and activities that focus on somatic components of a problem, as emotional states often involve the musculature and the expenditure of physical energy (Zajonc, 1980). *Cognitive interventions* deal with thoughts, beliefs, and attitudes students hold toward self and others. These strategies help with having students think differently about school situations, teachers, peers, parents, and so forth. *Behavioral interventions* are used to help students develop new behaviors or skills and/or control to eliminate existing behaviors that are counterproductive, used to possibly modify habits, routines, or interaction patterns with others. *Systemic intervention* strategies address relationship patterns with other people, tasks, or situations, including teachers, peers, parents, or anyone interacting with the students in their personal environments.

Due to student problems being multidimensional, counselors may be utilizing a combination of feeling, thinking, behaving, and interacting with others. The intent is to illustrate how selected interventions may be suitable for specific expressions of student problems, not oversimplifying the counseling process but, rather, to lay out the range of options that counselors have when working with specific student problems.

Family and peer interactions and interventions

Children with special needs pose unique issues in the counseling relationship since they have little power or control over their environment, so their world-views and/or self-esteem are also bound to have environmental limits. Children's behaviors are usually interconnected to the behaviors of others in the world, and the child's potential to change that environment is highly problematic without the involvement of significant others, be it at home, school, or within the community. Therefore, it is imperative that school counselors utilize systemic contacts with those surrounding the students, including parents, siblings, peers, friends, and teachers. The systemic view involves relationship patterns and their correlated behavioral and cognitive components. School counselors can work with the student on an individual basis and seek to produce systemic change through the child, or counselors can involve other participants in the child's system, seeking to invoke change in the interactional patterns of the system. If the problem is primarily learning related, then the process may be contained totally within the school setting. If the problem is family related, then the counselor may want to generate parental awareness and responsibility for the problem, at which time a referral to a family counselor would be warranted. At that point in time, the school counselor may or may not be part of the community counseling process, depending on the needs of the particular student. Issues related to peer interactions and community referrals are highlighted in Case Illustration 7.2, Gwen.

There have been recommendations for promoting social interactions between students with and without disabilities, including cooperative learning groups. These groups could provide both social and academic benefits to students with disabilities based on immediate concerns that are brought to the school counselor's attention. Additionally, school counselors who engage both groups of students in collaborative

CASE ILLUSTRATION 7.2

GWEN

Gwen is a six-year-old student who is currently in a regular education program. She was referred to the school counselor due to odd and strange behaviors in the classroom. Her performance has been average, but her social skills have been problematic. The other students think she is "weird" and do not seek her out, that is, for recess, open time in classroom, and so on. Gwen talks to herself quite frequently and seems to have imaginary friends. She is gentle and kind. The mother indicates that this is the way she is at home as well. Counseling interventions for Gwen include these features:

1. School counselor discusses these issues in individual counseling.

2. Counselor and teacher discuss and outline strategies to help with relationships with peers.

3. Gwen is referred to the school's Instructional Support Team (IST) committee, for possible Committee on Special Education (CSE) testing.

4. Gwen is referred to a local mental health agency for a full assessment.

5. The mother is given strategies by the school counselor to assist at home with odd behaviors and will continue to meet consistently throughout the school year.

problem-solving efforts to provide all students a voice for concerns will help them in development of self-awareness and communicating that awareness to others in a structured way. Empathy and understanding for those with disabilities is heightened and positive interactions will occur. An example of this shows a school counselor holding a 6-week Friendship Group of 12 students at the middle school setting, where six students are represented both from the regular education and special education settings. This type of group can promote communication, cooperation, and diversity through the use of direct service activities with students. Its design hopefully improves respect for differences and interaction among students with and without disabilities. A result from one session on attention-deficit hyperactive disorder (ADHD) for the Friendship Group at the middle school level may bring about an increased awareness on diversity from two different students. One student was referred to this particular group based on a formal IEP document and Other Health Impaired classification whereas the other student elected to voluntarily be a part of the group based on a teacher's recommendation. An activity on ADHD brings to light that both students have issues with attention and concentration within the classroom setting, although one was only formally assessed and given accommodations for these learning difficulties. Both students gained the awareness through this example that it is possible that *all* students have some needs when it comes to academics and that students may just be more alike than different. It certainly must be noted that another service delivery option for school counselors is to run this same type of group within the inclusive classroom setting. The difference is that the goal is to reach more students at one time concurrently.

Arman (2002) came up with a practical application of the group counseling model in working with students with disabilities. Teaching resiliency should be a key feature to any school counseling group, and it is best to identify students who might be helped through this type of group counseling model. Diversity among students such as ethnicity, socioeconomic status, and popularity in school increases the group's ability to develop a foundation of genuine caring, peer support, and appreciation for individual differences. Reality in social situations is learned when this diversity is achieved. During the recruitment period, the school counselor needs to be open to inclusion of all students referred to services and not just those who are commonly viewed as "successful" or "positive leaders" in the school.

These types of group counseling models are designed for working with six to eight students at a time. A group can be based on inclusive and self-contained students. Obtaining parental support, if possible, is recommended since some group homework activities include parental involvement. Last, prerequisites should include a willingness to talk and verbalize, being respectful, listening to others, following the group-originated norms, maintaining required grades for attendance, and maintaining confidentiality.

One role for the school counselor is to assist in the identification of students who are experiencing emotional and/or behavioral problems in school. Along with the MDT, school counselors should be able to assess whether learning disabilities or socioemotional problems are the primary contributors of the students' academic problems.

Students with disabilities can be helped to flourish when school counselors become more sensitive to the influence of the characteristics of students' disability types on their level of academic and socioemotional development. This section aims to achieve this objective in an informative and experiential manner for all those interested in helping facilitate a less bumpy transition from year to year for students with disabilities, charting the uneven course that oftentimes occurs when active Individualized Education Plans are implemented for students. It helps to distinguish a student's struggles based on the various disabilities, according to IDEA, such as autism, mental retardation, and so on. It will then strive to equip school counselors with practical strategies to reach out and impart knowledge to such students individually, in groups, or within the classroom setting. Furthermore, by understanding the classifications as they are described, oftentimes the school counselor is supporting and assisting the students' primary classroom teachers in an effort to streamline services. The next section, Indirect Student Services, addresses another key area of the delivery system model.

INDIRECT STUDENT SERVICES

Self-Advocacy

As stated previously, school counselors have a relatively distinct role in advocating for students across all levels in school systems. One way to follow through with that is to provide self-advocacy training to ensure students with disabilities successfully transition between school grade levels and to postsecondary education and/or careers (Hatch et al., 2009).

Self-advocacy training has much to do with externalizing disabilities and internalizing strengths as a learner for future endeavors. Students can learn these skills through active participation at their IEP meetings at school. School counselors can train students to communicate their strengths and weaknesses in a way to "get what they need" from teachers, counselors, administrators, and so on to succeed in school. This then helps students with communicating needs on a postsecondary basis with their future college or university and/or employer. It must be known that only 27% of students with disabilities enroll in postsecondary education compared to 68% of students without disabilities (Hatch et al., 2009). Of those students with disabilities who do proceed to postsecondary education, more are likely to enroll in 2-year colleges or vocational schools than to complete a degree program when compared to their peers without disabilities. Upon graduation from the public school system, students are no longer protected by IDEA and must request services in order to receive the same accommodations they received at the high school level. School counselors can prepare students through self-advocacy training and gain the assertiveness skills needed to follow through with such tasks, serving as a deterrent that may otherwise cause many students with disabilities to drop out of school prematurely. There is an indication that these skills are necessary to successfully transition to adult life, regardless of the paths individuals may take. They include all of the knowledge, attitudes, and skills students need while still in high school. When these particular students with disabilities were more active participants in their IEPs, receiving adequate knowledge of their individual disability, learning strengths and weaknesses, and being taught specific strategies such as how to ask and respond to questions related to them, they were found to be inherently more successful later in life.

Research was conducted through a grant funded by the Office of Special Educational Programs (OSEP), specifically called the School Counseling and Disabilities

Grant. This grant funded 48 professional school counselor trainees to provide counseling services to over 200 ninth-grade students with a high incidence disability between 2004 and 2008. The focus was to assist not only with self-advocacy training through the remaining years of high school but also with preparing them for life after high school. A survey given to 138 students in grades nine to 12, with an active IEP, revealed needs in students' attitude, knowledge, and skills in the area of college readiness and self-advocacy. Seventy-eight percent of the respondents reported they planned to go to college, yet only 58% of the students reported they "believed" they could succeed in college. Thirteen percent of students surveyed knew of disability services available to them in college. In regards to self-advocacy, only 46% of students reported they attended their IEP meetings, while 35% were active participants within them. So 54% of these students did not participate within their IEP meetings, and for those who did attend, 65% of those students did not participate or communicate to the IEP team in any way.

Grant teams met with students to address the gap in knowledge of college and postsecondary options by engaging them in certain training components such as self-advocacy training, commonly called "request advocacy." This occurs when students take initiative in asking for the appropriate accommodations they require. The training comprises one-on-one and small group instruction, modeling, and role-playing scenarios designed to help students gain the skills to advocate for themselves in the classroom, in their IEP meetings, and in their everyday lives. When a student communicates within an IEP format, this is sometimes called a "student-led IEP conference." Students were taught the differences between being assertive, aggressive, and passive to increase their understanding of appropriate and effective ways of communication.

The Why Try Curriculum was utilized within the study above to promote narrative and solution-focused counseling techniques to address the way students view themselves as successful learners. The goal is for students to become responsible for the decisions and choices that are needing to be made about them and to take charge of their lives. One activity called "Tearing Off Your Label" allowed students to identify all of the different ways they might be labeled or stereotyped in school, at home, or in the community. They were empowered to tear off their label and separate themselves from their stereotypes. This activity and curriculum is meant to lay the foundation for students to be active participants in their own education and transition plans for postsecondary life.

A key component of this initiative helped to change the way students viewed themselves as learners, where they were encouraged to externalize their disability and internalize their strengths. The first step was to gather material highlighting academic successes and positive feedback drawn from past schoolwork, such as passing grades, teacher comments on report cards, IEP meeting notes, and attendance and behavior records. This was all drawn together into a dynamic narrative about the student's past. Leaders introduced a lesson by asking the student about his or her perception and qualities that he or she thought made for a successful student. Then, a story was presented to the student that was about him or her but with altered names. Reflections occurred with what type of person this characterized student must be. Then, the story was retold to the student using real names, where the character's true identity revealed the student in a narrative sketch. The student was then asked if he or she was interested in continuing with the development of their "success" story.

College Readiness

Another prevention and/or indirect service that school counselors can provide to students are college readiness presentations through the use of classroom guidance activities. To address needs in this area, lessons can be used to focus on high school graduation and college entrance requirements, exit exam requirements, postsecondary options, as well as promoting any college and career night held at corresponding schools. As an example, classroom guidance presentations may target ninth-grade students through their English classes. A second presentation for the special education students can be redelivered to ensure comprehension of important details and understanding regarding the topic of choice, that is, postsecondary options (Hatch et al., 2009).

Parent Advocacy

Parental advocacy is also a vital role that school counselors can assist with in the school setting. To complement the college and career nights that schools may offer, an element teaching aspects of how the parents can support and advocate for their children during these nights is also important. Counselors can invite local college representatives to present information on admission processes and services available to special education students. For example, the director of the college disability center may speak about when and how a student will go about self-disclosing his or her disability and accommodations needed for success in the college setting to that corresponding office.

SUMMARY

The practice of school counseling is shaped by educational preparation standards (CACREP, 2009) and ASCA National Model practice standards (ASCA, 2012). Both CACREP and ASCA promote school counselor efforts and competencies to enhance students' academic, career, and personal-social development. School counselors provide service to students in four delivery systems.

The first delivery system, school counseling core curriculum, positions counselors in a developmental and preventive role of teaching competencies to students. The second system is individual planning. Counselors meet regularly with students to assist them in future planning and goal setting. Responsive services are a third delivery system for school counselors. Counselors respond to the immediate needs of students using such strategies as individual and group counseling, conflict resolution, and crisis counseling. Finally, school counselors deliver service to students indirectly via referral, collaboration, and consultation.

School counselors can implement those services within individual, group, and classroom settings and support teachers in their mission to help students with disabilities. As such, it is imperative that school counselors have a thorough understanding of the different disability categories, along with some basic counseling and teaching strategies for each. These help not only with providing direct service to these students but also with providing a strong ability to communicate those needs effectively with other school professionals, parents, and community service professionals, providing indirect services through the specialty of school counseling.

KEYSTONES

- Knowledge of systems of the ASCA National Model for school counseling is important.
- Ways in which school counselors can address the academic needs of students with disabilities was discussed.
- Knowledge of ways in which school counselors can deliver career-oriented services to students with disabilities was presented.
- School counselors promote the socioemotional development of students with disabilities.
- Delineation of direct and indirect services provided within the school setting is needed, and examples of how to implement each are important.
- Understanding the importance of lesson and treatment plans as it pertains to service delivery with students with disabilities is critical.
- Teaching self-advocacy to students with disabilities is a primary strategy within school counseling.

ADDITIONAL RESOURCES

Print

Baumberger, J., & Harper, R. (2007). *Assisting students with disabilities: A handbook for school counselors* (2nd ed.). Thousand Oaks, CA: Corwin.

Dollarhide, C., & Saginak, K. (2012). *Comprehensive school counseling programs: K–12 delivery systems in action* (2nd ed.). Upper Saddle River, NJ: Pearson.

Hatch, T., Shelton, T., & Monk, G. (2009). Making the invisible visible: School counselors empowering students with disabilities through self-advocacy training. *Journal of School Counseling, 7*(14). Retrieved from http://jsc.montana.edu/articles/v7n14.pdf

Romano, D., Paradise, L., & Green, E. (2009). School counselors' attitudes towards providing services to students receiving section 504 classroom accommodations: Implications for school counselor educators. *Journal of School Counseling, 7*(37). Retrieved from http://eric.ed.gov/?id=EJ886151

Web Based

ASCA Delivery System Worksheet: http://www.asca-web.org/New_Folder/PA%20Companion%20Guide/Delivery%20System.pdf

ASCA National Model: Delivery systems: http://www.ascanationalmodel.org/delivery-system

Toolkit on teaching and assessing students with disabilities: https://www.osepideasthatwork.org/toolkit/index.asp

U.S. Department of Education, Office of Special Education Programs' IDEA website: http://idea.ed.gov/explore/home

REFERENCES

American School Counselor Association (ASCA). (2004). *ASCA National Standards for Students*. Alexandria, VA: Author. Retrieved from http://ascamodel.timberlakepublishing.com/files/NationalStandards.pdf

American School Counselor Association (ASCA). (2012). *ASCA National Model: A framework for school counseling programs* (3rd ed.). Alexandria, VA: Author.

American School Counselor Association (ASCA). (2013). *The professional school counselor and students with disabilities*. Retrieved from http://www.schoolcounselor.org/asca/media/asca/PositionStatements/PS_Disabilities.pdf

Arman, J. F. (2002). A brief group counseling model to increase resiliency of students with mild disabilities. *Journal of Humanistic Counseling, Education, and Development, 41*(2), 120–128.

Berube, E., & Berube, L. (1997). Creating small groups using school and community resources to meet student needs. *The School Counselor, 44*, 294–302.

Brigman, G., & Campbell, C. (2003). Helping students improve academic achievement and school success behavior. *Professional School Counseling, 7*, 91–98.

Brigman, G., Campbell, C., & Webb, L. (2010). *Student success skills: Group counseling manual*. Boca Raton, FL: Atlantic Education Consultants.

Brigman, G., & Webb, L. (2004). *Student success skills: Classroom manual*. Boca Raton, FL: Atlantic Education Consultants.

Brigman, G., Webb, L., & Campbell, C. (2007). Building skills for school success: Improving the academic and social competence of students. *Professional School Counseling, 10*(3), 279–288.

Brown, D. (2012). *Career information, career counseling, and career development* (10th ed.). Boston, MA: Allyn and Bacon.

Brown, S. D., & Krane, N. E. R. (2000). Four (or five) sessions and a cloud of dust: Old assumptions and new observations about career counseling. In S. D. Brown & R. W. Lent (Eds.), *Handbook of counseling psychology* (3rd ed., pp. 740–766). New York, NY: Wiley.

Center for School Counseling Outcome Research & Evaluation. (2014). *Resources for counselors*. Retrieved from http://www.umass.edu/schoolcounseling/resources-for-counselors.php

Cobia, D. C., & Henderson, D. A. (2007). *Developing an effective and accountable school counseling program*. Upper Saddle River, NJ: Pearson Education.

Collaborative for Academic, Social, and Emotional Learning (CASEL). (2012). *2013 CASEL guide: Effective social and emotional learning programs—Preschool and elementary school edition.* Chicago, IL: Author.

Collaborative for Academic, Social, and Emotional Learning (CASEL). (2014). Social and emotional learning core competencies. Retrieved from https://casel.squarespace.com/social-and-emotional-learning/core-competencies

Cormier, S., & Nurius, P. S. (2003). Building your foundation as a helper. In *Interviewing and change strategies for helpers* (5th ed.; chapter 2). Pacific Grove, CA: Brooks/Cole.

Council for Accreditation of Counseling and Related Educational Programs (CACREP). (2009). Welcome to CACREP. Retrieved from http://www.cacrep.org/template/index.cfm

Dipeolu, A. O., Storlie, C., & Johnson, C. (2014). Transition to college and students with high functioning autism spectrum disorder: Strategy considerations for school counselors. *Journal of School Counseling, 12*(11). Retrieved from http://www.jsc.montana.edu/articles/v12n11.pdf

Durlak, J. A., & Weissberg, R. P. (2007). *Full report: The impact of after-school programs that promote personal and social skills.* Chicago, IL: Collaborative for Academic, Social, and Emotional Learning.

Durlak, J. A., Weissberg, R. P., Dymnicki, A. B., Taylor, R. D., & Schellinger, K. B. (2011). The impact of enhancing students' social and emotional learning: A meta-analysis of school-based universal interventions. *Child Development, 82*(1), 405–432.

Dymnicki, A., Sambolt, M., & Kidron, Y. (2013). *Improving college and career readiness by incorporating social and emotional learning.* Washington, DC: American Institutes for Research College & Career Readiness and Success Center.

Fleischman, K., Smothers, M. K., Christianson, H. F., Carter, L., Hains, A. A., & Davies, W. H. (2011). Experiences of adolescents with Type 1 Diabetes as they transition from middle school to high school. *Journal of School Counseling, 9*(4). Retrieved from http://www.jsc.montana.edu/articles/v9n4.pdf

Florida Department of Education. (2014). *Career and adult education.* Retrieved from http://www.fldoe.org/workforce/dwdframe/

Galassi, J. P., & Akos, P. (2004, March). Developmental advocacy: Twenty-first century school counseling. *Journal of Counseling and Development, 82,* 146–158.

Hamlet, H. S., Gergar, P. G., & Schaefer, B. A. (2011). Students living with chronic illness: The school counselor's role. *Professional School Counseling, 14,* 202–210. doi:10.5330/PSC.n.2011-14.202

Hatch, T., Shelton, T., & Monk, G. (2009). Making the invisible visible: School counselors empowering students with disabilities through self-advocacy training. *Journal of School Counseling, 7*(14). Retrieved from http://www.jsc.montana.edu/articles/v7n14.pdf

Individuals with Disabilities Improvement Education Act, of 2004, Pub. L. No. 108-446, 108th Congress. Retrieved from http://www.gpo.gov/fdsys/pkg/PLAW-108publ446/html/PLAW-108publ446.htm

Jarvis, R. S., & Keeley, E. S. (2003, April). From vocational decision making to career building: Blueprint, real games, and school counseling. *Professional School Counseling, 6,* 244–250.

Livneh, H., Wilson, L., & Pullo, R. (2004, February 1). Group counseling for people with physical disabilities. *Focus on Exceptional Children* [Newspaper]. Retrieved from HighBeam Research: http://www.highbeam.com/doc/1G1-136701477.html

Marriott Foundation. (2008). Bridges: From school to work. Retrieved from http://www.bridgestowork.org/

Marshak, L. E., Dandeneau, C. J., Prezant, F. P., & L'Amoreaux, N. A. (2009). *The school counselor's guide to helping students with disabilities.* San Francisco, CA: Jossey-Bass.

McEachern, A., & Kenny, M. (2007). Transition groups for high school students with disabilities. *The Journal for Specialists in Group Work, 32*(2), 165–177.

McGinnis, E. (2011). *Skill streaming the adolescent: A guide for teaching prosocial skills* (3rd ed.). Champaign, IL: Research Press.

Milsom, A. (2002). Students with disabilities: School counselor involvement and preparation. *Professional School Counseling, 5*(5), 331–338.

Milsom, A. (2006). Creating positive school experiences for students with disabilities. *Professional School Counseling Journal, 10*(1), 66–72.

Milsom, A. (2007). School counselor involvement in postsecondary transition planning for students with disabilities. *Journal of School Counseling, 5*(23). Retrieved from http://www.jsc.montana .edu/articles/v5n23.pdf

Milsom, A., & Hartley, M. T. (2005, June). Assisting students with learning disabilities transitioning to college: What school counselors should know? *Professional School Counseling, 8,* 436–441.

Missouri Career Education. (2014). Guidance and counseling grade–level expectations. Retrieved from http://www.missouricareereducation.org/doc/guidegle/GLE_Career_GrK-2.pdf

Naugle, K., Campbell, T. A., & Gray, N. D. (2010). Post-secondary transition model for students with disabilities. *Journal of School Counseling, 8*(40). Retrieved from http://www.jsc.montana.edu/ articles/v8n40.pdf

Owens, D., Thomas, D., & Strong, L. (2011). School counselors assisting students with disabilities. *Education, 132*(2), 235–241.

Payton, J. W., Weissberg, R. P., Durlak, J. A., Dymnicki, A. B., Taylor, R. D., Schellinger, K. B., & Pachan, M. (2008). *Positive impact of social and emotional learning for kindergarten to eighth-grade students: Findings from three scientific reviews (Executive summary).* Chicago, IL: Collaborative for Academic, Social, and Emotional Learning.

Praisner, C. L. (2003). Attitudes of elementary school principals toward inclusion of students with disabilities. *Exceptional Children, 69*(2), 135–145.

Roberts, L. A., Bouknight, T. M., & Karen, O. C. (2010). *The school counselor's role on behalf of college bound special education students.* Retrieved from http://counselingoutfitters.com/vistas/ vistas10/Article_79.pdf

Rowley, W. J., Stroh, H. R., & Sink, C. A. (2005, April). Comprehensive guidance and counseling programs' use of guidance curriculum materials: A survey of national trends. *Professional School Counseling, 8,* 296–304.

Sears, S. (2005). Large group guidance: Curriculum development and instruction. In C. A. Sink (Ed.), *Contemporary school counseling: Theory, research, and practice* (pp. 189–213). Boston, MA: Houghton Mifflin.

Sink, C. (2011). *Mental health interventions for school counselors.* Belmont, CA: Brooks/Cole.

Stevens, H., & Wilkerson, K. (2010). The developmental assets and ASCA's National Standards: A crosswalk review. *Professional School Counseling, 13,* 227–233. doi:10.5330/PSC.n.2010-13.227

Street, B., Bigaj, S., & Mahon, S. (2010). Build partnerships for career exploration using job shadows to explore the world of work. Retrieved from http://www.ivrs.iowa.gov/Transition/BuildPartnerships forCareerExploration.pdf

Tollerud, T. R., & Nejedlo, R. J. (2004). Designing a developmental counseling curriculum. In A. Vernon (Ed.), *Counseling children and adolescents* (3rd ed., pp. 391–423). Denver, CO: Love.

Trolley, B. C., Haas, H. S., & Patti, D. C. (2009). *The school counselor's guide to special education.* Thousand Oaks, CA: Corwin.

University of Washington. (2013). Do-It Disability Mentoring Day. Retrieved from http://www .washington.edu/doit/Programs/dmd.html

Vocational Information Center. (2012). General career information and guidance resources. Retrieved from http://www.khake.com/page95.html

Zins, J. E., Weissberg, R. P., Wang, M. C., & Walberg. H. J. (Eds.). (2004). *Building academic success on social and emotional learning: What does the research say?* New York, NY: Teachers College Press.

Zinsser, K. M., Weissberg, R. P., & Dusenbury, L. (2013). *Aligning preschool through high school social and emotional learning standards: A critical and doable next step.* Chicago, IL: Collaborative for Academic, Social, and Emotional Learning.

Chapter 8

Assessment, Evaluation, and Plans

Megyn Shea and Carol Dahir

New York Institute of Technology

Carolyn Stone

University of North Florida

"So here's the thing, ASCA members—whenever you get tired—and I know that you do—whenever you get frustrated or overwhelmed—and I know that you do—I want you to think about the extraordinary ripple effect of your work, because it's real. I want you to think about the impact you have not just on every child whose life you transform, but on the family that child will raise, on the business where that child will work, on the community that child will one day serve."

—First Lady Michelle Obama, Keynote Speech, American School
Counselor Association, National Conference, 2014

Throughout this chapter, serving all students will be emphasized. It cannot be stressed enough that counseling services must be equitable. According to the American School Counselor Association's (ASCA's) *Ethical Standards for School Counselors* (2010), it is our obligation to "ensure equitable academic, career, post-secondary access and personal/social opportunities for all students through the use of data to help close achievement gaps and opportunity gaps" (p. 2). It is not uncommon to find that both general education students and students with special needs are underserved by their school counseling program. It is our hope that readers will not just take on the belief system that all students should be served, but they will also actively work to improve the school counseling program to better address the needs of this population. Students with special needs, like all students, deserve to receive counseling services that will help them flourish. "Professional school counselors strive to assist all students in achieving their full potential, including students with disabilities, within the scope of the comprehensive school counseling program" (ASCA, 2013, p. 1).

The ASCA *Draft: Mindsets and Behaviors for Student Success* (2014) outlines five mind-sets that counselors should foster in all students, which includes those with disabilities. The mind-sets are attitudes and beliefs students hold about themselves that will likely have a significant impact on their academic success.

After reading this chapter, the reader will be able to define the following:

1. Assessment methods utilized in regard to students with disabilities

2. Additional specific standardized and nonstandardized measures used with this population

3. Behaviorally defined goals and methods of evaluation and data

ASSESSMENTS

School counselors address students' career, academic, and socioemotional developmental needs (ASCA, 2014). They utilize classroom guidance, also referred to as school counseling core curriculum, group counseling, and individual counseling, to ensure that all students are served by the school counseling program. Assessments assist school counselors in addressing the individual needs of students. This section will provide information on how school counselors can use assessments to address career, academic, and socioemotional needs of all students, including students with disabilities. In addition, we will provide information that can assist school counselors in the development of individual and program goals for all students, but we will emphasize working with populations with special needs.

Overview

In order to properly address assessment, we feel it is first important to define *assessment*. Surprisingly, there is a great deal of variation in the definitions of this term throughout the counseling profession. Additionally, *assessment*, *test*, *appraisal*, *instrument*, and *evaluation* are often used interchangeably, but some believe they have distinct meanings. We would like to provide you with alternate definitions and give you the definition we believe makes the most sense for the school counseling profession. The American Counseling Association (ACA) defines assessment as "the process of collecting in-depth information about a person in order to develop a comprehensive plan that will guide the collaborative counseling and service provision process" (ACA, 2014, p. 20). Whiston (2013) defined assessment as "a procedure for gathering client information that is used to facilitate clinical decisions, provide clients with information, or for evaluative purposes" (p. 392). A test is "an individual instrument in which the focus is on evaluation" (Whiston, 2013, p. 397). A joint committee of the American School Counselor Association (ASCA) and the Association for Assessment in Counseling and Education (AACE) developed the *Competencies for Assessment and Evaluation for School Counselors* (ASCA & AACE, 1998) in 1998. According to the ASCA-AACE Competencies:

> Assessment is the gathering of information for decision making about individuals, groups, programs, or processes. Assessment targets include abilities, achievements, personality variables, aptitudes, attitudes, preferences, interests, values, demographics, and other characteristics. Assessment procedures include but are not limited to standardized and unstandardized tests, questionnaires, inventories, checklists, observations, portfolios, performance assessments, rating scales, surveys, interviews, and other clinical measures.
>
> Evaluation is the collection and interpretation of information to make judgments about individuals, programs, or processes that lead to decisions and future actions. (ASCA & AACE, "Definitions of Terms" section, 1998)

To assist the reader in gaining a further understanding of this concept, Guided Practice Exercise 8.1 is offered.

For the purpose of this chapter, we will use the definition found in *The Standards for Educational and Psychological Testing* (1999), developed by a joint committee made up of the American Educational Research Association (AERA), the American Psychological Association (APA), and the National Council on Measurement in Education (NCME). Assessment is "any method used to measure characteristics of people, programs, or objects" (APA, NCME, & AERA, 1999, p. 2). We are choosing this definition because of its brevity, clarity, and broad use in the literature; however, we believe that all the definitions provided in this chapter can assist you in clarifying what assessment is.

In contrast to the definition, there is consistent agreement within the profession that school counselors should use assessments to best serve students. Assessments are believed to help school counselors identify and target specific counseling needs. The *Ethical Standards for School Counselors* (ASCA, 2010) provides

Guided Practice Exercise 8.1

ASSESSMENT DEFINITIONS

Table 8.1

Definitions of Assessment	*Resource*
The process of collecting in-depth information about a person in order to develop a comprehensive plan that will guide the collaborative counseling and service provision process	American Counseling Association, *ACA Code of Ethics*, 2014, p. 20
A procedure for gathering client information that is used to facilitate clinical decisions, provide clients with information, or for evaluative purposes	Whiston, 2013, p. 397
The gathering of information for decision making about individuals, groups, programs, or processes. Assessment targets include abilities, achievements, personality variables, aptitudes, attitudes, preferences, interests, values, demographics, and other characteristics. Assessment procedures include but are not limited to standardized and nonstandardized tests, questionnaires, inventories, checklists, observations, portfolios, performance assessments, rating scales, surveys, interviews, and other clinical measures.	ASCA & AACE, *Competencies in Assessment and Evaluation for School Counselors*, 1998
Any method used to measure characteristics of people, programs, or objects.	APA, NCME, & AERA, *Standards for Educational and Psychological Testing,* 1999, p. 2

1. Individual Activity: Table 8.1 lists a few definitions of assessment. Decide which definition makes the most sense to you. Why?

   _____

   _____

   _____

   _____

2. Group activity: As a class or in a small group, brainstorm all the ways that you have been assessed at school, at work, or other environment.

   _____

   _____

   _____

   _____

guidelines for evaluation, assessment, and interpretation. In this document, it is stated that professional school counselors

a. Adhere to all professional standards regarding selecting, administering, and interpreting assessment measures and only utilize assessment measures that are within the scope of practice for school counselors and for which they are trained and competent.

b. Consider confidentiality issues when utilizing evaluative or assessment instruments and electronically based programs.

c. Consider the developmental age, language skills and level of competence of the student taking the assessments before assessments are given.

d. Provide interpretation of the nature, purposes, results, and potential impact of assessment/evaluation measures in language the students can understand.

e. Monitor the use of assessment results and interpretations, and take reasonable steps to prevent others from misusing the information.

f. Use caution when utilizing assessment techniques, making evaluations, and interpreting the performance of populations not represented in the norm group on which an instrument is standardized.

g. Assess the effectiveness of their program in having an impact on students' academic, career, and personal/social development through accountability measures especially examining efforts to close achievement, opportunity and attainment gaps. (ASCA, 2010, "A.9. Evaluation, Assessment and Interpretation" section)

Ekstrom, Elmore, Schafer, Trotter, and Webster (2004) stated further that it is commonplace for school counselors to interpret scores from standardized achievement tests.

According to the National Career Development Association (NCDA) and the Association for Assessment in Counseling and Education (AACE; see AACE, 2010), effective assessment is also necessary to career counseling with students. Council for Accreditation of Counseling and Related Educational Programs (CACREP, 2009) also recognizes assessment as a strategy to identify student needs, barriers to learning, and as a means of evaluation of academic, career, and socioemotional development. Before moving into a discussion of specific types of assessments which exist, it is important to examine a few preliminary points in the next section.

Assessment Considerations

There are several areas to consider in regard to school counselor use of assessments. School counselors need to be aware of, and comfortable in using and interpreting both nonstandardized tests, as well as standardized tests. In one study, school counselors reported they were most likely to use observations and interviewing students as their primary assessment techniques (Blacher, Murray-Ward, & Uellendahl, 2005).

There are additional considerations, ethical in nature, which are important to address. One specific ethical concern that school counselors need to be cautious about is related to the selection, administration, or interpretation of scores from tests that have not been normed on the population (ACA, 2014). This is of particular importance when working with students with disabilities. If a standardized test has only been normed on people aged 17 to 24 from the general population but the intention is to have 10th-grade students with learning disabilities take the test, then measures outlined by the *ACA Code of Ethics* (2014) should be taken:

E.7.a. Counselors administer assessments under the same conditions that were established in their standardization. When assessments are not administered under standard conditions, as may be necessary to accommodate clients with disabilities, or when unusual behavior or irregularities occur during the administration, those conditions are noted in interpretation, and the results may be designated as invalid or of questionable validity. (ACA, 2014, p. 11)

These ethical principles are demonstrated in Guided Practice Exercise 8.2.

Guided Practice Exercise 8.2

COMPUTERIZED ASSESSMENTS

You have been a school counselor at ABC Middle School for 3 years. One of the responsibilities of the school counselors is to provide individual planning with new students where you discuss course preferences, student strengths, and previous school experiences and ultimately develop a course schedule. This year, your school implemented a new strategy, based on information from the district office, for placing students in reading and math courses. All new students will now be required to take a 15 to 20 minute computerized math assessment and a 20 to 30 minute reading assessment to help determine the level of math and reading courses they should be placed in. For students coming from another school in the district, these assessments are looked at in addition to grades in previous courses taken and the last several years of performance levels on state assessments. Unfortunately for students transferring from another district, you have no other assessment data other than the computerized assessments they take at the beginning of their first day of a new school because the cumulative folders take a few days to be transferred. Sadly, this also means that you do not have 504s or, in some cases, IEPs. Sometimes, you are able to get in touch with the previous school and have them immediately fax over a copy of the documentation, but this does not always work out as quickly as you would like. Many of the new students appear cautious and nervous on their first day, and you wonder how this might affect their assessment scores. After a couple months go by, you begin noticing another troubling issue. The computerized assessment results often do not reflect the same level of proficiency as the state standardized assessments. You decide to do some research about the validity and reliability of the computerized assessment. The company that makes the tests states, "the test is valid and reliable," but they give no specific information about the psychometric properties. (Note, this scenario is adapted from real events.)

In Small Groups:

1. Identify the ethical standards, listed previously in the chapter, that you believe apply to all the students taking the computerized assessment. Next, identify the ethical standards that apply to students with 504s and IEPs.

   _____

   _____

   _____

   _____

2. Next, given the circumstances in the scenario, develop strategies of how you will develop plans with future incoming students. Will there be differences in how you approach a student you believe will be in general education versus students that might need special accommodations?

   _____

   _____

   _____

   _____

3. Last, brainstorm how you might advocate for changing the placement practices. Who do you need to talk to? What evidence would you share?

   _____

   _____

   _____

   _____

Source: American Counseling Association (2014). ACA code of ethics. American Psychological Association, National Council on Measurement in Education & American Educational Research Association (1999). American School Counselor Association & Association for Assessment in Counseling. (1998). Whiston, S. C. (2013). Principals & applications of assessment in counseling (4th ed). Brooks/Cole, Cengage Learning. Belmont, CA.

Various types of assessments which can be utilized are further discussed in the next section. Suffice it to say that school counselors should only use assessments in which they have the training to competently select, administer, and accurately interpret results (AACE, 2003). The next area of consideration, what exactly are these various forms of assessments, is discussed next.

Assessment Types

Various types of assessments exist. As stated previously, while school counselors may not be trained in, or administer, all the assessment measures which are available, it is essential that they familiarize themselves with the various types and formats which exist.

Developmental

With regard to standardized and nonstandardized assessments, each serves important purposes and can help school counselors determine counseling needs for individual students, groups, and entire classrooms. *Standardized tests* refers to consistency in the administration, scoring, and administration of tests. These tests have been normed on a sample group of test takers. The adequacy of the norming population utilized in regard to standardized tests (also referred to as the standardization group) needs to be considered. Groth-Marnat (2009, pp. 10–11) suggested that three questions need to be asked when it comes to this determination of adequacy:

1. Is the standardization group representative of the population that will be taking the test?

2. Was the standardization group large enough? A small sample size creates less confidence in the reliability and validity of an assessment.

3. Does the test have subgroup norms? Examples of subgroups are different ethnic groups, age ranges, socioeconomic levels, and levels of education. The subgroup norms will provide greater confidence that comparisons can be made between the test and school children because of the diversity of students that will be taking the test.

Standardized assessments usually include a manual where counselors can find answers to the above questions. The manual will also outline the protocol for test administration. Testing conditions should be as similar to the testing conditions of the sample population as possible. The idea is to re-create the sample population testing conditions in order to have the highest validity and reliability possible.

Examples of standardized assessments include the following:

Armed Services Vocational Aptitude Battery (ASVAB). Multi-aptitude battery that measures current abilities and future academic and occupational success

Beck Depression Inventory for Youth. Commonly used by mental health counselors

Individual Intelligence Assessments. Commonly administered and interpreted by school psychologists

Personality Inventory. Myers-Briggs Type Indicator Instrument

State Achievement Tests. Survey achievement test to measure K–12 reading, writing, math, and other academic subject areas

The SAT. Aptitude assessment used to predict academic success in college

Standardized checklists. Career Planning Checklist for Middle School (http://www.educationplanner.org/students/career-planning/checklists/middle-school.shtml); Student Aid Checklists for Middle and High School (http://www.educationplanner.org/students/paying-for-school/student-aid-checklists/middle-school.shtml; http://www.educationplanner.org/students/paying-for-school/student-aid-checklists/high-school.shtml)

Strong Interest Inventory. Career interest inventory

The ACT Test. Curriculum and standards-based assessment used to predict academic success in college

In addition to standardized, there also exist a number of *nonstandardized assessments.* A nonstandardized assessment is one which looks at the abilities or performance of an individual, but does not provide the foundation for comparison of results among test takers, as do standardized tests.

Examples of nonstandardized assessments include the following:

Career Self-Assessment Inventory. Career Genogram; Holland Party Game

Checklists and rating scales. Instruments could be found or developed that address career, academic, or social/emotional development

Needs assessments. Often created using a checklist or rating scale format. The purpose of a needs assessment is to determine specific needs of the school population (i.e., students, parents, and staff). Needs assessments can be found on

School Counseling Association websites or by simply typing "school counselor needs assessment" into your search engine.

Interviews. Could be related to career, academic, or social/emotional development. The counselor could use a structured interview process where the same predetermined questions are asked of each student or an unstructured process where the counselor might have ideas about questions but takes a more interactive approach with the student.

Subject area tests. Often developed by teachers

In order for you, the reader, to familiarize yourself further with the various types of assessments which exist, Guided Practice Exercise 8.3 is shared.

In the next section, a specific type of assessment commonly used by school counselors, those related to career counseling, is discussed.

Career assessments

Assisting students with postsecondary and career decision making are arguably the most important tasks school counselors will engage in. Career development activities and counseling should begin in elementary school and continue through high school. Many school districts have a district-wide school counseling program where career development concepts are taught in a developmentally appropriate manner from K–12. A district-wide school counseling program is ideal because it ensures that all students are receiving guidance and counseling. Career, academic, and socioemotional assessments should be woven into career development lessons. For example, achievement tests can help inform areas of strength and interest. Subject area tests can be discussed in relation to work habits, achievement, and career options.

Students with disabilities should not be excluded; they should be able to participate in career development and counseling activities. In some cases, it may be

Guided Practice Exercise 8.3

TYPES OF ASSESSMENTS

1. Go back to the list of assessments your group generated in Activity 1. In your group, decide which of the assessments are standardized and which are nonstandardized.

necessary to provide accommodations for these students to complete assessments that contribute to the career decision-making process. It would be presumptuous to think that the same accommodation will work for all students with a similar disability (Osborn & Zunker, 2006). The following are examples of widely used accommodations outlined by Whiston (2013) for students with certain disabilities; but as stated previously, each student will need to be looked at without preconceived notions as to what will work best for him or her.

Students with visual impairments. Schools often use an aid to read an assessment aloud for students. Whiston (2013) cautioned that the tone and pace of the reader can impact the testing outcomes. Other widely used accommodations include changing the print (i.e., enlarging, Braille) or increasing time allowed to complete a test.

Students with hearing impairments. Using assessments that require less reading and use more pictures is sometimes a good option for students with hearing impairments. "Hearing has a direct link to language acquisition" (Whiston, 2013, p. 339), therefore reading can be greatly impacted. This chapter lists a few tests or assessments that are picture-based, but by no means is the list exhaustive. Counselors can find or create nonstandardized assessments that use pictures more often.

Students with motor disabilities. When selecting and designing assessments or group activities, school counselors should always include plans to accommodate those who have motor disabilities. Possible accommodations include using picture assessments, increasing test-taking time, or using computer assistive technology.

Students with cognitive impairments. It is inappropriate for school counselors to administer cognitive ability tests. However, school counselors must take students with cognitive impairments into consideration when administering career, academic, and socioemotional assessments. This chapter lists a couple of career assessments that are geared toward students with lower cognitive functioning.

Because cognitive ability will vary vastly within the student population, it is advisable to consult with school staff that is familiar with the student with disabilities population. For example, a school psychologist can offer a great deal of insight on possible modifications. School counselors would be remiss to not also consult with the special education teachers in the building when designing lessons. Another great resource for school counselors is local rehabilitation counselors who can help them with career resources for students with disabilities.

Osborn and Zunker (2006) reviewed such career assessments that may be appropriate for populations with special needs. Many of the assessments they reviewed may be appropriate for the entire school population, while others might only be appropriate for specific populations. School counselors should identify the needs of the specific students and then select the assessments that will address those needs. The following are a few of the assessments reviewed by Osborn and Zunker (2006):

- **Wide Range Interest-Opinion Test (WRIOT II).** The WRIOT is a career interest inventory developed for those who have severe cognitive disabilities.
- **Transition to Work Inventory (TWI).** Designed to identify necessary job accommodation needs of impaired students.
- **Social and Prevocational Information Battery-Revised (SPIB-R).** The SPIB-R can be useful for helping students identify life skills that are important when transitioning to community living.
- **Pictorial Inventory of Careers (PIC).** The PIC can help students explore career interests using pictures rather than sentences.

Case Illustration 8.1 will assist you in applying this material.

CASE ILLUSTRATION 8.1

SCHOOL COUNSELOR: REDUCING THE OVER-IDENTIFICATION OF STUDENTS FOR SPECIAL EDUCATION

You are a new school counselor at XYZ High School. The school counselors at XYZ provide career and postsecondary counseling and guidance to all the general education students. They go into the classroom where students complete career interest inventories, career and postsecondary searches, and rating scales. The counselors also meet two times a year with each student where they use interviews to assess interests. Unfortunately, the school counselors have not been going into the special education classes or meeting with special education students individually.

Activity:

What legal and ethical issues can you identify in this scenario?

How should you handle the situation?

Outline a brief plan to better serve the special education student population.

Special education assessments

In addition to career assessments, school counselors are often a part of the team that conducts a variety of assessments specific to students at risk (i.e., with special needs).

Functional Behavioral Assessment (FBA). The purpose of an FBA is to gather information about the problem behavior the student is displaying, using a variety of assessments, in order to get the best picture possible. A team of people that includes the school counselor, school psychologist, and teachers often completes the FBA. The team gathers the assessment information and identified interventions to improve behavior and/or academic performance (Kampwirth & Powers, 2012). These authors further specified the assessment methods in an FBA, which often include teacher interviews, a review of the student's cumulative folder, a parental interview, a student interview, rating scales, and classroom observations. In addition to the FBAs, school counselors are also involved in activities related to the *response to intervention* process.

Response to intervention (RTI). Response to intervention has become a common practice for schools that serve students with low performance and/or with special needs. The National Center on Response to Intervention (2010) offers the following definition:

> RTI integrates assessment and intervention within a multilevel prevention system to maximize student achievement and to reduce behavior problems. With RTI, schools use data to identify students at risk for poor learning outcomes, monitor student progress, provide evidenced-based interventions and adjust the intensity and nature of those interventions depending on the student's responsiveness, and identify students with learning disabilities or other disabilities. (p. 2)

The RTI framework consists of three levels: the primary level, the secondary level, and the tertiary level. The idea of the RTI framework is to determine students who need additional interventions beyond the primary level interventions. School counselors would be wise to connect their career, academic, and socioemotional interventions to the RTI framework. In the RTI framework, the bottom level, known as the primary level of prevention, or Tier 1, targets all students using evidence-based interventions in the areas of academic and socioemotional developmental needs. School counselors may look at this level as the delivery of their classroom lessons to the entire school population.

The secondary level, also known as Tier 2, is for some students who need more intense interventions. This level targets students who are considered the most at risk (National Center on Response to Intervention, 2010). School counselors might want to deliver their evidence-based small group interventions to the secondary level students. Students are identified to receive secondary prevention interventions through the evaluation of assessments.

The tertiary level of prevention, also known as Tier 3, is for a few students that need individualized plans. Students at this level do not display much improvement from the secondary level of interventions (National Center on Response to Intervention, 2010). School counselors should consider school and outside community resources for students that need this level of intense counseling services. Tertiary level students are identified through the monitoring of assessment data.

Once a comprehensive assessment is completed, school counselors, in collaboration with school-based professionals and families, can determine what the next steps are for both individual students and groups of students to succeed. These steps are articulated in either an Individualized Education Plan (IEP) or a 504 Plan, to be addressed in the next section.

INDIVIDUALIZED EDUCATION PLANS (IEP) AND 504 PLANS

This topic is not without some controversy in the profession. The extent to which school counselors should be involved in the planning and case management of IEPs and 504s varies. Because we believe it is important to have a unified voice when it comes to the role of the school counselor, we will once again refer to ASCA's position statement for working with students with disabilities. School counselors have a professional responsibility to consult and collaborate "with staff and families to understand the special needs of a student and understanding the adaptations and modifications needed to assist the student" (ASCA, 2013, p. 1).

It is appropriate for school counselors to act as consultants to the multidisciplinary team throughout the development and implementation of an IEP and a 504 Plan. In many cases, writing counseling services into an IEP or 504 Plan may not be appropriate; however, "providing short-term goal-focused counseling in instances where it is appropriate should be considered" (ASCA, 2013, p. 2). Acting as a collaborative consultant is not only appropriate, but also it is highly professional.

Administrative and supervisory responsibilities are often considered outside the scope of the professional school counselor's role. This is also true when it comes to IEP and 504 responsibilities. ASCA is quite clear about duties deemed inappropriate for school counselors:

- Making singular decisions regarding placement or retention
- Serving in any supervisory capacity related to the implementation of the IDEA

- Serving as the school district representative for the team writing the IEP
- Coordinating, writing, or supervising a specific plan under Section 504 of Public Law 93-112
- Coordinating, writing, or supervising the implementation of the IEP
- Providing long-term therapy (ASCA, 2013, p. 2)

Although activities such as supervising and administering IEPs and 504 Plans are considered inappropriate, other activities such as individual planning and goal setting are very important. The following sections outline how school counselors can work with students to help meet their individual needs without wandering into inappropriate territory. Goal setting for students with disabilities includes the development of measurable objectives that are regularly monitored, to ensure achievement of what is stated on the IEP or 504 Plan, and is discussed next.

GOAL SETTING FOR STUDENTS IN SPECIAL EDUCATION

Ongoing goal setting and evaluation of students' growth and development is an integral component of every special education student's education. IEP reviews and revisions are one component of ensuring that special education students have learning and behavioral goals that are manageable and attainable. School counselors can play a role in the development of these goals by participating in planning meetings and IEP reviews, as well as in ensuring that family members and teachers actively monitor the acquisition of these goals for both individual students with and without special needs. Most importantly, it is through the goal setting and planning process that each of our students understands the connection between school today and career and job satisfaction later. According to ASCA (2010):

> The professional school counselor advocates for counseling plans supporting students' right to choose from the wide array of options when they leave secondary education. Such plans will be regularly reviewed to update students regarding critical information they need to make informed decisions. (ASCA, 2010, "A.3.b." section)

School counselors must move beyond the legal obligations of IEP planning and acknowledge the ethical obligation we have to make sure our students have plans that will drive their future success. What role do school counselors play in the complex and sometimes daunting maze of regulations and accountability? Previously in this chapter, we touched on the role school counselors play in the IEP development. In this section, the issue of goal development and evaluation will be more specifically detailed.

The Process of Goal Setting

What does goal setting mean in a special education when it seems that IEPs are prescribed to drive both student learning and specific behavioral outcomes? Let us examine the goal setting process from several vantage points for both individuals and groups of students in special education, in alignment with the *ASCA National Model* (2005, 2012). This process, based on the fundamental principles of school counseling, will help these students acquire the competencies of the *ASCA National Standards for* Students (ASCA, 2004) and the new ASCA *Draft: Mindsets and Behaviors for Student Success* (2014) in the areas of academic, career, and socioemotional skills and attitudes. Specific means of service delivery in response to these goals are discussed in the next section.

Delivering Direct Student Services

Successful students, both general and special education, have learned to take ownership for their academic and affective learning and development. School counselors coordinate ongoing systematic activities designed to assist students individually in establishing academic and personal goals, and developing future plans. Individual student planning is a direct service delivered by school counselors in group, classroom, or individually, and it provides students with the knowledge and skill to plan, monitor, and evaluate their progress as they establish personal goals and develop future plans.

Students in special education must learn to plan, monitor, and evaluate their progress as they also learn to take ownership for their learning. As school counselors work closely with all students to support their academic, career, and personal social development, individual student planning can include developing behavioral, educational, or career/transition-planning goals. Professional school counselors possess the attitudes, knowledge, and skills to effectively work with these students to develop competence across the three domains: academic, career, and personal-social. Individual student planning consists of ongoing systemic activities and can include these opportunities:

- Individual/Small group appraisal: Students, with their school counselor and perhaps teacher and family member, engage in discussion about their abilities, interests, aptitudes, and achievements. Test results, career surveys, extracurricular activities, grades, and hobbies are examples of resources and data used to assist with the development of a written plan that also can include behavioral, educational, and career goals.
- Individual/Small group session: School counselors can work with students using personal-social, educational, and career-labor market information in

helping them to plan their short and long-term behavioral, educational, and career goals.

- Student monitoring: The school counselor works closely with each student to monitor progress and help her or him assess progress and identify and develop new supports and interventions as needed.
- Referral/Placement: School counselors collaborate with students, teachers, and family members to assist with transition planning from grade to grade, school level to school level, school to training programs, employment, or postsecondary and college opportunities.

These areas of academic or educational planning and goal setting are further delineated in the next section.

ACADEMIC/EDUCATIONAL AND BEHAVIORAL PLANNING AND GOAL SETTING

Students' needs will vary, and for the most part, targeted and measurable goals are unique to students and the goals of their IEPs. School counselors can collaborate with classroom teachers in self-contained or inclusive environments and conduct activities in goal setting: understanding and applying assessment information in a meaningful way to academic planning, postsecondary planning, and course selection.

Through the individual planning process, students can set educational or academic goals and identify specific strategies to help them achieve their goals. Individual planning documents the achievement of specific competencies that will ultimately support every student's attainment of the ASCA's *Draft: Student Mindsets and Behaviors for Students* (2014) and IEP goals.

Individual educational and academic planning should include family or parental involvement and provide multiple opportunities to personalize the educational experience. Examples of individual student goals to increase academic performance can include acquiring and practicing study skills, working on time management and planning skills, learning how to use test-taking strategies, organizing homework, developing a plan to seek help when needed, and choosing elective courses that match interests.

In addition to goals set with respect to academic and educational issues, this process is also vitally important to behavioral plans and change. Students in special education with learning or emotional disabilities can exhibit behaviors that require ongoing and focused remediation. Individual student planning can also help with behavioral goal setting through monitoring frustration, managing anger, acquiring self-confidence, coping with peer pressure, and acquaintance with self-control and self-discipline. As teachers and school counselors monitor IEP goals, individual student planning around behavioral issues can identify strategies to help students buy into taking responsibility for their actions. How this goal setting process applies to career planning is addressed in the subsequent section.

Career Planning and Goal Setting

Unique to every student, special or regular education is helping students realize their dreams. Career planning is inextricably intertwined with academic and educational goals. For a dynamic outcome, couple this with student motivation and the resiliency to overcome obstacles and challenges and professional school counselors who work diligently to help each student focus on future goals. Individual student planning is an essential component of career and transition planning. School counselors work diligently to help students in special education make the connection between their future plans and creating the pathway to achieve these goals. As no two students are the same in terms of ability, prior experience, and needs, or personality! So successful career and transition planning requires school counselors to work closely with teachers and families to make sure students understand the importance of their choices on future roles and goals. The importance of individual student planning and goal setting is illustrated in Guided Practice Exercise 8.4.

Guided Practice Exercise 8.4

INDIVIDUAL STUDENT PLANNING

Identify four different ways that you and your colleagues (teachers, counselors, and student support staff) can use individual planning with the students in special education in your school building.

SMART Goals

The SMART goal format (Doran, 1981) is frequently used for developing and writing overall program goals. SMART is an acronym for

S—specific, strategic
M—measurable
A—attainable and agreed on by everyone
R—results oriented
T—time bound

SMART goals are used to identify school-wide or program goals and develop the next steps needed to accomplish specific tasks. Just as school counselors frequently use data to identify specific school-based issues, SMART goals are a form of action plans that can focus on whole school initiatives. SMART goals can be developed for monitoring achievement, attendance, discipline, or behavioral issues. These goals are based on school data and should address those areas which are in need of improvement.

Example: Smart Goal Development

The following prompts may help you think about creating SMART goals to help you identify specific issues that address your special education students' success in school.

- By the end of the school year, the graduation rate for our special education students will increase from 55% to 65%.
- By the end of the school year, every special education student in eighth grade through 12th grade will have an educational and career plan in place for the following school year.
- By the end of the school year, the percentage of our elementary special education students who have discipline incidents will decrease by 10%.

Let's think through the steps in a SMART goal that calls for increasing the graduation rate for your special education students. First, answer the following questions:

- What is the Specific issue based on our school's data?
- How will we Measure the effectiveness of our interventions?
- How is it Attainable and agreed upon by everyone? What outcome would stretch us but is still attainable? What strategies will you use? Who needs to be involved?
- How will you monitor Results? Is the goal reported in results-oriented data (process, perception and outcome)? When will our goal be accomplished?
- What is the Time frame?

Now that you have answered all of the above questions, based on the information above, write a single goal statement sentence below.

Example: By the end of the school year, the graduation rate for special education students will increase from 55% to 65%.

In the last section, the issues surrounding the evaluation process of these assessments, goals, plans, and interventions are addressed.

EVALUATION

MEASURE(s) of Accountability

School counselors can evaluate their interventions and the impact their programs have on students' success through accountability measures. Accountability requires systematically collecting, analyzing, and using critical data elements to show improvement (Stone & Dahir, 2011). Examining demographic and performance data makes it possible to determine how policies and practices are affecting issues of equity, to identify results and to inform decision making. Data can help us look at student progress and results, inform, challenge our thinking, determine the need for systemic change, confirm progress, and reveal shortcomings in student achievement (Stone & Dahir, 2011).

MEASURE is an acronym that stands for Measure, Elements, Analyze, Stakeholders-Unite, Results, and Educate. MEASURE provides to novice and seasoned school counselors a simple six-step model for doing accountability work (Stone & Dahir, 2011). MEAURE provides a framework for school counselors to connect to the goals of the school as required by the American School Counselor Association's (ASCA) National Model (ASCA, 2005, 2012). School counselors take one or two school improvement goals and develop the primary focus for their program each year in moving the data toward positive results. School counselors bring a large majority of their strategies (small groups, individual counseling, and classroom guidance, parent contact, community resources, and school-wide behavior management programs) to bear on the critical data element(s) they are trying to move. Following is the application of a MEASURE to a hypothetical case of a real problem in schools across America.

Each year, the U.S. Department of Education, Office of Special Education Programs (OSEP) prepares the *Annual Report to Congress* on the implementation of Individuals with Disabilities Education Act (IDEA) showing data on special education placements to include ethnicity and gender. (Note, as of 2004, IDEA is now IDEIA: Individuals with Disabilities Education Improvement Act.) In 2011, 8.4% of students aged 6 through 21 were served under IDEA, Part B. Of this group, there is an overrepresentation of students who are African American in special education. Students who are African American were served at a higher rate by IDEA at the rate of 11.2% of the resident population aged 6 through 21. The percentages were very high in some states such as Iowa (18.9%), Minnesota (17.0%), Wisconsin (16.3%), Oregon (15.8%), and New Hampshire (15.1%) and, by contrast, much lower in three states: Mississippi (9.0%), Hawaii (8.9%), and Georgia (8.3%). Comparing rates by ethnicity, students who are White and Latino/ Hispanic are less likely to be served under IDEA with rates of 8.1% and 8.0%

respectively. Rates of emotional-behavioral disturbance are elevated within the African American population, roughly twice the national average.

This problem is not newly noted but has been the topic of debates for quite some time. On October 4, 2001, before the U.S. House of Representatives Committee on Education and the Workforce, a hearing on the over-identification of students with disabilities was conducted. Concerns raised at the hearing include the over-identification of minority students for special education services, particularly boys who are African American.

Only 27% of students who are African American and male and in special education graduate from high school (Kunjufu, 2009). "Special education has been used as an automatic answer to behavior and emotional problems that can and should be addressed in a variety of ways" (Kunjufu, 2009, p. 1). According to this author, the ideal student is quiet, can sit and pay attention at length, can work independently, and is passive, and these are not necessarily the attributes of many male students' learning styles nor always the culture of children who are African American. A master teacher can adapt his or her classroom to the learning styles of the students and not always expect students to adapt to the traditional classroom as seen in the effort of Tichman Elementary School. The details of this program are presented in Figure 8.1.

Figure 8.1   MEASURE Example

Mission, Element, Analyze, Stakeholders-Unite, Results, Educate,
A Six-Step Accountability Process for School Counselors

Name and Address of School: Tichman Elementary School

Paterson City, California

Principal: LaShanda Monroe

Name of Counselors Leading the Initiative: Hera Lorenza and Janice Converse

Enrollment: 1404

School Demographics:

Caucasian/Non-Hispanic:	30.7%
Native American:	.7%
Black:	46.5%
Asian:	4.3%
Hispanic:	17.7%
Female:	50.45%
Male:	49.55%
Free and Reduced Lunch:	79.00%

(Continued)

Figure 8.1   (Continued)

STEP ONE: MISSION

STEP TWO: ELEMENT

Element: Number of Black or African American Males receiving services for Emotional Disturbance
Baseline: Last school year, 35 or 11% of the 322 students who are Black or African American Males were receiving services for the designation Emotional Disturbance. This represents a disproportionately high percentage for this ethnic group and gender.
Goal: To reverse the trend of Black or African American Males who are disproportionately represented for Emotional Disturbances services by reducing the total number from 35 current service recipients to 30 or fewer. This number of 30 will also include any new placements into special education services for emotional disturbance during the current academic year.

STEP THREE: ANALYZE

Analyze by aggregating and disaggregating the data to better understand which students are or are not meeting success. You can disaggregate by gender, race, ethnicity, or in a multitude of ways to look at student groupings. This step answers the question, "what else do I need to know about the baseline data to help my students and close these gaps?"
The disaggregated Baseline Data Revealed:
Thirty five, or 11%, of the 322 students who are Black or African American Males are receiving services for Emotional Disturbances class.
8 students are in Grades K–1. 13 students are in Grades 2–3. 14 students are in Grades 4–5.
22 students have been receiving services for 1 month to 2 years. 11 students have been receiving services for 3 years to 4 years. 2 students have been receiving services for 5–6 years.

STEP FOUR: STAKEHOLDERS-UNITE

STAKEHOLDERS - UNITE to develop strategies and set timelines for moving the data element.
Beginning Date: August 2013 Ending Date: June 2014

Stakeholders	Strategies
School Counselors	• Classroom guidance lesson with role play to diffuse anger and to solve problems • Follow-up writing lesson plans for teachers to use such as having students read and write about people in history who used non-violent means to solve their problems

	• Small group counseling with identified groups of students on school success • Individual counseling • Managing resources and bringing in agencies who can work with students in danger of being identified for special education • Organized parents to develop service projects for students that could be done on school grounds • Developed a peer helper program where at-risk students were either the helper or the recipient
Administrators	• Implemented and supported a Pre-Referral Intervention Process • Made special assignments of students with emotional disturbances to master teachers who enjoyed working with challenging students and who had demonstrated success with challenging students • Supported training for the entire teaching staff on how to more successfully work with Black or AA students • Approved an in-school program to use in lieu of out-of-school suspension • Approved and established a single gender classroom on each of the three grade levels with the most discipline referrals
Teachers	• Implemented behavior modification suggestions identified during the Pre-Referral Intervention Process • Made a concerted effort to make their classrooms organized, safe, comfortable, structured • Adjusted to learning differences • Adjusted classroom structure to allow for more structured movement
Students	• Participated in small groups, behavior modifications programs, individual counseling programs • At risk students became peer helpers for other students • At risk students engaged in service projects
Parents	• Agreed to a weekly contact via phone, face-to-face, or email exchange
Parent Teacher Associations	• Provided the materials and awards for a behavior modification program • Provided manpower and food for the weekly award celebration
School Psychologists	• Implemented counseling strategies identified in the Pre-Referral Intervention Process
Social Workers	• Delivered interventions for students and families as an early intervention plan for students who are exhibiting disruptive behaviors that the teacher has not been able to solve
Community Agency Members	• Provided an event in which agencies were able to come and deliver workshops in which parents choose the topic they want to attend
Colleges and Universities	• Provided two school counseling interns to help conduct weekly small groups, individual counseling and classroom guidance lessons • University faculty provided a workshop on parentified youth

(Continued)

Figure 8.1 (Continued)

Stakeholders	Strategies
Classroom Teacher Assistants	• Provided support for the school counselors in the way of clerical help • Provided information to the school counselors about students who needed extra support because of a situation they were experiencing or because they were having a difficult day
Other Support Staff (front office, custodial, cafeteria)	• Alerted the school counselor and intern when a student was having a difficult day so that the counselor could try and intervene
School Improvement Team	• Provided verbal support for the efforts of the school counselor to curtail the over-identification of AA/Black youth for emotional disturbances

STEP FIVE: RESULTS

Results: Restate your baseline data. Where are your data now? Did you meet your goal? Yes X _____   No_____
Data Before (baseline): Thirty five, or 11%, of the 322 students who are Black or African American Males are receiving services for Emotional Disturbances class.
Data now: Thirty students who are Black or African American Males are receiving services for Emotional Disturbances class at the end of the school year. This includes two new staffings for the year and six students who were staffed out of the Emotional Disturbances class. One student moved making the final count at the end of the year 30. Two students are awaiting a change in status and will be staffed out before the beginning of the next school year.
Questions to Consider as you examine results and revise your MEASURE: Which strategies had a positive impact on the data? It appeared that the daily check-in and the weekly celebration that was part of the behavior modification program was most powerful. The six students who were staffed out of the program are doing well with behavior modification programs and the extra support from all the stakeholders. Teachers who were reluctant to have the students removed from special education status are now looking more closely at other students who can be reclassified as regular education because the schools interventions appear to be in place and working well. Which strategies should be replaced, changed, or added? All strategies employed by all stakeholders appeared to have contributed to the success of the MEASURE. The strategy that will be enlarged on and replicated more widely to include all 1st, 4th, and 5th grade classes next year is the daily behavior modification program with the weekly celebrations. Students seemed to respond best with the daily check-ins and the tangible way they could see their progressed tracked.

Based on what you have learned, how will you revise Step Four "Stakeholders-Unite"?

Next year, we need to include more community-based members and our faith-based community. We need to also establish some on school grounds just prior to the start of the school day clubs so that students feel more connected to the school. The school improvement team is working on seeing that this happens.

How did your MEASURE contribute to systemic change(s) in your school and/or in your community?

Teachers are less likely to reach for the paperwork and procedures for special education. The single gender classroom on each of the three grade levels with the most discipline referrals made a tremendous difference in the number of discipline referrals.

Teachers are willing to implement more positive behavior support for disruptive behaviors.

STEP SIX: EDUCATE

Educate others as to your efforts to move data. Develop a report card that shows how the work of the school counselor(s) is connected to the mission of the schools and to student success. The SPARC below is an example of a report card.

Principal's Comments	Results
Hera Lorenza and Janice Converse have taken on one of the most difficult challenges I have had the pleasure of witnessing since becoming a principal seven years ago. Hera and Janice are implementing solid strategies and changing attitudes and beliefs about regular education placement with solid interventions and special education placement. Hera and Janice have worked with members inside and outside the school to advantage our students and to find support for them. Each year our numbers have inched up for special education for African American/Black students as well as all other ethnicities. The strategies that have so positively curtailed the placement among our AA/Black students have also reduced placements considerably. Even though this was not the subject of the MEASURE, we have reduced emotional disturbance placement for the school by 24%. Additionally, the discipline referrals . . . —LaShanda Monroe, principal	Thirty students who are Black or African American Males are receiving services for Emotional Disturbances class at the end of the school year, down from 35 the previous year. This number includes 2 new staffings for the year and six students who were staffed out of the Emotional Disturbances class. One student moved making the final count at the end of the year 30. Two students are awaiting a change in status and will be staffed out before the beginning of the next school year. **Systemic Changes** Single sex classroom on selected grade levels A more frequent use of positive behavior management programs and less use of discipline interventions. Total school focus and support around a common problem.

(Continued)

Figure 8.1 (Continued)

School Improvement Issue(s)	Faces Behind the Data
Critical Data Element(s): Last school year, 35, or 11%, of the 322 students who are Black or African American Males were receiving services for the designation Emotional Disturbance. This represents a disproportionately high percentage for this ethnic group and gender. **Stakeholders Involved** Counselor(s): Conducted classroom guidance lessons, small groups, and classroom guidance lessons to help students solve problems. Developed and implemented behavior modification programs, a peer helper program, and managed resources to bring stakeholders into the effort to support students to move out of special education. Administrator: Supported a Pre-Referral Intervention Process, made teacher placements based on individual student needs, provided professional development specific to the goals of the MEASURE. Implemented a solid out-of-school suspension program. The principal supported a single gender classroom. Teachers: Implemented behavior modification efforts and attended workshops to learn how to make their classrooms and teaching more supportive of different learning and behavior differences.	"Josh" has been in the Emotional Disturbance self-contained class for four years. We conducted a trial period to help him move into regular education. He was placed in the single sex class with a master teacher who knows how to work with students who are volatile. A student intern was also assigned to this class and became another strong role model for this student. Josh has blossomed. He is starting a club for his classmates interested in chess. He has become a peer tutor for the three kindergarten students, and he is so responsible he walked to school six miles rather than miss his obligations to tutor his charges. "I did not want to disappoint them they were looking forward to seeing me." Josh is not the angry young man he seemed to be the year before—with an amazing change in his discipline record from 18 the year before to 4 this year. He was able to articulate in those 4 cases when he settled down as to why his behavior was not appropriate. This was a major change in just 6 months. Teachers recommended that Josh be given a trial period to be a safety patrol next year. Josh will be visiting a college campus this summer as people are trying to raise his aspirations and educational attainment. *The Educate Step is adapted with permission from SPARC a continuous improvement document by the California Department of Education and Los Angeles County Office of Education.*

Source: *Created by Carolyn Stone

The concept of MEASURE can be further applied via Guided Practice Exercise 8.5.

SUMMARY

Assessment is an essential tool in order to delineate the unique abilities and needs of each student and create best-practice interventions. It can be seen from this discussion

---

Guided Practice Exercise 8.5

MEASURE

Look at the MEASURE steps listed above. What concerns do you have about your students' with disabilities school success? Select a data element and draft your MEASURE.

Mission _____
Element _____
Analyze _____
Stakeholders-Unite _____
Results _____
Elements _____

---

that while school counselors will not be the primary professionals conducting batteries of assessments in the schools with students with special needs, they have a critical role in the process on a number of levels: conducting career assessments; coordinating with special education teams in the assessment process; gathering data; following up on goals generated from such assessments; and working with parents, teachers, and the community to ensure academic, career, and personal-social success for these students. Perhaps most importantly, they often have developed strong relationships with the students they serve, and can share nuances of the students' behavior with the team not otherwise known or evaluated by standardized materials. This connection can also serve the students and their families well, in the communication of the process and work outlined by these assessment results. Data collected via these evaluation methods can speak to the importance of the school counselors' role in working with students with special needs. Last, the importance of the role of school counselors in delivering equitable services to students with special needs cannot be understated.

KEYSTONES

- School counselors have an active role in the assessment process of students with disabilities, and they should be aware of the plethora of tools which may be used, including both standardized and nonstandardized measures.
- Two primary ethical considerations are related to assessment: the administration of tests within the training parameters of school counselors, and the selection of tests which are normed on similar groups for which the tests will be used.

- School counselors frequently conduct career assessments. In addition, while they are not the originators of such assessments, they are often involved within the special education team in the process of FBAs, IEPs, and RTI evaluations.
- It is essential that school counselors become comfortable in developing clearly specified goals in working with students with special needs and be able to gather accountability data. The MEASURE model (Measure, Elements, Analyze, Stakeholders-Unite, Results, and Educate) is a six-step strategy designed to facilitate this process.

ADDITIONAL RESOURCES

Print

American School Counselor Association (ASCA). (1997). *Executive summary: The national standards for school counseling programs.* Alexandria, VA: Author.

Barona, A., & de Barona, M. (2006). School counselors and school psychologists: Collaborating to ensure minority students receive appropriate consideration for special educational programs. *Professional School Counseling, 10*(1). Retrieved from http://eric.ed.gov/?id=EJ767391

Elmore, P. (1998). Competencies in assessment and evaluation for school counselors. Retrieved from http://eric.ed.gov/?id=ED457432.]

Elsner, D., & Carey, J. (n.d.). School counseling program implementation survey. Retrieved from http://www.umass.edu/schoolcounseling/school-counseling-program-implementation-survey.php

Lehr, C., & Thurlow, M. (2003). Putting it all together: Including students with disabilities in assessment and accountability systems. Retrieved from http://www.cehd.umn.edu/NCEO/onlinepubs/Policy16.htm

Milsom, A. (2006). Creating positive school experiences for students with disabilities. *Professional School Counseling, 10*(1). Retrieved from http://eric.ed.gov/?id=EJ767379

Mynatt, B. S., & Gibbons, M. M. (2011). Preparing students with disabilities for their future careers. Retrieved from http://counselingoutfitters.com/vistas/vistas11/Article_08.pdf

Roessler, R., Hennessey, M., Hogan, E. M., & Savickas, S. (2009). Career assessment and planning strategies for postsecondary students with disabilities. *Journal of Postsecondary Education and Disability, 21*(3), 126–137.

Scarborough, J. L. (2005). The School Counselor Activity Rating Scale: An instrument for gathering process data. *Professional School Counseling, 8*(3), 274–283.

Web Based

Center for Parent Information and Resources: Assessment and Accommodations: http://nichcy.org/research/ee/assessment-accommodations

AACE: Competencies in Assessment and Evaluation for School Counselors: http://aac.ncat.edu/documents/atsc_cmptncy.htm

EzAnalyze (offers free data collection tools for school counselors): http://www.ezanalyze.com

ERIC Database: New Assessment Measures for School Counselors: http://ericae.net/db/edo/ED388888.htm

Positive Behavioral Interventions & Supports: OSEP Technical Assistance Center provides forms to assist in FBA assessment: http://www.pbis.org/common/cms/files/pbisresources/EfficientFBA_FACTS.pdf

Survey Monkey (offers survey assistance): https://www.surveymonkey.com

The Education Trust (promotes high academic achievement for all students at all levels—pre-kindergarten through college): http://www.edtrust.org

The National Career Development Association (plethora of resources for working with disabled students): http://www.ncda.org/aws/NCDA/pt/sp/interests_disabilities#list_disabilities-I850-NCDA

REFERENCES

American Counseling Association (ACA). (2014). *ACA code of ethics*. Alexandria, VA: Author. Retrieved from http://www.counseling.org/resources/aca-code-of-ethics.pdf

American Psychological Association (APA), National Council on Measurement in Education (NCME), & American Educational Research Association (AERA). (1999). *Standards for educational and psychological testing*. Washington, DC: American Educational Research Association.

American School Counselor Association (ASCA). (2004). *ASCA National Standards for Students*. Alexandria, VA: Author.

American School Counselor Association (ASCA). (2005). *The ASCA National Model: A framework for school counseling programs*. Alexandria, VA: Author.

American School Counselor Association (ASCA). (2010). *Ethical standards for school counselors*. Retrieved from www.schoolcounselor.org

American School Counselor Association (ASCA). (2012). *The ASCA National Model: A framework for school counseling programs* (3rd ed.). Alexandria, VA: Author.

American School Counselor Association (ASCA). (2013). *The professional school counselor and students with disabilities*. Alexandria, VA: Author.

American School Counselor Association (ASCA). (2014). *Draft: Mindsets and behaviors for student success*. Alexandria, VA: Author.

American School Counselor Association (ASCA) & Association for Assessment in Counseling and Education (AACE). (1998). *Competencies in assessment and evaluation for school counselors*. Alexandria, VA: Author. Retrieved from http://aac.ncat.edu/documents/atsc_cmptncy.htm

Association for Assessment in Counseling and Education (AACE). (2003). Responsibilities of Users of Standardized Tests (RUST; 3rd ed). Retrieved from http://aac.ncat.edu/documents/rust.html

Blacher, J. H., Murray-Ward, M., & Uellendahl, G. E. (2005). School counselors and student assessment. *Professional School Counselor, 8*(4), 337–343.

Council for Accreditation of Counseling and Related Educational Programs (CACREP). (2009). *2009 standards for accreditation*. Alexandria, VA: Author.

Doran, G. T. (1981). There's a S.M.A.R.T. way to write management's goals and objectives. *Management Review, 70*(11), 35–36.

Ekstrom, R. B., Elmore, P. B., Schafer, W. D., Trotter, T. V., & Webster, B. (2004). A survey assessment and evaluation activities of school counselors. *Professional School Counseling, 8*, 24–30.

Groth-Marnat, G. (2009). *Handbook of psychological assessments* (5th ed.). Hoboken, NJ: Wiley & Sons.

Kampwirth, T. J., & Powers, K. M. (2012). *Collaborative consultation in the schools* (4th ed.). Upper Saddle River, NJ: Pearson Education.

Kunjufu, J. (2009). *Black boys and special education—Change is needed!* Retrieved from http://www.teachersofcolor.com/2009/04/black-boys-and-special-education-change-is-needed/

National Center on Response to Intervention. (2010). *Essential components of RTI—A closer look at response to intervention*. Washington, DC: U.S. Department of Education, Office of Special Education Programs, National Center on Response to Intervention.

Osborn, D. S., & Zunker, V. G. (2006). *Using career assessment results for career development* (7th ed.). Belmont, CA: Thomson Brooks/Cole.

Stone, C., & Dahir, C. (2011). *School counselor accountability: A measure of student success* (3rd ed.). Upper Saddle River, NJ: Pearson Education.

Whiston, S. C. (2013). *Principals & applications of assessment in counseling* (4th ed.). Belmont, CA: Brooks/Cole, Cengage Learning.

Chapter 9

Inclusion Considerations

DOMENICO CAVAIUOLO

East Stroudsburg University

"Inclusion, it is just education."

—Author

Inclusion can be a difficult concept to understand and an even more difficult practice to implement. The role of school counselors has most often been to advise students, but many are given the added responsibility to work with students with disabilities at various educational levels. The role and function of school counselors may not be only to assess students' emotional and/or social needs or their motivation toward school; today, some are being asked as well to facilitate and support teachers in various educational areas such as curriculum implementation, strategies for including students, or in conducting group sessions to aid social skill development (Friend & Bursuck, 2013). Depending on the educational level (elementary, middle, or high school), the role of school counselor may be either directive or collaborative with teachers. It should be noted, depending on the state and school district, school counselors may play different roles and/or have different responsibilities. Regardless, school counselors can play a critical function in the lives of students with disabilities, particularly in their educational planning and in the implementation of inclusion. School counselors are not just bystanders in the inclusion of students with disabilities, they are facilitators who can assist teachers to gain a greater understanding of students' needs and abilities and offer possible solutions for placement in the least restrictive environment (LRE).

This chapter will provide the school counselor with an understanding of the legal and philosophical positions of inclusion, as well as strategies and programs, to support inclusive practices at all levels of education. At the end of this chapter, you will be able to discern the following:

1. Clearly define LRE and the process for implementation.

2. Understand how to prepare students with and without disabilities for inclusion.

3. Understand the legal concept in response to disciplinary action toward students with disabilities and inclusive practices.

4. Understand the various accommodations and strategies that can support inclusive practices in school.

5. Understand how to support the needs of students with various disabilities in the least restricted environment.

CURRENT ISSUES IN SPECIAL EDUCATION

Inclusion for students with disabilities has been an inconsistent practice (U.S. Department of Education, 2012). Why this wide range of practices exists within states is not clear. Perhaps it is the lack of a clear definition of inclusion and its relationship to the LRE mandate. Or perhaps it is the way inclusion and LRE is viewed as a placement of practice. Other factors may include a lack of leadership, experience, training, and/or skills by school districts to practice and implement inclusion. Regardless of the reason, inclusive practices are not consistently implemented or understood.

Since the beginning of PL 94-142, discussed in Chapter 3, inclusion has been perceived differently (U.S. Department of Education, 2012). Additionally, as students with disabilities move through the educational process from elementary to middle and finally to high school, their inclusion into these settings also differs (Steere, Rose, & Cavaiuolo, 2007). An even greater factor to consider with inclusion is the student's level of disability.

When exploring practical considerations for inclusion, it is important to understand what the legal requirements are so that students with disabilities and their families are provided with equal access to the educational system. One important issue in special education is the legal requirement of LRE.

The Least Restrictive Environment

Arguably one can say that the least restrictive environment (LRE) mandate provides a guideline for establishing an inclusive setting for students with disabilities. The legal definition states:

To the maximum extent appropriate, children with disabilities, including children in public or private institutions or other care facilities, are educated with children who are not disabled, and special classes, separate schooling, or other removal of children with disabilities from the regular educational environment occurs only when the nature or severity of the disability of a child is such that education in regular classes with the use of supplementary aids and services cannot be achieved satisfactorily. (The IDEIA 2004 LRE Mandate, 20 U.S.C § 1412(a)(5)(A))

Closer examination of this mandate indicates that special education planning teams should first consider placement in the regular educational setting with supplementary aids to allow the student with the opportunity to be successful. Depending on the student's disability, be it cognitive, emotional, and/or physical impairment, supplementary aids are provided to support student placement in the general education classroom. Therefore, when a student is deemed eligible for special education and an Individualized Educational Program (IEP) is developed, the team should first decide what supplementary aids would benefit the student to participate and function within the general education classroom with same age peers. If after the use of supplementary aids the student is not appropriate for the classroom, then an alternate placement may be considered. Diagram 9.1 demonstrates how LRE *should* be considered during the IEP process.

The Continuum of Education Concept

The educational placement of students has been a controversial issue since the beginning of the Education for All Handicapped Children Act (EHA) of 1975.

Diagram 9.1   LRE Model for Inclusion

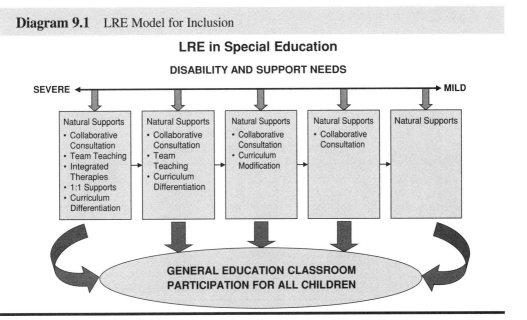

Perhaps one of the factors that add to this confusion is that the special education law allows for the continuum of services. This concept allows the varied educational levels to exist in which students with disabilities may be placed. As discussed in the previous section, the LRE requirement should first consider the general education placement with the use of supplementary aids, and only when deemed ineffective should an alternative placement be considered. The basis for deciding on the effectiveness of the educational placement is if students are making educational progress. The continuum model places students based on disability categories and not on the support needs of students. That is, when considering the placement of a student, the disability becomes a factor in deciding where the student is placed. For example, students with autism spectrum disorders (ASD) may be placed in autistic support classrooms, and students with intellectual disabilities may be placed in life skills classrooms. If the placement does not consider the student's individuality and unique needs and is based on the disability alone, inclusion is not likely to occur. Diagram 9.2 provides a view of the continuum placement approach.

It may be this confusion that professionals need to resolve; is LRE a procedural implementation strategy that requires a "trial" period before alternative placements are considered or simply a placement model? Parents of students with disabilities may not understand LRE or the concept of inclusion or even the potential benefits of placing their child in an inclusive classroom (Gyamfi, P., Walrath, C., Burns, B., Stephens, R., Gen, Y., & Stambaugh, L., 2010). If parents lack this awareness, placement of students is then decided by school administrators and professionals. If school administrators and professionals do not see the value of inclusion, philosophy, and resources or consider the legal application, then the continuum placement model becomes the general practice allowing students with disabilities to be placed in segregated classrooms. It is *critically important* that the placement of students with disability be *need based* and not decided by the disability.

Diagram 9.2   Continuum of Service and Placement Approach

The Continuum of Services in Special Education

DISABILITY AND SUPPORT NEEDS

HIGH ← → LOW

| Institution and Residential School | Separate Special Schools | Segregates Classroom in Home School | Resource Room | Inclusion: General Education |

SUPPORT

The question is, Are schools responsible to ensure that families understand the legal implementation of LRE and be presented with options for inclusion?

The debate over students with disabilities being included in the classroom has changed, from should they be in the general education classroom to what are the most appropriate strategies to help the student be included (Soukup, Wehmeyer, Bashinski, & Bovaird, 2007). Many studies have demonstrated the positive effects of inclusion on students with disabilities (Downing & Peckham-Hardin, 2007; Downing, Spencer, & Cavallaro, 2004), and other studies have focused on the effects of students without disabilities (Carter & Hughes, 2006). In addition, there has been a dramatic increase of students with severe and profound disabilities in the general education classroom (U.S. Department of Education [USDOE], 2006); this may be attributed to parental advocacy in requesting placement of their children in the general education setting (Downing & Peckham-Hardin, 2007). It should also be noted that several studies have also demonstrated the benefits on teachers when students with disabilities are included in their classrooms (Carter & Hughes, 2006; Copeland, S. R., Hughes, C., Carter, E. W., Guth, C., Presley, J. A., Williams, C. R., & Fowler, S. E., 2004). For example, greater collaboration between special education and general education teachers, more shared teaching responsibilities, and a greater concern for students with severe disabilities was reported. These benefits occur as a function of implementing inclusive practices that affect the type of curriculum used and how it is delivered.

Nature of the Curriculum

The type of curriculum appropriate for students will vary depending on the student's disability and level of need. The students' postschool expectations will have a major impact on how the school's educational services will be provided for students at all levels (Steere, Rose, & Cavaiuolo, 2007). In the past, the issue of whether a student's educational program should be academic or functional has generally been based on the student's disability. For example, students with a learning disability generally receive learning support services that would help them develop strategies toward academic success for potential postsecondary education. Students with significant disabilities might receive a life skills educational program (Steere, Rose, & Cavaiuolo, 2007). When considering the different levels of a student's education, regardless of the level of disability, students can be included together using a balance curriculum of a mix of academic and functional skill development (Wehman & Kregal, 2012). This can also occur at the middle level when a student turns 14 years of age. When students are in high school and/or continue to receive special education after 18 years of age, they should be receiving transition-based services that will lead to a post school outcome of work and community living (Steere et al., 2007).

Over the past 10 years, a student population of autism and autism spectrum disorders (ASD) has significantly increased throughout our public education system (Centers for Disease Control, 2014). Inclusion has not been so easy to attain for many of these students at any level of their education (U.S. Department of Education, 2012). Perhaps this has been challenging to schools because of the uniqueness of this population and the difficulty in considering what is an appropriate education for them. To complicate the issue further, students with Asperger's syndrome have emerged as a unique population to support, both academically and functionally. Unlike the "typical" student with autism, individuals on the high-functioning end of the spectrum show average to high levels of intelligence as well as developing language early (Montgomery, Stoesz, & McCrimmon, 2012); these students typically do not have language difficulties. Many of these students may have the academic ability to learn in school with or without support and achieve the required graduation credits to complete high school and receive a diploma, but they may not have the functional skills and ability to live independently as one might need to attend college (Gobbo & Shmulsky, 2014). Many of the students on the autism continuum are challenged by the lack of social skills and communication skills and have behavioral issues (Friend & Bursuck, 2013), as well as executive functioning skills (Gobbo & Shmulsky, 2014). These issues are highlighted in Case Illustration 9.1.

CASE ILLUSTRATION 9.1

"WISH WE DIDN'T HAVE TO SIT NEXT TO THE WEIRD KID"

Imagine the student who is shy and lacks confidence in herself. She is intelligent and understands the math concepts but lacks the confidence in her abilities. When asked a question about a math problem, even though she can figure out the math problem and has the answer, she is nervous and anxious. She looks down at her desk and yells out, "I don't know." Her classmates look at her and think she is strange; they do not associate with her. To her classmates she is "the weird kid." Her teachers think she is a sweet and kind person, but they also see her as a student who does not like to communicate, has awkward social skills, and gets anxious when assignments are discussed and are due. However, despite fear of failure, she is very hard working and seems to get As and Bs in her classes. She is a student with autism spectrum disorder—Asperger's syndrome.

Although students on the higher function end of the continuum may achieve their academic goals, the functional skill development of these students is not so clear. The question becomes, should a student with ASD who meets all of the academic requirements but is not able to successfully function in the community graduate from high school? Whereas most general education students are able to generalize their learning into practical life skills, many students with ASD-Asperger's will need direct instruction that is context related to learn these skills, yet often they do not receive this type of instruction. The aforementioned important question is being asked by many parents of students with ASD-Asperger's. School counselors can evaluate and help to answer this very important question. A concern of families is when their child shows extreme deficits in social and/or functional skills—without such skills, their success in postsecondary education is questionable. If a student has difficulty functioning independently on a college campus or at a job, it may have a negative impact on the person's academic performance. For those students with ASD interested in going on to postsecondary education, school counselors can assist students by helping them develop an awareness of their disability and teaching them self-determination and self-advocacy skills that can lead to an appropriate plan for transition into college life. Although the goal of public education is to help all students be contributing members of their community, students with disability require a direct instructional approach to help them transition into adult life. (It should be noted that the American Psychiatric Association's 2013 *Diagnostic and Statistical Manual of Mental Disorders,* fifth edition, now has one category, Autism Spectrum Disorders [ASD], to include all forms of autism; Asperger's is no longer a separate category.)

Transition Out of Special Education

Transition from school to adult life is seen differently for students with mild disabilities than for those with more significant disabilities. As previously mentioned, some students will benefit from an academic curriculum, and others will benefit most from a functional curriculum. When a student reaches the age of 16, which is the federal requirement for transition planning (IDEA of 2004), regardless of the level of disability, transition must be discussed. However, for some students with disabilities, such as learning disabilities, who may be college bound, transition planning may be overlooked (Steere et al., 2007). Equally important is when transition is not emphasized for students with ASD-Asperger's who are in academic courses. When a student is considered to be on an academic track, often the Post-Secondary Outcome statement in the IEP typically becomes, "The student plans on attending college after high school." It seems that when a student is seen as college bound, transition planning is not emphasized. This limited scope of transition planning can be problematic to students, particularly those with ASD-Asperger's. The areas of concern for some students with ASD-Asperger's may not be easily identifiable by teachers or school counselors and may thus go unnoticed and subsequently not addressed (Sciutto, Richwine, Mentrikoski, & Niedzwiecki, 2012). When this happens, the IEP is not complete, and the critical areas of transition remain unplanned. One way that the IEP can begin to address the transition of students with disabilities is by encouraging them to gain part-time employment as a way to develop work skills. When the focus is solely on academics with little or no instruction in areas that will allow the student to live and function in his community, the student's education will have little relevance in the student's life. School counselors should be cognizant of this important concern and help to address this problem by monitoring student IEPs. However, for students with significant disabilities, transition planning is usually not a concern because it is seen as critical. Aspects of transition planning are addressed in Case Illustration 9.2.

CASE ILLUSTRATION 9.2

TRANSITION TO POSTSECONDARY EDUCATION AND WORK

Latisha is a quiet young girl with the dream of going on to college and becoming a nurse. However, she has struggled with all of her subjects since elementary school when she was identified with a learning disability. Beginning in fourth grade, she received specialized reading support as well as support in her other subject areas. She was behind her grade-level peers but was motivated and worked hard to learn. During middle school, she continued to receive academic support for her learning disability. During the beginning of eighth grade, when she turned 14 years of age, the special education planning team requested that Latisha and her parents meet to consider the courses and her 4-year plan for when she would attend high school. The high school guidance counselor attended the meeting as well. Latisha and her parents made it clear that she wanted to go on to college. Since her older sister was attending a college, she did not want to be left behind. As part of the transition plan of the IEP, it was now important to plan services through high school with the goal of preparing her for college. The counselor laid out a typical 4-year program that would qualify a student to attend college. Although the subjects presented to her and her parents looked very challenging, she was motivated to work hard. The counselor recommended that Latisha join a support group of other students with learning disabilities to talk about their special challenges and to share strategies for overcoming those challenges. The counselor also offered to monitor her progress and said when the time came that colleges would provide the type of support (accommodations) she would need; since these would be available to her, she could then choose the college that would offer the best opportunity to succeed.

Another student in the transitional planning stage is Ramone, an eighth-grade student with significant intellectual and physical disabilities (cerebral palsy). It was clear from the first day of school that he would need a strong support system from family as well as from his teachers and peers. He receives physical therapy PT, OT, and speech therapy regularly and has been since he entered class in the school district. Although Ramone has severe disabilities, his family wanted to be sure he had the opportunity to make friends and to be included in school and his community. His family made sure he participated in many of the community athletic teams, some of which were exclusively for individuals with disabilities and others which were not. He is an active member of his church and hands out bulletins at the end of the services every Sunday. Ramone has been included in activities and regular classes for most of his education, and now that he is about to enter high school, the family and the IEP team must make a decision about his postschool life. It was suggested that the Life Skills Class would provide Ramone with the functional skills he will need to function and survive in the community as an adult. The family was interested but concerned that he would not be with his peers who have known him since elementary school. The counselor, who had Ramone on her caseload, attended the meeting and suggested that he could continue to participate in many extracurricular activities that would maintain his relationships with peers. Ramone was interested in sports and photography, so it was suggested that he join the photography club and perhaps be a sports manager. He could be paired up with a peer who could support him in the club or at the sporting events. It was also suggested that Ramone begin to receive community-based instruction, as well as vocational exploration. The counselor suggested a 4-year high school plan that would include a balance of classroom instruction in areas that would teach him functionally relevant skills in such subjects as consumer science, career planning, and physical education. He could participate in several classes that were for the general education population. He could spend part of his time in these classes and part of his time in the life skills class and part of his time in community-based learning. The counselor also suggested that when Ramone turns 18 years of age and his peers would be graduating, he too could walk during graduation with his peers but return to continue special education until he turned 21 years of age. During the final years of school he could receive community-based learning all day with the focus on job exploration. Most of his day would be outside of the school

(Continued)

(Continued)

building. The counselor was very instrumental in helping the family understand their options and what to expect when Ramone became an adult. The counselor provided the family with information on the adult service system and helped them apply for social security benefits for Ramone and for disability services from the county's developmental disabilities and the state's vocational rehabilitation offices. Ramone had a plan for transition that would lead to a results-oriented outcome.

STRATEGIES TO INCREASE AND ENHANCE INCLUSION

Inclusion should be based on use of best practices, also known as evidence-based practices. These practices are often the tools that special educators use as supplementary aids to support students in learning and to include them in the classroom. Special educators and school counselors can facilitate inclusion by offering ideas, suggesting strategies, and even suggesting participating in direct intervention. This section will provide some of those strategies that can enhance inclusion for students with disabilities.

Preparation of Students With and Without Disabilities

The preparation to include students with disabilities begins when they are children, when they receive early intervention services. At this early stage, parents experience the challenges of having children with a disability and having to make decisions regarding services. Although the services may be therapeutic in nature, this is the first step in understanding their child's needs and how it will affect their life as well as the family's future. As children with disabilities first begin to interact with children without disabilities, these experiences expose parents to the role of being an advocate. Through these experiences, parents are also exposed to support groups that will help them understand about their child's disability while learning how to negotiate the educational system.

Just as we prepare all students to accept individual differences with regard to race, religion, color, ethnicity, and/or sexual orientation, so this acceptance also includes individuals with disabilities. In a world of many individual differences, preparing students without disabilities to be accepting and welcoming of diversity is very important. With appropriate strategies, students without disabilities can be better prepared to accept a classmate with a disability.

Students who have had early interaction with peers with disabilities, such as in early childhood programs, are more likely to have a positive experience (Raver, 2009). The early experiences of interacting, playing, and learning together can lead to greater acceptance of individual differences. However, many students do not have the opportunity in their early education years to be with peers with disabilities. When students enter early childhood education and elementary school with limited experiences with individuals with disabilities, their introduction may need to be facilitated. Teachers have several options to facilitate inclusive experiences with students.

Children's literature

Early childhood education is an excellent place to begin to expose children to disability issues and to peers with disabilities (Raver, 2009). In these early years, from kindergarten to fifth grade (and beyond), teachers and counselors can introduce disabilities to students through literature. Children's books with the theme of children who have varying disabilities are plentiful (Prater, 2000). Books provide views of the world that are different from one's own experiences and give the opportunity to see another person's perspective. There are many books available (Prater, 2000) that are appropriate for young students from kindergarten to fifth grade that can teach them to gain an awareness and acceptance of disabilities (Prater & Dyches, 2008). Prior to the 1980s, individuals with disabilities were portrayed as evil and sinister people (Blaska & Lynch, 1998), but today society has modified its view toward people with disabilities along with an emphasis on inclusion (Prater & Dyches, 2008). As the media continue to present people with disabilities on TV and in movies, particularly if they are portrayed in a positive way, this positive imagery will help to mold society's views. Many children's books can be used as a resource for teaching acceptance, which is more than just tolerance (Prater & Dyches, 2008). Early studies have demonstrated that reading books has had an effect on changing attitudes in a positive way in children (Sawyer & Comer, 1991). Just as books that represent racial and cultural diversity are used to create an understanding of those issues, books about individuals with disabilities can help to create an understanding and awareness of their classmates with disability (Blaska & Lynch, 1998). Using children's literature to develop student awareness and acceptance is an excellent strategy for young children to formulate a positive image of individuals with disabilities that will last throughout their school years and into adult life. School counselors have an opportunity to enhance this practice by reading stories to children and discussing the important themes of the stories with students and by being a role model for other students. Another strategy that can be used to introduce individuals with disabilities to peers in the early childhood and elementary level is *circle of friends*.

Circle of friends

Circle of friends is a concept that can promote student acceptance and inclusion in the classroom (Jorgensen, Schuh, & Nisbet, 2006). Through this process, students learn to build a network of friends around a student with disability. This is a visual process with a series of circles and drawings. It begins by first having students explore their own friendships and relationships. This would be visually displayed in the circles with the focus person being represented in the center. The inner circle represents people who are the most intimate of friends, which includes family; the next circle would be people considered to be close to them such as classmates, neighbors, and family relations. The next circle would list acquaintances such as the teammates from a sports team the students may be on or people the students know by name. The last and outermost circle would be people who are considered helpers or paid professionals such as teachers and counselors. The purpose of this activity is to help students realize how many people are in their lives, also known as *social capital* (Condeluci, 2010). The process is repeated with the student with disabilities, which usually highlights the differences in the number of friendships. As students consider the differences, they are asked to participate as an active member of the focus student's circle of friends. The expectation is that even with a small number of children in the student's circle of friends, those students would eventually invite other individuals and classmates to befriend the student. School counselors can facilitate such activities and monitor the students' participation with students with disabilities. School counselors can meet with the circle of friends weekly by having a "lunch buddy meeting," for example, to encourage and problem-solve issues that may come up during the week. School counselors can make not only a direct impact on the inclusion of the student but also can help to establish potential long-lasting social relationships between peers.

Circle of friends is only one approach that is designed to introduce peers to each other while developing relationships and social skills with individuals with disabilities and their peers without disability; this is something school counselors can facilitate. Other strategies exist that promote friendships between students with and without disabilities. One program, Special Friends program, is designed to enhance the educational experience of students and improve the bond between the school and children, usually in the elementary grades. The program facilitator spends 30 minutes each week for 12 to 14 weeks giving students individual attention that makes them feel important and more connected with school and the adults they see there each day (Friend & Bursuck, 2013). Peer Tutoring program (Harper, Maheady, Mallette, & Karnes, 1999) is described as students helping one another based on their ability. For example, while one student may excel in math, another student may be top-notch in English. These two students can work together to help each other understand difficult concepts, while deepening their own knowledge of the subject. In the Cross-Age Tutoring program, the tutor is older than the tutee. However, sometimes the term *peer tutoring* is used to include both types of mentoring (Friend & Bursuck, 2013). Additional ideas might involve pairing students together based on shared interest so as to have a natural basis for becoming friends (Friend & Bursuck, 2013), and still another approach may be via adapting activities so that students with disabilities are able to participate in those activities such as in the game of musical chairs where the chairs are removed but the players remain (Turnbull, Pereira, & Blue-Banning, 2000). Of course teachers can encourage student interaction by reinforcing positive behaviors toward each other. Teachers can also incorporate social interventions and friendships in their instruction as well as model to students how to interact with their peers with disability. Teacher's modeling can also occur with the strategy of cooperative learning. Case Illustration 9.3 demonstrates how circle of friends strategy might be used in a school setting.

CASE ILLUSTRATION 9.3

CIRCLE OF FRIENDS

Joshua is a student with severe physical and intellectual disabilities. He is being included in a first-grade classroom. He is being introduced to his peers in the class using the circle of friends approach. The counselor introduces the concept of circle of friends to the class and uses Joshua as the example. The counselor begins to identify Joshua's inner circle of friends as being his mother, father, older brother, and two sets of grandparents. The second circle identifies his support staff (personal care attendant), teacher, and therapist (PT, OT, speech therapist). The next circle lists his doctors and his bus driver who picks him up and drops him off from school daily. This is all written on large poster paper for all of the class to see. The counselor asks the students if these are who they might consider as friends and playmates. The counselor leads a discussion between the students, and they all come to the conclusion that Joshua does not have many close friends other than his family. Now the counselor asks for a volunteer to go through the Circle of Friends activity. Jose volunteers and begins to tell the class about all of his relationships in his life, many family members, relatives, friends, and neighbors; the counselor writes all of the names of the people he identifies. Before long, the four circles are filled with many names, relationships, and people. The students in the class are asked to compare Joshua's Circles of Friends with that of Jose's. When this is illustrated to the class, the class members ask questions about why Joshua does not have any friends. They are told that he is new to the class and does not know anyone to befriend. The class is asked if anyone would like to help Joshua by taking him to the lunchroom and sitting with him during lunch. The class is told that Joshua likes sports and has a big

(Continued)

(Continued)

dog and uses a communication device. On the device are several pictures of himself with his family, with his dog, and at various sporting events he has attended. Some students take interest in his dog and others in the sporting events he has gone to and others are very fascinated by the communication device. Students were then invited to sit with Joshua at lunch and during recess to socialize and interact. Students were interested in getting to know Joshua. Later in the school year, Joshua is invited to his first birthday party ever, and when he has his birthday, all of his classmates attend.

Cooperative learning

Cooperative learning is an excellent approach to teaching collaborative skills while ensuring learning and interaction between students. The practice of cooperative learning brings diverse learners, individuals who are ethnically different, as well as students with varying academic levels, together in a setting where they can learn and interact toward a common goal (Friend & Bursuck, 2013). Research on the effects of cooperative learning has demonstrated success in improved academic achievement (Johnson, Johnson, & Cary, 2010), acceptance of individual differences, and relationship building with diverse students including those with disabilities (Putnam, Markovchick, Johnson, & Johnson, 1996).

Cooperative learning is characterized by five essential elements (Brown & Ciuffetelli, 2009; Siltala, 2010). The five elements that are key to cooperative learning are (a) positive interdependence, where each member of the group has a role and responsibility that is needed by the whole group to achieve their goal; (b) face-to-face interaction, where students explain to each other their understanding of the lesson or assignment; (c) individual and group accountability, in which each student is responsible for her or his own learning and work; (d) social skills, the interpersonal skills that are taught to be able to successfully cooperate with each other. This element may require a facilitator to teach the collaborative skills to the students; and (e) group processing, where students assess their effectiveness as a group and how they are progressing toward a synergetic outcome. School counselors can play a role in cooperative learning by enhancing the skills and social relationships between students. Counselors can facilitate group functions, model, and help students to understand each other and their differences while encouraging social skill development. The role of a school counselor can support students and teachers as the groups progress. Another strategy for including students that can incorporate cooperative learning is co-teaching.

Co-teaching

Co-teaching has become an extremely popular approach to inclusive practices (Friend & Bursuck, 2013). This strategy occurs when two or more educators and/or professionals are in the classroom providing and sharing instruction. It should be noted that although this strategy can be very effective, the use of co-teaching can be impacted by the availability of resources, funding, and openness to using co-teaching. There are several different approaches to co-teaching that have been outlined by Friend and Bursuck (2013). The teachers and/or professionals involved in teaching and supporting student learning may be general education teachers, special education teachers, and a specialist such as a speech therapist or school counselors. These teachers and professionals can share the responsibility for teaching content and/or supporting student learning. As part of the co-teaching model, school counselors may become involved in specific objectives to address such areas as communication skills, social skills, and/or encouraging positive interaction. Being able to participate in the classroom can offer important "teachable moments"; this is where school counselors can facilitate the objectives from the students' IEP goals that include communication skills, social skills, and positive interaction. As we have provided strategies for school counselors to facilitate inclusion, there are also many challenges in working with students with disabilities. Inclusive processes are addressed in Guided Practice Exercise 9.1.

Guided Practice Exercise 9.1

INCLUSIVE PRACTICES

During the school year, list all of the strategies observed that are best practices in the area of inclusive education as discussed in this chapter. For example, identify the various types and the teachers that use accommodations to meet student learning styles. Identify the various types and the teachers that differentiate their lessons to assimilate students with a broad range of abilities and disabilities (i.e., ASD, intellectual disabilities). Are general and special education teachers collaborating around student needs? How are teachers collaborating (meetings or through e-mails or phone conversations, etc.)? Are staff meetings compliant sessions as compared to problem-solving opportunities? What opportunities exist for students to socialize and develop social skills in formal and informal learning settings? Are teachers facilitating social interactions, and how is that being done? Generate more areas that can be observed in your school that are important toward the development and maintenance of inclusive practices. At the end of the year, reflect on your list and highlight the good practices being used that you have noticed and recognize those teachers for their efforts and work to enhance inclusive practices in the school. If you noticed a lack of any practice to enhance inclusion in your school, use the information as a way to help identify training needs for teacher in-service days.

SPECIFIC CHALLENGES FOR SCHOOL COUNSELORS IN WORKING WITH STUDENTS IN SPECIAL EDUCATION

Expectations

Expectations of students with disabilities can be critical for student success as well as for their inclusion in school and society. The expectations of individuals with disabilities come from various sources and can be a challenge to school counselors to overcome. Some of the challenges to student expectations come from parents and teachers.

Parental expectations

One variable that can affect students' success and inclusion in school are parental expectations (Doren, 2012). Parental expectations vary depending on the disability of the child, their economic status, and/or minority status (Doren, 2012); if parents are not aware of the potential benefits of inclusion on their children, expectations may be low. Many studies have demonstrated the positive effects of inclusion on students with disabilities such as improved academic gains in a number of areas including mastery of IEP goals, on-task behavior, and motivation to learn (Downing & Peckham-Hardin, 2007; Downing et al., 2004). IEP considerations are highlighted in Guided Practice Exercise 9.2.

Guided Practice Exercise 9.2

IEP MEETINGS

As you attend IEP meetings, observe the interaction between families and the professional staff and how the meeting is facilitated and also observe and consider the following: As the present levels of educational performance are being discussed, are students deficits and disabilities the main areas discussed or are the unique characteristics the main focus? Is the general educational setting the first placement option being considered before other alternate placement options? Are accommodations and/or curriculum modifications presented as support options for student placement needs? Are parents encouraged to participate and offer input into the decisions about students? Are parents asked for their feedback and/or opinions about students and the direction of the IEP? Are parents fully aware and do they understand the IEP process? Is the language used during the meeting clear and not full of professional jargon that parents may not understand? If the student is of transition age (14 or 16 years of age and older), have parents been asked to create a postschool outcome statement for which the IEP and transition goals can be developed? Was the student invited and present at the meeting to discuss the postschool expectations?

Still other studies have demonstrated the benefits of inclusion on the attitudes of students without disabilities toward peers with disabilities: more interactions between them and no interference in their academic performance (Carter & Hughes, 2006). Inclusion of students with disabilities, particularly those with severe disabilities, has been in greater demand by parents (Downing & Peckham-Hardin, 2007). As parents envision what can be possible for their children, and best practices continue to have benefits for both students with and without disabilities, inclusion is becoming a preferred choice by parents of students with disabilities. However, for a child with significant disability, the parental expectations may be different. For example, parents of children with severe disabilities may want their children to learn to live, work, and be able to function within the community (Doren, 2012). In contrast, others want their children to be academically ready to go on to postsecondary education. Positive parental encouragement and high expectations of their children are important factors toward their children's success in school, be it postsecondary education or employment. Often, parents can increase their awareness of educational issues and potential expectations through the support they get from other parents (Turnbull, Turnbull, Erwin, Soodak, & Shogren, 2011).

Parents can gain insight of the educational system by becoming involved in parent support and advocacy organizations. There are many national organizations that can lead parents to advocacy and support organizations within their state. Figure 9.1 provides a listing of many national disability organizations and their websites.

Parental organizations can provide information and training, so parents can be better informed of their rights such as being able to bring an advocate to their IEP meetings and providing information on their legal rights for an appropriate education. For example, the University of Kansas, Beach Center on Disability, has been providing training to families through their publications and programs for many years. One specific program is the Parent-to-Parent program that offers parents the opportunity to receive emotional and informational support from another parent who may be in a similar situation (Santelli, Turnbull, Marquis, & Lerner, 1997). By matching an experienced parent with parents who may be just beginning to advocate for their children, the experienced parent can help guide and provide information that can make their experience less stressful. The Beach Center at the University of Kansas offers many resources for parents as well as a list of

Figure 9.1   List of National Disability Advocacy Organizations

Autism:

- National Autism Association: www.nationalautismassociation.org
- Autism Society: www.autism-society.org
- Autism Speaks: www.autismspeaks.org
- Autistic Self Advocacy Network (ASAN): www.autisticadvocacy.org

Intellectual Disabilities:

- The Arc of the United States: www.thearc.org
- American Association on Intellectual and Developmental Disabilities: www.aaidd.org
- National Dissemination Center for Children with Disabilities: www.nichcy.org

Learning Disabilities:

- National Learning Disabilities of American: www.idaamerica.org
- National Center for Learning Disabilities: www.ncid.org

Physical and Neurological Disabilities:

- Cerebral Palsy
    - United Cerebral Palsy Association: www.ucp.org
    - March of Dimes: www.askus@marchofdimes.com
    - Easter Seals: www.info@easterseals.com
- Tramatic Head Injury
    - Brian Injury Association of America: www.braininjuryinfo@biausa.org
    - National Institute on Disability and Rehabilitation Research: www.ed.gov/about/offices/list/osers/nidrr.com

Mental Health/Mental Illness:

- National Alliance on Mental Illness: www.nami.org
- Mental Health Advocacy: www.mhaadvocacy.org

Center for Independent Living:

- National Council on Independent Living: www.ncil.org
- Independent Living: USA: www.ilusa.com
- Centers for Independent Living: www2.ed.gov/programs/cil/index/html

guidelines for starting a Parent-to-Parent program (www.beachcenter.org). An outcome of these parent programs may be to help them envision positive expectations for their children's educational and/or life skills future.

School counselors can enhance expectations of students by helping parents be aware of the impact they have on their children (Doren, 2012). They may also be able to assist secondary education teachers and transition specialists to help their students develop functionally relevant and self-determination skills, as well as provide support or access to employment after graduation. For example, Carter, Austin, and Trainor (2012) found that when parents had the expectation of their child with disability being employed after high school, the child was 5 times more likely to gain employment than other students with disabilities. High expectations by parents are vital for their children's educational motivation as well as for a positive transition into community life (Francis, Gross, Turnbull, & Parent-Johnson, 2013).

Based on these studies, as well as the findings of Doren (2012), parental expectations can be considered a major factor for student success. Doren's (2012) research highlights several implications that can be important for school counselors to consider as a way to offer support to students, families, and teachers: (a) help parents have a clear set of expectations for their children based on experiences, (b) provide parents with information about accommodations and what services may be available for their children that will lead to a successful postschool outcome, and (c) help to promote self-determination and independence that will lead to a positive postschool outcome. The first two points can be offered to parents in the form of informational or individual sessions while the third point can be provided as a group instruction session with students. These important factors can improve the inclusion of students with disabilities in schools.

Teachers' expectations

As important as parental expectations are, teacher expectations are equally as important. Parental expectations, as noted by Doren (2012), can change and be influenced by teacher expectations. Having high expectations for students with disabilities by teachers and parents may be an important factor toward their success, not only in their education but also as adults. However, teachers must challenge students who have disabilities enough to grow both academically and emotionally with the goal of not being so rigorous that they fail. There may be one factor that can significantly contribute toward teachers' willingness to include students with disabilities. Other factors include expectations of students, attitudes with respect to students with disabilities, and their values toward inclusive education (Cross, Traub, Hutter-Pishgahi, & Shelton, 2004). In the study by Cross et al. (2004), several elements were presented as important toward achieving a successfully implemented inclusive school; and one was a positive attitude by staff. Their findings suggested that having a solid parent-professional relationship, having a therapeutic intervention to reflect students' needs, and having specific adaptations were important elements for an inclusive school. It can be assumed that in order for these elements to come to fruition, a philosophy of inclusion is expected by the school district's administration and supported by the building principals. When there is strong leadership to guide schools toward inclusion, along with the commitment to provide training and support to teachers, the outcome of inclusion is more likely to occur (DiPaola, Tschannen-Moran, & Walther-Thomas, 2004). In order for administrators, teachers, and other professionals to implement inclusive practices, the message of inclusion must be communicated effectively to all stakeholders. Effective communication is important to the implementation of any change or initiative in schools.

Communication

Overview

Effective communication is an essential quality for teachers and school counselors when interacting with parents, students, and colleagues. Communication involves talking, listening, and addressing conflicts (Dettmer, Thurston, & Dyck, 2005). Communicating with teachers, parents, and students is necessary not only for conveying messages and ideas, but also effective communication fosters partnerships and builds trust among all stakeholders. Conversely, poor communication can create barriers and can hinder the relationship between professionals, students, and parents. Effective communication provides a foundation for collaboration among colleagues, parents, and students (Dettmer et al., 2005). A positive communicative relationship is important for the success of inclusion.

School counselors are usually one of the first people students will go to when they are feeling distressed, challenged by the rigor of the curriculum, bullied, or feel lonely. Subsequently, these issues may have a negative academic impact on students in the classroom. Parents will contact school counselors about their child, making inquiries about their child's learning challenges, behaviors, or direction for the future. Teachers likewise may go to school counselors when they need support around a student who is having difficulties emotionally or behaviorally. Effective communication with each of the stakeholders is important for the success of students and for a positive inclusive experience (Semke, Garbacz, Kwon, Sheridan, & Woods, 2010). Communication can occur through many modalities, and either formally or informally, given the current technology, social media (e-mails, Twitter, texting, Facebook, etc.) technology has made it easier to communicate more than ever before.

Professional interactions and communicating with colleagues is not always easy. How to effectively communicate with stakeholders has not been covered sufficiently in formal teacher preparation programs but may be sometimes offered through professional development training (Dettmer et al., 2005). Understanding the skills of effective communication, as well as the barriers to communication, is beyond the scope of this chapter, so only highlights will be presented for further exploration. According to Dettmer et al. (2005), the skills for positive communication outcomes between two or more people can have the following elements: rapport building, responsive listening, assertion skills, conflict management, and collaborative problem-solving skills. These characteristics are important for successful communication. The element of rapport building is the process of building trust for one another. People are more likely to accept an idea from someone they like and trust than someone they do not. Effective communication has more to do with listening, which is also known as *responsive listening,* or *active listening*. Active listening demonstrates a genuine caring for the person's opinions and message. Assertion skills involve being able to communicate the message without negatively affecting the relationship of the person being spoken to. Once trust and rapport have been achieved and one has clearly listened to the message, then it is time to assert your thoughts and opinions in a respectful manner. The final two elements of communication offer insight to managing conflicts and resolving problems. Problem solving can take on many different strategies that can lead to a positive outcome. Stephen Covey (1989) of *The Seven Habits of Highly Effective People* speaks of "always think win-win." Just as these elements can lead to effective communication, barriers to communication can lead to negative outcomes.

It is important to avoid barriers to any form of communication. Barriers can be presented in nonverbal forms. For example, body language such as during interaction can show signs of not being interested or lack of respect for the person. Another nonverbal barrier to communication that is difficult to change is the personal attitudes and diverse values that may affect how people interact with each other. What is important is how teachers and other professionals are able to acknowledge personal attitude toward another person, and yet, though that may affect how they respond, they are fair in the decisions and interaction toward others. For example, conversational style may be seen differently with diverse groups (Palawat & May, 2012). Some cultural groups use silence, proximity of the speaker, eye contact, facial expressions, hand gestures, or intonation of their voice to reflect their communication. Misinterpreting the person's communication intent can hinder the relationship and cause a feeling of distrust (Salend & Duhaney, 2005). For example, when meeting with an Asian American parent who does not make direct eye contact, it should not be assumed that the lack of eye contact is a sign of resistance, lack of caring, or lack of cooperation. This may be a cultural behavior that is not consistent with American cultural norms. Misunderstanding this cultural behavior may lead to feelings of mistrust and disrespect. Being culturally sensitive is important for all school counselors as schools become increasingly diverse. Effective communication conveys trust, caring, and respect that allows school counselors a way to be more effective in dealing with colleagues, parents, and students.

Parents

Communicating with parents does not always have to be challenging. A specific strategy in communicating with families of students with disabilities may help counselors and teachers support parents in their efforts to becoming a partner in their child's education. Edwards and Da Fonte (2012) highlighted a five-point plan to foster a successful partnership with families of students with disabilities through effective communication. The five points are strategies to support the aforementioned discussion on accomplishing effective communication: Point 1, be positive, proactive, and solution oriented; Point 2, respect families' roles and cultural backgrounds in their children's lives; Point 3, communicate consistently, listen to families' concerns, and work together; Point 4, consider simple, natural supports that meet individual needs of students; and Point 5, empower families with knowledge and opportunities for involvement in the context of students' global needs. For example, teachers and counselors might, for Point 1, remember to be sure to share more positive comments about students than negative; for Point 2, they might attend functions within the community that the students live in to get to know the community and the families better; for Point 3, teachers might set up a communication schedule with parents; for Point 4, teachers can be flexible in accommodations and other strategies and be sure to communicate the changes to the families; for Point 5, teachers might provide information on community agencies and services to families so that they can review and make decisions about them. These are excellent suggestions for counselors and teachers to follow when communicating and partnering with families.

Students

Communicating with students with disabilities may also pose a unique challenge to school counselors and is particularly true if students have a deficit due to either a functional or organic communication disorder (Anderson & Shames, 2006). A third communication challenge is in communicating with students who use *augmentative alternative communication* (AAC). Augmentative alternative communication includes all forms of communication (other than oral speech) that are used to express thoughts, needs, wants, and ideas. We all use AAC when we make facial expressions or gestures, use symbols or pictures, or write. People with severe speech or language problems rely on AAC to supplement existing speech or replace speech that is not functional. Special augmentative aids, such as picture and symbol communication boards and electronic devices, are available to help people express themselves. This may increase social interaction, school performance, and feelings of self-worth. These devices may be used by students with physical disabilities or students with autism spectrum disorders (ASD). Important here is communicating respect and trust in students for a successful relationship between counselors and students. Some important considerations in communicating with students with disabilities that will show respect and help build trust are summed up in Figure 9.2.

This discussion on communication is important because it is how information is shared, including the message of inclusion. How the message is sent, delivered, and received has a great impact on the success of inclusion when providing information to teachers, parents, and students. For example, sharing information as to how inclusion benefits teachers and students can help to create a better understanding of the rationale behind the philosophy.

Attendance Issues

Attendance problems in school may be a function of two broad areas; first, students who have lost interest in school perhaps due to the lack of relevance to their lives and, second, those who live in poor socioeconomic conditions (poverty) or have a lack of support (Hughes, 2013). Lack of connectedness to school, concerns about issues at home, caretaking roles at home, and being bullied are other factors that may contribute to school interest and/or attendance problems. Students affected by poverty may not all be students in special education, although there are many students in special education that come from low-income families (Hughes, 2013). The effects of poverty and the relationship of poverty and disability cannot be overlooked. Poverty has a huge impact on children and families, which contributes to unemployment, job loss, school dropout, drug and alcohol abuse, and incarceration (Hughes, 2013). More than one fourth of children with disabilities are living in families that are below the poverty level in this country

Figure 9.2   Tips in Communicating With Students With Disabilities

1. When speaking with someone in a wheelchair, lower the body level, so the speaker's face is level to that of the person in the wheelchair.

2. Listen intently to the person speaking, and if the message is not clear, let the speaker know that it has not been understood rather than acquiescing and not really knowing what the person said.

3. Be patient with the person communicating; give the person time to speak, and/or when they are using technology, to communicate. Pay attention to the person, even when it is taking a long time to say what he or she is trying to say.

4. Do not interrupt the person while they are speaking; allow them to finish what they are saying even if you know what they are going to say.

5. Learn how the technology works that allows the person to communicate and what to do when the technology breaks down. Have a backup form of communication.

(Parish, Rose, & Andrew, 2010). In addition, most of these students with disabilities that live in poverty are minorities—about 27% of African Americans and Hispanic Americans combined as compared to 10% of Whites (U.S. Census Bureau, 2011). It is widely known that minorities are overrepresented in special education (Salend & Duhaney, 2005), and this trend seems to be mostly concentrated in areas where tax revenues underfund schools and are understaffed (Orfield, 2009). This overrepresentation may be due to several or a combination of factors that include a bias toward a cultural group, lack of resources available to families, living within a depressed area, a lack of parental attention, and/or a lack of available health care. Understanding these facts should raise concern about the equality of education to all people in the United States. It also reminds us of the complexity of our society as well as the complexity of special education. The competition between high- and low-achieving schools and high-stakes testing makes it difficult for schools in areas of high concentration of minorities and poverty that poses a unique problem with students' motivation toward school (Hughes, 2013).

Health Impairments and Medical Concerns

Absences in school for students in special education are medical issues known as *special health care needs* (Bryan, Stiles, Burstein, Ergul & Chao, 2007). This term refers to chronic medical issues that affect many students. This includes physical problems, cognitive issues, developmental delays, and behavioral-emotional conditions (Bryan et al., 2007), and students receiving special education and related services have physical disabilities, chronic medical problems, or health impairments that interfere with their learning (Friend & Bursuck, 2013). Students with physical disabilities are individuals who may be limited in ambulation and also have problems with internal bodily functions. These disabilities include spina bifida, spinal cord injury, and muscular dystrophy, all of which may require the attention of the school nurse or the need for medical attention. For example, some students with a severe form of spina bifida known as myelomeningocele will have varying degrees of leg weakness and inability to control bowels or bladder as well as other physical disabilities (Turnbull, Turnbull, Shank, & Smith, 2010). Students with muscular dystrophy have weakened muscles that will progressively debilitate the person to where she or he will have difficulty walking and may need a wheelchair for mobility. In both examples, student absences may be a common occurrence due to medical appointments, recovering from an infection, or simply the need to rest due to their weakened condition. If absences are excessive and the student is missing an inordinate number of school days, home instruction may be necessary. However, home instruction may impact students' ability for social connections and association with peers.

Other impairments that may require medical attention as part of the student's IEP are conditions such as seizures, asthma, attention disorders or attention-deficit hyperactivity disorders (ADHD), diabetes, heart conditions, leukemia, and sickle-cell anemia or cancer, all of which can lead to student absences. For example, sickle-cell anemia causes extreme swelling of the joints and extreme fatigue; these students are more likely to miss school and will need assistance making up missed instruction. Cystic fibrosis is another impairment that causes a buildup of mucus in the lungs that can lead to chronic respiratory infections and possible pneumonia. It is important for school counselors to be aware of students with potentially deleterious condition so that they can be prepared to assist the student and their peers for the severity of these conditions.

Behavioral Issues

Students with behavioral-emotional conditions may also be at risk for absences from school. The definition of emotional disturbance in the Individuals with Disabilities Education Act (IDEA) of 1997 is characterized by (a) an inability to learn that is not explained by intellectual, sensory, or other health factors; (b) an inability to build or maintain satisfactory interpersonal relationships with peers and teachers; (c) inappropriate types of behavior or feelings under normal circumstances; (d) a general pervasive mood of unhappiness or depression and a tendency to develop physical symptoms or fears associated with personal or school problems (includes schizophrenia; Pratt, Gill, Barrett, & Roberts, 2013). (Note, as of 2004, IDEA is known as IDEIA, the Individuals with Disabilities Education Improvement Act.) This definition clearly indicates the need for psychological and/or medical interventions. The absences of students with behavioral-emotional problems may be misunderstood by school personnel as a lack of interest, motivation toward school, or parental neglect when actually students may be experiencing a psychological breakdown. Emotional conditions, such as depression, anxiety, obsessions, or compulsions (Turnbull et al., 2010), may go unnoticed. Tragically, some of these internalized behaviors, particularly depression, can lead to suicide. Suicide is the third leading cause of death in people between the ages of 10 and 24 years of age (U.S. Department of Health and Human Services, 2012), and nearly 5,000 die annually. Although this number does not represent only students receiving special education services, some percentage of students is contained in that number. Many may have gone unnoticed who could have been eligible for services if diagnosed. School counselors should be aware of the warning signs and create initiatives and programs to prevent such tragedies. The mental health of youth in this country has become an increasing concern, and the need to address these concerns is critical for our schools and society's well-being (U.S. Department of Health and Human Services, 2012).

The inclusion of students with behavioral-emotional challenges is a very slow process. In 2002, students with behavioral-emotional disturbances were less likely to be included in the general education class than the same students in 2009 (U.S. Department of Education, National Center for Educational Statistics, 2012). However, placement of such students in facilities outside the school such as separate schools, separate residential facilities, homebound, and correctional facilities increased slightly and continues to be the largest group of students that are placed outside of their home school district (U.S. Department of Education, National Center for Educational Statistics, 2012). The lack of support to include students with behavioral-emotional disorders in their home school may be the biggest barrier to their inclusion (Turnbull et al., 2010). One approach used to support students with behavioral-emotional disorders in schools is *wraparound services* (Turnbull et al., 2010). Wraparound is an intensive, holistic method of engaging with individuals with complex needs (most typically, children, youth, and their families) so that they can live in their homes and communities and realize their hopes and dreams. With the support of therapeutic support staff and the school counselor, these students will have a greater chance of being included. However, this student group continues to be one of the most challenging to include. Some will need intensive therapeutic interventions that schools often do not provide; consequently, alternative schools are the recommended placement for such students. Issues surrounding challenging behaviors and the need for thorough evaluations are addressed in Case Illustration 9.4.

CASE ILLUSTRATION 9.4

IMAGINE YOU ARE A PARENT AT YOUR FIRST IEP MEETING

Imagine you are a parent at your child's first IEP meeting. Your daughter's first-grade teacher is there along with the director of special education for the school district, the speech and language therapist, occupational therapist, and the special education consulting teacher—all sitting around the table. You are here alone to represent your daughter, Melanie. Everyone around the table introduces himself or herself to you, and all of them tell you that they are there to support Melanie in her education. As the meeting begins, you are handed a document and asked to sign that you received your Parental Rights in Special Education. You are not quite sure what the document is, but you sign that you have received it. The director of special education begins by asking each of the teachers and professionals around the table to give their evaluation of Melanie. It is agreed that Melanie is a student on the autism spectrum disorder. After they give their reports, they offer their recommendation for where Melanie should be placed. They all suggest that she should be placed in a classroom with similar students like her called the Autistic Support classroom. You listen but feel disheartened with the fact that they are speaking of Melanie not by name but referring to her by disability. No one at the meeting mentioned anything about placing Melanie in the general education first-grade classroom. The teachers and other professionals continue without asking you what your opinions are about what they have just recommended for your daughter. You feel as if you are in a train and other trains go past you at a high rate of speed making you confused with what is happening. During a brief lull in the meeting, you say, "Why is Melanie not going into first grade with her friends from her day care?" The director of special education tells you that the placement in the Autistic Support classroom is the most appropriate place for Melanie and that she has nothing to fear. The teachers and other professionals were not very attentive to your comments. They did not seem to be active listeners to what you said. Their response does not satisfy your fears that Melanie will not receive a good education or that she will not see her friends and learn. You feel stunned and confused about the whole experience, and no one seemed to hear what you had to say.

SPECIAL CONSIDERATIONS FOR INCLUSION

Students with chronic or acute conditions, such as those previously discussed who will need intensive medical and therapeutic interventions, may not be provided for in the school setting. However, school counselors can coordinate with schools and medical staff on the needs and challenges of such students. Students with these conditions may also need to miss school days, which may require homebound instruction. The IEP team should discuss these possibilities and design alternative strategies for educating students based on their needs. Students with behavioral-emotional disorders pose a unique challenge to school administrators and counselors, but with effective teacher training, behavioral interventions, and psychological support, students will have the opportunity to be educated in the least restrictive environment.

INTERVENTIONS

Responding to behavioral challenges is one of the biggest concerns facing schools today (Westling & Fox, 2009). Students that exhibit behavioral challenges may include individuals with autism spectrum disorders (ASD). In reality, behavioral incidents can occur by any student with or without a disability, and their behaviors may be dependent on factors that are environmental such as a stressful living condition or child abuse as well as peer rejection or bullying at school (Turnbull et al., 2010). The behaviors of students can range from aggressive, abusive, and/or self-injurious to stereotypical such as hand flapping, echolalia, or excessive body rocking. These behaviors are seen as socially inappropriate and hinder students' ability to learn, as well as leading to potential medical complications, particularly in individuals whereby the behaviors are self-injurious or aggressive. Whereas 30 years ago behaviors were seen as something to be eliminated without considering the function to or for the student (Cooper, Heron, & Heward, 2007), today the field has progressed by considering the function of the behavior to the individual and working to replace the negative behavior with appropriate and acceptable alternatives. Today, *positive behavior supports,* typically termed (PBS), is a common approach in dealing with behavioral concerns in students (Horner et al., 1990).

Positive Behavioral Supports

The concept of PBS considers not only the behavior itself but also the factors that surround the behavior, as well as the purpose or function of the behavior. That is, practitioners consider all aspects of the person's life, including the environment in which the context of the behavior occurs. In addition, the focus is not only an interest in changing the negative behavior but also an attempt to improve the quality of life of the person by changing the environment (Westling & Fox, 2009). The changing environment may be moving from a more restrictive setting to one that is less restrictive such as an inclusive classroom where positive role models can help students learn appropriate behaviors. In addition, there are two important concepts when working to correct inappropriate behaviors. First is to consider that many behaviors individuals exhibit are a form of communication; there is an attempt to communicate something. Since some may not have an effective means of communicating (i.e., verbal or augmentative), the only way they may be able to get attention is by behaving aberrantly. The second important consideration about PBS is that the intervention is not only designed to reduce a problem behavior, but also it is an attempt to understand the context of that communication and replace it with an appropriate prosocial behavior (Carr et al., 2002). The application of both of these concepts to address the aberrant behaviors of individuals is extremely important for the maintenance of prosocial behaviors.

The concept of PBS has great significance to inclusion as a supplementary aid. This should be of particular interest to school administrators and school counselors. In order to comply with IDEA (Turnbull, Wilcox, Stowe, & Turnbull, 2001) and meet the LRE mandate, before any action to remove students from the general education environment for behavioral problems, a Functional Behaviorial

Assessment (FBA) must be completed and a Behavior Support Plan (BSP) implemented; the BSP is considered to be supplementary aid. In instances where the behavior of a student is the result of a more egregious action, the amendments to IDEA (Turnbull et al., 2001) have provided clear guidelines. The IDEA (Turnbull et al., 2001) requires an FBA and a support plan be administered when (a) a student is being considered for suspension from school for up to 10 days; and (b) when the student's behavior is impeding on the learning of others or himself or herself (Turnbull et al., 2001). It becomes important that school districts and administrative personnel, including school counselors, be aware of the procedure so that students' rights are not violated. Figure 9.3 provides a visual of the procedure to be considered.

Whereas PBS is an individual intervention approach to address behavioral concerns, it does not need to be the first response in a school's plan for creating a positive and safe learning environment for all students. Response to intervention (RTI) outlined in Individuals with Disability Education Improvement Act (IDEIA)

Figure 9.3   Procedure for Implementing Behavioral Interventions

Student behavior as determined by teacher

Teacher implements classroom plan to correct behavior

Conduct a Functional Behavior Assessment
(If the plan is deemed ineffective)

Develop Positive Behavior Support Plan

Monitor and assess the effectiveness of the plan

If plan is not effective, redo FBA or consider alternative placement

of 2004 (PL 108-446) provides a model with intervention levels that begins with a school-wide program to encourage prosocial behaviors in students throughout the school building. Response to intervention is defined as a method of academic intervention used to provide early, systematic assistance to children who are having difficulty learning or behavioral challenges. RTI seeks to prevent academic failure and behavioral concerns through early intervention, frequent progress measurement, and increasingly intensive research-based instructional interventions for children who continue to have difficulty. RTI is a multileveled approach for aiding students that is adjusted and modified as needed.

School-Wide Positive Behavior Supports

In addition to the individual support plan, school-wide positive behavior supports (SW-PBS) have also been used effectively (Horner, Sugai, & Anderson, 2010) in both elementary and secondary schools with success (Bradshaw, Mitchell, & Leaf, 2010). The system of school-wide PBS is a preventive approach. It considers the school's social culture and matches the appropriate plan to achieve both social and academic success while preventing behavior problems (Horner et al., 2010). The individual supports are provided to students as needed when the school-wide approach is not meeting the student's needs to control the behavior. One of the key ingredients to the success of SW-PBS is to teach appropriate social behaviors and skills while reinforcing through individual recognition or a collective reward for achieving specific results within the school setting (Horner & Sugai, 2005). For example, schools can give students reward tickets for any number of positive interactions, behaviors, or acts exhibited that are considered to be "good" or "kind." The tickets can then be exchanged for items in the cafeteria or school store. School counselors and administrators can be very instrumental in establishing such practices in schools by monitoring and acknowledging student progress. The purpose of SW-PBS and individual PBS is to provide a safe learning environment for all students as a proactive and preventive strategy.

Curricular Adaptations

As we have noted in this chapter, there are many strategies and curriculum issues that support the inclusion of students with disabilities in schools. In some instances, good teaching skills, materials, and attention to individual learning styles may be sufficient for students with disabilities in order to learn and be successfully included. However, for other students with disabilities, modifications or accommodations to the curriculum may be needed (Friend & Bursuck, 2013). Depending on the nature of the students' disability, either modifications or accommodations are used to support students' inclusion and learning needs. First, it must be determined if students will need a modification or accommodation and how these two terms differ: Modifications change the expected outcomes of the curriculum whereas accommodations do not. For example, students with significant disabilities may need a functional curriculum; this is a *modified* curriculum because it is not an academic program but addresses independent living skills. For other students with disabilities, a modified curriculum may require only a minor content change (i.e., reducing the number of possible answers to a test from four to three or solving eight math problems rather than 10).

Students with mild disabilities, such as learning disabilities, may receive an *adapted* curriculum that does not significantly change the curriculum content. The adapted curriculum does not change the content but only how it is instructed to the student. Usually the adaptation is consistent with the student's preferred learning needs and the expected outcomes are the same for all students. For instance, students with learning disabilities who have reading processing difficulties may need reading materials given to them in an audio version, such as a CD. The content of the curriculum is not changed or altered but simply provided to students in a different manner. In the cases where an accommodation is provided, an IEP is not required and a 504 Plan is provided (Friend & Bursuck, 2013). School counselors are generally responsible for writing 504 Plans for students when an IEP is not needed.

Accommodations

As stated above, accommodations do not alter or change the content of the curriculum and a 504 Plan is sufficient to legally provide the accommodation. There are critical features of effective accommodations: (a) determine students' learning style, (b) determine the teaching methods used in the classroom by teachers, and (c) determine the difference in teachers' teaching approach with that of the students' preferred learning needs and determine which accommodation will best match the students' ability to learn the content (Gartner & Kerzner-Lipsky, 2002). These authors have developed a process to assess students and teachers and a method to determine an appropriate accommodation for the student. This approach is individualized and specific to a student's needs. School counselors may be very helpful in assessing student learning styles and/or teacher teaching methods. From the information obtained about a student's preferred learning style, teachers can determine if their methods of teaching match up to the student. Teachers can also be assessed and get feedback on their teaching methods. From this information, school counselors can determine if lessons are presented in ways that benefit students. The concept of using multiple teaching strategies is consistent with the concept of universal design, which will be discussed in the next section. Accommodations can be very important to students by allowing them an equal opportunity for learning and being successful in school.

Universal Design

Individual accommodations are being replaced with the concept of universal design, also known as universal design for instruction (UDI). This concept is an educational application that uses principles of learning that are accessible for all students including students with disabilities (Meyer, Rose, & Gordon, 2014). Universal design for instruction allows all students to benefit from instruction when it is made accessible (Hitchcock, Meyer, Rose, & Jackson, 2002). This approach focuses on addressing accommodation for students' individual learning styles without singling them out. This concept has important implications for including all students, as well as students with mild to severe disabilities (Westling & Fox, 2009). These authors further indicated that the concept of UDI recognizes that classrooms consist of heterogeneously diverse learners each with unique learning abilities; they highlighted positive academic results with its use. In the universal designed curriculum, all teaching materials, goals, methods, and assessments are flexible to accommodate all learners and range of abilities (Rose, 2000).

Universal design is not only beneficial for students with mild disabilities (i.e., learning disabilities); it has also been seen as an effective method for students with severe disabilities. Dymond et al. (2006) used the principles of universal design in a high school classroom with a heterogeneous group consisting of students without disabilities, mild disabilities, and severe cognitive disabilities. The results of the study provided evidence of changes in both teachers and students. For teachers, there was greater collaboration between special education and general education teachers, more shared teaching responsibilities, and a greater concern for students with severe disabilities. The authors also noted greater interaction by teachers with students with severe disabilities and more student engagement between students with and without disabilities. Principles of Universal Design are illustrated in Case Illustration 9.5.

CASE ILLUSTRATION 9.5

PRINCIPLES OF UNIVERSAL DESIGN

Ms. Moss has a class of diverse learners in her fifth-grade intercity classroom. There are students who are classified as needing special education services as well as students who do not qualify for services but have learning challenges due to their social conditions and preparation. All are included in this fifth-grade class. Ms. Moss was interested in creating a learning environment that was conducive to every student's learning ability level and learning style. Rather than trying to create separate lessons for each student, she decided to implement a universal design instructional (UDI) approach. She began to do some research and found several websites that helped her plan and design a UDI lesson (www.cast.org, www.udlcenter.org, and http://udl-irn.org.). First, she wanted to know how her students learned best and asked the school counselor to help her assess student learning styles. She also reviewed student records and IEPs for those who had them. Next, she asked the school counselor to give her feedback on her teaching approach and how often she lectured, versus doing hands-on projects, group work, or independent time. She also reviewed how she assessed and tested her students. Once she had all of this information, she began to plan for one lesson to design universal strategies for instruction. For a lecture, she added images, video clips, and animation to PowerPoint slides; for other lesson elements, she added tangible items to demonstrate concepts, pre-taught vocabulary words on topics, and showed images to help student understanding of the meaning; provided students with graphic organizers and concept maps; provided several options for learning, such as games, discussion groups, and computer programs; used peer tutoring; and allowed students to create their own learning experience based on strengths, interests, and preferences. When deciding on assessment strategies, she decided to test student knowledge through discussions, projects, presentations, and written exams. This required much time for Ms. Moss to plan and implement, but it reaped results. She noticed her students more engaged and interested, she spent less time on classroom management, and student performance on assessments improved. She enjoyed teaching using her newfound method of universal design instruction.

Application Activities

1. Analyze your school's inclusion policy and programs. To what degree are students with disabilities included in academic classes or in other extracurricular activities?

2. If you work at the secondary level, determine how planning for transition from special education to adult services is handled by your district. What role do you or could you plan in the transition planning process as a school counselor?

3. Analyze and determine your school-wide positive behavior support system. How does this system tie into classroom-wide behavior support systems used by individual teachers within your school? If your school does not have a school-wide positive behavior support system, list two ideas that can be the beginning for the design of a school-wide program.

4. If you work in the early childhood or elementary school level, identify four books that will illustrate the acceptance of individuals with disabilities (i.e., autism spectrum disorder, intellectual disability, physical disability—for example, a person uses a wheelchair, an individual has sensory impairment). Develop a lesson plan to read a book to a class and discuss the acceptance issues in the book.

Modifications

For many students with significant and severe disabilities, where universal design is not appropriate, instructional modifications may be required. Modifications are changes to the curriculum that are impacted by federal and state standards. For example, using UDI for a math lesson to teach addition to a student with severe disabilities may not be beneficial whereas a functional lesson such as money recognition would be more appropriate. It may be a change in the content of the curriculum or in the expected outcome for students (Price & Nelson, 2007). Modifications may be minor or significant; for example, during a geography lesson, while *all* students are learning the same subject, the lesson may be taught at different levels of difficulty, for example, where *most* students are locating major cities on the U.S. map and where one student with special needs is working to locate streets in his own town. Another example of a modification is reducing the criteria of an objective. For example, the teacher can accept fewer answers to a quiz or have the students complete fewer math problems than other students in the class. A third level of modification might be to teach different content, where the students are learning functionally relevant information, such as independent living and work skills. This modification approach whereby the curriculum is altered at different levels is an approach that can offer the opportunity for students with varying disabilities to participate in the general education environment.

Modifying the curriculum to increase the engagement of students with mild to severe disabilities in the general education classroom begins with the philosophy that all students should be educated together—first introduced by Brown, Nietupski, and Hamre-Nietupski (1976). The idea of teaching relevant skills to students when the academic curriculum is not a critical need has motivated much discussion and controversy over the years. Despite the authors' guidelines for including students with severe disabilities, these students have generally received their education separated from their peers without disability (U.S. Department of Education, 2012). The inclusion of students with mild to severe disabilities has been an elusive concept despite the demonstrated best practices and research on the benefits of this approach (Downing, 2005; Friend & Shamberger, 2008; Villa, Thousand, Nevin, & Liston, 2005). The idea of creating an inclusive, functional curriculum should not be an onerous process. Designing a balanced approach to teaching what students need to know within the context of the general education curriculum can be achieved (Wehman & Kregal, 2012). Later, as students move from elementary to middle school, the emphasis may turn from classroom instruction to community-based instruction (Westling & Fox, 2009). For students with severe disabilities, learning in the context of a "real" setting such as that found in a community-based learning environment is needed and therefore appropriate as compared to academic instruction. When students with mild to severe disabilities reach the age of transition, the curriculum should prepare students to live, work, and function in the community commensurate to their level of ability (Steere et al., 2007).

In addition, the LRE doctrine should be kept in mind when modifications are considered. Modifications should be seen as levels of support based on student need and ability. When modifying assignments for students with disabilities, though the activities may be different from those for other students, they should continue to be aligned with the general education curriculum (Friend & Bursuck, 2013). As first introduced by Udvari-Solner (1992), curriculum modifications can occur through changes in the instructional groupings of students, the teaching format, the environmental conditions, the curriculum goals or outcomes, the instructional materials, or the level or type of personal assistance provided; or by creating an alternative activity when the aforementioned strategies are not effective. These strategies have consistently been shown to be effective and are still of value as teachers modify their lessons and materials to allow for the greatest amount of inclusion of students with disabilities. For example, when considering instructional groupings, cooperative learning strategies as previously discussed is a good method for teaching diverse learners (Johnson & Johnson, 2009). Consistent with Udvari-Solner's (1992) suggestions, curriculum modifications can occur in changes in the teaching format. For example, this type of modification can be the use of co-teaching strategies (Friend & Bursuck, 2013). Another consideration might be changes in the environmental condition. For example, for students of transition age, the most context relevant condition might include community-based instruction (Bambara, Browder, & Koger, 2006). Yet another suggestion might be changing the level or type of personal assistance provided. A strategy here might be peer tutoring or peer-mediated instruction (Bryant, Bryant, Gersten, Scammacca, & Chavez, 2008). When all of the supplementary aids and services have been exhausted, then the last rung in the LRE continuum can be applied, and an alternate placement may be considered.

Technology

Yet another important supplementary aid for supporting the inclusion of students with disabilities is through technology. Technology may be the single most important contribution to people with disabilities. The impact of technology on the lives of people with disabilities goes far beyond the classroom: It has increased the independence and productivity of people with disabilities in multiple ways. A colleague mentioned an important excerpt taken from an IBM brochure: "Technology makes life easier for most people, but technology for people with disabilities makes things possible" (personal communication, April 18, 2014). The use of technology ranges from traditional and basic forms such as computers and laptops to the complex forms used to assist and aid students to participate, communicate, and function within the classroom. Technology has provided teachers with additional tools for teaching, such as the utilization of SMART boards, e-books, computer-based or web-based learning, and online tutorials and/or classes (Friend & Bursuck, 2013). The use of technology, particularly in special education, has received federal legislative support and is associated with amendments to IDEA.

Several federal laws have been enacted over the years beginning with the 1988 Technology-Related Assistance for Individuals with Disabilities Act (PL 100-407), and the later amendments to the law (PL 103-218, 1994). Also, the Assistive Technology Act of 1998 (PL 105-394), and amendments to IDEA, 1997 and 2004, have included provisions for assistive technology devices and assistive technology services for students in special education. The term *assistive technology* (AT) has been used to indicate any item, piece of equipment, or product system, whether acquired commercially, modified, or customized, that is used to increase, maintain, or improve functional capabilities of a child with a disability (IDEIA, 2004). The 2004 amendments of IDEA required that assistive technology be considered when determining the child's needs and services in the IEP. The need for AT should be considered at three different points in the IEP process: first, during the present levels of performance to discuss if AT will have an impact on the student's achievement; second, when setting the goals and objectives; and third, when determining the student's placement to determine if AT will impact the student in different settings (Parette & Peterson-Karlan, 2007).

Technology has a wide range of applications that can be beneficial to students with a variety of disabilities. Devices can be relatively simple low-technology items or more complex high-technology items. The need for AT begins with an assessment that determines the benefits and needs in relation to the students followed by the selection of the needed AT device (Best, Reed, & Bigge, 2005). Many school districts will have access to AT professionals that can assess and recommend appropriate technology for students. In addition, many states have AT lending libraries that allow individuals who have been recommended for a specific type of device to borrow the device to determine if it is appropriate for the student. It is suggested that schools contact their state Department of Education for a list of AT lending library centers and providers in their state. One issue that has raised concern and controversy in schools is the cost of AT devices and who owns the right to those devices.

Financial responsibility for AT devices has been an issue. Wehmeyer (1999) found that one reason why persons with intellectual disabilities do not receive AT devices is due to the cost. However, IDEA (2004) requires the IEP team to determine the student's need for AT as part of a free and appropriate education (Parette & Peterson-Karlan, 2007). Consequently, if the need for an AT device is determined necessary by the IEP team for the student to receive an appropriate education, schools must provide the device at no cost to the student and/or family. However, funding for the device may be limited to school use only unless it is specified that the device could be used at home (Westling & Fox, 2009). Families can request that students have access to their AT device for home use by including such a statement in the IEP. Because funding for some AT devices may be a concern, the Technology-Related Assistance for Individuals with Disabilities Act of 1998 (PL 100-407) provides states with the opportunity for long-term federal funding to support AT program needs. School counselors, professionals, and parents should be aware that funding for AT devices can be provided by federal programs such as Medicaid programs, state Developmental Disabilities Offices, state Vocational Rehabilitation Offices, and some private insurance. School counselors and other professionals should help in determining the best way to support the need for AT devices for students that need them.

SUMMARY

Throughout this chapter, strategies and ideas have been presented to assist school counselors in supporting the philosophy and practical application of inclusion. We have discussed aspects of inclusion from a philosophical perspective to a legal mandate. Strategies for inclusion were presented as well as how to prepare students with and without disabilities to participate in an inclusive setting as well as challenges to enhancing inclusion. Communicating with colleagues and parents about the benefits of inclusion and how to increase awareness and understanding was presented. Finally, accommodations and universal design strategies were presented along with the importance of technology in support of an appropriate education. One final point should be made about students with disabilities and postsecondary education. Clearly, students with learning disabilities and many with autism spectrum disorders (ASD) can be successful in postsecondary education. As school counselors guide and plan for students with these disabilities in regard to the selection of postsecondary education, students can continue to receive accommodations (by institutions if requested by qualified students).

Once students leave education and enter postsecondary or higher education, IDEA entitlements no longer apply. Students must be determined eligible for accommodations based on their disability. It is important to note that although postsecondary education must provide accommodations for students, they are not required to modify the instruction for students. In addition, higher education institutions are not responsible for providing support or instructional aides, therapeutic interventions, or purchase needed equipment such as computers. However, state vocational rehabilitation agencies may be able to purchase equipment for students they deem eligible for their services. Students must be able to self-identify and self-advocate in order for them to receive services. The one aspect that does carry over into higher education and community employment and living is Section 504 of the Rehabilitation Act and of the Americans with Disabilities Act. It is important that students understand their disability and their accommodations needs and be able to request them wherever they are needed. Therefore, it is important to help students to understand the impact of their disability and what accommodations work best. In some cases, accommodations should be faded from use whenever possible to determine the student's continued level or need in postsecondary education. As part of this preparation for postsecondary education, students should be taught their rights under Section 504 of the Rehabilitation Act and the Americans with Disabilities Act. It is important that students have the ability to advocate for themselves and the self-determination skills to request needed accommodations. The following website may offer some information on the accommodations provided in postsecondary education and how to qualify for them: http://Eric.ed.gov/?id=ED370293.

School counselors can impact the inclusion of students with varying disabilities at all levels of education by understanding student needs, the legal mandates, and the strategies that can enhance the inclusion for all students. Now, it is up to the school counselors to participate in this important outcome and facilitate this process of inclusion.

KEYSTONES

- School counselors play a critical role in the lives of students with disabilities, particularly in regard to their educational planning and in the implementation of inclusion. As such, they must understand the principles of LRE and the inclusion process.
- School counselors should be aware of the legal mandates and guidelines that exist with respect to disciplinary action toward students with disabilities and with inclusive practices.
- School counselors need to be aware of best-practices inclusion strategies in order to prepare students with and without disabilities to participate in an inclusive setting.

ADDITIONAL RESOURCES

Print

Brownell, M. T., Smith, S. J., Crockett, J. B., & Griffin, C. C. (2012). *Inclusive instruction: Evidence-based practices for teaching students with disabilities*. New York, NY: Guilford.

Dettmer, P., Knackendoffel, A. P., & Thurston, L. P. (2013). *Collaboration, consultation, and teamwork for students with special needs* (7th ed.). Upper Saddle River, NJ: Pearson/Allyn & Bacon.

Friend, M. (2014). *Special education: Contemporary perspectives for school professionals* (4th ed.). Upper Saddle River, NJ: Merrill/Pearson.

Rose, D., Meyer, S., & Hitchcock, C. (2005). *The universally designed classroom: Accessible curriculum and digital technologies.* Cambridge, MA: Harvard Education Press.

Turnbull, A., Turnbull, R., Erwin, E. J., Sookak, L. C., & Shogren, K. A. (2011). *Families, professionals, and exceptionality: Positive outcomes through partnerships and trust* (6th ed.). Upper Saddle River, NJ: Merrill/Pearson.

Web Based

CAST. Universal design strategies also known as universal design for learning (UDL): www.cast.org/udl/

UDL strategies are for creating instructional goals, methods, materials, and assessments that work for all students, not just students with special needs. It is not the one-size-fits-all solution but a flexible approach that is customized and adjusted for individual needs.

The Beach Center on Disabilities: www.beachcenter.org

Provides interventions, support, publications, and training to parents and professionals on practices to affect the quality of life of people with disabilities in all areas, from school to community living.

Technical Assistance Center on Positive Behavioral Interventions and Supports, established by the U.S. Department of Education's Office of Special Education Programs (OSEP): www.pbis.org

ERIC Database: http://Eric.ed.gov/?id=ED370293

Information on accommodations provided for students who qualify at the postsecondary education level.

A list of colleges and universities that offer an inclusive college opportunity for individuals with intellectual disabilities: www.thinkcollege.net

Home of the National Longitudinal Transition Study-2 (NLTS2): www.nlts2.org

Provides documents and research on a national level on the results of students who moved from secondary education into adult life. The NLTS2 is funded by the U.S. Department of Education.

REFERENCES

American Psychiatric Association. (2013). *Diagnostic and statistical manual of mental disorders* (5th ed.). Washington, DC: Author.

Anderson, N. B., & Shames, G. H. (2006). *Human communication disorders* (7th ed.). Boston, MA: Allyn & Bacon.

Bambara, L. M., Browder, D. M., & Koger, F. (2006). Home and community. In M. E. Snell & Brown (Eds.), *Instruction of students with severe disabilities* (6th ed., pp. 526–568). Upper Saddle River, NJ: Merrill/Pearson Education.

Best, S. J., Reed, P., & Bigge, J. L. (2005). Assistive technology. In S. J. Best, K. Wolff Heller, & J. L. Bigge (Eds.), *Teaching individuals with physical or multiple disabilities* (5th ed., pp. 179–226). Upper Saddle River, NJ: Pearson/Merrill.

Blaska, J. K., & Lynch, E. C. (1998). Is everyone included? Using children's literature to facilitate the understanding of disabilities. *Young Children, 53*(2), 36–38.

Bradshaw, C., Mitchell, M., & Leaf, P. (2010). Examining the effects of schoolwide positive behavioral interventions and support on student outcomes: Results from a randomized controlled effectiveness trial in elementary schools. *Journal of Positive Behavior Interventions, 12*(3), 133–148.

Brown, H., & Ciuffetelli, D. C. (Eds.). (2009). *Foundational methods: Understanding teaching and learning.* Toronto, Ontario, Canada: Pearson Education.

Brown, L., Nietupski, J., & Hamre-Nietupski, S. (1976). Criterion of ultimate functioning. In A. Thomas (Ed.), *Hey, don't forget about me!* Reston, VA: CEC Information Center.

Bryan, T., Stiles, N., Burstein, K., Ergul, C., & Chao P.-C. (2007). "Am I supposed to understand this stuff?" Youth and special health care needs readiness for transition. *Education and Training in Developmental Disabilities, 42*(3), 330–338.

Bryant, D. P., Bryant, B. R., Gersten, R., Scammacca, N., & Chavez, M. M. (2008). Mathematics intervention for first and second grade students with mathematics difficulties. The effects of tier 2 intervention delivered as booster lessons. *Remedial and Special Education, 29*(1), 20–32.

Carr, E. G., Dunlap, G., Horner, R. H., Koegel, R. L., Turnbull, A. P., Sailor, W., . . . Fox, L. (2002). Positive behavior support: Evolution of an applied science. *Journal of Positive Behavior Intervention, 4*(1), 4–16.

Carter, E. W., Austin, D., & Trainor, A. A. (2012). Predictors of postschool employment outcomes for young adults with severe disabilities. *Journal of Disability Policy Studies, 23*(1), 50–63.

Carter, E. W., & Hughes, C. (2006). Including high school students with severe disabilities in general education classes: Perspectives of general and special educators, paraprofessionals, and administrators. *Research and Practice for Persons with Severe Disabilities, 31*(2), 174–185.

Centers for Disease Control. (2014). Autism spectrum disorder (ASD). Retrieved from www.cdc.gov/ncbddd/autism/data.html

Condeluci, A. (2010). Social capital—The real route to inclusion. Retrieved from http://www.bianc.net/docs/Family%20Conference/Condeluci%20TASH_article.pdf

Cooper, J. O., Heron, R. E., & Heward, W. L. (2007). *Applied behavior analysis* (2nd ed.). Upper Saddle River, NJ: Pearson.

Copeland, S. R., Hughes, C., Carter, E. W., Guth, C., Presley, J. A., Williams, C. R., & Fowler, S. E. (2004). Increasing access to general education: Perspectives of participants in a high school peer support program. *Remedial and Special Education, 25*(6), 342–352.

Covey, S. R. (1989). *The seven habits of highly effective people.* New York, NY: Simon and Schuster.

Cross, A. F., Traub, E. D., Hutter-Pishgahi, L., & Shelton, G. (2004). Elements of successful inclusion for children with significant disabilities. *Topics in Early Childhood Special Education, 24*(3), 169–183.

Dettmer, P., Thurston, L. P., & Dyck, N. J. (2005). *Consultation, collaboration, and teamwork for students with special needs* (5th ed.). Boston, MA: Pearson.

DiPaola, M., Tschannen-Moran, M., & Walther-Thomas, C. (2004). School principals and special education: Creating the context for academic success. *Focus on Exceptional Children, 37*(1), 1–12.

Doren, B. (2012). The relationship between parent expectations and postschool outcomes of adolescents with disabilities. *Exceptional Children, 79*(1), 7–23.

Downing, J. E. (2005). Inclusive education for high school students with severe intellectual disabilities: Supporting communication. *Alternative and Augmentative Communication, 21*(2), 132–148.

Downing, J. E., & Peckham-Hardin, K. D. (2007). Inclusive education: What makes it a good education for students with moderate to severe disabilities? *Research and Practice for Persons with Severe Disabilities 32*(1), 16–30.

Downing, J. E., Spencer, S., & Cavallaro, C. (2004). The development of an inclusive charter elementary school: Lessons learned. *Research and Practice for Persons with Severe Disabilities, 29*(1), 1–24.

Dymond, S. K., Renzaglia, A., Rosenstein, A., Jung Chun, E., Banks, R. A., Niswander, V., & Gilson, C. L. (2006). Using a participatory action research approach to create a universally designed inclusive high school science course: A case study. *Research and Practice for Persons with Severe Disabilities, 31*(4), 293–308.

Education for All Handicapped Children Act of 1975, 20 U.S.C.1400 et seq.

Edwards, C. C., & Da Fonte, A. (2012). The 5-point plan: Fostering successful partnerships with families of students with disabilities. *Teaching Exceptional Children, 44*(3), 6–13.

Francis, G., Gross, J., Turnbull, R., & Parent-Johnson, W. (2013). Evaluating the effectiveness of the family employment awareness training in Kansas: A pilot study. *Research and Practice for Persons with Severe Disabilities, 38*(1), 44–57.

Friend, M., & Bursuck, W. D. (2013). *Including students with special needs: A practical guide for classroom teachers*. Boston, MA: Allyn & Bacon.

Friend, M., & Shamberger, C. (2008). Inclusion. In T. L. Good (Ed.), *Twenty-first century education: A reference handbook* (Vol. 2, Pt. 11, chap. 64, pp. 124–131). Thousand Oaks, CA: Sage.

Gartner, A., & Kerzner-Lipsky, D. (2002). *Inclusion: A service, not a place, a whole school approach.* Port Chester, NY: Dude.

Gobbo, K., & Shmulsky S. (2014). Faculty experience with college students with autism spectrum disorders: A qualitative study of challenges and solutions. *Focus on Autism and Other Developmental Disorders, 29(1)*, 13–22.

Gyamfi, P., Walrath, C., Burns, B., Stephens, R., Gen, Y., & Stambaugh, L. (2010). Family education and support services in systems of care. *Journal of Emotional and Behavioral Disorders, 18*(1), 14–26.

Harper, G. F., Maheady, L., Mallette, B., & Karnes, M. (1999). Peer tutoring and the minority child with disabilities. *Preventing School Failure, 43*(2), 45–51.

Hitchcock, C., Meyer, A., Rose, D., & Jackson, R. (2002). Providing new access to the general curriculum. *Teaching Exceptional Children, 35*(2), 8–17.

Horner, R. H., Dunlap, G., Koegel, R. L., Carr, E. G., Sailor, W., Anderson, J., . . . O'Neill, R. E. (1990). Toward a technology of "nonaversive" behavioral support. *Journal of the Association for Persons with Severe Handicaps, 15*(3), 125–132.

Horner, R. H., & Sugai, G. (2005). School-wide positive behavior support: An alternative approach to discipline in schools. In L. Bambara & L. Kern (Eds.), *Positive behavior supports* (pp. 359–390). New York, NY: Guilford Press.

Horner, R. H., Sugai, G., & Anderson, C. (2010). Examining evidence base for school-wide positive behavior support. *Focus on Exceptional Children, 42*(8), 1–14.

Hughes, C. (2013). Poverty and disability: Addressing the challenge of inequality. *Career Development and Transition for Exceptional Individuals, 36*(1), 37–42.

Johnson, D., Johnson, R., & Cary, R. (2010). Cooperative learning in middle schools: Interrelationships and relationships and achievement. *Middle Grade Research Journal, 5*(1), 1–18.

Johnson, D. R., & Johnson, F. P. (2009). *Joining together: Group theory and group skills* (10th ed.). Upper Saddle River, NJ: Merrill/Pearson Education.

Jorgensen, C. M., Schuh, M. C., & Nisbet, J. (2006). *The inclusion facilitator's guide*. Baltimore, MD: Brookes.

Meyer, A., Rose, D. H., & Gordon, D. (2014). *Universal design for learning: Theory and practice*. Wakefield, MA: CAST Professional.

Montgomery, J. M., Stoesz, B. M., & McCrimmon A. (2012). Emotional intelligence, theory of mind and executive functions as predictors of social outcomes in young adults with Asperger syndrome. *Focus on Autism and Other Developmental Disabilities, 28*(1), 4–13.

Orfield, G. (2009). Reviving the goal of an integrated society: A 21st century challenge. Los Angeles, CA: The Civil Rights Project/Proyecto Derechos Civiles at UCLA. Retrieved from http://www .civilrightsproject.ucla.edu/

Palawat, M., & May, M. E. (2012). The impact of cultural diversity on special education provision in the United States. *Journal of the International Association of Special Education, 13*(1), 58–63.

Parette, H. P., & Peterson-Karlan, G. R. (2007). Facilitating student achievement with assistive technology. *Education and Training in Developmental Disabilities, 42*(4), 387–397.

Parish, S. L., Rose, R. A., & Andrew, M. E. (2010). TANF's impact on low-income mothers raising children with disabilities. *Exceptional Children, 76*(2), 234–253.

Prater, M. A. (2000). Using juvenile literature with portrayals of disabilities in your classroom. *Intervention in School and Clinic, 35*(3), 167–176.

Prater, M. A., & Dyches, T. T. (2008). *Teaching about disabilities through children's literature.* Westport, CT: Libraries Unlimited/Teacher Ideas Press.

Pratt, C. W., Gill, K. J., Barrett, N. M., & Roberts, M. M. (2013). *Psychiatric rehabilitation* (3rd ed.). Burlington, MA: Elsevier Academic Press.

Price, K. M., & Nelson, K. L. (2007). *Planning effective instruction: Diversity responsive methods and management* (3rd, ed.). Belmont, CA: Thomson Higher Education.

Putnam, J., Markovchick, K., Johnson, D., & Johnson, R. (1996). Cooperative learning and peer acceptance of students with learning disabilities. *Journal of Social Psychology, 136*(6), 741–752.

Raver, S. A. (2009). *Early childhood special education—0–8 years: Strategies for positive outcomes.* Upper Saddle River, NJ: Merrill/Pearson Education.

Rose, D. H. (2000). Universal design for learning. *Journal of Special Education Technology, 15*(1), 67–70.

Salend, S. J., & Duhaney, L. M. (2005). Understanding and addressing the disproportionate representation of students of color in special education. *Intervention in School and Clinic, 40*(4), 213–221.

Santelli, B., Turnbull, A., Marquis, J., & Lerner, E. (1997). Parent-to-parent programs: A resource for parents and professional. *Journal of Early Intervention, 21*(1), 73–83.

Sawyer, S., & Comer, D. E. (1991). *Growing up with literature.* New York, NY: Delmar.

Sciutto, M., Richwine, S., Mentrikoski, J., & Niedzwiecki K. (2012). A qualitative analysis of the school experiences of students with Asperger syndrome. *Focus on Autism and Other Developmental Disabilities, 27*(3), 177–188.

Semke, C. A., Garbacz, S., Kwon, K., Sheridan, S. M., & Woods, K. E. (2010). Family involvement for children with disruptive behaviors: The role of parenting stress and motivational beliefs. *Journal of School Psychology, 48*(4), 293–312.

Siltala, R. (2010). *Innovativity and cooperative learning in business life and teaching.* Turku, Finland: University of Turku.

Soukup, J. H., Wehmeyer, M. L., Bashinski, S. M., & Bovaird, J. A. (2007). Classroom variables and access to the general education curriculum. *Exceptional Children, 74*(1), 101–120.

Steere, D. E., Rose, E., & Cavaiuolo, D. (2007). *Growing up: Transition to adult life for students with disabilities.* Boston, MA: Allyn & Bacon.

Turnbull, A., Turnbull, R., Erwin, E. J., Soodak, L. C., & Shogren, K. A. (2011). *Families, professionals, and exceptionality: Positive outcomes through partnerships and trust* (6th ed.). Upper Saddle River, NJ: Merrill/Pearson.

Turnbull, H. R., Turnbull, A., Shank, M., & Smith, S. J. (2010). *Exceptional lives: Special education in today's schools* (4th ed.). Boston: MA: Pearson.

Turnbull, H. R., Wilcox, B., Stowe, M., & Turnbull, A. (2001). IDEA requirements for use of PBS. *Journal of Positive Behavior Interventions, 3*(1), 11–18.

Turnbull, P., Pereira, L., & Blue-Banning, M. (2000). Teachers as friendship facilitators. *Teaching Exceptional Children, 23*(5), 66–70.

Wehman, P., & Kregal, S. (2012). *Functional curriculum for elementary and secondary students with special needs.* Austin, TX: Pro-Ed.

Wehmeyer, M. L. (1999). Assistive technology and students with mental retardation: Utilization and barriers. *Journal of Special Education Technology, 14*(1), 48–58.

Westling, D. L., & Fox, L. (2009). *Teaching students with severe disabilities* (4th ed.). Upper Saddle River NJ: Pearson Education.

Villa, R. A., Thousand, J. S., Nevin, A., & Liston, A. (2005). Successful inclusive practices in middle and secondary schools. *American Secondary Education, 33*(3), 33–50.

U.S. Census Bureau. (2011). *Income, poverty, and health insurance coverage in the United States: 2010*. Washington, DC: Author: Retrieved from http://www.census.gov/prod/2011pubs/p60-239.pdf

U.S. Department of Education (USDOE). (2006). *Twenty-eighth annual report to Congress on the implementation of the Individuals with Disabilities Education Act*. Washington, DC: Author.

U.S. Department of Education. (2012). *29th annual report to Congress on the implementation of the Individuals with Disabilities Education Act, 2007*. Washington, DC: Author.

U.S. Department of Education, National Center for Educational Statistics. (2012). Inclusion of special-needs students. Retrieved from http://nces.ed.gov/nationsreportcard/about/inclusion/asp

U.S. Department of Health and Human Services. (2012). *2012 national strategy for suicide prevention: Goals and objectives for action*. Washington, DC: Author. Retrieved from www.surgeon general.gov/library/reports/national-strategy-suicide-prevention/index.html

Udvari-Solner, A. (1992). Curricular adaptations: Accommodating the instructional needs of diverse learners in the context of general education [Monograph]. Retrieved from Eric database. (ERIC No. ED354685)

Chapter 10

Fundamentals of Transitions

DONNA WANDRY

West Chester University of Pennsylvania

> *"Transitions themselves are not the issue, but how well you respond to their challenges!"*
>
> —Jim George, Christian Author and Speaker

Student transition from one point to another in an educational system is an inevitable occurrence. Transitions can be seen as temporal processes that cross social, academic, and procedural lines (Tilleczek, 2008). According to the seminal work of Bronfenbrenner (1979), "Every transition is both a consequence and an instigator of developmental processes" (p. 27).

The transition points are numerous, and the number of factors impacting the transitional experience at each juncture is significant. Assisting students with and without disabilities to successfully navigate these points of passage is a task for all school personnel and a potentially key role for school counselors.

After reading this chapter, the following objectives will be met by readers:

1. Identification of at least one key transitional challenge for youth with disabilities at each point of transition, from early intervention services to elementary school, elementary and middle school to high school, and high school to postsecondary school settings

2. Identification of at least three points of special education or disability law that govern transitional movement for individuals with disabilities

3. Identification of at least five points of engagement for school counselors as partners with special education in facilitating successful student transitions.

TRANSITION VERSUS TRANSITIONS

Definition

The term *transition* is defined as passage from one state, stage, subject, or place to another (Transition, n.d.). This connotes that the life span for any individual contains a number of transition points, each with its own characteristics and challenges. Tilleczek (2008) posited that the process is part of a "nested transition" (p. 68) that includes transition from childhood to adulthood; transitions along pathways to success through schools, communities, and families; and transition from grade to grade. School personnel benefit from understanding the variety and complexities of transition points for all students in general, and in particular for students with disabilities.

Horizontal and Vertical Transitions for All Students

Horizontal transitions

Students experience many transitions throughout their lives. Some of them are predictable, and others are unique to individual circumstances. Clark and Patton (2006) described these transitions as *vertical* (e.g., life span related and predictable) or *horizontal* (unique to individual circumstances). Horizontal transitions refer to movement from one situation or setting to another. In the lives of students, this could mean changing schools or teachers, while remaining at the same grade level.

Vertical transitions

The life span–related (i.e., vertical) transitions are associated with predictable life events, such as beginning school, leaving elementary school, and growing older, although there may be variations within cultures in terms of timing and expectations. Coordinated planning for these transitions can minimize the anxiety that may arise and make transitions smoother, but in reality, little comprehensive planning occurs in the lives of most individuals (Wehmeyer & Patton, 2012).

Additional Horizontal and Vertical Transitions for Students With Disabilities

For students with disabilities, one of the most common horizontal changes may be in the form of change of placement or service pattern. One of the most important and frequently discussed horizontal transitions is the movement from separate settings to more inclusive ones.

On a smaller scope, this may mean changes made during the school years of students with disabilities, as the special education team makes decisions about the least restrictive environment in which a student may receive appropriate levels of supports to achieve maximum growth. On a larger scope, this is an example of a transition that is not age specific, as opportunities for such movement are available throughout the life span for persons with disabilities (Wehmeyer & Patton, 2012).

Two primary areas of vertical transition for students with disabilities supported by mandates under the Individuals with Disabilities Education Act (IDEA) are (a) in the movement from early intervention to preschool services, and (b) in the movement from postsecondary to adult roles. (Note, as of 2004, IDEA is now known as IDEIA, the Individuals with Disabilities Education Improvement Act.) In essence, although other transitions occur throughout the K–12 years, the transitions at the front and at the end of special education eligibility are the two most closely defined by legislation.

Part C to Part B

Up to age 3, eligible children are covered by Part C of IDEA. Part C focuses on helping the family meet the developmental needs of their child, such as learning to sit up, walk, or talk. These services are called "early intervention services." Typically provided in natural environments, such as the child's home or child-care setting, these services and outcomes for the child and family are defined in an Individual Family Service Plan (IFSP). At age 3, supports and services change as eligible children move from Part C to Part B of IDEIA, which provides services during ages of 3 to 22. Preschool services are covered in Section 619 of Part B. At the time of movement from Part C to Part B services, the IFSP is replaced by an Individualized Education Plan (IEP; PACER, 2012).

School to adult roles

Transition from secondary education to adulthood represents a period during which adolescents with disabilities face multiple responsibilities and changing roles that include establishing independence, attending postsecondary education or training, developing social networks, choosing a career, participating in their communities, and managing health care and financial affairs (Wehmeyer & Webb, 2012). Students who are eligible for special education may be served until age 22 under the aegis of IDEA. At that point, they "age out" of eligibility. Others may choose to exit with their age peers via graduation, thus, electively ending their affiliation with school services. Sadly, another exit option is dropping out, which, again, ends affiliation with school services unless the student opts to return. Statistics regarding disability rates are variable, depending on *the type* of disability and interaction with other factors such as ethnic membership. According to a literature meta-analysis conducted by Wilkins and Huckabee (2014), the graduation rate is approximately 75% for students in general, but it is only about 50% for special education–served students. Students from certain disability categories have particularly high rates of dropout; those with emotional disturbance had the highest dropout rates of all disability groups (40%). Dropout rates were also high for students with specific learning disabilities (21%), other health impairments (20%), and intellectual disabilities (20%). Graduation rates are particularly low for African American and Hispanic/Latino students with disabilities (40% and 48%, respectively).

In any case, no student may be served past the age of 22 under IDEA. Therefore, and in full recognition that supports will be needed at varying levels beyond the school years, IDEA mandates and provides procedures in planning and executing successful transitions for students with disabilities into postschool roles in postsecondary education, workplace, home, and community settings.

The 2004 reauthorization of the IDEA required that transition services be considered for all students receiving special education services aged 16 and over, although many state plans place the age at 14, and defined *transition services* as a "coordinated set of activities for a child with a disability that

- is designed to be within a results-oriented process, that is focused on improving the academic and functional achievement of the child with a disability to facilitate the child's movement from school to post-school activities, including postsecondary education, vocational education, integrated employment (including supported employment); continuing and adult education, adult services, independent living, or community participation;
- is based on the individual child's needs, taking into account the child's strengths, preferences, and interests; and
- includes instruction, related services, community experiences, the development of employment and other post-school adult living objectives, and, if appropriate, acquisition of daily living skills and functional vocational evaluation." [34 CFR 300.43 (a)], [20 U.S.C. 1401(34)]

CHALLENGES ASSOCIATED WITH TRANSITIONS FOR STUDENTS WITH DISABILITIES

Whether vertical or horizontal in nature, transitions present challenges across multiple domains, such as academic, social, self-advocacy, and decision-making processes. According to Turner (2007), educators recognize that transitions may provide opportunities to promote positive development for students but, if unmanaged, can result in anxiety or stress that affects learning and relationships. However, when a school counseling program promotes effective transitions, outcomes can reflect higher graduation rates and more students from underrepresented populations being included in higher level courses (North Carolina Department of Public Instruction [NCDPI], 2007). All students face transitional challenges to one degree or another; therefore, it is helpful to discuss inherent challenges that all students may face at various transition points and elaborate to address further challenges faced by those with disabilities.

THE PREK–EIGHT YEARS

General

This section describes both horizontal and vertical examples of school transitions all students may experience as they undergo mobility within and between grade levels at the preschool through elementary and middle school years. Possible challenges all students may face as they navigate the PreK–Eight school years include changing classes and grade-level changes.

For students who are accustomed to being with the same teacher for all subject areas, in addition to the traditional challenges of being on time for class and locating lockers and classrooms, the requirement to change classes can cause struggles with remembering homework and settling down for the onset of teacher instruction (Black, 2008). Parents may worry as much about the stresses this can cause, as well as its effect on their child's social and emotional adjustment, as they do about report card grades.

Although school counselors have the intervention expertise to facilitate grade-level changes, the practice may not be well executed by school professionals (Augst & Akos, 2009). Particularly in the vertical transition from preschool to kindergarten, dramatic changes occur in class size, parental involvement, academic demands, social relationships, and behavioral expectations (McIntyre, Eckert, Fiese, Reed, & Wildenger, 2010; Pianta & Kraft-Sayre, 2003).

For students with disabilities, additional challenges may surface during the PreK–Eight school years related to their disability.

An example of these challenges for students with disabilities is illustrated in the Case Illustration 10.1.

CASE ILLUSTRATION 10.1

PREK–EIGHT, MIKE

Mike is a 10-year-old, third-grade student identified as having a learning disability. He has made remarkable growth academically and socially after being held back in third grade. His mother has been very pleased with his growth in the last school year; however, she is still having a difficult time accepting her son's disability. Ms. Isabelle did not want her son in a self-contained special education classroom and fought very hard to keep him in a general education classroom.

Mike's mother is very involved with her son and has enrolled him in the Boys and Girls Club where he attends two to three days a week. His family spends weekends doing things together, for example, going shopping, watching movies, bowling, mini vacationing, cooking and baking, and so on. Mike enjoys baking and decorating cakes and would one day like to go to cooking school and learn how to design cakes. He bakes at home with his mother and states that he enjoys the closeness they share in the kitchen.

Mike takes pleasure in playing with his friends at school and at the Boys and Girls Club. He stated that he has enjoyed school more these past 2 years, especially his new friends, his teachers, and the fact that he is doing better in all his classes. Mike reports that he does not enjoy his physical education class—especially the exercise section of the class; however, he is often more interested in playing the sports aspect of the class.

In addition, Mike is very pleasant and well mannered and is liked very much by his peers. Academically, he strives to do his best in all subjects and is creative with his drawings. Mike also stated that he does not like going to the resource room because the work is boring (e.g., the endless and mindless worksheets) and does not like being pulled out of class. Mike has shown great improvement with his social and behavioral skills (i.e., he is handling his emotions better and taking control of his frustrations and emotions). His acceptance of not being able to have everything his way or right away has enabled him to become a well-liked classmate and someone other students can look up to.

Mike's greatest academic challenges are in spelling, basic reading skills, written expression, and reading comprehension—he needs support and assistance in content areas that incorporate reading, comprehension, and writing. In addition, his organizational skills need to be refined. He typically stays on task, but if the assignment is too difficult, he tends to daydream or starts flipping through his desk contents and book bag or disrupts other students while they are completing the class work.

Questions for Critical Thinking:

1. Mike is getting ready to transition to middle school next year. What transitional challenges do you think he might encounter in academics? School day structure? Social interactions?
2. What opportunities do you find for him to engage in self-advocacy as he moves to middle school, and how would you facilitate that as a counseling professional?
3. What skills could you see him building at this point that will also be of benefit as he moves to high school and post–high school environments?

As stated earlier in the chapter, under IDEA, eligible students with disabilities may be served from birth through age 22. The particular section of IDEA that guides service from birth through age 2 is Part C; services for students aged 3 to 22 is provided under Part B of the act. At the time of transition from Part C to Part B, the law requires that specific timely transition planning actions be taken to support the child's transition to preschool and other appropriate community services by the third birthday. These actions include (a) development of the Individual Family Service Plans (IFSPs) with transition steps and services; (b) notification to the school district, if the child is potentially eligible for Part B; and (c) organization of a transition conference, if the child is potentially eligible for Part B (Montana Office of Public Instruction, 2013).

A critical decision takes place at this juncture, as eligibility for Part C services does not automatically guarantee eligibility for Part B services. At this transitional planning stage, parents have the right to "opt out" of having the school district informed that their child will be turning 3 years old in the next 12 months. As this notification is an alert to the district that determining eligibility for Part B services will be the next step, opting out essentially severs special education services when that child turns three, therefore eliminating the potential benefits of special education services for their child. However, parents may rescind their decision to opt out at any point prior to age three, and the provider of the Part C services would assist them in delayed notification to the receiving school district. This critical decision should be a key discussion point in the transitional steps planning of the IFSP.

If the decision is made to pursue Part B eligibility, the transition steps should include (a) an explanation of Parts B and C procedures and safeguards, (b) discussion of program options and next steps with family and school district, (c) obtainment of the consent for referral and evaluation, and (d) review to determine if all current evaluations and/or assessments have been given to the school district. This ensures that a seamless transference occurs between the birth through aged 2 services and the aged 3 through 22 services for an eligible child with a disability.

Once in school, as mentioned earlier, horizontal movement toward less restrictive, more inclusive settings is an important option for students with disabilities that must be considered first in meeting educational needs. This transitional phase from more restrictive to less restrictive settings may be problematic in terms of adjustment to general education requirements as well as teacher receptivity. General education teachers may have strong reservations about additional workload, the effect of inclusion, adequacy of preservice and in-service professional development, and administrator support (Shade & Stewart, 2001). Similarly, building principals tend to be strongly uncertain about inclusive practices (Praisner, 2003). Therefore, students with disabilities moving into inclusive settings may experience not only academic and social challenges but also the uncertainties of the inclusive teachers and administrators.

Conversely, movement to more restrictive environments can also necessitate professional attention to the student's transitional needs. For example, movement from a regular school to an alternative placement to address behavioral needs possesses its own transitional challenges. Involved staff in the traditional setting should be notified of the pending move and assist in building a network of support in the new setting (Young, 2007); this advice has positive implications as well for placement changes from more to less restrictive environments.

For all grade-level changes, transition may be a difficult process for students and for parents. However, the concerns of parents with students with special needs exceed those of their counterparts without the presence of disability. McIntyre and her colleagues (2010), in a study of parents of children both with and without disabilities who were transitioning into kindergarten, found that concerns by the parents of children with special needs exceeded those of their counterparts in all areas, but with significance in the areas of following directions, making needs known to others, behavior problems, and toilet training. This finding is particularly interesting since these students had already received a large amount of support at the preschool level via IEPS and family focused services; it may be posited that there was fear of services being altered or ineffective in light of new classroom challenges.

Secondary Level

At a point in the adolescent years, students progress from elementary to secondary (which may include elementary to middle, or middle to high school) settings.

The transition from middle to high school is a seminal transition, referred to as "one of the defining parameters of development in the second decade of life" (Barber & Olsen, 2004, p. 3). This condition can be seen in Hall's (1904) seminal work regarding the "sturm und drang" of adolescence. He posited that "storm and stress" was evident in adolescents' tendency to question and contradict their parents, in their mood disruptions, and in their propensity for reckless and antisocial behavior. While his theories are not accepted by most contemporary psychologists as being universal and inevitable (Arnett, 1999), there is validation that adolescents are more likely than elementary school children to have problems such as symptoms of anxiousness, insecurity, and depression. When this predilection coincides with transitional challenges in new environments, the effect can be monumental for students. These feelings of anxiety can be further exacerbated as students move into high school, where teachers and students alike may have a sense of increased isolation compared to middle school (Ellerbrock & Kiefer, 2013). Researchers have determined that failure and dropout rates increase at the ninth-grade level, while achievement declines (Allensworth & Easton, 2005; Tilleczek, 2008), and behavioral problems resulting in suspension and expulsion may increase significantly (Jerald, 2006). The dropout rate for students with disabilities was cited earlier in the chapter; further, the average yearly income for dropouts is only about $25,000 a year, at the poverty level for a family of four (Department of Health and Human Services [DHHS], 2012).

Many school districts have invested in counseling programs that educate parents and students in the postsecondary planning processes, such as college searches and career guidance. In addition, an emerging practice is the use of Individual Learning Plans (ILPs) for all students. An ILP helps identify a particular student's strengths, challenges, interests, and learning styles and then matches that profile to resources and tools that can maximize his or her learning potential within a given classroom setting. This resource and record follows students as they grow and mature, reaching beyond the formal educational process into all aspects of professional and personal life (Parent Driven Schools, n.d.). Therefore, this planning process can be another path to support effective postsecondary transitions for youth.

For students with disabilities, there are added challenges at a time in their life when postsecondary transition becomes the main focus. An example of these challenges for students with disabilities is depicted in Case Illustration 10.2.

As students with disabilities move from grade to grade at the secondary level, changes in support systems may occur. For example, Thurlow (2001) found that assessment accommodations are used by greater percentages of students at the elementary school level than at either the middle school or high school levels and posited that this unfortunately may have correlation to a reduced amount of offered instructional accommodations as the student ages. This decreased amount of accommodation as a part of specially designed instruction likely will have an effect on student performance, as well as on resultant student and parent reactions.

CASE ILLUSTRATION 10.2

SECONDARY LEVEL, JIMMY

Jimmy is a 17-year-old student with mild intellectual disabilities. Intelligence test results indicate significant deficits in verbal performance and short-term memory. He has a history of poor school attendance and displays immature and inappropriate behavior at school. Jimmy works part-time in the evenings, bagging ice at an ice factory, and is currently enrolled in a community work-study experience as a general helper, where he stocks shelves and vending machines, bags groceries, and collects money from the vending machines. He is transported to each of the work sites from school. He is currently placed in a self-contained special education classroom for all subjects except an elective class (auto mechanics), and he is currently not passing the class, even with accommodations.

After graduation, Jimmy will most likely be competitively employed. His teachers and job coach report that he lacks some essential general job skills needed for successful employment. In addition, he feels strongly that he does not know about jobs or community-based employment training settings he might pursue when school is over.

Jimmy will most likely live with relatives when school is completed even though he has expressed the desire to live with friends in an apartment. He does not understand how to make this happen given that he currently lacks the skills in dealing with the personal care and everyday tasks such as managing his money, cooking, and laundry. Even though he currently uses the public transportation system to reach his part-time job, he often runs into difficulties when he deviates from his usual route.

Jimmy has had very limited exposure to the different recreational resources and services available in his community. He tends not to use many community-based programs that provide recreational activities.

Jimmy has not developed a strong set of self-determination skills, such as assertiveness, choice making, decision making, and goal setting. He has a false sense of confidence related to his understanding of his own strengths and weaknesses. He often experiences difficulties getting along with other people and from time to time displays inappropriate behaviors. As a result, he has not developed strong, meaningful relationships.

Questions for Critical Thinking:

1. What are the domain areas in which Jimmy will need supports as he moves toward school completion?

2. What role do you see yourself playing as a counseling professional in Jimmy's IEP development?

3. From what types of community agency supports might Jimmy benefit after he exits school? What types of school-based related services might benefit him now?

Another related challenge may be viewed in light of encouraging secondary level students with disabilities in their emerging independence. As will be discussed in more depth later in the chapter as *self-determination*, students will need to understand, embrace, and learn to advocate for needed accommodations. If, indeed, the amount of offered accommodations decreases as students age, it becomes increasingly incumbent on the students to advocate for their own support needs. Teachers, schools counselors, and other professionals—involving students in the process of determining goals and assisting parents and others to respect their voices about which accommodations might best help them achieve those goals—are recognizing them as valued participants, and this can ultimately lead to feelings of increased control and responsibility in their education (Thurlow, Thompson, Walz, & Shin, 2001).

While the program and class and teacher change and their inherent challenges represented at the PreK–Eighth level may replicate themselves in the secondary settings for students with disabilities, a new type of transitional challenge emerges at the secondary level. This challenge, as mentioned earlier in this chapter, is in the form of postsecondary planning as mandated by IDEA.

The importance of this process is evident in data that show lower success rates for people with disabilities across several domains. The National Longitudinal Transition Study of Special Education Students (NLTS), sponsored by the U.S. Department of Education, Office of Special Education Programs, provided data regarding the adult outcomes of more than 8,000 youth with disabilities in several waves, starting in 1983 and culminating in 2010 (Newman, Wagner, Cameto, Knokey, & Shaver, 2010). This longitudinal study used a weighted sample, which generalized to youth with disabilities across the nation. Findings indicate that postsecondary education enrollments for students with disabilities are only half of their nondisabled peers' rate and that they were employed at significantly lower rates in lower tier jobs, for shorter mean times and at significantly lower pay, than their nondisabled peers. Concurring data show that while the employment rate for adults without disabilities is at 76%, it is only at 30% for their counterparts with disabilities (U.S. Department of Labor, 2013). Further, youth with disabilities, as they moved into adult roles, were significantly less likely than their nondisabled peers to live independently, partly as a function of their lower earning power, but also partly because the essential daily living and self-determination skills necessary to this process were not developed.

As a function of the IDEA mandate, uniquely new discussions must be held regarding the onset of transition planning, which must be present as an instructional provision of the IEP that is in place when the student turns 16 (although most states have adhered to the earlier timeline established in the 1997 reauthorization and therefore remain at an onset age of 14). This transition planning includes such areas as

- delivery of appropriate assessments to determine needs, preferences, and interests across adult domains of employment, community access, personal-social skills, and so on;
- IEP planning and course of study decisions that will support optimal preparation for individualized postschool goals based on those assessments; and
- creation of partnerships with postschool providers to create a seamless system of service delivery in the pursuit of those goals.

Each of these will be presented in a separate manner, although all three have a shared context of providing, as the law mandates, appropriate instruction based on student needs.

Transition assessment

Age-appropriate assessment is an important and mandated component of successful transitional planning. Because traditional psychometric techniques have limited usefulness in evaluating student achievement, particularly in areas related to transition education, alternative approaches are required. An alternative is to directly observe student performance on relevant tasks in a systematic, standardized manner. Skills can be measured best by comparing students to themselves as opposed to comparing them to other students. This is especially important in evaluating students with disabilities, since their progress may not reflect gains typically sought with other youth.

As secondary transition assessment is best served via criteria-based venues, it may include informal assessments (interviews, questionnaires, direct observation, situational assessments, and curriculum-based assessments) or formal assessments (adaptive behavior scales, specific aptitude tests, self-determination assessments, and interest and work value inventories). The objective of comprehensive assessments is to define planning and services in the Individualized Education Plan (Sitlington, Neubert, Begun, Lombard, & Leconte, 2007).

Transition planning in the IEP

Course of study decisions are an outcome not only of assessment but also of transition planning in the IEP to establish instructional needs based on those assessments; therefore, it is important to understand the key points of transition planning first. Transition planning is to cover domains of employment, postsecondary education, and, as appropriate, daily living skills. The results of the assessments should become an integral part of the mandated Present Level of Academic and Functional Performance statement on the IEP, upon which that planning is to be based. The meaning of academic performance is clear. As for the term *functional performance*, the U.S. Department of Education notes the term is generally understood as referring to skills or activities that are not considered academic or related to a child's academic achievement, and is often used in the context of routine activities of everyday living (Academic achievement, 2006, 71 Fed. Reg. at 46661). Therefore, "routine activities of everyday living" can refer to skills and activities of daily living skills, such as

- self-care and home care;
- social skills, such as making friends, communicating with others, and engaging in self-determination;
- behavior skills, such as knowing how to behave across a range of settings; and
- mobility skills, such as walking and navigating one's environment.

Once the baseline skill sets are determined, they are examined within the context of anticipated postschool goals. This assists in establishing IEP goals that will systematically move the student in building the skills necessary to move successfully into those postschool roles across multiple domains (home, school, work, community). IEP goals for transition planning are to be developed with no less gravitas nor rigor than any other IEP goals, containing full attention to behavior, condition, and criteria for related instructional delivery.

Course of study decisions

Bridgeland, Dilulio, and Morrison (2006) found that a major reason why students drop out of high school is that they do not see the relevance and importance of the course work they are taking. The more specific that IEP teams can be in identifying course work that directly relates to students' postsecondary goals, the more likely it is that students are motivated to complete their educations. Courses of studies represent long-range plans for ensuring students' access to the course work and other educational experiences they need to be adequately prepared for adult life (Storms, O'Leary, & Williams, 2000).

Recommendations for designing courses of study include (a) involving students meaningfully in the development of their courses of study, (b) basing course selection upon students' postsecondary goals, (c) developing courses of study as soon as students consider taking high school course work, and (d) review students' Present

Levels of Academic and Functional Performance (PLAAFP) statements, to identify needs that can be addressed through strategic selection of courses and other educational experiences.

The course of study is a multiyear description of course work from the students' current to anticipated exit year that is designed to help achieve the students' desired postschool goal(s). The courses of study must align with the postsecondary goals. Courses of study must be reviewed annually as part of the IEP renewal process. They should reflect an educational program and plan that specifies all courses and educational experiences from the first IEP to be in effect when the student turns 16, or younger if determined appropriate by the IEP team or state regulations. It must be kept in mind that, in order to meet goals pertaining to employment, daily living, and personal-social skills, stepping outside the standard academic course work to identify related educational experiences likely will be necessary. Specifically, course of study decisions should relate to the students' achieving their desired measurable postsecondary goals, making sure that multiple years of classes and educational experiences are specified, not just one year.

Partnerships with providers

Although students with disabilities benefit from instruction appropriate to meeting their postschool goals, the concept of secondary transition planning relies upon the premise that it is a team effort. IDEA of 2004 is clear in its charge—to ensure that all children with disabilities have available to them a "free appropriate public education that emphasizes special education and related services designed to meet their unique needs and prepare them for further education, employment, and independent living" (§300.1). Unfortunately, Bruce and Bridgeland (2012) reported that less than one third of counselors (32% high school and 30% middle school) collaborate with outside organizations to support career and college readiness, indicating the need for improvement so school counselors may fully contribute to this aspect of transition planning for students with disabilities.

The law is also clear in its charge that transition services are a "coordinated set of activities designed within a results oriented process" (Individuals with Disabilities Education Improvement Act (IDEIA) of 2004, 34 CFR 300.43 (a) 20 U.S.C. 1401(34)). The activities should specify what will occur, who is responsible, and when the transition activity will take place. *Coordinated* connotes that the transition activities planning and the responsibility for completing the activities are shared. Schools and outside agencies cannot, by themselves, do all of the activities necessary to help the student achieve her or his desired measurable postsecondary goals. The activities must be a well-planned and shared effort among all parties if the student is going to achieve her or his measurable postsecondary goals.

In addition, school counselors must remember that essential members of the IEP planning team are to be the student and the parents. Although the participants in effective transition assessment, planning, and implementation span multiple disciplines and systemic structures, the primary focus, as across the entire service spectrum for individuals with disabilities, must rest upon serving the individual needs of the primary consumers: the youth and, peripherally, the family. Effective transition programs, simply stated, have high degrees of productive parental and student participation (Kohler & Field, 2003; Zhang, Ivester, Chen, & Katsiyannis, 2005). Family members remain a primary source of economic and psychological support during the transition period (Glidden & Jobe, 2007). They also help their young adults negotiate this life change by aiding in resource exploration, goal setting, and instruction and reinforcement of independent living skills (Sitlington, Clark, & Kolstoe, 2000).

As IEP teams design transition services, related service personnel serving students must consider the need to provide services that support students' adjustment to adult life. Participation in the IEP by public and private community service providers, such as independent living, vocational, and therapeutic professionals who may assume primary support roles when the student exits the educational system, is critical.

Self-determination

As students with disabilities prepare for postschool roles, the ability to self-advocate becomes not only a desired behavior but also a practical one. Once students exit the K–12 system, they no longer benefit from being sought out and identified by the system as a person requiring supports or accommodations. Therefore, they must develop the skills to self-disclose and seek accommodations as appropriate in postsecondary school, work, residential, and community settings. However, less than half of individuals with disabilities self-disclose their disability or seek supports in employment or postsecondary education, partially from lack of awareness to do so and partially from fear of stigma and/or subsequent employer or instructor maltreatment (Madaus, 2008; von Schrader, Malzer, & Bruyere, 2013).

Self-determination, of which self-advocacy is a part, is defined as "a combination of skills, knowledge, and beliefs that enable a person to engage in goal-directed, self-regulated, autonomous behavior. An understanding of one's strengths and limitations, together with a belief of oneself as capable and effective are essential to self-determination. When acting on the basis of these skills and attitudes, individuals have greater ability to take control of their lives and assume the role of successful adults in our society" (Field, Martin, Miller, Ward, & Wehmeyer, 1998, p. 2).

Table 10.1   Appendix C: Domains of Transition Activity

Below is a table that includes domains for which we engage in secondary transition planning. Within each domain area, list at least three skills that may be included in that area. Then, list a type of assessment that could be done to measure a student's skills in each of those three areas with its respective domains. Finally, define for yourself a role you could play as a counseling professional in administering the assessment, planning for instruction, and delivering instruction/ intervention in at least one of those seven domains.

Primary Domains of Transition

- Employment
- Education/Training
- Independent Living/Daily Living Skills

Other Areas of Consideration

- Community Involvement
- Leisure Pursuits
- Physical and Emotional Health
- Personal Responsibility and Relationships

The framework of being able to exercise self-determined behaviors requires individuals with disabilities to be able to know and understand their own strengths and needs, articulate their needs appropriately, and engage in problem solving to evaluate efficacy of their own self-advocacy. As this is a skill that has validity throughout the K–12 years, and has particular currency at transitional points when new environments are encountered, counselors assisting teachers in helping their students develop and engage in the skill will have ramifications into adulthood. These points are illustrated in Guided Practice Exercise 10.1.

Guided Practice Exercise 10.1

KEY DOMAINS OF TRANSITION ACTIVITY

Table 10.1 shows key domains for which we engage in secondary transition planning. Within each domain area, list at least three skills that may be included in that area. Then list a type of assessment that could be done to measure a student's skills in each of those three areas with its respective domains. Finally, define for yourself a role you could play as a counseling professional in administering the assessment, planning for instruction, and delivering instruction and intervention in at least one of those seven domains.

SCHOOL COUNSELING TASKS ASSOCIATED WITH TRANSITIONS FOR ALL STUDENTS

ASCA and CACREP

Two key organizations have informed the preparation and continuing professional development of school counselors. The American School Counselor Association (ASCA) supports school counselors' efforts to help students focus on academic, personal-social, and career development so they achieve success in school and are prepared to lead fulfilling lives as responsible members of society. ASCA provides professional development, publications and other resources, research, and advocacy to professional school counselors around the globe. The specific position statement as to the role of the school counselor in regard to transitions is "providing assistance with developing academic and transition plans for students in the IEP as appropriate" (ASCA, 2013, p. 49). The Council for Accreditation of Counseling and Related Education Programs (CACREP, n.d.) accredits masters and doctoral degree programs in counseling and its specialties that are offered by colleges and universities in the United States and throughout the world. Both ASCA and CACREP provide constructs for school counselors that can align smoothly in practice with fostering successful student transitions. Specific to the issue of transition and the expectations tied to school counselor competency is the following statement, which is found in the CACREP 2009 Standards: "knows how to design, implement, manage, and evaluate transition programs, including school-to-work, postsecondary planning, and college admissions Counseling" (CACREP, n.d., p. 40). These alignments are described below.

ASCA

School counselors have or gain the expertise to play key roles in both student induction and horizontal as well as vertical transitions (Augst & Akos, 2009). Their vantage point allows insight into individual student success and failure experiences, as well as which courses are most optimal to success, which policies hold students back, and which supports help (Education Trust, 2011). To support this synergy, the American School Counselor Association has developed the ASCA National Model; within that model, program components specifically for addressing student transitions are embedded within the four components of foundation, delivery system, management system, and accountability system (Dimmitt & Carey, 2007).

PreK–Eight transition. The ASCA Model focuses on orienting incoming students and families as a way to foster feelings of membership, both through informal communication and formal curriculum units that align with teachers' actions;

the goals of this communication are to promote safety and learning and to meet socioemotional needs. Information about academic and behavioral expectations, which evolve as students progress through the elementary and middle school years, contribute to the communication. Further, management of counseling resources via data-driven written agreements between counselors and administrators, as well as use of advisory councils, are designed to ensure practitioner clarity and consistency (ASCA, 2004).

Secondary transition. The ASCA Model sets the stage for postsecondary transition during the middle school years, providing early information about career options, goal setting, and decision making. It also reinforces correct course selection in the middle school years to facilitate academic success in the secondary setting. The counseling focus at the secondary level is to successfully balance students' academic focus with counseling activities that can actually foster grades, career knowledge, and socioemotional functioning. Further, effective data keeping allows close scrutiny of student grades, course-taking patterns, postsecondary choices, achievement-gap patterns, and remediation efficacy (Dimmitt & Carey, 2007).

CACREP

In addition to professional organization guidelines for school counselors found in the ASCA National Model, many counselor education programs preparing the professionals are accredited by the Council for Accreditation of Counseling and Related Educational Programs (CACREP). Counselor education preparation programs that adhere to the accreditation standards of CACREP, under current 2009 standards, must train school counselors in several areas that support secondary transition for all students across age ranges. These include understanding theories of individual and family development and transitions across the life span and, in addition, knowing how to (a) design, implement, manage, and evaluate programs to enhance the academic, career, and personal-social development of students; and (b) design, implement, manage, and evaluate transition programs, including school-to-work program, postsecondary planning, and college admissions counseling; this is to be accomplished through individual and group counseling and classroom guidance to promote the academic, career, and personal-social development of students.

Specifically under the domain of career development, CACREP-accredited programs meet content requirements in (a) career development theories and decision-making models; (b) career, avocational, educational, occupational and labor market information resources, and career information systems; (c) career development program planning, organization, implementation, administration, and evaluation; (d) interrelationships among and between work, family, and other life roles and factors, including the role of multicultural issues in career development; (e) career and educational planning, placement, follow-up, and evaluation; (f) assessment instruments and techniques relevant to career planning and decision making; and (g) career counseling processes, techniques, and resources, including those applicable to specific populations in a global economy (CACREP, n.d.).

When one examines the scope of training and professional development constructs under which both ASCA and CACREP operate, as well as the mandatory language of IDEA described earlier in the chapter, it should be easy to see where an alliance of those constructs and the tenets of IDEA converge relative to transition needs. In addition to deployment of counseling skills to address transitional concerns noted throughout the chapter, the following sections outline other critical roles school counselors can play in facilitating smoother transitions for students with disabilities, in partnership with special education, families, and related personnel.

Additional or Modified Roles on Behalf of Students With Disabilities

Team structures

In addition to assisting with the transitional issues that all students encounter, counselors should seek to be proactive participants in assessment practices, eligibility determinations, IEP planning, partnership building, and self-determination supports as described earlier in this chapter.

Critical secondary documents

In addition to practices noted above and earlier in the chapter, school counselors can also play an integral role in critical documentation that should follow students with disabilities once they exit the K–12 system. These two sets of documents, the Summary of Performance and the IEP *Evaluation Report*, will help ensure a smoother transition into postschool services and supports. Specifics regarding these documents are delineated below.

Summary of Performance. Individuals with Disabilities Education Act (IDEA) of 2004 requires that "the public agency provide a summary of academic and functional performance, including recommendations to assist the student in meeting postsecondary goals, for students whose eligibility terminates because of graduation with a regular high school diploma or because of exceeding the age eligibility for FAPE under State law" (§300.305[e][3]).

While not a formal part of the IEP, the information in the Summary of Performance (SOP) can be an important tool in reinforcing self-determination and securing accommodations in postschool settings. SOPs should be based on young adults' unique needs and goals after they graduate or age out from high school, although IDEA does not spell out specifically what the SOP must contain. Since specific information that must be included in a student's SOP will vary by state, parents (and practitioners) should become familiar with their state's requirements (Wrightslaw, n.d.).

IEP Evaluation Report. When students who are special education-eligible transition from one point of the K–12 system to another, whether a vertical or a horizontal move, effective transfer of eligibility documentation and service provision is critical. Therefore, during those transitions from kindergarten to elementary, elementary to secondary, secondary to high school, grade to grade, and teacher to teacher take place, it is essential that current verification documentation transfer as well. School counselors, as part of an IEP team, may want to define their role in addressing students' transitional stresses and have it noted under the related services section of the IEP.

When those same students transition into postschool environments, particularly postsecondary education, they will find themselves seeking accommodations based on the artifacts of their disability. Without a current IEP and *Evaluation Report* (IEPs being completed yearly and *Evaluation Reports* being completed every 3 years), there exists no verification of ongoing services or support needs. Therefore, the young adults may find it difficult to obtain needed supports and accommodations, even if they do self-disclose their disabilities and support needs. This is not to say that the individuals will receive those supports under the aegis of IDEA; however, the disability documentation and record of continuing service provision helps validate the individuals' requests for accommodations in their next environments. As a possible part of the team providing services to this individual in preparation for exiting into postschool roles and environments, the school counselors should be active advocates for making sure all eligibility documentation is current and therefore portable into the next environment.

SUMMARY

School counselors can and should be an integral part of any team that serves students with disabilities during the K–12 years. Poised to lead, those counselors can play essential roles in ensuring that our nation's schools prepare all students for a productive future (Education Trust, 2011). Because professional school counselors are advocates, they should be an active voice in IEP team meetings, assisting with providing assessment and relevant background information, and acting upon their commitment to support and enhance the lives of all students, including those with disabilities (Owens, Thomas, & Strong, 2011).

KEYSTONES

- School counselor program standards specify transition components within the four quadrants of the ASCA Model: foundation, delivery system, management system, and accountability system.
- School counselors must have an understanding of theories of individual and family development and transitions across the life span. In addition, they need to know how to (a) design, implement, manage, and evaluate programs to enhance the academic, career, and personal-social development of students, and (b) design, implement, manage, and evaluate transition programs, including school-to-work program, postsecondary planning, and college admissions counseling.
- School counselors must have an understanding of (a) career development theories and decision-making models; (b) career, vocational, educational, occupational and labor market information resources, and career information systems; (c) career development program planning, organization, implementation, administration, and evaluation; (d) interrelationships among work, family, and other life roles and factors, including the role of multicultural issues in career development; (e) career and educational planning, placement, follow-up, and evaluation; (f) assessment instruments and techniques relevant to career planning and decision making; and (g) career counseling processes, techniques, and resources, including those applicable to specific populations in a global economy.
- School counselors can set the stage for postsecondary transition during the middle school years, providing early information about career options, goal setting, and decision making and by reinforcing appropriate course selection in the middle school years to facilitate academic success in the secondary setting.
- School counselors play an integral role in documentation that follows students with disabilities once they exit the K–12 system. These documents, the Summary of Performance and the IEP *Evaluation Report*, help ensure a smoother transition into postschool services and supports.

ADDITIONAL RESOURCES

Print

National Collaborative on Workforce and Disability for Youth. (2005). *The 411 on disability disclosure workbook*. Washington, DC: Institute for Educational Leadership.

National Secondary Transition Technical Assistance Center. (2013). *Age Appropriate Transition Assessment Toolkit* (3rd ed.). Charlotte, VA: University of North Carolina at Charlotte.

Sitlington, P. L., Neubert, D. A., Begun, W., Lombard, R. C., & Leconte. P. J. (2007). *Assess for success: Handbook for Transition Assessment* (2nd ed.). Arlington, VA: Council for Exceptional Children.

West, L. (2010). *Integrating transition planning into the IEP process.* Arlington, VA: Council for Exceptional Children.

(West offers information for educators "new to transition.")

Web Based

Parent-Friendly Supports:

Center for Parent Information and Resources. Newark, NJ: www.parentcenterhub.org

"The Center for Parent Information and Resources (CPIR) serves as a central resource of information and products to the community of Parent Training Information (PTI) Centers and the Community Parent Resource Centers (CPRCs), so that they can focus their efforts on serving families of children with disabilities."

Parent Educational Advocacy Training Center. Falls Church, VA: www.peatc.org

PEATC offers, among many other family centered supports, a transition series for training parent and professional teams in building transition partnerships, called NEXT STEPS.

Professional Organizations:

American School Counselor Association Position Statements: http://www.schoolcounselor.org/asca/media/asca/PositionStatements/PositionStatements.pdf

In this document, aspects of the school counselor role in regard to many areas are delineated. Relevant to this discussion is the topic on students with disabilities.

Council on Accreditation of Counseling and Related Educational Programs 2009 Standards: http://www.cacrep.org/wp-content/uploads/2013/12/2009-Standards.pdf

Expectations of and standards for school counselor preparation programs are outlined in this comprehensive manual.

Secondary Transition

Division (of Council on Exceptional Children) on Career Development and Transition (DCDT): www.dcdt.org

Professional organization dedicated to secondary transition.

National Secondary Transition Technical Assistance Center (NSTTAC): www.nsttac.org

A federally funded TA center with a plethora of material or resources.

Secondary Transition Assessment:

Casey Life Skills: www.caseylifeskills.org

Zarrow Center for Learning Enrichment. Norman, OK: www.ou.edu/zarrow

The Zarrow Center for Learning Enrichment, housed at University of Oklahoma, "facilitates successful secondary and postsecondary educational, vocational and personal outcomes for students and adults with disabilities through self-determination oriented evaluation, research, development, transition education instruction, and dissemination of best educational and support practices."

Self-Determination:

Choicemaker Self-Determination Assessment and Curriculum: www.ou.edu/zarrow

The ChoiceMaker Self-Determination Assessment is a curriculum-referenced tool that measures students' self-determination skills and progress Curriculum. Educators use the ChoiceMaker Self-Determination Assessment to assess middle and high school students' with mild to moderate disabilities self-determination skills and opportunities at school to exercise these skills across three areas: (a) choosing educational, vocational, and personal goals; (b) students' involvement in their IEP meetings; and (c) students' attainment of IEP goals, including developing a plan, implementing the plan, self-evaluation of plan progress, and adjusting any of the plan parts.

Parents and practitioners can guide youth through the process of considering benefits and disadvantages of disclosure.

The self-determined learning model of instruction (SDLMI): www.thebeachcenter.org

The SDLMI is an instructional model that teaches students to engage in self-regulated and self-directed learning. The SDLMI, which is based on component elements of self-determined behavior, such as goal setting, problem solving, and decision making, assists a curriculum augmentation for students with disabilities and help students to promote self-determination and access to the general curriculum.

State Laws:

U.S. Department of Education (Office of Special Education Programs [OSEP]):

http://findit.ed.gov/search?utf8=%E2%9C%93&affiliate=ed.gov&query=stae+laws+and+special+education

An expansive amount of information on a wide variety of federal and state laws related to special education may be found at this website.

Wrightslaw: State Laws: http://www.google.com/cse?cx=partner-pub-4630897488592702%3A0441753484&ie=UTF-8&q=state+laws&sa=Search&siteurl=wrightslaw.com%2F&ref=search.iminent.com%2FSearchTheWeb

The Wrightslaw website provides a plethora of information in regard to special education. This specific link is tied to specific topics such as evaluation, restraint, inclusion, and physical education laws in various states.

Summary of Performance: http://www.nsttac.org/content/summary-performance-resources

This link provides guidance on Summary of Performance development and use.

REFERENCES

Academic achievement; Comment. (2006). Vol. 71 Fed. Reg. No. 156 (August 14, 2006) at p. 46661. Retrieved from https://www.federalregister.gov/articles/

Allensworth, E. M., & Easton, J. Q. (2005). *The on-track indicator as a predictor of high school graduation*. Chicago, IL: Consortium on Chicago School Research.

American School Counselor Association (ASCA). (2004). *ASCA National Standards for Students*. Alexandria, VA: Author.

American School Counselor Association (ASCA). (2013). The professional school counselor and students with disabilities. Retrieved from https://www.schoolcounselor.org/asca/media/asca/PositionStatements/PS_Disabilities.pdf

Arnett, J. J. (1999). Adolescent storm and stress, revisited. *American Psychologist, 54*(5), 317–326.

Augst, K., & Akos, P. (2009). Primary transitions: How elementary school counselors promote optimal transitions. *Journal of School Counseling, 7*(3). Retrieved from http://www.jsc.montana.edu/articles/v7n3.pdf

Barber, B. K., & Olsen, J. A. (2004). Assessing the transitions to middle and high school. *Journal of Adolescent Research, 19*(1), 3–30.

Black, S. (2008, October). Switching classes. *American School Board Journal, 195,* 47–49.

Bridgeland, J. M., Dilulio, J. J., & Morison, K. B. (2006, March). *The silent epidemic: Perspectives of high school dropouts.* Washington, DC: Civic Enterprises in association with Peter D. Hart Research for the Bill & Melinda Gates Foundation.

Bronfenbrenner, U. (1979). *The ecology of human development: Experiments by nature and design.* Cambridge, MA: Harvard University Press.

Bruce, M., & Bridgeland, J. M. (2012). *2012 National Survey of School Counselors: True north: Charting the course to college and career readiness.* Washington, DC: National Office for School Counselor Advocacy.

Clark, G. W., & Patton, J. R. (2006). *Transition Planning Inventory—Updated version.* Austin, TX: ProEd.

Council for Accreditation of Counseling and Related Educational Programs (CACREP). (n.d.). *2009 Standards.* Retrieved from http://www.cacrep.com/doc/2009%20Standards%20with%20cover.pdf

Department of Health and Human Services (DHHS). (2012). *Information on poverty and income statistics: A summary of 2012 current population survey data.* Washington, DC: U.S. Government Printing Office.

Dimmitt, C., & Carey, J. (2007). Using the ASCA national model to facilitate school transitions. *Professional School Counseling, 10*(3), 227–232.

Education Trust. (2011). *Poised to lead: How school counselors can drive college and career readiness.* Washington, DC: The Education Trust.

Ellerbrock, C. R., & Kiefer, S. M. (2013, February/March). The interplay between adolescent needs and secondary school structures: Fostering developmentally responsive middle and high school environments across the transition. *The High School Journal, 96*(3), 170–194.

Field, S., Martin, J., Miller, R., Ward, M., & Wehmeyer, M. (1998). *A practical guide for teaching self-determination.* Reston, VA: Council for Exceptional Children.

Glidden, L. M., & Jobe, B. M. (2007). Measuring parental daily rewards and worries in the transition to adulthood. *American Journal of Mental Retardation, 112*(4), 275–288.

Hall, G. S. (1904). *Adolescence: Its psychology and its relation to physiology, anthropology, sociology, sex, crime, religion, and education.* Englewood Cliffs, NJ: Prentice-Hall.

Individuals with Disabilities Education Improvement Act, 20 U.S.C. § 1400 (2004). Retrieved from http://www.copyright.gov/legislation/pl108-446.html

Jerald, C. D. (2006). *Identifying potential dropouts: Key lessons for building early warning systems.* Washington, DC: Achieve.

Kohler, P. D., & Field, S. (2003). Transition-focused education: Foundation for the future. *Journal of Special Education, 37*(3), 174–183.

Madaus, J. W. (2008). Employment self-disclosure rates and rationales of university graduates with learning disabilities. *Journal of Learning Disabilities, 41*(4), 291–299.

McIntyre, L., Eckert, T., Fiese, B., Reed, F., & Wildenger, K. (2010). Family concerns surrounding kindergarten transition: A comparison of students in special and general education. *Early Childhood Education Journal, 38*(4), 259–263.

Montana Office of Public Instruction. (2013). Children transitioning from IDEA Part C to IDEA Part B. Retrieved from http://opi.mt.gov

Newman, L., Wagner, M., Cameto, R., Knokey, A.-M., & Shaver, D. (2010). *Comparisons across time of the outcomes of youth with disabilities up to 4 years after high school: A report of findings from the National Longitudinal Transition Study (NLTS) and the National Longitudinal Transition Study-2 (NLTS2)* (NCSER Report 2010-3008). Menlo Park, CA: SRI International.

North Carolina Department of Public Instruction (NCDPI). (2007). *Transition planning for 21st century schools*. Retrieved from State Board of Education: www.ncpublicschools.org

Owens, D., Thomas, D., & Strong, L. A. (2011). School counselors assisting students with disabilities. *Education, 132*(2), 235–240.

PACER. (2012). Preparing for transition from early intervention to an Individualized Education Program (ACTion Sheet: PHP-c158). Minneapolis, MN: PACER Center.

Parent Driven Schools. (n.d.). Individual Learning Plans. Retrieved from http://www.parentdriven schools.com/ilp.htm

Pianta, R. C., & Kraft-Sayre, M. (2003). *Successful kindergarten transition: Your guide to connecting children, families, and schools*. Baltimore, MD: Paul H. Brookes.

Praisner, C. L. (2003). Attitudes of elementary school principals toward the inclusion of students with disabilities. *Exceptional Children, 69*(2), 135–145.

Shade, R., & Stewart, R. (2001). General education and education pre-service teachers' attitudes toward inclusion. *Preventing School Failure, 46*(1), 37–41.

Sitlington, P. L., Clark, G. M., & Kolstoe, O. P. (2000). *Transition education and services for adolescents with disabilities*. Boston, MA: Allyn & Bacon.

Sitlington, P. L, Neubert, D. A., Begun, W. H., Lombard, R. C., & Lecconte, P. J. (2007). *Assess for success: A practitioner's handbook on transition assessment* (2nd ed.). Thousand Oaks, CA: Corwin.

Storms, J., O'Leary, E., & Williams, J. (2000). *The Individuals with Disabilities Education Act of 1997 transition requirements: A guide for states, districts, schools, universities and families*. Minneapolis: University of Minnesota, The College of Education & Human Development, U.S. Department of Education, Office of Special Education Programs.

Thurlow, M. L. (2001). *Use of accommodations in state assessments—What data bases tell us about differential levels of use and how to document the use of accommodations* (Technical Report 30). Minneapolis: University of Minnesota, National Center on Educational Outcomes.

Thurlow, M. L., Thompson, S. J., Walz, L., & Shin, H. (2001). *Student perspectives on using accommodations during statewide testing*. Minneapolis: University of Minnesota, National Center on Educational Outcomes. (ERIC Document Reproduction Service No. ED474766)

Tilleczek, K. (2008). Building bridges: Transitions from elementary to secondary school. *Education Canada, 48*(1), 71.

Transition. (n.d.). In *Merriam-Webster's online dictionary*. Retrieved from http://www.merriam-webster.com/dictionary/transition

Turner, S. L. (2007). Introduction to special issue: Transitional issues for K–16 students. *Professional School Counseling, 10*(3), 224–226.

U.S. Department of Labor, Bureau of Labor Statistics. (2013). *Labor Force Statistics from the Current Population Survey*. Retrieved from http://bls.gove/data/

von Schrader, S., Malzer, V., & Bruyere, S. (2013). Perspectives on disability disclosure: The importance of employer practices and workplace climate. Retrieved from http://link.springer.com/article/10.1007%2Fs10672-013-9227-9

Wehmeyer, M. L., & Patton, J. R. (2012). Transition to postsecondary education, employment, and adult living. In D. Zagar, M. L. Wehmeyer, & R. Simpson (Eds.), *Educating students with autism spectrum disorders: Research-based principles and practices* (pp. 247–261). New York, NY: Taylor & Francis.

Wehmeyer, M. L., & Webb, K. W. (Eds.). (2012). *Handbook of adolescent transition and disability*. New York, NY: Taylor & Francis.

Wilkins, J., & Huckabee, S. (2014). *A literature map of dropout prevention interventions for students with disabilities*. Clemson, SC: National Dropout Prevention Center for Students with Disabilities, Clemson University.

Wrightslaw. (n.d.). Transition: Summary of Performance. Retrieved from http://www.wrightslaw
.com/info/trans.sop.htm

Young, A. (2007). Horizontal transitions: A commonly overlooked opportunity for student empowerment. *Principal Leadership, 7*(7), 31–33.

Zhang, D., Ivester, J., Chen, L. J., & Katsiyannis, A. (2005). Perspectives on transition practices.
Career Development for Exceptional Individuals, 28(1), 15–25.

Chapter 11

Culturally Responsive Counseling and Collaboration

YORK WILLIAMS

West Chester University of Pennsylvania

> *"I know there is strength in the differences between us.*
> *I know there is comfort, where we overlap."*
>
> — Ani DiFranco, Singer, Songwriter, and Poet

Special education includes a variety of disciplines across the educational setting and involves many professionals with intersecting duties and tasks. A number of team members and related service providers may communicate and collaborate in order to identify and meet the needs of students with disabilities. While many Individualized Education Plan (IEP) team members play multiple roles in the educational life of a student with a special education need, the purpose of this chapter is to clarify the role of school counselors whose primary duty, among many others, is to be culturally responsive and inclusive collaborators across the school setting for identified students.

After reading this chapter, the reader will be able to meet these objectives:

1. Define characteristics of *culturally and linguistically diverse* (CLD) students with special needs.

2. Define the role of a culturally competent school counselor.

3. Identify strategies to include CLD students with special education needs and their families in the educational decision-making process.

Rogoff (2003) maintained that culture is complex and dynamic and that it is much more than holidays, foods, and customs, that is, token gestures: It reflects our beliefs, how we learn, what we value, and the ways we interact with others. In addition, culture is not a static or unitary construct. Simply put, students do not just have one culture but multiple cultures. Unfortunately, some views of culture tend to stereotype individuals and box them into categorical identities (e.g., students who are poor, Black, immigrant, students with disabilities, Latino, or low achieving). A comprehensive definition of culture must include variables across race, ethnicity, language, sexual orientation, age, social economic status (SES), disability, and ability.

Gay (2000) defined *culturally responsive teaching* (CRT) as using the cultural knowledge, prior experiences, and performance styles of diverse students to make learning more appropriate and effective for them and to meet the needs of diverse students by relating pedagogy and practice to their strengths and needs. Gay (2000) also described culturally responsive teaching as having these characteristics:

- Acknowledges the legitimacy of diverse cultures across language, dispositions, habits, attitudes, and lifestyles
- Builds upon collaborative partnerships between the home, school, and community of the student
- Entails learning styles and differences
- Entails diversities of one's self and others, beyond tolerance
- Incorporates multicultural literatures, media, artifacts, religions, topics, and other values associated with the culture of discussion in order to invoke meaningful dialogue

For school counselors, CRT requires the aforementioned in addition to understanding the unique role that "the learning disability" and ability plays in the lives of students who are eligible for special education, English language learners (ELLs) services, and/or gifted education (Ford, 2013; Williams, 2008). English language learners (ELLs) are students who are typically unable to communicate fluently or learn effectively in English, and who often come from non-English-speaking homes and backgrounds, and who typically require specialized or modified instruction in both the English language and in their academic courses. Gifted students are usually characterized as those who show evidence of high performance capability in areas such as intellectual, creative, artistic, or leadership capacity, or in specific academic fields, and who require enrichment, acceleration, or access to a compacted curriculum. This chapter focuses on the need for counselors to become culturally responsive by adopting CRT pedagogy and practice in order to meet the unique academic and socioemotional needs of students receiving special education *beyond the disability*.

AN OVERVIEW OF SCHOOL COUNSELORS' ROLES IN SPECIAL EDUCATION

Based on data from the National Survey of School Counselors and Administrators (College Board Advocacy and Policy Center, 2012), school counselors, in general, are seeing not only an increase in the size of their student caseloads and those with moderate to severe mental health issues, but also they are servicing more students with Individualized Education Plans (IEPs) and 504 Plans. Coupled with this caseload increase in students with special needs, school counselors now have increasing responsibilities related to students' academic standards and performance, such as those dictated by the No Child Left Behind (NCLB) Act of 2001 (U.S. Department of Education, 2004) and the *Reauthorization of the Elementary and Secondary Education Act* (ESEA) of 2010 (U.S. Department of Education, 2010). This growing body of school students is also more diverse, which involves a more complex set of educational needs (Hughes, Valle-Riestra, & Arguelles, 2002; Lo, 2010; Salas, 2004). Both the primary professional organization for school counselors, American School Counselor Association (ASCA), and the major counselor educator accrediting body, the Council for Accreditation of Counseling and Related Educational Programs (CACREP), further speak to the expectations of, and guidelines for, school counselors who work with students in special education from CLD backgrounds. ASCA has adopted guidelines for school counselors to follow in order to support the overall needs of these students across the school settings. The following are taken from ASCA's position statements in regard to students with special needs:

American School Counselor Association (ASCA) Position Statements

Professional school counselors encourage and support the academic, career and personal/social development for all students through comprehensive school counseling programs. Professional school counselors are committed to helping all students realize their potential and meet or exceed academic standards regardless of challenges resulting from disabilities and other special needs. (ASCA, 2013, p. 52)

Hence, school counselors should

- be able to articulate and demonstrate an understanding of student diversity;
- be able to accomplish measurable objectives demonstrating best practices that meet the needs of CLD and learning diverse students and families;

- believe that all students have potential and can learn and lead productive lives;
- demonstrate their attitudes and beliefs that all students deserve access to a comprehensive program that confers a free appropriate public education (FAPE).

Students With Disabilities

School counselors have always played important roles in working with students who have special needs. State and federal laws require schools to provide an equitable education for all students, including those with special needs. Components of these laws offer a plethora of opportunities for school counselors to be collaborators in the special education process. Procedural due process, IEPs, the least restrictive environment (LRE), and other plans and strategies for students with accommodations and modifications provide opportunities to use the school counselors' skills to benefit students who have identified special needs. School counselors work with students with special needs both in special class settings and in the regular classrooms. They are key professionals on the team who assist with accommodations and provide an awareness of federal regulations, and they are a key component in assisting with transitions to postsecondary options. It is particularly important that not only is the school counselor role in these procedures clearly defined and in compliance with laws and local policies but also that school counselors know their students beyond the disability or other health need. Part of knowing comes through culturally responsive practices, school collaboration, and home-school partnerships (Darling-Hammond & Garcia-Lopez, 2002; Han & Thomas, 2010; Sánchez & Thorp, 2008). Some of the experiences of being students with disabilities are reflected in the Guided Practice Exercise 11.1.

Guided Practice Exercise 11.1

DIVERSITY AND DISABILITY IN THE SCHOOL

Over the next few days, reflect on your experience as a student in any grade, K–12. Now, think about your strengths as a student and what you were able to accomplish without supports. Next, consider your areas of need such as in writing, speaking, listening, and reading and consider how you were able to ask teachers or school staff for assistance in any or all of these areas. Last, reflect on how your teachers, school staff, and peers related to you when you required this extra support and assistance. Now, openly and honestly reflect on the questions below and write down a few bullet-point responses to share over the course of your subsequent discussions of this chapter.

- How did it feel to have so many of your peers and others celebrate your strengths with you?
- How do you think students with disabilities who are also members of an under-represented minority group or other diverse group feel when they have very few peers, if any at all, to celebrate their accomplishments?
- How did it feel to ask for assistance with any academic area and excel? Can you now imagine having a disability and never actually feeling that you have excelled academically or at least understood the content with minimum proficiency?
- In schools, who did you turn to for support when you had social and emotional difficulties that intersected with any of these questions listed above? What might this feel like to have no one in the school or home who can support your journey through some of the complex questions listed above?

Now, write a short two-paragraph e-mail to students who come from culturally and linguistically diverse (CLD) backgrounds and who have a learning disability, address-ing any areas of concern based on your understanding of the reflection questions noted above. This e-mail letter should attempt to make these students feel that they can come to you, a professional school counselor, for assistance in any of these areas discussed here. The test, however, for you is to demonstrate through this short letter e-mail that you truly *understand* their needs, experiences, and strengths, as illustrated here, and if not, perhaps ask them questions to guide your understanding of their school-based experiences related to their diversity and disability. (The e-mail letter can be done *pre* and *post* your reading of this chapter so as to compare your discourse around the top-ics explored here and to measure growth in understanding of this content and, more importantly, of the needs of the students.)

Further delineation of school counselor responsibilities when working with students in special education who are also from CLD backgrounds is addressed in the next section.

SCHOOL COUNSELORS' RELATED ROLES ACROSS DIVERSE LEARNING NEEDS

One of the school counselors' primary tasks is to provide counseling if this service is mandated as a related service in a student's IEP. School counselors have a responsibility to be a part of designing portions of these plans related to the comprehensive school counseling program. However, school counselors may serve as a member of the IEP team whose primary interest is to assist the school to provide the student with a FAPE. School counselors typically

- coordinate 504 planning meetings;
- serve as members of the child study team; and
- supervise the implementation of the 504 Plan.

School counselors *do not*
- make sole decisions regarding student placement in special education;
- serve as the local education agency (LEA) or in any supervisory role related to the implementation of Individuals With Disabilities Education Improvement Act of 2004 (IDEA) services; or
- coordinate special education or related services.

Based on the aforementioned above, those school counselors who are the sole counselor of a school must not only fulfill the expectations of the school administration and district mission statements and philosophies, but also they are required to fulfill both state and federal requirements in regard to students who are classified as having a disability and who have counseling as a related service on their IEPs. This duty requires school counselors to know the student beyond the IEP and 504 Plan, and work as collaborative team members among teachers, school, and home (Brotherson, Summers, Bruns, & Sharp, 2008).

In addition to the tasks specified in the previously identified disabilities, further discussion is warranted when school counselors are working with students with disabilities who are also culturally and linguistically diverse. There is an increase of culturally and linguistically diverse (CLD) students who have special education and other needs. Students from low-income homes, single parent homes, foster families, second language families, and more serve as examples of CLD students who are also served under the IDEA of 2004. Diversity no doubt impacts the ways students learn but also how teachers and other personnel support the needs of the students. When students are experiencing learning or behavioral problems, in many cases, school counselors are the first point of contact between the school and teachers. This role is supplemented by the need for school counselors to understand the needs, wants, dispositions, and home life of the student. Questions about language, race, class, gender, and identity are often first identified by school counselors. In addition, school counselors may also be valuable assets in the identification of another potentially confounding variable, that of differential stimuli (i.e., environmental, emotional, sociological, physiological, and psychological) that can impact learning styles (Dunn, 2000). Similarly, it may be worthwhile to consider the students' capabilities and limitations within the various areas (i.e., musical, visual, verbal, logical, bodily, interpersonal, intrapersonal, naturalistic, and existential) specified in the theory of multiple intelligences (Gardner, 2011). With this knowledge, school counselors are then able to assist the IEP team to develop a well-rounded understanding of the students and to place those identified students' needs within context. To illustrate this point, Case Illustration 11.1 of Tina is presented below.

CASE ILLUSTRATION 11.1

TINA

Tina is a 12-year-old sixth grader. Tina lives at home with her mother and grandmother, who both speak several languages in the home. However, Tina is the only child in the home and the only one who speaks English, but she is having some difficulty communicating in her reading and English language arts (ELA) courses in school. The ELA teacher, Ms. Watson, attempted to reach out to Tina's mom but had difficulty understanding her in a recent phone conversation. At present, Tina is failing both courses and seems to be growing more distant as the teacher attempts to reach out to her to find out what is wrong. Additionally, no one else on the sixth-grade team has expressed any concerns about Tina's academic or social progress, or has failed her for the first two marking periods of the school year. It is now April, and the team is planning on recommending non-special education students for summer school. However, there has still been limited communication with Tina's mom or any other guardian.

- What might be the role of the culturally competent guidance counselor?
- Should the grade-level teachers meet to discuss interventions with the guidance counselor?
- What unique next steps can you envision that the school counselor should take now that the grade-level teachers may not have expertise?
- What next steps do you recommend for the school counselor, the family, Tina, and the grade-level team?

Case Summary: Tina

As for Tina, the school counselor must be aware of her needs, strengths, and the needs of the home. The two together can help build the school counselor's culturally

(Continued)

(Continued)

responsive lens in order to construct a framework of support around Tina. This framework will outline an attempt to

- understand issues with teaching and learning within the school setting;
- build a competent and respectful dialogue between the home family members and school teachers;
- recommend Tina to the *child study team* (CST) in order for her to undergo a pre-referral, which is a crucial first step in the evaluation process; and
- possibly help identify Tina's learning styles and needs, and recommend a *response to instruction and intervention* (RtII) and/or counseling to address her motivation, self-awareness, and any other needs that may result from the referral and dialogue with her family.

In summary, school counselors need to develop perspectives regarding their role in promoting culturally responsive schools including assisting students with needs across language, such as ELLs, special education, diverse learning styles, and other needs. Such initiatives can be a major influence in meeting the challenges and seizing the opportunities of true cultural diversity (Baca & de Valenzuela, 1994; Echevarría & Graves, 2006). The needs and issues of students with disabilities who come from CLD backgrounds have been addressed in this section. Students do not exist in a vacuum; therefore, in the following section, considerations of families who are also from CLD backgrounds are reviewed.

Families

Children from CLD backgrounds generally bring to the school a set of behaviors and expectations that are fostered both at home and in their communities. Most families, regardless of cultural background, place a high value on education, considering it to be the prime factor in improving socioeconomic status. Paradoxically, the expectations, however, of many students from CLD backgrounds and their families and communities are often at odds with the realities of schools and the educational process (Darling-Hammond & Garcia-Lopez, 2002; Han & Thomas, 2010; Lee, 1995; Sánchez & Thorp, 2008). For example, a single parent, working evenings and raising an entire family, may expect that the school might inform him or her of his or her child's progress and/or any abrupt behavioral challenges as they occur. In contrast, the school may find that the parent should become aware through inquiring with his or her child and through checking for these changes through e-mail, calling into the school, or by checking an online grading system provided by the district. The two entities want what is best for the student, but getting there may come only through convergence as a part of the process of collaboration and culturally competent communication.

Another important note of consideration is in regard to cultural insensitivities. Lee (2005) maintained that these are inherent in the educational system and tend not to validate the experiences of the culturally diverse home and family life. Moreover, students who come from CLD families are often excluded from serious consideration in the education of their children. Ford (2005, 2013) maintained that this type of thinking stems from deficit thinking about the family, that is, assumptions about unemployed parents, parents disconnected from supporting their child's school life and resistant to school collaboration because they do not show up at school events, and more stereotypes. The aforementioned could be related to a working single parent, or foster parent, who has more than one child with special and other needs. It is not unusual, therefore, to find that relations between the school and many communities are severely strained in many instances (Lee, 1995; Williams, 2007; Williams, 2008). School counselors' collaboration becomes critical in order to address perceptions held from both sides of the students' stakeholders (i.e., teachers and home), and to provide and foster a culturally responsive understanding that supports the whole student, beyond the identified disability. Oftentimes, the school counselor takes on the role of a child advocate under the framework of special education and may often unwittingly be the resource that prevents parents from filing for due process against the school regarding their child's FAPE.

Most importantly, school counselors provide ways to bridge the home and family life of the CLD student. In order for such bridges to be constructed, it is necessary that school counselors form working alliances with parents and families from CLD backgrounds and the special education team. An important role of the school counselor is promotion of the development and incorporation of a wide variety of family and community resources in the educational process (Cartledge & Lo, 2006), such as parent nights, language nights, grandparent and foster parent retreats, gifted and ELL events, and more. In regard to students, it is also essential to communicate with the family about positive events and results, not only about negative concerns or bad news. It is important to be mindful of culturally competent communication between the home and school, and as demonstrated here, school counselors can assist in this dialogue. These concepts are illustrated in Case Illustration 11.2.

CASE ILLUSTRATION 11.2

JATOLLA

Jatolla is a 14-year-old ninth-grade student who lives with her mother and her mother's paramour. Jatolla does not see her biological father, who is reportedly incarcerated. Jatolla is classified as Other Health Impairment with ADHD and has an IEP. Lately, Jatolla has been withdrawn and seems to be experiencing symptoms associated with anxiety disorder and depression. Her family social worker, Mr. Hart, has been active with the school in order to make sure that Jatolla has a FAPE and can make progress in the general curriculum. Mr. Hart has also been attempting to provide supports for the mother, who has been experiencing issues with drug addiction and some alleged criminal activity related to this addiction. Mr. Hart has contacted the school and left messages regarding Jatolla's declining grades and other behaviors that he has observed. However, he is concerned because he has not heard from Jatolla's teachers regarding any sudden changes in behavior. Mr. Hart is also concerned that Jatolla may want to drop out of school given the seriousness of these and other more complex family issues currently taking place in the home. Mr. Hart is looking for direction from you, the school counselor.

- What discussion will you have with Mr. Hart and Mom regarding Jatolla?
- Is it appropriate to share information with Jatolla's teachers regarding growing problems in the home?
- At what point does this situation become an issue for administration or the IEP team to pursue rather than the school counselor?
- Are there other steps that can be taken to help Jatolla in the educational setting?

Case Summary: Jatolla

In Jatolla's case, the school counselor must assist the IEP team by making them aware of her social, emotional, and academic needs and the problems she is experiencing in school and home, even if the teachers have not observed any stark differences. Balanced with confidentiality, the collaborative role between the school counselor and the county social worker will provide supports for Jatolla to be more successful within the school setting. Mr. Hart had legitimate concerns about Jatolla's declining grades across disciplines and the social and functional behaviors he has observed. Through the school counselor's interagency collaborative efforts and home-school collaboration, the school teachers and IEP team members will have access to important information that can assist the team in providing further supports for Jatolla. This collaborative effort also underscores the importance of working with others who are outside of the home and who may have a vested interest in the well-being of all school students and those with needs similar to Jatolla's.

The school counselor will also be instrumental in assisting with the following:

- Understanding issues with teaching and learning across the school setting
- Building competent and respectful dialogue between the home and school teachers around these sensitive issues taking place in the home life of Jatolla
- Helping to make additional recommendations to the child study team (CST) in order for Jatolla to possibly undergo additional assessments that may lead to a reevaluation that will identify additional learning, social, emotional, or other needs, in addition to supplementary aides and services
- Developing some school counseling supports, as well as wraparound and/or therapeutic behavior supports for Jatolla for an interim period of time

In summary, school counselors may need to develop new perspectives regarding their role in promoting inclusive and culturally responsive schools which support all students, including those like Jatolla, who had needs including counseling, social, and emotional behaviors. This type of professional support is in addition to the student's identified special education needs under IDEA of 2004.

COUNSELING TO IMPROVE TEACHING AND LEARNING

Interventions, modifications, and accommodations are the responsibility of every educator who has any meaningful contact with the students. There will need to be collaboration among such professionals. However, the role of the school counselor, as defined by ASCA, is not fully explained; the definition lacks information about the school counselor's recommended level of assistance or interaction required to support students with special education needs (Trolley, Haas, & Campese Patti, 2009). But most can agree on one fundamental consideration: These interventions and modifications must be diverse themselves, and not simply become a bandage to problems such as negative behaviors, absenteeism, or tardiness. School counselors and educators in general must focus on the holistic needs of the students, beyond those solely tied to the students' disability. This focus identifies the assumptions, needs, wants, and home life that impact the student's experiences through teaching and learning. The aforementioned points are illustrated in Case Illustration 11.3 below: Damere.

CASE ILLUSTRATION 11.3

DAMERE

Damere is a nine-year-old male in fourth grade who lives with his father. Damere sees his biological mother at least once a month, but after each visit, he has a major behavioral disruption at home and at school. Damere just started at this school this year. He is classified as Other Health Impaired (OHI). Damere has also been diagnosed by a psychologist as having an emotional behavior disorder (EBD). His father is currently trying to access therapeutic supports outside of school to address his behaviors. In school, Damere is rapidly falling behind. Recently, general education teachers have complained to the counselor, his special education teacher, and even other parents about him disrupting students in class and putting his hands on other students throughout the school day. Damere has been sent to in-school suspension three times in one month. You are the school counselor and have just been contacted by Damere's general education teachers and his father. They ask for your help in dealing with this situation.

- What discussion will you have with the parent regarding Damere?
- In this situation, what is culturally appropriate?
- At what point does this situation become an issue for administration to pursue rather than the school counselor or special education teacher?
- What steps can be taken to help Damere in the educational setting?

Case Summary: Damere

As noted here, the role of the school counselor becomes one of mentor and mediator. Because of the intensity of the behaviors and the perceptions held by Damere's parents, there is a need for a culturally competent mediator, that is, a school counselor who can address the needs of all the key players who have a vested role in Damere's education. Such a school counselor will be able to identify the strengths and needs of students such as Damere, who does not have a "voice" and whose parents are unable to supplement important information to assist the school or team to aid their child. In Damere's case, the school counselor acts in concert with the school leadership team to ward off any wrongful penalties, suspensions, or any other issues that might lead to expulsion. Because the school counselor had the capital knowledge and competency to dig deeper and examine issues presented by students and more freedom than that of the traditionally licensed classroom teachers, the school coun-selor's cultural responsiveness becomes part of the intervention giving Damere the ability to save Damere from himself. The school counselor must assist the IEP team and make them aware of Damere's needs and strengths. Of course, simultaneously, the grade-level teacher(s) should be collaborating with the school counselor, parents, paraprofessionals, and others in order to build a framework of support for Damere. This dual approach can continue to strengthen not only the school counselor's cultur-ally responsive lens but also the lens of the special education teacher who works with Damere. This framework will attempt to satisfy the following needs:

- Identify Damere's issues with teaching and learning within the school setting.
- Build a competent and respectful dialogue between the home and school teach-ers around these sensitive issues taking place in Damere's home life.
- Recommend Damere to the CST in order for him to undergo possible addi-tional assessments that may lead to a reevaluation that will identify additional learning, social, emotional, or other needs and/or supplementary aids or aides and services.
- Possibly identify wraparound and/or therapeutic behavioral supports and coun-seling for Damere. Also, response to instruction and intervention (RtII) for behav-ior is strongly recommended as well as a Positive Behavior Support Plan (PBSP), which would no doubt follow the Functional Behavioral Assessment (FBA).

In summary, school counselors need to develop perspectives regarding their role in promoting inclusivity and culturally responsive awareness schools that support all students, including those like Damere, who had needs across behavior and social functioning domains. This type of professional support led by school counselors is essential, and this support should be considered in addition to any program for students identified for special education needs and other recommended supports noted above that fall under the umbrella of the IDEA and the IDEA of 2004.

Schools

In order for counseling services to be most effective, school counselors and other team members must find ways to engage students, families, and members of the greater community, then, identify barriers to and solutions for this participation. Through these partnerships and collaborations, school leaders and counselors will be able to address ways parents and others can more positively view the school and the special education process and enhance the development of trust with diverse families. Additionally, one area of importance that schools need to attend to is that of the diversity in language and cultural customs. These differences can leave parents feeling alienated from or intimidated by the schools. In order to address these feelings of isolation and mistrust, a good faith effort on the part of school counselors is warranted that demonstrates that they are willing to meet parents *where they are at* in terms of circumstances and worldview. This attitude translates into a practice of culturally competent collaboration that can help to dispel the fear or alienation many parents from low SES and CLD backgrounds experience in their interactions with schools. Home visits, phone calls that offer resources, and friendly and professional check-ins are some examples of meeting parents and strengthening the branch of partnership through culturally competent collaboration. Oftentimes, if parents misunderstand and mistrust, it can easily turn to self-defensiveness and anger toward the school (Williams, 2007). If this occurs, the special education process for the child is hindered and potential success impeded.

It is therefore important for school counselors to work with their school to move beyond the disability and toward a model of cultural inclusivity. The idea of a monolithic society cannot coexist in a school that embraces students from CLD backgrounds and possess diverse learning needs and supports. As the 21st century ensues, a new American culture has emerged, where diversity and pluralism are accepted hallmarks of society. Students from CLD backgrounds who possess diverse learning styles also hold diverse worldviews characteristic of the general student population, parallel with that of pluralism. These students are the future leaders of this new nation, and as these students mature, they will need guidance in this developmental process from culturally responsive and competent school counselors. This inclusive framework requires school counselors to develop expertise and be able to competently respond to diversity variables such as culture, learning styles, race, class, gender, disability, and ability. Essentially, they need to develop the knowledge, skills, and dispositions to provide the most effective services to students with disabilities within the context of cultural realities. When all the aforementioned is taken into consideration, school counselors, as culturally responsive practitioners, have the potential to be on the cutting edge of promoting access, equity, and educational justice to all students, beyond the disability.

We are in an era of ever evolving models and geographical locations of schools and educational services delivery, such as traditional and newer charter, urban, suburban, rural, private, and cyber schools. The most important component of providing equity, parity, and access to students with special education and other needs is to construct schools that possess the core value of integrating a culturally responsive and inclusive framework. It has become paramount that schools provide equal access to educational opportunities to students from CLD backgrounds. Even more so, under

IDEA and IDEA of 2004, it is critical that these schools support the diverse learning styles and needs of the students with disabilities through a variety of approaches. Lee (2001) identified the following as salient aspects of culturally responsive schools:

- Adopt a "salad bowl" as opposed to a "melting pot" philosophy of education.
- Forge a sense of community out of cultural diversity.
- Capitalize on cultural diversity and maintain academic standards.
- Use standards with the same high academic expectations for all students.
- Use a curriculum that is neither Eurocentric nor Afrocentric nor Asiancentric.
- Use a curriculum that is "centrically" centered fairly and accurately.
- Reflect the contributions of many cultures.
- Go "beyond Black History Month" (i.e., infuse multiculturalism and diversity in a nonstereotypical manner throughout the curriculum and the school year).
- Provide students with forums outside of the classroom to communicate with and learn about peers from diverse cultural backgrounds.
- Put mechanisms in place to deal with racial and cultural tensions.
- Employ committed educators who engage in ongoing staff development and are not afraid to take risks or improvise when necessary.
- Recruit a diverse staff of educators.
- Engage high levels of parental involvement, including via educators who consider language and cultural customs in their interactions with parents.
- Define cultural diversity to include people with disabilities, people with diverse sexual orientations, people with diverse religious traditions, and older people (p. 258).

Although no one school will possess all of these characteristics, it is important for schools to strive to incorporate as many as possible. Schools are complex and so too are the students who attend them. Therefore, this complexity, scored with diversity and learning disability, requires schools to become as inclusive and culturally responsive as possible so that no one is left behind. School counselors may need to develop new perspectives regarding their role in promoting culturally responsive schools including students with language needs such as English language learners (ELLs), those in special education and with diverse learning styles, and those with other needs. Such initiatives can be a major influence in meeting the challenges and seizing the opportunities of true cultural diversity (Baca & de Valenzuela, 1994; Echevarría & Graves, 2006).

Communities

Community collaborative endeavors may be operationalized in several important ways. For example, it may be important to coordinate paraprofessional development programs to involve selected people from diverse communities to assist with the students related services. These individuals may play an important role in helping to bridge language and cultural barriers, which ultimately can lead to interventions that can result in positive academic, career, and personal-social success for the identified students and their families. Additionally, these collaborations can include the students' behavioral health supports, mental health providers, and related service providers, as well as extended family members, those the IEP team may not usually or normally be able to access, especially during times of turbulence and/or concerns around the students' FAPE.

Further, more innovative approaches to culturally responsive community collaborations may involve *thinking outside the box* about how and where culturally responsive school-related counseling services can be delivered, in addition to developing fundamental awareness of and respect for cultural differences in helping to seek worthwhile attitudes and behaviors. An example of this would be a reconfiguration of the school counseling day, whereby Extended School Day (ESD) services are offered that provide student counseling and encourage parental or guardian involvement. Altering the counseling day for some members of the special education and counseling staffs would allow for the possibility of greater access to this related service for family and community members. The latter is especially important for working class families who do not have the benefit of a stay-at-home parent or an after school caretaker. In these families, typically the parents are working two or more jobs in order to provide the basic necessities for the child (Baker, Gersten, & Keating, 2000; Invernizzi, Juel, & Rosemary, 1997). Meetings normally scheduled during the day would hinder their ability to attend and/or result in financial or job jeopardy.

Another example of innovative and culturally responsive community collaboration would involve home visits. School counselors, proceeding with caution and school district support, could conduct home visits during afternoon and evening hours to work with students who have identified special education needs that can be addressed through counseling sessions. In addition to the home, after school counseling sessions may be held in other places within the community, not just the home. For example, they could be conducted at a family support center, the community library, a church, or at the parents' place of comfort. Utilizing this approach, students and families feel valued and are viewed as members of the child's whole education team. This approach underscores the African proverb, It Takes a Village to Raise a Child. Indeed, it takes more than just the special education team to provide a FAPE.

Similarly, school counseling activities could be conducted during afternoon hours in community centers such as religious institutions or youth clubs: places where people can gather and experience both a feeling of safety and cultural validation. Counseling initiatives in such centers could be co-facilitated by community stakeholders and paraprofessionals who are more familiar with a community's language and cultural customs. Under IDEA, the *village* becomes more than just the student's IEP team, and it might include innovative pedagogies and best practices to promote student learning and engagement.

CULTURALLY RESPONSIVE SCHOOL PROGRAMMING

The inclusive framework of culturally responsive guidance practices in schools should entail a focus on the needs of the whole student. In addition, myths such as "there is no such thing as the *color-blind* rule" (i.e., all students are the same) must be dispelled. A fundamental theme of culturally responsive counseling and guidance is based on the assumption that there must be a shared understanding of the cultural experiences of students and how these experiences intersect with students' academic, career, and personal-social development.

Through related services such as individual and group counseling, as well as large group guidance in psycho-educational lessons and interventions, the culturally responsive school counselors should be able to help students from a variety of cultural backgrounds with diverse disabilities to develop healthy self-concepts. They also need to help these students learn to own and respect their own cultural diversity, within the context of educational, career, and personal-social goals. The aforementioned will require that school counselors be effective facilitators of student development. As effective student development facilitators, five distinct functions emerge for culturally responsive school counselors, which are presented in Figure 11.1 (Lee, 2001, 2005).

Figure 11.1 Five Functions of Culturally Responsive School Counselors

1. Promoting the development of positive self-identities among students with disabilities

2. Facilitating the development of positive interpersonal relations among students with disabilities and who come from CLD backgrounds

3. Encouraging academic achievement for identified students protected under the IDEA and Section 504, as well as for those students who are considered at risk and are experiencing issues embedded in the achievement gap

4. Promoting the attitude and skills for school success grounded in a culturally inclusive framework for students with special and other needs

5. Facilitating the career exploration and choice process among young people to support secondary transitions, which are required of students under the IDEA who are aged 16 or younger

Source: Adapted from Lee, C. C. (2001) Culturally responsive school counselors and programs: Addressing the needs of all students. *Professional School Counseling, 4,* 257–260. Lee, C. C. (2005). Urban school counseling context, characteristics, and competencies. *Professional School Counseling, 8,* 184–188.

School counselors can begin by promoting the development of positive self-identities among students with disabilities. The first function might be accomplished by conducting self-awareness groups that emphasize self-appreciation through a validation of cultural heritage and learning styles. Counselors might consider using culturally specific curriculum materials to cultivate self-pride. In addition, education to address autism awareness and different learning styles could be beneficial to students, educators, administrators, and families.

A variety of events and activities could be organized such as those presented in Figure 11.2.

In addition to the development of positive self-identities of these students, the second function highlights the importance of the development of positive interpersonal relations among students with disabilities and who come from CLD backgrounds. Growth groups might be used to accomplish this goal by having students from diverse backgrounds explore with each other the nature and importance of positive interpersonal relationships. Cultural variations on the notion of community might be incorporated into group interactions as a way to develop mutual respect and understanding among youth from diverse backgrounds (Carter & Vuong, 1997; Hayes, 1996; Lee, 2001). To facilitate this dialogue, interest and learning styles inventories can be utilized by teachers across multiple curriculum areas. School counselors can also assist in this process by exploring with students such areas as extended family, kinships, group, and family identities that relate to practices across special education and secondary transition practices.

School counselors could employ such tools as simple genograms and family trees to facilitate this dialogue. Additional tools that could be utilized to obtain further information include picture maps, social media, and literature.

Figure 11.2 Examples of Diversity—Through Disability

January 4	World Braille Day
February 28	Rare Disease Awareness Day
March	Brain Injury Awareness Month
April 2	Autism Awareness Day
May	Cystic Fibrosis Awareness Month
June 27	National PTSD Awareness Day
August	Spinal Muscular Atrophy Awareness
September 9	Fetal Alcohol Syndrome Awareness Day
October	ADHD Awareness Month
November	Diabetes Awareness Month
December 2	Special Education Day

Source: Special Needs Awareness Calendar. Adapted from FriendshipCircle.org.

Figure 11.3   Learning Styles

Modality	Descriptors	Learn Best Through the Use of . . .
Visual Learners (input)	• Learn by observation • Can recall what they have seen • Can follow written or drawn instructions • Like to read • Use written notes • Benefit by visualizing, watching TV/video/films	• Charts, graphs, diagrams, and flow charts • Sight words • Flashcards • Visual similarities and differences • Pictures and graphics • Maps • Silent reading • Written instructions • Computer assisted learning
Auditory Learners (input) Verbal-Linguistic Intelligence	• Prefer listening and taking notes • Listen for patterns • Consult peers to ascertain that they have the correct details • Can recall what they have heard • Can follow oral directions • Repeat words aloud for memorization • Use oral language effectively	• Discussion, dialog, debate • Memorization • Phonics • Oral reading • Hearing anecdotes or stories • Listening to tapes or CDs • Cooperative learning groups
Kinesthetic Learners (input)	• Are often physically adept • Learn through experience and physical activity • Benefit from demonstration • Learn from teaching others what they know	• Playing games • Role playing • Read body language/gestures • Mime • Drama • Learn or memorize while moving (pacing, stationary bike, finger or whole body games)
Tactile Learners (input)	• Learn by touching and manipulating objects • Often learn inductively rather than deductively • Tend toward psychomotor over abstract thinking • Prefer personal connections to topics • Follow directions they have written themselves/that they have rehearsed • Benefit from demonstrations	• Learning by doing • "Hands-on" • Creating maps • Building models • Art projects • Using manipulatives • Drawing, designing things • Writing/tracing
Active	• Can be impulsive • Risk-takers • Do not prefer lectures	• Prefer "doing, discussion, explaining" vs. listening and watching

(Continued)

Figure 11.3 (Continued)

Modality	Descriptors	Learn Best Through the Use of . . .
	• Prefer group work • Tend to be interpersonal • Not inclined to too much note-taking	• Prefer active experimentation • Like acting and role playing • Like team competition
Reflective	• Prefer to think about concepts quietly before any action • Learn by thinking • Like writing • Tend to be intrapersonal and introspective	• Tend toward deductive learning • Prefer reflective observation • Intrapersonal skills valued • Journals • Learning logs
Global Understanding	• Make decisions based on intuition • Spontaneous and creative; "idea" person • Often a risk-taker • Tend to reach conclusions quickly • Intake information in large chunks rather than details • Nonlinear thinkers • "See the forest before they see the trees."	• Interpersonal connection important to them • Stories and anecdotes • Seeing the "whole" rather than in parts • Highly interesting project and materials • Functional games and activities • Think-pair-share; Praise-question-polish • Teacher feedback; person-to-person communication
Analytical Understanding	• Sequential, linear learners • Prefer information in small chunks, steps • Can follow the rules for mathematic equations • Prefer a logical progression • "See the trees before they see the forest."	• Intrapersonal skills valued • Journals • Learning logs • Sequentially organized material, timelines, diagrams • Moving from "part" to the "whole" • Puzzles, logic games

Source: Baltimore County Public Schools.org (n.d.): http://www.bcps.org/offices/lis/models/tips/styles.html

Not only might the students' comprehension and expression of knowledge be taught but how they learn best (i.e., learning styles) may also play a pivotal role in their success. Samples of such learning styles and activities are presented in Figure 11.3.

The third function entails academic achievement for identified students protected under IDEA and Section 504, as well as those students who are considered at risk and are experiencing issues embedded in the achievement gap. It is important that the school counselors explore opportunities to collaborate with all staff members to address disparities across student performance and support a broader understanding of achievement, which for some students may focus on specific goals in their IEP or accommodations in their 504 or ELL plans. For other students, the school counselors may advise school staff on how to support reading, writing, and mathematics in the home connected to the Common Core State Standards (CCSS). Under the CCSS, states must align their curriculum with rigorous standards to address overall measurable student outcomes across core academic subject areas (ESEA of 2010, U.S. Department of Education, 2010). Additionally, the school counselors become important in supporting school-based academic and behavior interventions that can be part of response to intervention and instruction (RtII).

Based on models of intervention, such as RtII, schools provide remedial and developmental instruction across the core academic areas of needs identified through school-wide curriculum-based assessments. After students are identified in Tier 1, then students that move to Tier 2 are provided with more intense instruction. Students that move to Tier 3 are those typically in need of even more specifically designed instructional strategies and are thought to be eligible for special education services under IDEA or Section 504 services. School counselors can assist the staff to monitor progress and needs along with either the IEP team and/or the child

Figure 11.4 Factors Affecting Teaching and Learning

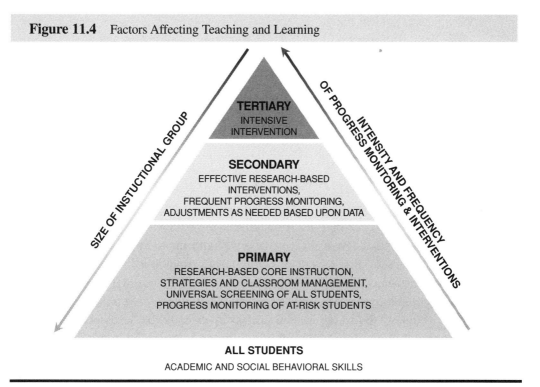

Source: Factors Affecting Teaching and Learning. Used by permission of Epic Ohana, Inc.

study team of the school (Fuchs, Mock, Morgan, & Young, 2003). School counselors may consider other relevant factors that may impact student performance and minimize teaching and learning as illustrated in Figure 11.4.

The fourth function entails promoting the attitude and skills for school success grounded in a culturally inclusive framework for students with special needs. These involve promoting the development of positive attitudes toward academic achievement among all students and facilitating the development of academic skills and competencies beyond race, class, gender, and disability or exceptionality. With respect to this view, school counselors must work to see each student as having the same potential as any other student. To accomplish the former, school counselors should consider developing guidance activities that focus on inherent cultural potential that incorporates the educational experiences of influential people from diverse backgrounds. Additionally, counseling guidance activities need to be planned in areas such as academic planning, study skills test taking, time management, and remediation intervention. Such workshops are necessary to ensure that all students have an opportunity to develop the skills to achieve, given cultural differences in learning styles (Lee, 2001). Hence, students with disabilities are a part of the general student population, and we must value and understand their unique differences toward learning in order to truly appreciate their important contribution to the general student body.

The final, fifth function is facilitating the career exploration and choice process among young people to support secondary transitions. For young people from many cultural backgrounds, the issues of career interest and choice become complex and challenging dimensions in their development for many reasons, including racism and socioeconomic disadvantage (Herring, 1998), a need for role models, and an understanding of parental expectations and realities, from the elementary through the secondary level. Therefore, it is important to provide students from CLD backgrounds with relevant guidance to the work world (Murrow-Taylor, Foltz, McDonald, Ellis, & Culbertson, 1999). For example, a comprehensive guidance program needs to include information forums on nonstereotypical jobs and careers that include perspectives from those in the field who have disabilities. Also, school counselors can sponsor "career days" and invite career role models who have disabilities from a variety of cultural backgrounds to school to share with students their perceptions of and experiences in the work world. For older students, internships and cooperative experiences with culturally diverse businesses that employ people with disabilities and professionals could be developed (Skinner & Lindstrom, 2003). School counselors can work in partnership with the family, special education teachers and/or secondary transition workers, Office of Vocation Rehabilitation (OVR) workers, and additional community agencies to develop programming that includes culturally diverse mentors. The overall framework should include culturally inclusive secondary education opportunities, relevant and realistic employment, and, if appropriate, independent living opportunities that show how disabilities can be accommodated and supported (Hughes et al., 2002; Lo, 2010; Salas, 2004). This continuum of support does not end in 12th grade.

As outlined here, the role of school counselors is one of a facilitator and partner in student development through a culturally responsive and inclusive framework, and this role goes beyond traditional school counseling practices and acknowledges the students' potential beyond their disability. Specific guidance provisions are necessary for heightening awareness, expanding skills, and maximizing options on the part of all students regardless of their disability and cultural background (Lee, 2001, 2005). The latter is done through facilitated school, home, and community collaboration. An example of the importance of knowing the CLD student and family's wants and needs at the point of secondary transitions in high school is illustrated in Figure 11.5.

Advocates

In addition to the five functions previously discussed, school counselors often become student advocates. Frequently, school counselors are faced with unique dilemmas regarding programming and working with a gamut of teachers who are all required to support the student. For example, students who have more severe disabilities and who may be ELLs may also require specialized secondary transition services, which may transcend the role of the traditional classroom special education teacher. School counselors may need to collaborate with such professionals as a home interpreter, a worker from OVR, a secondary level ELL worker, and the students' related service providers in occupational therapy and physical therapy. Regarding students with special education needs, there may also be adjustment issues, behavioral concerns, and other problems that are beyond the scope of

Figure 11.5   Knowing Needs and Wants of Students and Families

`Ohana Conferencing is a collaborative effort that brings together families, extended and hanai family, CWS, service providers, and the support system of children who are involved with CWS. Families know their own strengths, issues, and resources and this process provides families a voice.

In an `Ohana Conference, families work with CWS and use what they know to make the best decisions for the safety of their children and create a plan for strengthening the family. The `Ohana Conference is voluntary and is a positive, solution-oriented process. The `Ohana Conference is grounded in the core goals and values of child safety, preserving family relationships, and timely permanent placement of children.  EPIC `Ohana is the only organization in the State of Hawai'i providing family engagement services through `Ohana Conferencing.

Source: EPICOhana.info, n.d., "Ohana Conferencing": http://www.epicohana.info/oc.aspx

the classroom teachers and other school professionals and administrators. Therefore, school counselors may be responsible for facilitating student adjustment to the system and perhaps adjusting the system to the students.

Some of the dilemmas which arise may be tied to educators' efforts to try to neatly fit students into a square peg or cookie cutter mold, especially those students with diverse learning needs and other challenges. In addition, systematic insensitivity may abound in regard to disability and cultural diversity. The solution to this dilemma is found in a culturally responsive and inclusive school counseling approach utilized to support the whole student. According to Lee and Waltz (1998), this shift in thinking entails a redefinition of the school counseling role to account for the fact that problems are not always found in students, but often exist in the school as an educational system. Therefore, an important task is for these professionals to advocate for these students, and possibly change the school climate as indicated above.

School counselors are vested with this responsibility of becoming an advocate for students served under IDEA. This advocacy role represents a shift in the way traditional school counselors were trained to address disability, FAPE, and universal design for learning (UDL) for students. Culturally responsive school counselors can intervene in the educational system on behalf of students in ways designed to eliminate institutional barriers and cultural insensitivities. In addition, school counselors as "student advocates" become a critical resource in assisting the school to address inappropriate suspensions, bullying, placement, and FAPE concerns.

Two important school counselor components form the basis of the student advocate role. The first component is facilitating educator awareness of systemic barriers to accessing a FAPE for students served under IDEA. School counselors, acting as student advocates, can identify factors that may impinge upon student progress. The second component is facilitating the professional development of teachers and school administrators with respect to culturally responsive approaches to education.

To implement the first component with fidelity, school counselors serving as student advocates may need to conduct individual and group consultations with teachers, administrators, and other school personnel to identify potentially culturally alienating or insensitive factors in educational attitudes, behaviors, or policies. It is especially important that educators and administrators become aware of their own personal cultural and disability biases and examine how these might impact the development of students who come from CLD backgrounds with special education needs.

The second component may be implemented through professional development groups and workshops organized by the school child study team (CST) or school counseling staff for teachers and other educators on ways to incorporate culturally diverse experiences and disability sensitivity into a whole school program. These workshops might entail a counseling program, initiated under administrative auspices, a review of curriculum, and master plans to ensure that cultural diversity and disability sensitivity is reflected in all areas related to academic, career, and personal-social development. School counselors may also need to be an integral part of discussions related to least restrictive environments (LRE), more restrictive environments (MRE), inclusion practices, and related services that are essential to the student's FAPE. In addition, school counselors may be able to minimize any potential conflicts that may result and help to avoid a due process challenge that could potentially result in costly court and attorney's fees. The aforementioned is often born from a lack of culturally responsive and inclusive pedagogy that would assist all IEP team members to understand the students' needs and programs for the students in a holistic manner. Last, school counselors may play a pivotal role in reaching out to parents, helping to address their questions, concerns, and feelings, as well as addressing any conflicts with the school, in an attempt to bring both sides together in the best interest of the students.

SUMMARY

Each year, the United States' population becomes more and more diverse. It is projected that by the year 2050, people of color will make up roughly 50% of the national population (U.S. Census Bureau, 2005). With the growing diversity in our nation's population, and those who have a disability, comes an increased recognition of the importance of working in ways that are knowledgeable, respectful, and affirming of other cultures' ways of caring and being for all students. Holcomb-McCoy (2003) maintained that for school counselors, practicing in a culturally competent manner demands a paradigm shift in how one conceptualizes students and student issues. This shift requires one to understand the influence of a number of factors on students' academic and social functioning at school. These considerations are presented below.

KEYSTONES

School Counselors' Roles as a Diverse Culturally Inclusive Collaborator
- School counselors work as team members with students who have special and other needs teachers, paraprofessionals, and legal guardians to support their FAPE.

- School counselors must adopt a stance of inclusive collaborator in order to be most effective at reaching and meeting the students' needs.
- School counselors must model best practices and culturally responsive and inclusive collaboration in order to further support the student from initial identification of a learning disability to eligibility in support services or other means no matter how the referral process results.

School Counselors' Related Roles Across Diverse Learning Needs
- School counselors have dual roles, including acting as providers of related services, direct workers, evaluators, and screeners in the special education and 504 eligibility frameworks.
- School counselors must know the whole student and his or her needs beyond the disability.
- School counselors must develop a deeper understanding of the roles and functions of learning disability and the diversity that exists across the students' learning styles, needs, and strengths.

Cultural Competent Counseling to Improve Teaching and Learning
- School counselors may be required to dig a bit deeper into the outside-of-school lives of students in order to address issues related with underperformance and school failure that are unrelated to the students' learning disability.
- School counselors must work with the CST, behavior support personnel, occupational and speech and language personnel, and others in order to provide needed support for the student and assistance to the family.
- School counselors must be open to working within opposition and tension when there are issues with a student, where there is also a lack of diversity within the school staff and among the teachers, and where there is missing a culturally responsive and inclusive lens that is required and needed to understand and program for the whole student.

Culturally Responsive Counselors and Culturally Diverse Families and Communities
- School counselors must develop a deeper understanding of the diverse student and his or her family, beyond the disability, which is also impacted by the demographic shifts in modern society.
- School counselors must be willing to work with the family and student through various modalities and to communicate their needs and wants effectively to the school and staff.
- School counselors must be willing to intercede on behalf of families from CLD backgrounds in order to make schooling a positive experience for their children and to develop lasting partnerships with parents on the students' behalf.

Culturally Responsive Community Collaboration
- School counselors must be willing to collaborate with members within the diverse school community by first developing an understanding of its relationship in the life of the student and his or her family.
- School counselors must be willing to find stakeholders within the school community that will support the initiatives and efforts of culturally responsive inclusive collaboration in order to build strong relationships between the school and community.
- School counselors must be willing to think outside of the box in order to implement community and school-based activities, such as ESD Counseling, family diversity and inclusion nights, and ELL festivals.

Effective Components of a Culturally Responsive School
- All students and schools do not comprise each component noted as effective. However, the majority of these components should be a common practice and a part of any school educating today's CLD student.
- School counselors can guide their schools to become culturally responsive through partnerships with the school leadership teams and teachers. This partnership should be one that is modeled on knowing the expectations, values, and needs of its diverse student body.
- School counselors can assist the school in developing an all-inclusive and culturally responsive framework by inviting guest speakers, conducting diversity workshops, and supporting students in plays, performances, and assemblies who come from CLD backgrounds.

Developing Culturally Responsive Student Self-Worth
- School counselors can work to promote the development of positive self-identities among students with learning disabilities and cofacilitate the development of positive interpersonal relations among students with disabilities and who come from CLD backgrounds.
- School counselors can support the academic achievement for identified students protected under the IDEA and Section 504 as well as those students who are considered at risk and are experiencing issues embedded in the achievement gap.
- School counselors can promote the attitude and skills for school success grounded in a culturally inclusive framework for students with special and other needs including diverse students' career choices and aspirations.

Culturally Responsive Counselors as Student Advocates
- School counselors unwittingly become advocates for students with disabilities and other learning needs, since they are in the best position to explore the needs, home life, and other related matters for the student.

- School counselors' advocacy efforts improve the services, delivery, and overall FAPE for all students, beyond the disability.
- School counselors can serve as student advocates by modeling best practices for all school staff and supporting the overall vision of a culturally responsive and inclusive school.

ADDITIONAL RESOURCES

Print

Aronson, J., & Steele, C. M. (2005). Stereotypes and the fragility of human competence, motivation, and self-concept. In C. Dweck & E. Elliot (Eds.), *Handbook of competence & motivation* (pp. 436–455). New York, NY: Guilford.

Ford, D. Y. (2013). *Recruiting and retaining culturally different students in gifted education.* Waco, TX: Prufrock Press.

Ford, D. Y., & Milner, H. R. (2006). Counseling high achieving African Americans. In C. C. Lee (Ed.), *Multicultural issues in counseling: New approaches to diversity* (pp. 63–78). Alexandria, VA: American Counseling Association.

Tatum, B. D. (2007). *Can we talk about race? And other conversations in an era of school resegregation.* Boston, MA: Beacon Press.

Web Based

Diversity Web Wide: http://www.diversityweb.org/

A resource for higher education, part of an initiative designed to create relevant pathways for training preservice teachers and professionals on how to invent collaboration and cross organizational connections, via the World Wide Web and more traditional forms of print communication

Educating Teachers and Other Professionals for Diversity: http://www.ncrel.org/sdrs/areas/issues/educatrs/presrvce/pe300.htm

An article addressing the critical issue of preparing future teachers to promote "meaningful, engaged learning for all students, regardless of their race, gender, ethnic heritage, or cultural background."

Multiculturalism: Beyond Ethnicity Towards Diversity: http://www.library.csustan.edu/lboyer/multicultural/main.htm

A variety of web resources on multicultural education and diversity, including background articles, websites for K–12 teachers, bibliographies, biographies, ethnic cooking, religion, and more.

REFERENCES

American School Counselor Association (ASCA). (2013). *ASCA position statements.* Retrieved from https://www.schoolcounselor.org/asca/media/asca/PositionStatements/PositionStatements.pdf

Baca, L., & de Valenzuela, J. S. (1994). Reconstructing the bilingual special education interface. *NCBE Program Information Guide Series, 20.* Retrieved from http://www.ncela.gwu.edu/ncbepubs/pigs/pig20.htm

Baker, S., Gersten, R., & Keating, T. (2000). When less may be more: A 2-year longitudinal evaluation of a volunteer tutoring program requiring minimal training. *Reading Research Quarterly, 35(4),* 494–519.

Brotherson, M. J., Summers, J. A., Bruns, D., & Sharp, L. (2008). Family-centered practices: Working in partnership with families. In P. Winton, J. McCollum, & C. Catlett (Eds.), *Practical approaches to early childhood professional development* (pp. 53–80). Washington, DC: ZERO TO THREE.

Carter, R. B., & Vuong, T. K. (1997). Unity through diversity: Fostering cultural awareness. *Professional School Counseling, 1*(1), 47–49.

Cartledge, G., & Lo, Y. (2006). *Teaching urban learners: Culturally responsive strategies for developing academic and behavioral competence.* Champaign, IL: Research Press.

College Board Advocacy and Policy Center (2012). *The College Board national survey of school counselors and administrators.* Retrieved from http://media.collegeboard.com/digitalServices/pdf/nosca/Barriers-Supports_TechReport_Final.pdf

Darling-Hammond, L., & Garcia-Lopez, S. P. (2002). What is diversity? In L. Darling-Hammond, J. French, & S. P. Garcia-Lopez (Eds.), *Learning to teach for social justice* (pp. 9–38). New York, NY: Teachers College Press.

Dunn, R. (2000). Learning styles: Theory, research, and practice. *National Forum of Applied Educational Research Journal, 13*(1), 3–22.

Echevarría, J., & Graves, A. (2006). *Sheltered content instruction: Teaching English language learners with diverse abilities* (3rd ed.). Boston, MA: Allyn and Bacon.

Ford, D. Y. (2005). Ten strategies for increasing diversity in gifted education. *Gifted Education Press Quarterly, 19*(4), 2–4.

Ford, D. Y. (2013). *Recruiting and retaining culturally different students in gifted education.* Waco, TX: Prufrock Press.

Fuchs, D., Mock, D., Morgan, P. L., & Young, C. L. (2003). Responsiveness-to-intervention for the learning disabilities construct. *Learning Disabilities Research & Practice, 18*(3), 157–171.

Gardner, H. (2011). *Frames of mind: The theory of multiple intelligences.* Philadelphia, PA: Persus Books.

Gay, G. (2000). C*ulturally responsive teaching.* New York, NY: Teachers College Press.

Han, H. S., & Thomas, M. S. (2010). No child misunderstood: Enhancing early childhood teachers' multicultural responsiveness to the social competence of diverse children. *Early Childhood Education Journal, 37(6),* 469–476.

Hayes, S. A. (1996). Cross-cultural learning in elementary guidance activities. *Elementary School Guidance and Counseling, 30,* 264–274.

Herring, R. D. (1998). *Career counseling in schools: Multicultural and developmental perspectives.* Alexandria, VA: American Counseling Association.

Holcomb-McCoy, C. C. (2003). Multicultural competence in school settings. In D. B. Pope-Davis, H. L. K. Coleman, W. M. Ling, & R. L Torporek (Eds.), *Handbook of multicultural competencies in counseling and psychology* (pp. 406–419). Thousand Oaks, CA: Sage.

Hughes, M. T., Valle-Riestra, D. M., & Arguelles, M. E. (2002). Experiences of Latino families with their child's special education program. *Multicultural Perspectives, 4*(1), 11–17.

Individuals with Disabilities Education Improvement Act (IDEIA) of 2004, 20 U.S.C. § 1400 et seq. (2004).

Invernizzi, M., Juel, C., & Rosemary, C. A. (1997). A community tutorial that works. *The Reading Teacher,* 50, 304–311.

Lee, C. C. (Ed.). (1995). *Counseling for diversity: A guide for school counselors and related professionals.* Boston, MA: Allyn & Bacon.

Lee, C. C. (2001, April). Culturally responsive school counselors and programs: Addressing the needs of all students. *Professional School Counseling,* 4, 257.

Lee, C. C. (2005). Urban school counseling context, characteristics, and competencies. *Professional School Counseling*, 8(3), 184–188.

Lee, C. C., & Walz, G. (1998). *Social action: A mandate for counselors*. Alexandria, VA: American Counseling Association, ERIC Counseling, and Student Services Clearinghouse.

Lo, L. (2010). Perceived benefits experienced in support groups for Chinese families of children with disabilities. *Early Child Development and Care, 180*(3), 405–415.

Murrow-Taylor, C., Foltz, B. M., McDonald, A. B., Ellis, M. R., & Culbertson, K. (1999). A multicultural career fair for elementary school students. *Professional School Counseling*, 2(3), 241–243.

Pransky, K., & Bailey, F. (2002). To meet your students where they are, first you have to find them: Working with culturally and linguistically diverse at-risk students. *Reading Teacher, 56*(4), 370–383.

Rogoff, B. (2003). *The cultural nature of human development*. New York, NY: Oxford University Press.

Salas, L. (2004). Individualized Educational Plan (IEP) meetings and Mexican American parents: Let's talk about it. *Journal of Latinos and Education, 3*(3), 181–192.

Sánchez, S. Y., & Thorp, E. K. (2008). Teaching to transform: Infusing cultural and linguistic diversity. In P. J. Winton, J. A. McCollum, & C. Catlett (Eds.), *Practical approaches to early childhood professional development: Evidence, strategies, and resources* (pp. 81–97). Washington, DC: ZERO TO THREE.

Skinner, M. L., & Lindstrom, B. D. (2003). Bridging the gap between high school and college: Strategies for successful transition of students with learning disabilities. *Preventing School Failure, 47*(3), 132–137.

Trolley, B., Haas, H., & Campese Patti, D. (2009). *The school counselor's guide to special education*. Thousand Oaks, CA: Corwin.

U.S. Census Bureau. (2005). *Detailed poverty tables: 2003*. Washington, DC: Author.

U.S. Department of Education. (2004). *No Child Left Behind Act*. Retrieved from http://www.ed.gov/index.jhtm

U.S. Department of Education. (2010). *Reauthorization of the elementary and secondary education act* (ESEA). Retrieved from http://www.ed.gov/blog/topic/esea-reauthorization/

Williams, E. R. (2007). Unnecessary and unjustified: African American parental perceptions of special education. *Educational Forum, 71*(3), 250–261.

Williams, Y. (2008). Deconstructing gifted and special education, policy and practice: A paradigm of ethical leadership in residentially segregated schools and communities. In V. Ikpa & K. McGuire (Eds.), *Advances in educational leadership and policy: K–16 issues impacting student achievement in urban communities*. New York, NY: Information Age.

Chapter 12

Psychosocial and At-Risk Considerations

BARBARA C. TROLLEY

St. Bonaventure University

"If I regarded my life from the point of view of the pessimist, I should be undone. I should seek in vain for the light that does not visit my eyes and the music that does not ring in my ears. I should beg night and day and never be satisfied. I should sit apart in awful solitude, a prey to fear and despair. But since I consider it a duty to myself and to others to be happy, I escape a misery worse than any physical deprivation."

— Helen Keller, American Author, Activist, and Lecturer

School counselors are not strangers to issues such as bullying, substance abuse, social isolation and stigmatization, grief, sexual identity and involvement, social networking conflicts, and self-injurious behaviors. Imagine, however, that the student entering your office, in addition, has a disability. Some of these concerns are those that all students face, but may be magnified or compounded for students in special education. In contrast, other concerns may be intimately tied to the manifestations associated with one of the 13 special education classifications, such as the impulsivity and anger outbursts often seen with emotional disorders, the lack of social cues associated with autistic disorders and deaf-blindness, the inability to attend due to certain learning disabilities, or the chronic fatigue and school absences experienced by students with other health impairments. In this chapter, an overview of these issues is presented, and practical tools are offered, in an effort to assist school counselors in maximizing the success of these students, especially in regard to the personal-social domain of the American School Counselor Association's ASCA National Model (http://ascanationalmodel.org/foundation). However, while the exact role of the school counselor in regard to students in special education may vary, and there are proponents on either side as to the extent these professionals should be involved, the fact is that there are many students with IEPs on school counselor caseloads. Owens, Thomas, and Strong (2011), in referencing statistics put out in 2007 by the U.S. Department of Education, indicated that the number of students with disabilities in the United States alone has increased by a million in the past decade. When one considers the fact that approximately 96% of students with disabilities are in general education schools and three quarters of these students spend most of the day in general education classrooms (Myers, 2005), it behooves school counselors to become familiar with the needs of, and effective interventions for, this population.

Specifically, after reading this chapter, you will be able to meet these objectives:

1. Identify three primary psychosocial concerns related to disability for students in special education.

2. Define three key risk factors that result in psychosocial concerns for students in special education.

3. Identify both three general and three specific tasks school counselors can undertake to better serve this population.

4. Gain access to a comprehensive list of programs and resources which address psychosocial issues for students in special education.

PSYCHOSOCIAL RESPONSES TO DISABILITY

Overview

A plethora of psychosocial issues exist in regard to students with disabilities. Disabilities can be either congenital (present at birth; developmental/genetic in nature) or acquired (present after birth; due to an injury or illness). At the core of having either type of disability is that of grieving and adaptation. Put in simple terms, how does that student who walked in your door deal with the losses associated with disability, such as sensory, intellectual, and emotional functioning, come to grips with this reality, and move on? Perhaps you can remember your own transition from elementary to middle school. If you were like most, you probably had preschool anxiety about finding your classroom on time, not getting lost, being able to work your locker combination, and having enough time to eat your lunch. If these things were not enough to worry about, you heard from your older sibling that upper classmen like to "orient" the new students with frightening rituals and that much "drama" exists in middle school, which involves social grouping and exclusion, teasing, and pressures to "fit in." You prepare yourself the best you can by practicing with the lock, memorizing your schedule, and picking out the newest fashion trend to wear the first day in hopes that you will learn the new rhythm of middle school and be accepted by your peers. These issues of social adjustment and the psychological discomfort that accompanies this adjustment are certainly normative. But now imagine that you enter this new social milieu, this somewhat critical and evaluative setting knowing that you "look" or "act" or "learn" in ways that are clearly different from those of the "typical" student. You struggle with your lock combination, you take longer to process what the teacher just said, your gait is slightly off, or you are not able to participate in gym. Worse yet, you have to leave the regular classroom and go to those "special classes." Students with disabilities are clearly presented with unique obstacles to their adaptation to their school setting. They have the normative issues with which to cope, with the added concerns associated with the disability (the impairment) and the related handicaps (architectural and attitudinal barriers).

Grief Reactions and Developmental Stage

Much of the literature in this area is focused on people with disabilities in general, and is not specific to the student population. However, many of the issues discussed are generic and applicable to most populations. Falvo (2010) has indicated that many emotional reactions to disability can occur, such as grief, which can incorporate anger and depression and eventual acceptance; fear and anxiety; and guilt. Olsson, Bond, Johnson, Forer, and Boyce (2003) further identified five broad themes in a population of adolescents with chronic illnesses: control, emotional reactions, acceptance, coping strategies, and a search for meaning. Similarly, Livneh and Antonak (2005) addressed core concepts of stress; crisis; loss and grief; body image, self-concept, and quality of life issues; uncertainty and unpredictability; and stigma in regard to people with disabilities. The school counselor is often confronted with issues of sadness, frustration, stress, and volatility in their work with students with special needs. It would be important to differentiate the source of the reactions. For example, a student who is angry, acting out, and depressed could be demonstrating these behaviors due to a variety of reasons:

- The nature of the disability (e.g., he or she is identified with an emotional disorder)
- The grief response to having the disability (e.g., the student has just learned that he or she has a learning disability)
- The developmental stage of the student (e.g., a 13-year-old is becoming oppositional with teachers)

Depending on the developmental stage of the student, these reactions may also be differently manifested. Younger children may express these emotions in acting out behavior while older ones may be better able to verbalize these reactions or seek nonhealthy means of coping, such as abuse of substances, which will be discussed later in this chapter. It would also be important for the school counselor to evaluate the degree of learned helplessness which is present, which may be fostered by well-intentioned but overprotective parents and peers, and the impact of the disability on the students' academic performance. A student in special education who is depressed and referred to the school counselor may be dealing with the adjustment to a newly diagnosed disability, chronic response to an ongoing condition, a diagnosed mental health disorder, the impact of self-medicating to "cope" with the disability, and/or ongoing escalation of academic failure or social ostracism due to the nature of the disability, and/or sporadic attendance. It is helpful if school counselors select their interventions based on the origin and reinforcement of the depression.

Stress and Stigma

Falvo (2010) further stated that areas of stress for people with disabilities may be concern about the impact of the disability on their quality of life, negative self-concept and body image, uncertainty, and stigma. It is not uncommon for students with temporary use of crutches to resist using the school elevator or to refuse offers of help in order to maintain their sense of independence and fitting in with the norm. Similarly, while many students without disabilities would probably appreciate a "free pass" from gym class once in a while, to have involvement in physical education totally suspended can result in students with disabilities feeling isolated and on the outside. Those with visible physical disabilities, such as mobility issues, an amputated limb, speech impediments, and bodily disfigurations, may find themselves alone, withdrawing, socially awkward, and potentially the target of bullies. Hahn (1988) provided much insight into aesthetic versus existential anxiety in regard to people with disabilities. Socially, much pressure exists to be physically appealing, which is constantly emphasized in various media formats. This strain can be even greater during the time of preadolescence, when issues of gender identity, dating, and school social events of dances and proms occur. School counselors need to assess both the perceptions of the students in special education, as well as the peer responses to them. A simple case example illustrated in Case Illustration 12.1 will help to clarify this point.

While one may wonder in the above case as to the rationale for the parents' insistence on this non-disclosure policy, and there may be many diverse parental motivations behind this request, the resulting stigma and stereotyping of students with disabilities may be at the foreground.

CASE ILLUSTRATION 12.1

MAKING FRIENDS IN A NEW SCHOOL

Alex is a 13-year-old young man diagnosed with Asperger's who transferred to a new school. He is trying to make new friends, but his repetitive, monotone speech and lack of awareness of social cues and concepts are creating difficulties in this process. Not only is Alex not making friends, but he is also starting to be teased and harassed by his classmates as being "weird." The parents do not want the teacher or other school staff to disclose the nature of his disability. While initially stymied, the school counselor decides on a three-pronged approach. First, a general psycho-educational presentation on a gamut of disabilities, including those on the autism spectrum, and appropriate ways to respond is given in the classroom. This lesson assists both students and teachers in terms of educating them about, and increasing their sensitivity to, disability. Second, the school counselor works with Alex in terms of social skills training, helping him to identify social cues, and self-defeating behaviors. Third, the school counselor pairs Alex with a peer mentor to assist him in day-to-day social interactions and to role model socially acceptable responses.

Florian et al. (2006) examined the cross-cultural perspectives of the classifications of children with disabilities and discussed the need to reduce the unnecessary stigmatization of such labels. While classification of students with disabilities is essential to understanding the nature of the problem, and will hopefully provide a road map to effective intervention, lack of understanding of these classifications, combined with stereotyping, can be destructive and stigmatizing. Even the term *special* has a gamut of interpretations: one that is treasured, extraordinary, superior, unusual, different, or separate. *Special* may be seen as an endearing quality or one that is interpreted sarcastically, in a demeaning sense. Interestingly, an entire article has focused on this construct of "special" (Hausstatter & Connolley, 2012). While it is essential that those working with students in special education not be immobilized by semantics, a fundamental concept for school counselors to be aware of is the impact of words used in regard to this population. In addition to education, use of person-first language and efforts to erase common slang terms (e.g., *dummy*, *retard*) are ways that school counselors can advocate for students in special education.

Family Responses

In addition, family members of the students in special education are not immune to these grief issues, and the reactions of parents are frequently concerns that are presented to school counselors to address. This point is illustrated in the Guided Practice Exercise 12.1.

It is therefore essential that these professionals have some sense of what the impact of the disability is on the family as this will in turn reverberate on the student. Knowing the family dynamics will not only aid school counselors in understanding the issues facing the student, but also it may aid them in ascertaining what support systems are available to the student. In a classic article by Anderegg, Vergason, and Smith (1992), three stages of grief for parents of children with

---

Guided Practice Exercise 12.1

TRANSITION IN PARENTAL EXPECTATIONS

Imagine you are a parent of an eighth grader. You are excited about your child's transition to high school, and have long thought about her future in college. You have started a college fund and have even explored potential options. You want your child to have an opportunity that you yourself did not have growing up. You have pushed her reading difficulty at times to the back of your mind, attributing it to the increased use of electronic rather than print forms of text. You explain away the fact that your younger child is at the same reading level as your eighth grader by the fact that each of your children reach developmental milestones at various times. In the spring, you receive a call from your child's school counselor, asking you to come in for an appointment. Thinking this is a standard appointment in preparing for the transition, you are not prepared for the focus of the meeting. The school counselor, as gently as possible, shares his concerns that your child may have a learning disability and would like your permission for further testing.

- What might be the parent's reactions and initial thoughts?
- What skills can the school counselor use to communicate his concern in a manner that promotes engagement with, and support of, the parent?
- What knowledge is essential for the school counselor to have in order to provide quality services to the student and her family?
- What tasks can the school counselor do as a part of the team to assist this student and her family?

disabilities were identified: confronting, adjusting, and adapting. If the student has a congenital disability, the family may have experienced these stages early on, and pre-morbid levels of family functioning and adaptation are not ascertainable as with situations of acquired disabilities. However, many complex variables such as marital and sibling interaction, the mental health of the individuals in the family, access to and the quality of family support, and disability demographics, such as severity, prognosis, and visibility, may impact on the family's experience of and successful transition through these stages.

Developmental stages may exacerbate additional loss issues. For example, Podvey, Hinojosa, and Koenig (2013) discussed the need for family intervention as children with disabilities transition from early intervention to preschool education programs. At each level of school, the focus on the empowerment and increased independence of the student is associated with parental role changes, which can evoke feelings of loss and abandonment. Families may also experience the loss of "normalcy" for the child with a disability and go through stages of "chronic sorrow" (Gordon, 2009; Hobdell et al., 2007; Kurtzer-White & Luterman, 2003). Parents worry and believe that typical developmental milestones will not be achieved: dating, driving, college graduations, full-time employment, marriage, and grandchildren. School counselors, especially in cooperation with special education teachers, school psychologists, and social workers, can assist parents in understanding the nature of disabilities, school committees, the evaluation processes, and special education language. This can be done individually as well as via group parental meetings. Some of the most commonly used acronyms that school personnel and parents alike will need to know are described below. For a comprehensive list of acronyms, see Trolley, Haas, and Patti (2009). A sample of the most commonly used acronyms is presented in Table 12.1.

These professionals can also provide a source of support for these families, be nonbiased mediators between parents and the school, and be an excellent source of referrals for the child and family for more intensive counseling work and medical evaluations.

Friendships

One additional area of primary focus for students in special education, and one that most frequently is brought to school counselors, is that of friendships. These concepts are demonstrated in Case Illustration 12.2.

A multiple array of stumbling blocks for students in special education can negatively impact their ability to form solid, long-lasting friendships. Many disabilities involve potential communication deficits, such as those with hearing impairments, speech and language disorders, traumatic brain injuries, and other

Table 12.1	Acronyms
Acronym	**Definition**
BIP	Behavior Intervention Plan
CCS	Common Core Standards
CSE	Committee on Special Education
FAPE	Free Appropriate Public Education
FBA	Functional Behavioral Assessments
FERPA	Family Educational Rights and Privacy Act (aka the Buckley Amendment)
IDEA	Individuals with Disabilities Education Act
IDEIA	Individuals with Disabilities Education Improvement Act
IEP	Individualized Education Program
IST*	Instructional Support Team
NCLB	No Child Left Behind (Act and Law)
RTI	Response to Intervention

Source: Center for Parent Information and Resources (retrieved 3/12/15). Disability and Special Education Acronyms, Newark, NJ.

*Note, there are numerous variations in the terminology which signifies the notion of an Instructional Support Team within and across states.

CASE ILLUSTRATION 12.2

THE FIELD TRIP

Imagine having been diagnosed with Asperger's, being one to two years older than the peers in your class, and having made one very good friend. The difficulty is that your friend is on a different team and classroom. You are set to go on a field trip to the local museum. The change in structure and routine is already evoking anxiety, as is the antici-pation of walking by yourself, as others in your class fall into their *cliques*, and some of these peers may be staring at you. The teachers have assigned you and your friend to separate buses to be with your classmates. They are reluctant to make any adjustments as they insist they have to keep track of their own students. A pre–field trip meeting involv-ing the teachers, the school counselor, and your parents takes place. The teachers are supported for their safety concerns, but they are then educated as to the nature of your disability. The ability of you to take the same bus as your friend is addressed as a means of prevention, and it will minimize time that most likely would be needed to deal with your reactions to the change in routine. The facts that both buses are ultimately going to the same place and that parental chaperones have lists of the students they are watching are pointed out. At the end of 20 minutes, it was agreed you and your friend can ride the same bus. Your anticipatory anxiety is greatly reduced, and you go and have a great time.

health impairments. Specifically, much current research has spotlighted the communication and social challenges of students on the autism spectrum, some of which can be seen in the above case (Carter, Brock, & Trainor, 2014; Griffin, Taylor, Urbano, & Hodapp, 2014). While the etiology and expression of the communication problems vary, the result is that these students struggle with ways to express their thoughts and feelings to peers, and likewise to understand what peers are sharing with them. While nonverbal cues are of assistance, they can be easily misread, culturally influenced, and may not be available (e.g., if students have visual impairments). You are in fifth grade and trying to invite your classmates to your birthday party. You start to hand out invitations and start stuttering when you begin to explain what they are. Kids start laughing, calling you names, and walk away.

In addition, behaviors such as aggression and isolation, associated with emotional disturbances and autism spectrum disorders, may create fear or aversion in typically developing peers. Those with ongoing medical complications, found in other health impairment classifications, often involve frequent absences which affect both academic and interpersonal relationships. Students with mobility issues may have restrictions placed on physical education and recess activities. Imagine sitting inside on a beautiful sunny day, while your friends are all outside playing kick ball. Your asthma has escalated; you are not allowed to run. To make matters even worse, the teacher is there with you, and the last child out turned around and yelled, "Teacher's pet!" You are left lonely, embarrassed, and disheartened.

Further research has suggested that the existence of co-morbid disabilities, such as *learning disabilities* and *attention deficit disorders*, have even a more negative impact on social skills than the existence of a sole disability (Smith & Wallace, 2011). Whatever the origin of the concern, the outcome can be similar in that students in special education often have difficulty in developing and maintaining friendships due to deficits in communication and social skills, as well as interrupted attendance and inclusion. As described in a report published by the National Association of School Psychologists, social skills were categorized into four main areas: survival, interpersonal, problem solving, and conflict resolution (http://www.nasponline.org/resources/factsheets/socialskills_fs.aspx). Youth who are typically developing often find these areas to be challenging. If the normal development of social skills is further impeded by a disability, then these students can find themselves isolated and lonely, acting out with potential subsequent disciplinary actions, and/or subject to teasing (this topic is discussed further in the risk factor section). In a study by Uusitalo-Malmivaara et al. (2012), students in special education were found to be less happy than their typically developing peers, and the most frequently cited value choice of these students was to have more friends.

Inclusion

A related confounding variable is that of inclusion. Many argue that exposure to typically developing peers, and associated role modelling of appropriate social behaviors, is of great benefit to students with disabilities. Opponents pose a variety of counterarguments: Students with disabilities cannot keep pace academically or socially with peers, and teachers do not have time or training to address the diversity of individualized needs; typically developing peers may ostracize, fear, or tease those with disabilities; and/or typically developing peers may learn inappropriate behaviors from them. One of the most critical factors tied to the success of an inclusion program is that of teacher attitudes (Mastin, 2010). Considerations that may impact these attitudes include teachers' demands and supports. Hsien, Brown, and Bortoli (2009) further addressed the connection of teacher education and training as related to their perceptions of inclusion, with those having higher credentials as being more positive. While school counselors cannot alter classroom sizes or educational standard requirements, they can be a source of support for teachers, a resource for materials and tools, an educational avenue in terms of disability classifications and interventions, and a resource for advocacy for change.

Think back to when you were in school and times and demands were much simpler. Now, fast-forward to the present day. You are a teacher, dealing with a gamut of standard requirements, under pressure to make sure your students are adequately performing, and have students of five different cultures of origin in your class. It is August, and you are told that an additional three students with special needs are to be included in your class. You are a general education teacher, and you have limited training in special education. The school counselor becomes aware of your situation and invites you down for a cup of coffee in the office. Your concerns are empathically heard, you are given resources on the disabilities the students have, and a joint consultation meeting with the special education teacher, school psychologist, and aide is arranged. You go from feeling overwhelmed to feeling supported and not alone.

In summary, many of the above responses to having a disability may create specific presenting problems that school counselors must address, for the student in special education, the family, and the general student population. In addition, students in special education may also be at higher risk for developing a number of additional psychosocial concerns, which are addressed in the following section.

RISK FOR SPECIFIC PSYCHOSOCIAL PROBLEMS

Overview

Wasburn-Moses (2011), in citing the work of Fulerkson, Harrison, and Hedger (1999), discussed the issue of students with disabilities in alternative school placements being exposed to a variety of at-risk issues, including sexual and substance abuse, suicide, violence, and psychological concerns. These are just a sample of the specific types of psychosocial risk issues to which students with disabilities are exposed. School counselors must be aware of the vulnerability of this population to these various areas of psychological and social distress and impairment.

Abuse and Neglect

A plethora of literature exists in which the physical and sexual abuse and neglect in children with disabilities has been discussed. It is, however, difficult to determine exact numbers of children with disabilities who have been abused as child abuse registries are not required to identify the existence of disability in reported cases, and states vary according to reporting procedures, and even in the definitions of abuse and neglect (U.S. Department of Health and Human Services, 2011). There is also the difficulty that at times disability symptoms are confused with those of maltreatment (Hibbard & Desch, 2007). It is heartbreaking enough to have someone you trust sexually or physically abuse you. If you, the child survivor, also have a speech impediment or lower functioning autism, it is almost impossible to imagine the horror of experiencing this abuse and not being able to tell anyone what is happening. You are trapped in verbal darkness while being subjected to nightly rape or a beating.

In spite of the previously mentioned limitations, some attempts have been made to examine this issue. The U.S. Department of Health and Human Services (2011), based on the Child Maltreatment data of 2009, reported 11% of child maltreatment victims had a reported disability; this information was based on 49 states that reported disability information in child abuse cases. This statistic of 11% of child abuse victims having a disability (intellectual disabilities, learning disability, hearing or visual impairment, emotional disturbance, behavioral problems, or physical or medical problems) was supported in the report on child maltreatment put out by the Department of Health and Human Services in 2011. Within this report, it was stated that this statistic may actually be low as not every child who has experienced maltreatment has a diagnostic classification.

Many factors can be associated with the increased risk of this population to various forms of maltreatment including the devaluation of those with disabilities; lack of proper training of professionals, who complete such assessments, in regard to working with children with disabilities; perceptions of these children as less credible; and positive biases toward caregivers of these children. Manders and Stoneman (2009), in their study of child protection workers, found that these professionals were more likely to attribute some of the behavior of the children with disabilities as factors that contributed to the abuse and that they had empathy for the parents who were abusive. Furthermore, Cederborg, Danielsson, La Rooy, and

Lamb (2009), in their research of children with intellectual disabilities who had been sexually abused and who had had evaluation contamination type questions repeated to them, discovered that 40% of the participants changed their answers, thus making their testimony in court less credible. Similarly, while children with disabilities were found to be more likely to be abused sexually than their peers without disabilities, they tended to disclose less and when they did, had delayed response time (Hershkowitz, Lamb, & Horowitz, 2007). Many variables may mediate these results, and the response of systems to allegations of abuse of children with abuse must be examined.

In an extensive review of the literature spanning 1996 to 2009, Stalker and McArthur (2012) found that students with disabilities were subject to more maltreatment than their peers without disabilities, that workers often failed to take into account their needs and heightened vulnerability, and that few studies took into account the reports of the abuse of these children. School counselors, while recipients of training and mandated reporters for child maltreatment, should also have a working knowledge of the special considerations of working with students with disabilities in terms of awareness of risk factors, indicators, and interventions. With the amount of time students spend in school and the pivotal role school counselors have in connecting with youth, these professionals may be the first to be aware of potential maltreatment. It is imperative that clear policies for reporting, and resources for referrals, are known and accessible to all school staff, especially those providing psycho-educational services to the student population.

Substance Abuse

In addition to being at higher risk for child abuse, students in special education are also more susceptible to issues of substance abuse (Fowler & Tisdale, 1992; Kress & Elias, 1993). According to the National Institute on Drug Abuse, youth with psychiatric conditions, such as conduct disorders, learning disabilities, and attention deficit disorders, are at higher risk of substance abuse, and there is an interactive effect in that the abuse of substances early on can increase the risk or accelerate the course of later psychiatric disorders (http://www.drugabuse.gov/news-events/nida-notes/2007/02/addiction-co-occurring-mental-disorders). The exact mechanism of these interactions is not known; however, suffice it to say that students in special education are more vulnerable to such abuse, which can add to or precipitate additional psychosocial issues. While exposed to similar peer pressures and media influences as their typically developing peers, students with disabilities may have access to more prescribed medications, face increased peer pressures and isolation, have more medical problems, and have fewer coping skills and more behavioral problems (McCombs & Moore, 2002). You are new in school and have been diagnosed with ADHD (attention-deficit hyperactivity disorder) and been given stimulant medication to help you focus in school. Your "friends" find out and offer you $5 a pill. Others tell you of those in school who have different drugs that really make you feel good. This is the first time you have been subjected to peer pressure, have few friends, and have been feeling irritable and anxious. Given these circumstances, it would not be surprising that you begin to try other drugs and make a little money off your prescription, which you do not think is helping anyway.

While many substance abuse prevention programs exist across school districts, their overall effectiveness, in general, and their availability and suitability for students in special education are of concern. In a report by the U.S. Department of Health and Human Services related to disability and substance abuse, the concern is raised that such programs may not match the learning needs of the over 5 million students in special education in this country (http://www.hhs.gov/od/about/fact_sheets/substanceabusech26.html). School counselors could play an active role as part of a school team that would educate staff, parents, and students as to this population being at higher risk for substance abuse and in the development of prevention programs that are better suited for the specific needs of these students. Particular attention may be given to frequently prescribed medications for this population, with a focus on their potential psychologically and physically addictive properties.

Cyberbullying

In addition, while every student is at risk in this decade of becoming the target of, or perpetrator of, cyberbullying, the factors associated with both positions of low social support and status, along with academic and home concerns (Calvete, Orue, Est`evez, Villar`don, & Padilla, 2010; Katzer, Fetchenhauer, & Belschak, 2009), are those often found in the student population who are in special education. While these are issues confronting all youth, the incidence and prevalence of these presenting problems increase for those students with disabilities. An important consideration is that if the issue of cyberbullying is not addressed, oftentimes, those who are "victims" become the aggressors. Wright and Li (2013) found that children who were diagnosed with ADHD who had been cyber victimized and/or rejected by peers within six months became more aggressive themselves. The themes of loneliness, lack of social support, and depressed mood for youth with the aforementioned disability were key factors in escalating their risk in being victimized by bullies. It is essential that intervention occur in a timely manner, as well as prevention efforts, in order to prevent this vicious cycle from perpetuating. School counselors are key players in the school team who can assist in the development of therapeutic and educational programs to stand alone or supplement disciplinary measures when cyberbullying occurs. Reflect on the following exchange that a high school girl with spina bifida discovers on Facebook:

> Has everyone seen Denise [the girl with spina bifida] trying to talk to Joe in the cafeteria today? Does the *Hunchback of Notre Dame* really think she will be asked to the prom? Even if she was, they would have to add an extra yard of material and Velcro to her prom dress to cover that mountain on her back! Anyway, we are all going to Maggie's house after the prom, but don't tell Denise. She hurts our eyes and it's bad enough if she comes to the prom.

Obesity

An additional concern is that of obesity for students with disabilities. The Centers for Disease Control (2010) reported that over a third of children in the United States are overweight or obese (http://www.cdc.gov/HealthyYouth/obesity/facts.htm). If one further considers the results of a recent study by Reinehr, Dobe, Winkel, Schaefer, and Hoffmann (2010), which showed that children with disabilities were at least 2 times as likely to be overweight or obese than their peers without disabilities, then this issue is at epidemic proportions for this population. This concern is an international one as evidenced by the results of the study by Slevin, Truesdale-Kennedy, McConkey, Livingstone, and Fleming (2012) who found that children with intellectual disabilities in Northern Ireland had a higher prevalence of being overweight or obese; ate more fatty and sugary foods as part of at least a quarter of their diet; were involved in sedentary activities, such as watching TV or playing video games; and were less involved than peers without disabilities in physical activities. This can become a vicious cycle. You are a youth with Asperger's and are very good in using the computer, enjoy the time you spend on it as you have few friends, and often have to use the Internet for homework assignments. You often get frustrated and overwhelmed with the homework and wind up playing computer games and getting snacks.

Reinehr et al. (2010) further discussed that those with neuromuscular or neurological disorders, due to swallowing difficulties, may actually have eating disorders and be underweight or malnourished. If the disability is a diagnosed eating disorder, variations from a healthy weight will also occur. While many schools are utilizing a Body Mass Index (BMI) to evaluate the status of student weight, there is some controversy as to whether this is the most effective measure to use and how it is communicated, and followed up on, with the student. Whether it is an issue of more limited mobility; lack of independent choice of food or self-feeding ability; physical education restrictions (due to physical, sensory, or cognitive deficits and balance and coordination impairments); physical or emotional challenges; or hormonal imbalances, weight is a key issue for youth, especially in the prepubescent and adolescent years. Most readers have been exposed to teasing of others or themselves in regard to being "fat" or "chubby" or have experienced in some way the negative self-perceptions associated with weight issues.

While national focus is spotlighting healthy eating for all youth, it is particularly important to be cognizant of this potential psychosocial problem for students with disabilities. Monitoring breakfast and lunch programs, providing healthy classroom snacks, and addressing healthy eating in a psycho-educational workshop for students and parents are all tasks that school counselors can address. Education of families and school staff may be needed as to dietary variations associated with different disorders. For example, those on the autism spectrum may be attracted to more high caloric foods; they often have sensory issues that make them oversensitized to textures and tastes, and they tend to be very picky eaters (Martins, Young, & Robson, 2008; Volkert & Vaz, 2010; Williams, Dalrymple, & Neal, 2000). Those with spina bifida, Prader-Willi syndrome, and Down's syndrome can overeat due to cerebral dysfunctions (Reinehr et al., 2010). Youth who are depressed, bored, or isolated, as with adults, may use food as a means of comfort.

In addition, being creative in limiting the sedentary position of these students and developing cooperative programs with health care facilities and youth organizations, such as the YMCA and YWCA and the Boys & Girls Clubs of America, can also provide school counselors with intervention tools, as well as steps to prevention. It would also be another place whereby school counselors could advocate for more accessible recreational opportunities for students with disabilities, under the supervision of trained staff. Last, school counselors may need to work with parents who are overprotective and avoiding exercise for their child with a disability, by allaying their fears and looking at *safe* physical options for the child.

Suicide

In light of the higher risk this population holds for a plethora of presenting problems, along with the symptomatology and stigma associated with the disability, it is not surprising that this population of students may be at higher risk for suicide. Carter and Spencer (2006) found that students with both visible and invisible disabilities were bullied more, were less popular, had fewer friends, and experienced more loneliness. In particular, students with learning disabilities have been identified as being at greater risk for suicide (Bender, Rosenkrans, & Crane, 1999; Daniel et al., 2006; Huntington & Bender, 1993). This was explained in part due to the depression experienced and to characteristics associated with the disorder such as impulsivity and social skill deficits. It is hard enough dealing with the issues associated with the disability, but then to experience harassment and exclusion and have minimal to no supports is devastating. Wachter and Bouck (2008) further discussed identifying variables and intervention tools that special educators should be aware of in working with students with high-incidence disabilities, in terms of suicide potential. It would be of value for all school staff to be aware of such issues and communicate on a regular basis, working as a team to facilitate the health of these students, of which the school counselor could be a prime facilitator and educator. It is important to examine coexisting risk issues such as the presence of substance abuse or a co-morbid mental diagnosis of depression in working with students in special education. Examination of demographic factors, such as culture and the incidence of suicidal potential in students in special education, is another fertile area to explore (Medina & Luna, 2006). While a specific "suicide profile" does not exist, the suicide rate in the general adolescent population remains high. The Centers for Disease Control (CDC) ranks it as the third leading cause of death in those between the ages of 10 and 24 (http://www.cdc.gov/violenceprevention/pub/youth_suicide.html).

If one considers all of the compounding issues with which students in special education are confronted, such as lack of social support, teasing, potential substance abuse, depression, and access to medications, it is essential that the higher risk potential of this population is considered. Medina and Luna (2006), in their research of Mexican American students in special education, found variables such as depression, social and interpersonal conflict, school failure, family distress, and substance abuse as being tied to suicide ideation, or attempts, in this group. Similar to the issues surrounding substance abuse prevention programs, it is important that suicide prevention programs in schools are tailored to the needs and abilities of the students in special education and are evaluated for their effectiveness. School counselors can play a pivotal role and be the first line of prevention and intervention in regard to potential lethality issues of students in special education. Ongoing collaboration and communication with additional school staff, preliminary lethality assessments, and referrals for services, psycho-educational presentations to families and staff, development of partnerships in the community, and advocacy for the implementation of evidenced-based suicide prevention programs in schools are just a few of the tasks that these professionals can undertake.

Case Illustration 12.3 will help to exemplify the impact and response to several of these risk issues.

In this section, a sampling of areas that pose even higher risk for students in special education has been explored. In the following discussion, a synopsis of psychosocial issues is presented, and suggestions for school counselors in working with students in special education are further addressed.

CASE ILLUSTRATION 12.3

WHERE TO START?

Melissa is a 16-year-old high school student that has been a student in special education since the age of 10. She has been classified with a learning disability. Experiencing much frustration in the classroom, being unable to immediately respond to teacher questions, having difficulty in written assignments, and experiencing delayed processing of concepts, she is becoming increasingly depressed and anxious. She is close to giving up on school as she feels like a failure. Melissa has responded to these challenges by overeating and, more recently, by smoking marijuana. Her sporadic school attendance, along with her inadequate social skills, has negatively affected her ability to make friends. Her recent weight gain has made her the subject of peer teasing, with female classmates posting hateful texts on social network sites, calling her a "fat slob" and a "loser." Her social studies teacher has become aware that Melissa is becoming more withdrawn and is turning in fewer assignments, and she has contacted the school counselor. The school counselor has known Melissa for 3 years and has developed a fairly good rapport with her. This positive interaction has occurred through regular check-ins with Melissa, visibility in Melissa's classrooms during psycho-educational presentations, informal contact with her in the hall and cafeteria, and via more formalized parent-teacher and CSE meetings. At the start of the meeting, the school counselor is struck by Melissa's flat affect, disheveled appearance, and teary eyed responses. The first task the school counselor undertakes is that of an initial lethality assessment. She informs Melissa that she cares about her, reminds her of the limits of confidentiality, and indicates she will be contacting her parents with a psychiatric referral. She further explains that the referral is for further assessment of her depression, as well as an evaluation of the need for prescribed medication. Upon learning about the marijuana use, she informs Melissa that it is essential that she is fully open with the doctor about this, and she indicates she will be talking with the doctor as well, once the referral is made and consents are obtained. The school counselor also recommends that Melissa be seen by her general practitioner for a complete physical and attention to the weight gain and make appointments for outside counseling services for the mood issues and social concerns. The school counselor indicated that Melissa's transition plan is in place and that it can be reviewed, with additional supports for academic success put into place. Last, the school counselor states she will address the issue of the cyberbullying with school administrators and make sure that school and the Dignity for All Students Act (DASA) policies are being followed.

ADDRESSING PSYCHOSOCIAL ISSUES

It is fairly evident from the prior discussion that students in special education face many psychosocial issues, which may be generally grouped into two categories:

- Grieving/Emotional Responses (e.g., depression, anxiety, and anger; feelings of failure and learned helplessness)
- Socialization Concerns (e.g., stigma; lack of friendships; segregation and isolation)

School counselors are often the first referral source by teachers, administrators, and families when requests are made for help in assisting these students in feeling better about themselves, making friends, becoming more a part of the school climate, and doing better academically. While these professionals may not have the time or expertise to address all of these concerns, they are at the very least a sounding board and resource for many.

Awareness, Knowledge, and Activities

Initial considerations for school counselors include the following:

- Awareness of school policy and their defined roles in working with students in special education
- Recognition of their areas of expertise and limitations
- Involvement in ongoing professional development opportunities in regard to special education
- Differentiation of issues related to the disability and those that are tied to typical developmental stages
- Advocacy for these students within and outside of the school setting
- Development of community partnerships to assist these students and their families
- Understanding of special education laws and mandates, such as IDEA (Individual with Disabilities Education Act), national (e.g., Common Core Standards), state education laws and initiatives, and professional organization expectations and standards
- Knowledge and utilization of evidenced-based programs for working with students in special education. For example, while social skills programs are frequently a model of choice to use with students with disabilities, applied behavioral analysis is more effective (Burns & Ysseldyke, 2009).

Many diversified tasks can also be done which can further the potential for success of students in special education. Trolley et al. (2009) have specified a gamut of undertakings school counselors can assume throughout the school year in regard to students with disabilities. Sample activities include but are not limited to

- conduction of psycho-educational lessons in classrooms, and for school staff and parents;
- involvement in school committees such as ISTs and 504 planning meetings;
- attendance at CSE meetings for their students;
- development of a resource handbook for referrals;
- individualization of counseling services specified in IEPs;
- visitation of the school's resource rooms and self-contained classrooms; and
- ongoing collaboration and communication with special education teachers and directors, general education teachers, school psychologist and social workers, and community agencies and professionals.

It is also important for school counselors to be aware of areas that require administrative input such as behavioral concerns which warrant disciplinary action or placement and retention decisions. While their feedback may be ascertained, they should not be the primary decision maker in these cases. In an effort to better facilitate the work of school counselors in relation to students in special education, it is important for these professionals to be aware of evidenced-based resources that are available. These tools are discussed further in the next section. Coping with and adaptation to disability are long-term processes that require understanding and support. School counselors can use the resources listed next to assist students in special education in developing knowledge and skills in order to cope and adapt to the disability.

Resources

Many programs have been developed to address the psychosocial issues of students in special education. Many of these have focused on the area of social skill enhancement. In the report by the National Association of School Psychologists previously discussed, a number of social skills programs to assist school counselors and staff in their work with students in special education and the general population are shared: "Stop and Think" Social Skills Program, Primary Mental Health Project, The EQUIP Program, The PREPARE Curriculum, and The ACCEPTS Program (http://www.nasponline.org/resources/factsheets/socialskills_fs.aspx).

Furthermore, a plethora of social skills programs have been developed for many diverse disabilities such as for students on the autism spectrum, having a learning disability, and those who have intellectual disability, once known as mentally retarded (Aljadeff-Abergel, Ayvazo, & Eldar, 2012; Carlson et al., 2009; Cifci Tekinarslan, Sazak Pinar, & Sucuoglu, 2012; Jamison, Forston, & Stanton-Chapman, 2012; Xin & Stutman, 2011). As stated earlier, it is important that any program that is implemented is evidence based. Myers' (2013) book on social skills strategies for children with disabilities is an excellent collation of such practices. A research-based social skills program is *Skillstreaming*. Based on the premises of modeling, role playing, performance feedback, and generalization, this program exists to teach social skills across a range of developmental stages (McGinnis, 2011a, 2011b, 2011c).

As previously mentioned, applied behavioral analysis (ABA) is an empirically based intervention, utilizing individualized instruction, to teach social skills to youth with disabilities (Cooper, Heron, & Heward, 2008). Based on learning theory, its application has had a plethora of ranges. Examples of this evidenced-based practice include teaching behavior management skills to children on the autism spectrum in environments, helping youth with language delays to develop their verbal repertoires, and assisting young children with developmental disabilities develop self-monitoring behaviors (Greer & Ross, 2007; Hernandez & Ikkanda, 2011; Plavnick, Ferreri, & Mauvin, 2010). It should be noted that specialized training and credentialing is required in order to provide such ABA interventions.

As previously discussed, it is not only the student in special education who is impacted by psychosocial issues but also the family. School counselors, therefore, may not only see students with disabilities in their offices, but also siblings of these students who are also struggling with psychological and social concerns related to their brothers' or sisters' impairment. For example, they may be grieving the loss of the ability to do things with their siblings if there is a physical disability present, and they may be angry, resentful, or guilty that their sibling gets more of their parents' attention, and/or have limited time for social outings. Resources to help siblings are more limited. One comprehensive curriculum for siblings of students with special needs is that of Sibshop (http://www.siblingsupport.org/ sibshops). This curriculum is one of the few that exist that target this specific population. Another program which brings the awareness of students with disabilities to a wider audience is that of Circle of Friends (http://www.circleofriends .org). This inclusion program has such features as the involvement of peers without disabilities in teaching social skills to those who do have a disability, weekly student phone calls to those with special needs in order that they may practice phone social skills, disability presentations within the school and community, and twice a year meetings with parents of the children with disabilities. A very concise checklist of strategies that parents can use in teaching their young children about prosocial skills is titled Research into Action: A Checklist of Everyday Strategies to Promote Prosocial Development (see Hyson & Taylor, 2011). While many of these strategies are simplistic applications most parents utilize for all children, some of the strategies may need to be adapted depending on the specific disability of the child.

The above are just a sampling of resources that school counselors may access in addressing the psychosocial issues of students in special education. Additional tools are presented in the online resource section associated with this text. Suffice it to say that guiding principles in selecting resources are finding ones that have proven effective, are accessible, and are within the competency of the school counselors' training to perform. Huberman, Navo, and Parrish (2012) provided a nice review of effective strategies used in special education programs across high-performing districts. It is highly recommended that school counselors collate a file, either hard copy or electronic, of resources related to special education, to use for themselves and to share with fellow professionals and families.

SUMMARY

In reviewing the gamut of psychosocial issues students with disabilities may experience, their heightened vulnerability to additional sources of concern, and the "normal" psychosocial concerns associated with various developmental stages, in addition to considering the individuality of each student despite being a part of a group of those commonly classified, it would be next to impossible to predict what problems school counselors may encounter or the exhaustive list of tools they would need to assist students in special education. Compounding this process is that of the interactive effects of development with the disability. For example, students in special education approaching the dating stage of school relationships may experience the *normal angst* of talking to a potential boyfriend or girlfriend but heightened with the stigma of having a disability. It was the intent of this chapter to give an overview of some of the mutual concerns this population may face, raise the awareness of their higher potential for co-occurring disorders, and to weave throughout this discussion the roles school counselors can play in working with these students.

As can be seen, the primary considerations of this chapter pertain to the gamut of psychosocial issues with which students in special education are confronted, which can compound the typical developmental concerns all students face. In addition to their own grieving reactions to the disability and the need to cope and adapt, often these students are at higher risk for additional challenges such as being stigmatized; bullied, and/or abused; developing obesity and substance abuse issues; and depression. Thus, while these students need assistance in academics, they also need support and opportunities to address disability-related and risk area matters. The school counselor is one of the key players that can assist these students with the psychosocial problems, through counseling, education, advocacy, and prevention.

Whereas the debates over what, if anything, school counselors should be doing with students in special education—and the positive and negative connotations of the word *special*—will most likely ensue for some time to come, in the meantime, there are children and teens who are trying to achieve academic, personal-social, and career success and fulfillment. In humanity, all are joined by their similarities and differences, and at some point, all will be confronted with a disability in their family or themselves. Why not begin to "pay it forward," helping one child at a time?

KEYSTONES

This chapter is perhaps best concluded with a few reminders for school counselors:

- As with any specific area of concern, it is important to examine their own attitudes and biases toward working with students in special education. While typically psychosocial concerns focus on the negative aspects of disability, positive biases exist and may be just as detrimental to students.
- School counselors should be aware of the district's defined roles of staff working with students, specifically in regard to their defined position and anticipated duties in regard to the special education process, as well as state and federal laws, and acts.
- Even though many commonalities exit across disabilities and standardized assessments, it is important to remember to assess the needs of each individual child.
- These professionals, as with all, need to be aware of what they are trained to do and what is beyond their competence level. The latter entails referrals to outside services and knowledge of resources.

ADDITIONAL RESOURCES

Print

Hughes, L., Banks, P., & Terras, M. (2013). Secondary school transition for children with special educational needs: A literature review. *Support for Learning, 21*(1), 24–34.

Humphrey, N., Lendrum, A., Barlow, A., Wigelsworth, M., & Squires, G. (2013). Achievement for all: Improving psychosocial outcomes for students with special educational needs and disabilities. *Research in Developmental Disabilities, 34*, 1210–1225.

Jones, M. (2002). Deafness as culture: A psychosocial perspective. *Disability Studies Quarterly, 22*(2), 51–60.

Murray, C., & Greenberg, M. (2006). Examining the importance of social relationships and social contexts in the lives of children with high-incidence disabilities. *Journal of Special Education, 39*(4), 220–233.

Tresco, K., Lefler, E., & Power, T. (2010). Psychosocial interventions to improve the school perfor-mance of students with attention-deficit/hyperactivity disorder. *Mind and Brain: The Journal of Psychiatry, 1*(20), 69–74.

Web Based

General
National Association of Special Education Teachers: http://www.naset.org/

National Dissemination Center for Children with Disabilities: http://www. http://nichcy.org/

Special Education Resources: http://www.specialednet.com/resources.htm

Journals
Comprehensive Lists
George Mason University: http://specialed.gmu.edu/?page_id=3

Samples
American Annals of the Deaf: http://gupress.gallaudet.edu/annals/

American Journal of Speech-Language Pathology: http://ajslp.asha.org/

Disability and Health Journal: http://www.aahd.us/page.php?pname=health/initiatives/journal

Disability Studies Quarterly: http://www.dsq-sds.org/

Journal of Developmental Disabilities: http://www.oadd.org/publications/journal/jddfront.htm

Journal of Disability Policy Studies: http://dps.sagepub.com/

Journal of Intellectual Disabilities: http://www.sagepub.com/journalsProdDesc.nav?prodId= Journal201355

Journal of Learning Disabilities: http://ldx.sagepub.com/

Journal of Special Education: http://www.sagepub.com/journals/Journal201881

The International Journal of Special Education: http://www.internationaljournalofspecial education.com/

The Review of Disability Studies: An International Journal: http://www.rds.hawaii.edu/

Publication Lists
Bright Hub: file:///C:/Users/Owner/Desktop/Special%20Education%20%20Articles%20On% 20Technology,%20Classroom%20Inclusion,%20Special%20Education%20Law%20&%20 Intervention.htm

A plethora of publications; handouts related to many diverse disabilities.

Child Abuse Victims With Disabilities
The National Children's Advocacy Center: http://www.nationalcac.org/

Disabilitiesbibliography4.pdf A compilation of publications related to the maltreatment and chil-dren with disabilities. Published by The National Children's Advocacy Center.

ERIC: file:///C:/Users/Owner/Desktop/ERIC%20-%20Search%20Results.htm

Expansive number of publications related to special education.

Office of Special Education & Rehabilitative Services, U.S. Education Department: http://www2
.ed.gov/about/pubs/intro/index.html?src=ln

Comprehensive publications on a gamut of diverse topics related to special education.

Social Skills Programs

Circle of Friends: http://www.circleoffriends.org/

This inclusion program has such features as the involvement of peers without disabilities in teaching
social skills to those who do have a disability, weekly student phone calls to those with special needs
in order that they may practice phone social skills, disability presentations within the school and
community, and twice a year meetings with parents of the children with disabilities.

Primary Mental Health Project (Cowen et al.): http://www.sharingsuccess.org/code/eptw/
profiles/48.html

Targets children K–Third and addresses social and emotional problems that interfere with effective learning. It has been shown to improve learning and social skills; reduce acting, shyness, and
anxious behaviors; and increase frustration tolerances.

Sibshop: http://www.siblingsupport.org/sibshops

A comprehensive curriculum for siblings of students with special needs. Sibshops acknowledge
that being the brother or sister of a person with special needs is for some a good thing, others a
not-so-good thing, and for many, somewhere in-between. They reflect a belief that brothers and
sisters have much to offer one another—if they are given a chance. Sibshops are a spirited mix of
new games (designed to be unique, offbeat, and appealing to a wide ability range), new friends,
and discussion activities.

The Sibshop curriculum is used throughout the United States, Canada, England, Ireland, Iceland,
Japan, New Zealand, Guatemala, Turkey, and Argentina.

Skillstream Training: http://www.skillstreaming.com/

Originally developed by Dr. Arnold P. Goldstein and Dr. Ellen McGinnis, Skillstreaming is a highly
acclaimed, research-based prosocial skills training program book series published by Research
Press. Skillstreaming employs a four-part training approach—modeling, role-playing, performance
feedback, and generalization—to teach essential prosocial skills to children and adolescents. Each
book provides a complete description of the Skillstreaming program, with instructions for teaching
a wide variety of prosocial skills and a CD including reproducible forms and handouts.

"Stop and Think" Social Skills Program (Knoff): http://www.projectachieve.info

Part of Project ACHIEVE (Knoff and Batsche). Project has demonstrated success in reducing
student discipline referrals to the principal's office, school suspensions, and expulsions; fostering positive school climates and prosocial interactions; increasing students' on-task behavior; and
improving academic performance.

The ACCEPTS Program (Walker et al.): http://www.proedinc.com/customer/productView
.aspx?ID=625&SearchWord=ACCEPTS%20PROGRAM

Offers a complete curriculum for teaching effective social skills to students at middle and
high school levels. The program teaches peer-to-peer skills, skills for relating to adults, and
self-management skills.

The EQUIP Program (Gibbs, Potter, & Goldstein): http://www.researchpress.com/scripts/product.
asp?item=4848#5134

Offers a three-part intervention method for working with antisocial or behavior disordered adolescents. The approach includes training in moral judgment, anger management/correction of thinking errors, and prosocial skills.

The PREPARE Curriculum (Goldstein): http://www.researchpress.com/scripts/product.asp?item=5063

Presents a series of 10 course-length interventions grouped into three areas: reducing aggression, reducing stress, and reducing prejudice. It is designed for use with middle school and high school students but can be adapted for use with younger students.

National Children's Advocacy Center: http://www.nationalcac.org/online-training/children-with-disabilities-harold-johnson.html

A presentation in which the issue of working with children who have been abused is addressed. Training is designed for use with middle school and high school students but can be adapted for use with younger students.

REFERENCES

Aljadeff-Abergel, E., Ayvazo, S., & Eldar, E. (2012). Social skills training in natural play settings: Educating through the physical theory to practice. *Intervention in School and Clinic, 48*(2), 76–86.

Anderegg, M., Vergason, G., & Smith, M. (1992). A visual representation of the grief cycle for use by teachers with families of children with disabilities. *Remedial and Special Education (RASE), 13*(2), 17–23.

Bender, W., Rosenkrans, C., & Crane, M. (1999). Stress, depression, and suicide among students with learning disabilities: Assessing the risk. *Learning Disability Quarterly, 22*(2), 143–156.

Burns, M., & Ysseldyke, J. (2009). Reported prevalence of evidence-based instructional practices in special education. *Journal of Special Education, 43*(1), 3–11.

Calvete, E., Orue, I., Est`evez, A., Villar`don, L., & Padilla, P. (2010). Cyberbullying in adolescents: Modalities and aggressors' profile. *Computers in Human Behavior, 26*(5), 1128–1135.

Carlson, E., Daley, T., Bitterman, A., Heinzen, H., Keller, B., Markowitz, J., & Riley, J. (2009). *Early school transitions and the social behavior of children with disabilities: Selected findings from the pre-elementary education longitudinal study. Wave 3 overview report from the pre-elementary education longitudinal study* (PEELS) (NCSER Report 2009-3016). Washington, DC: National Center for Special Education Research, U.S. Department of Education.

Carter, B., & Spencer, V. (2006). The fear factor: Bullying and students with disabilities. *International Journal of Special Education, 21*(1), 11–23.

Carter, E., Borck, M., & Trainor, A. (2014). Transition assessment and planning for youth with severe intellectual and developmental disabilities. *Journal of Special Education, 47*(4), 245–255.

Cederborg, A. C., Danielsson, H., La Rooy, D., & Lamb, M. E. (2009). Repetition of contaminating question types when children and youths with intellectual disabilities are interviewed. *Journal of Intellectual Disability Research, 53*(5), 440–449.

Cifci Tekinarslan, I., Sazak Pinar, E., & Sucuoglu, B. (2012). Teachers' and mothers' assessment of social skills of students with mental retardation. *Educational Sciences: Theory and Practice, 12*(4), 2783–2788.

Cooper, J., Heron, T., & Heward, W. (2008). *Applied behavior analysis* (2nd ed.). Upper Saddle River, NJ: Pearson/Prentice Hall.

Daniel, S., Walsh, A., Goldstone, D., Arnold, E., Reboussin, B., & Wood, F. (2006). Suicidality, school dropout, and reading problems among adolescents. *Journal of Learning Disabilities, 39*(6), 507–514.

Falvo, D. (2010). *Medical and psychosocial aspects of chronic illness and disability.* Sudbury, MA: Jones and Bartlett.

Florian, L., Hollenweger, J., Simeonsson, R., Wedell, K., Riddell, S., Terzi, L., & Holland, A. (2006). Cross-cultural perspectives on the classification of children with disabilities: Part I. Issues in the classification of children. *Journal of Special Education, 40*(1), 36–45.

Fowler, R. E., & Tisdale, P. C. (1992). Special Education students as a high-risk group for substance abuse: Teachers' perceptions. *School Counselor*, *40*(2), 103–108.

Gordon, J. (2009). An evidence-based approach for supporting parents experiencing chronic sorrow. *Pediatric Nursing, 35*(2), 115–119.

Greer, R. D., & Ross, D. E. (2007). *Verbal behavior analysis: Inducing and expanding new verbal capabilities in children with language delays.* New York, NY: Pearson.

Griffin, M., Taylor, J., Urbano, R., & Hodapp, R. (2014). Involvement in transition planning meetings among high school students with autism spectrum disorders. *Journal of Special Education, 47*(4), 256–264.

Hahn, H. (1988). The politics of physical differentness: Disability and discrimination. *Journal of Social Issues, 44*(1), 39–47.

Hausstatter, R., & Connolley, S. (2012). Towards a framework for understanding the process of educating the "special" in special education. *International Journal of Special Education*, *27*(2), 181–188.

Hernandez, P., & Ikkanda, Z. (2011). Behavior management of children with autism spectrum disorders in dental environments. *The Journal of the American Dental Association, 142*(3), 281–287.

Hershkowitz, I., Lamb, M., & Horowitz, D. (2007). Victimization of children with disabilities. *American Journal of Orthopsychiatry, 77*(4), 629–635.

Hibbard, R., & Desch, L. (2007). Clinical report: Maltreatment of children with disabilities. *Pediatrics Update, 119*(5), 1018–1025.

Hobdell, E., Grant, M., Valencia, I., Mare, J., Kothare, S., Legido, A., & Khurana, D. (2007). Chronic sorrow and coping in families of children with epilepsy. *Journal of Neuroscience Nursing, 39*(2), 76–82.

Hsien, M., Brown, P. M., & Bortoli, A. (2009). Teacher qualifications and attitudes toward inclusion. *Australasian Journal of Special Education, 33*(1), 26–41.

Huberman, M., Navo, M., & Parrish, T. (2012). Effective practices in high performing districts serving students in special education. *Journal of Special Education Leadership*, *25*(2), 59–71.

Huntington, D., & Bender, W. (1993). Adolescents with learning disabilities at risk? Emotional well-being, depression, suicide. *Journal of Learning Disabilites, 26*(3), 159–166.

Hyson, M., & Taylor, J. (2011). Caring about caring: What adults can do to promote young children's prosocial skills. *Young Children, 74*–83.

Jamison, K., Forston, L., & Stanton-Chapman, T. (2012). Encouraging social skill development through play in early childhood special education classes. *Young Exceptional Children, 15*(2), 3–19.

Katzer, C., Fetchenhauer, D., & Belschak, F. (2009). Cyberbullying: Who are the victims? A comparison of victimization in Internet chartrooms and victimization in school. *Journal of Media Psychology, 21*(1), 25–36.

Kress, J., & Elias, M. (1993). Substance abuse prevention in Special Education populations: Review and recommendations. *Journal of Special Education*, *27*(1), 35–51.

Kurtzer-White, E., & Luterman, D. (2003). Families and children with hearing loss: Grief and coping. *Developmental Disabilities Research Reviews, 9*(4), 232–235.

Livneh, H., & Antonak, R. (2005). Psychosocial adaptation to chronic illness and disability: A primer for counselors. *Journal of Counseling & Development, 83*(1), 12–20.

Manders, J., & Stoneman, Z. (2009). Children with disabilities in the child protective services system: An analog study of investigation and case management. *Child Abuse & Neglect, 33*(4), 229–237.

Martins, Y., Young, R., & Robson, D. (2008). Feeding and eating behaviors in children with autism and typically developing children. *Journal of Autism and Developmental Disorders, 38*(10), 1878–1887.

Mastin, D. (2010). *General and special education teachers' attitudes toward inclusion of Down syndrome students* (Doctoral dissertation, Walden University). Available from ProQuest Dissertations and Theses database. (ERIC No. ED514449)

McCombs, K., & Moore, D. (2002). *Substance abuse prevention and intervention for students with disabilities: A call to educators.* ERIC Clearinghouse on Disabilities and Gifted Education. (ERIC No. ED469441)

McGinnis, E. (2011a). *Skill streaming in early childhood: A guide for teaching prosocial skills* (3rd ed.). Champaign, IL: Research Press.

McGinnis, E. (2011b). *Skillstreaming the adolescent: A guide for teaching prosocial skills* (3rd ed.). Champaign, IL: Research Press.

McGinnis, E. (2011c). *Skillstreaming the elementary school child: A guide for teaching prosocial skills* (3rd ed.). Champaign, IL: Research Press.

Medina, C., & Luna, G. (2006). Suicide attempts among adolescent Mexican American students enrolled in special education classes. *Adolescence, 41*(162), 299–312.

Myers, H. N. F. (2005). How elementary school counselors can meet the needs of students with disabilities. *Professional School Counseling, 8*(5), 442–450.

Myers, H. N. F. (Ed.). (2013). *Social skills deficits in students with disabilities: Successful strategies from the disability field.* Lanham, MD: Littlefield.

Olsson C., Bond, L., Johnson, M., Forer, D., & Boyce, M. (2003). Adolescent chronic illness: A qualitative study of psychosocial adjustment. *Annual Academy of Medicine, Singapore, 32*(1), 43–50.

Owens, D., Thomas, D., & Strong, L. (2011). School counselors assisting students with disabilities. *Education, 132*(2), 235–241.

Plavnick, J., & Ferreri, S. (2011). Establishing verbal repertoires in children with autism using function-based video modeling. *Journal of Applied Behavior Analysis, 44*(4), 747–766.

Plavnick, J., Ferreri, S., & Maupin, A. (2010). The effects of self-monitoring on the procedural integrity of a behavioral intervention for young children with developmental disabilities. *Journal of Applied Behavior Analysis, 43*(2), 315–320.

Podvey, M., Hinojosa, J., & Koenig, K. (2013). Reconsidering insider status for families during the transition from early intervention to preschool special education. *Journal of Special Education, 46*(4), 211–222.

Reinehr, T., Dobe, M.,Winkel, K., Schaefer, A., & Hoffmann, D. (2010). Obesity in disabled children and adolescents: An overlooked group of patients. *Dtsch Arztebl Int., 107*(15), 268–275.

Slevin, E., Truesdale-Kennedy, M., McConkey, R., Livingstone, B., & Fleming, P. (2012). Obesity and overweight in intellectual and non-intellectually disabled children. *Journal of Intellectual Disability Research.* Article first published online September 7, 2012. doi:10.1111/j.1365-2788.2012.01615.x

Smith, T., & Wallace, S. (2011). Social skills of children in the U.S. with comorbid learning disabilities and AD/HD. *International Journal of Special Education, 26*(3), 238–247.

Stalker, K., & McArthur, K. (2012). Child abuse, child protection and disabled children: A review of recent research. *Child Abuse Review, 21*(1), 24–40.

Trolley, B., Haas, H., & Patti, D. (2009). *The school counselor's guide to special education.* Thousand Oaks, CA: Corwin.

U.S. Department of Health and Human Services. (2011). *Child maltreatment 2011.* Administration on Children, Youth and Families Children's Bureau. Retrieved from https://www.acf.hhs.gov/sites/default/files/cb/cm11.pdf#page=59

Uusitalo-Malmivaara, L., Kankaanpaa, P., Makinen, T, Raeluoto, T.,Rauttu, K., Tarhala, V., & Lehto, J. (2012). Are special education students happy? *Scandinavian Journal of Educational Research, 56*(4), 419–437.

Volkert, V., & Vaz, P. (2010). Recent studies on feeding problems in children with autism. *Journal Applied Behavior Analysis, 43*(1), 155–159.

Wachter, C., & Bouck, E. (2008). Suicide and students with high-incidence disabilities: What special educators need to know. *Teaching Exceptional Children, 41*(1), 66–72.

Wasburn-Moses, L. (2011). An investigation of alternative schools in one state: Implications for students with disabilities. *Journal of Special Education, 44*(4), 247–255.

Williams, P., Dalrymple, N., & Neal, J. (2000). Eating habits of children with autism. *Pediatric Nursing, 26*(3), 259–264.

Wright, M. F., & Li, Y. (2013). The association between cyber victimization and subsequent cyber aggression: The moderating effect of peer rejection. *Journal of Youth and Adolescence, 42,* 662–674.

Xin, J., & Sutman, F. (2011). Using the SMART board in teaching social stories to students with autism. *Teaching Exceptional Children, 43*(4), 18–24.

From the Editors' Chair

Writing a text book is part research—part experience—but mostly the articulation of the author's unique perspective on practice and profession. Each author has made personal decisions on how to organize the book and what, from the mass of information available, should be included. These decisions reflect the author's bias—personal interest—values and professional identity. We, as editors of the series, have invited each author to respond to the following questions as a way of providing the reader a glimpse into the *person* and not just the product of the author. In the case of this edited work, we are asking the editors to respond as a reflection of their experience producing this work.

It is our hope that these brief reflections will provide a little more insight into our view of our profession—and ourselves as professionals.

Rp/Nz

Question: There is certainly an abundance of insightful points found within this text. But if you were asked to identify a single point or theme from all that is presented that you would hope would stand out and stick with the reader, what would that point or theme be?

BT: It is a challenge to narrow down key points to just one theme or focus from so many excellent points. With that said, one key point is that school counselors have a *great deal* to contribute to students in special education such as the (a) possession of multiple therapeutic and psycho-educational skills, (b) ability to work within a team and take on leadership roles, (c) engagement with a strong national professional organization which has a set of clear guidelines and standards and whose mission is to help *all* students succeed in academic, career, and personal-social domains, and (d) ongoing continuous contact with students in general education, in which many more students with special needs are included. A second theme is one of individuality, personhood, and worth; disabilities are experienced differentially, the student is not defined by the disability, and every child has potential and strengths. Last, *it takes a village to raise a child.*

VM: A difficult question to answer, but I believe a single theme that is presented and stands out is the important work that the school counselor will be involved in on behalf of the children with disabilities they serve. There is much to do, but it is exciting work which the school counselor is prepared to undertake. The text offers a lot of support for this important work and emphasizes that the school counselor is not alone, as he or she will work with a team that knows and cares about the child as well.

Question: In the text, there is a great deal of research cited—theories presented. Could you share from your own experience how the information presented within the text may actually look—or—take form in practice?

BT: Fundamental to the core of interventions with students with special needs is behavioral theory. This theory in practical application exists in such areas as Functional Behavioral Assessments, Behavioral Intervention Plans, Positive Behavior Interventions and Supports, applied behavioral analysis, and behavioral intervention specialists. The common theme in practice is to set clear, specific, age-appropriate (developmentally not chronologically), measurable goals that reflect the individuality of each child with special needs. IEPs should not read the same across children but reflect the unique expression of the disability for the child and his or her needs. Additional practical considerations involve uniformity of intervention implementation by individuals and across time, and utilization of best practices in terms of strategies and evaluation methods. The fundamental need of a trusting relationship between school counselors and the child with special needs is incorporated across theories. Consider solution-focused brief therapy, which incorporates behavioral concepts, being utilized, as it often is in the school setting. Now imagine the student is being asked the *miracle question*, that is, "if you woke up tomorrow and the problem is gone, what happened, how do you feel, what do you observe, how are things better?" It is challenging for most to even address that a problem exists, even more so, to talk about desires, feelings, and change. A bond between school counselors and their students lays the foundation for this work to be done.

VM: As we are aware, theory and research drives intervention. First, the theory drives the research and then the research follows with best practices. The current and past pivotal research found in the text forms best practices for school counselors. In my own practice, I have gone to the research to help me with the best curricula, tools, strategies, and so on in my work. The law now directs us to do so. The text offers you the opportunity to dive into theory and research further to support you too in your work.

Question: As editors of this text—what might this book reveal about your own professional identity?

BT: The process of coediting this book has reaffirmed my passion for work with children and the core principles of rehabilitation: affirming strengths, not just recognizing pathology; working within a team; advocating and educating others about disability; empowering and believing in those with disabilities; and being sensitized to issues of disability and social justice. All of these basic concepts are essential to working with children with special needs, whether it be in helping them to academically perform at their best potential, seek postsecondary goals that are realistic and satisfying, and develop social skills that will lead to meaningful personal relationships and social skills.

VM: I think the biggest area of my own professional identity that the text addresses is the importance of interdisciplinary work—teamwork and collaboration. If done right, we all benefit, and the most important person that benefits is the child. I love to learn from other disciplines, and this text was written in that collaborative spirit.

Question: What final prescription—direction—might you offer your readers as they continue in their journey toward becoming professional counselors?

BT:
- Digest and apply the knowledge you have obtained.
- Trust your internal frame of reference.
- Communicate, consult, collaborate, and document.
- Continue your education; it is a life-long journey.
- Admit and learn from mistakes.
- Recognize you are a role model to students and adults alike.
- Understand you are the guide or navigator; the student is ultimately the "captain" of the ship and the most important person in the equation.
- Respect each and every child, parent or guardian, educator, and administrator. This does not mean you have to agree with everything they say or accept unacceptable behavior. It does mean that the worth and dignity of every individual must be recognized. *Every* person is special and has needs.

VM: At this point, it may sound cliché, but continue learning! Try to be the best that you can be every day. Communicate well with all you encounter. Take care of yourself so you can take of those you serve.

Index

About the Editors

Vicki A. McGinley, professor, is a faculty member at West Chester University of PA in the Special Education Department. She has taught both undergraduate and graduate courses in foundations, communication and behavioral disorders, action research, family systems, and legal issues. She has served in two states as a due process hearing officer and serves as a university fact finder as well as mediator. Presently, her teaching and service work focus on diversity issues, specifically, teaching in the urban environment and international education. She was recently awarded a research and teaching Fulbright Scholarship to work in Eastern Europe. Her publications reflect her teaching and have been in the areas of urban education, legal issues, best pedagogical practices, inclusive practices, and working with families.

Barbara C. Trolley has spent over three decades working in the counseling field. Currently, she is a professor in counselor education at St. Bonaventure University, where she trains graduate students for careers in school and mental health counseling. As the chair of her university's disability committee and coordinator of the autism training program, Trolley is committed to working with issues of diversity and youth. Besides the lead author of books on school counseling and cyberbullying, as well as numerous professional articles in the area of rehabilitation and grief counseling, Trolley is the creator and editor of the *New York State School Counseling Journal.* She and her coauthors of *Cyber Kids, Cyberbullying, Cyber Balance* have spent the past 4 years conducting countless workshops and media presentations on cyberbullying at the local, state, and national levels. Before coming to the academic world, she spent almost a decade working as a therapist and administrator, addressing child and family issues, especially around child abuse and grief.